axioms

AF184413

MDPI

Editorial

New Developments in Geometric Function Theory II

Georgia Irina Oros

Department of Mathematics and Computer Science, University of Oradea, 410087 Oradea, Romania; georgia_oros_ro@yahoo.co.uk

1. Introduction

This Special Issue is a sequel to the successful first volume entitled "New Developments in Geometric Function Theory". Following the same idea as the previous Special Issue, this project aimed to gather the latest developments in research concerning complex-valued functions in the Geometric Function Theory field.

Scholars' contributions were accepted on topics which included but were not limited to:

- New classes of univalent and bi-univalent functions;
- Studies regarding coefficient estimates including the Fekete–Szegő functional, Hankel determinants and Toeplitz matrices;
- Applications of different types of operators in Geometric Function Theory, including differential, integral, fractional or quantum calculus operators;
- Differential subordination and superordination theories in their classical form, also concerning their recent extensions, and strong and fuzzy differential subordination and superordination theories;
- Applications of different hypergeometric functions and orthogonal polynomials in Geometric Function Theory.

New results obtained by using any other techniques which can be applied in the field of complex analysis and its applications were also welcome. Hopefully, new lines of research associated with Geometric Function Theory have been highlighted and will provide a boost in the development of this field.

2. Overview of the Published Papers

Following a comprehensive review process, 14 articles were accepted for publication in this Special Issue.

Research by Sunday Olufemi Olatunji, Matthew Olanrewaju Oluwayemi and Georgia Irina Oros (Contribution 1) associates the powerful numerical tool provided by Gegenbauer polynomials with the prolific concepts of convolution and subordination. The investigation presented in this paper concerns a new subclass of functions introduced using an operator defined as the convolution of the generalized distribution and the error function using the concept of subordination. The research presented here targets a current topic of interest in Geometric Function Theory, namely coefficient-related studies. Investigations into this subclass are considered in connection to Carathéodory functions, the modified sigmoid function and Bell numbers to obtain coefficient estimates for the contained functions. The initial results regarding the coefficient estimates obtained by the authors can be used for further specific investigations regarding the coefficients of the functions from this class, such as estimations of Hankel determinants of different orders, Toeplitz determinants or the Fekete–Szegö problem.

Ibtisam Aldawish, Basem Frasin and Ala Amourah (Contribution 2) introduce a new family of normalized bi-univalent functions in the open unit disk associated with the Horadam polynomials using the concept of subordination and they estimate the second and the third coefficients in the Taylor–Maclaurin expansions of functions belonging to

Citation: Oros, G.I. New Developments in Geometric Function Theory II. *Axioms* **2024**, *13*, 224. https://doi.org/10.3390/axioms13040224

Received: 25 March 2024
Accepted: 26 March 2024
Published: 28 March 2024

this class. Furthermore, the Fekete–Szegö inequality is evaluated for the functions in the newly defined family. Making use of the Bell distribution series could inspire researchers to derive the estimates of the Taylor–Maclaurin coefficients and Fekete–Szegö functional problems for functions belonging to new subclasses of bi-univalent functions defined by means of the Horadam polynomials associated with this distribution series.

Rasoul Aghalary, Ali Ebadian, Nak Eun Cho and Mehri Alizadeh (Contribution 3) present a new method of studying harmonic functions in Geometric Function Theory. In this paper, a specified class of new log-harmonic functions is constructed taking the convex-exponent product combination of two elements. Sufficient conditions for this class to be starlike log-harmonic are given as a result of this study. Earlier work in the literature is proven to be generalized by the outcome of this research, and examples connected to the new results are presented in order to encourage future investigations.

In their research (Contribution 4), Maryam Al-Towailb and Zeinab S. I. Mansour use quantum calculus aspects in order to introduce a q-analog of the class of completely convex functions. This class of functions is a generalization of the class of completely convex functions. Specific properties, including the convergence of q-Lidstone series expansions of q-completely convex functions, are proven in the study, and it also provides a sufficient and necessary condition for a real function to have an absolutely convergent q-Lidstone series expansion.

The main aim of the study conducted by Abbas Kareem Wanas, Fethiye Müge Sakar and Alina Alb Lupaş (Contribution 5) was to investigate two new classes of bi-univalent functions described through a generalized q-calculus operator using the generator function for the Laguerre polynomial. Initial Taylor–Maclaurin coefficient estimates for functions of these newly introduced bi-univalent function classes are obtained, and the well-known Fekete–Szegö inequalities are examined for each of these classes.

The study performed by Abdullah Alsoboh, Ala Amourah, Fethiye Müge Sakar, Osama Ogilat, Gharib Mousa Gharib and Nasser Zomot (Contribution 6) provides deeper insights into the theory and applications of bi-univalent functions. A new family of analytic bi-univalent functions that are injective and possess analytic inverses is introduced by employing a q-analogue of the derivative operator and the concept of subordination. Moreover, the upper bounds of the Taylor–Maclaurin coefficients of these functions are established, which can aid in approximating the accuracy of approximations using a finite number of terms. The upper bounds are obtained by approximating analytic functions using Faber polynomial expansions. The results obtained in this article can be generalized in the future using post-quantum calculus and other q-analogs of the fractional derivative operator.

The primary objective of the study published by Sercan Kazımoğlu, Erhan Deniz and Luminiţa-Ioana Cotîrlă (Contribution 7) is to investigate the criteria for univalence and convexity of the integral operators that employ Miller–Ross functions. Differential inequalities related to the Miller–Ross functions and well-known lemmas are employed in the proofs of the new results. By using Mathematica (version 8.0), some graphics are generated that support the main results. The original results presented here could stimulate and inspire researchers, just as all the operators introduced before in studies related to functions of a complex variable have done. Other geometric properties related to these operators could be investigated and they could also prove useful in introducing special classes of functions based on these properties.

By utilizing the concept of the q-fractional derivative operator and bi-close-to-convex functions, Hari Mohan Srivastava, Isra Al-Shbeil, Qin Xin, Fairouz Tchier, Shahid Khan and Sarfraz Nawaz Malik (Contribution 8) define and investigate a new subclass of normalized analytic functions in an open unit disk employing a novel fractional differential operator. By using the Faber polynomial expansion technique, the l-th coefficient bound for the functions contained within this class is provided, and a further explanation for the first few coefficients of bi-close-to-convex functions defined by the q-fractional derivative is also given. The Fekete–Szegö problem is also considered for this class and some examples are provided. It is also demonstrated how some previously published results could be improved and generalized as a result of the primary findings of this study, as well as their corollaries and consequences.

In their research (Contribution 9), Abeer A. Al-Dohiman, Basem Aref Frasin, Naci Taşar and Fethiye Müge Sakar discover some inclusion relations of a certain harmonic class with other classes of harmonic analytic functions defined in an open disk by applying a convolution operator associated with the Mittag–Leffler function. Several special cases of the main results are also obtained as corollaries of the main results. Following this study, one can find new inclusion relations for new harmonic classes of analytic functions using the convolution operator presented in this study.

Mohsan Raza, Mehak Tariq, Jong-Suk Ro, Fairouz Tchier and Sarfraz Nawaz Malik (Contribution 10) aim to introduce a class of starlike functions that are related to Bernoulli's numbers of the second kind using the concept of subordination. Coefficient bounds, several radii problems, structural formulas, and inclusion relations are established, and sharp Hankel determinant problems of this class are presented. The newly defined class can be further investigated for determining the bounds of higher-order Hankel and Toeplitz determinants, and the same estimates can also be derived for logarithmic coefficients and for the coefficients of inverse functions.

Hasan Bayram, Kaliappan Vijaya, Gangadharan Murugusundaramoorthy and Sibel Yalçın (Contribution 11) introduce two novel subclasses of bi-univalent functions by leveraging generalized telephone numbers and binomial series through convolution. The analysis of the initial Taylor–Maclaurin coefficients is performed and Fekete–Szegö inequalities are established for these functions.

In the research presented by Sondekola Rudra Swamy and Luminita-Ioana Cotîrlă (Contribution 12), a new pseudo-type κ-fold symmetric bi-univalent function class that meets certain subordination conditions is introduced and studied with regard to coefficient bounds. For functions in the newly defined class, the upper bounds are obtained for certain coefficients that are further used for the evaluation of the Fekete–Szegö problem. In addition, pertinent links to previous results are highlighted and a few observations are given.

The goal of the study presented by Ebrahim Analouei Adegani, Mostafa Jafari, Teodor Bulboacă and Paweł Zaprawa (Contribution 13) is to estimate the upper bounds of the coefficients of the functions that belong to a set of bi-univalent functions with missing coefficients defined by using subordination. The results improve some previous results concerning different subclasses of bi-univalent functions that have been recently studied. In addition, important examples of some classes of such functions are provided, which can aid in the understanding of issues related to these functions. The authors expect that this method can be applied to the classes of harmonic and meromorphic functions in future work.

The notion of third-order strong differential subordination is investigated by Madan Mohan Soren, Abbas Kareem Wanas and Luminiţa-Ioana Cotîrlă (Contribution 14), who propose a new line of investigation for third-order strong differential subordination. Several intriguing properties are given within the context of specific classes of admissible functions. Certain definitions are extended to fit the third order strong differential subordination theory, presenting new and interesting results. Several properties of the results of third-order strong differential subordinations for analytic functions associated with the Srivastava–Attiya operator are given. Studies of the dual theory of third-order strong differential superordination could be inspired by the results presented in this paper.

3. Conclusions

A book published under the same title, "New Developments in Geometric Function Theory II", is available and contains the 14 papers that were published in this Special Issue. In the papers released as part of this initiative, a wide range of topics are discussed. Therefore, this Special Issue should be of interest to researchers studying Geometric Function Theory and its related fields.

List of Contributions:

1. Olatunji, S.O.; Oluwayemi, M.O.; Oros, G.I. Coefficient Results concerning a New Class of Functions Associated with Gegenbauer Polynomials and Convolution in Terms of Subordination. *Axioms* **2023**, *12*, 360. https://doi.org/10.3390/axioms12040360.
2. Aldawish, I.; Frasin, B.; Amourah, A. Bell Distribution Series Defined on Subclasses of Bi-Univalent Functions That Are Subordinate to Horadam Polynomials. *Axioms* **2023**, *12*, 362. https://doi.org/10.3390/axioms12040362.
3. Aghalary, R.; Ebadian, A.; Cho, N.E.; Alizadeh, M. New Criteria for Convex-Exponent Product of Log-Harmonic Functions. *Axioms* **2023**, *12*, 409. https://doi.org/10.3390/axioms12050409.
4. Al-Towailb, M.; Mansour, Z.S.I. A q-Analog of the Class of Completely Convex Functions and Lidstone Series. *Axioms* **2023**, *12*, 412. https://doi.org/10.3390/axioms12050412.
5. Wanas, A.K.; Sakar, F.M.; Alb Lupaş, A. Applications Laguerre Polynomials for Families of Bi-Univalent Functions Defined with (p, q)-Wanas Operator. *Axioms* **2023**, *12*, 430. https://doi.org/10.3390/axioms12050430.
6. Alsoboh, A.; Amourah, A.; Sakar, F.M.; Ogilat, O.; Gharib, G.M.; Zomot, N. Coefficient Estimation Utilizing the Faber Polynomial for a Subfamily of Bi-Univalent Functions. *Axioms* **2023**, *12*, 512. https://doi.org/10.3390/axioms12060512.
7. Kazımoğlu, S.; Deniz, E.; Cotîrlă, L.-I. Geometric Properties of Generalized Integral Operators Related to The Miller–Ross Function. *Axioms* **2023**, *12*, 563. https://doi.org/10.3390/axioms12060563.
8. Srivastava, H.M.; Al-Shbeil, I.; Xin, Q.; Tchier, F.; Khan, S.; Malik, S.N. Faber Polynomial Coefficient Estimates for Bi-Close-to-Convex Functions Defined by the q-Fractional Derivative. *Axioms* **2023**, *12*, 585. https://doi.org/10.3390/axioms12060585.
9. Al-Dohiman, A.A.; Frasin, B.A.; Taşar, N.; Sakar, F.M. Classes of Harmonic Functions Related to Mittag–Leffler Function. *Axioms* **2023**, *12*, 714. https://doi.org/10.3390/axioms12070714.
10. Raza, M.; Tariq, M.; Ro, J.-S.; Tchier, F.; Malik, S.N. Starlike Functions Associated with Bernoulli's Numbers of Second Kind. *Axioms* **2023**, *12*, 764. https://doi.org/10.3390/axioms12080764.
11. Bayram, H.; Vijaya, K.; Murugusundaramoorthy, G.; Yalçın, S. Bi-Univalent Functions Based on Binomial Series-Type Convolution Operator Related with Telephone Numbers. *Axioms* **2023**, *12*, 951. https://doi.org/10.3390/axioms12100951.
12. Swamy, S.R.; Cotîrlă, L.-I. A New Pseudo-Type κ-Fold Symmetric Bi-Univalent Function Class. *Axioms* **2023**, *12*, 953. https://doi.org/10.3390/axioms12100953.
13. Analouei Adegani, E.; Jafari, M.; Bulboacă, T.; Zaprawa, P. Coefficient Bounds for Some Families of Bi-Univalent Functions with Missing Coefficients. *Axioms* **2023**, *12*, 1071. https://doi.org/10.3390/axioms12121071.
14. Soren, M.M.; Wanas, A.K.; Cotîrlă, L.-I. Results of Third-Order Strong Differential Subordinations. *Axioms* **2024**, *13*, 42. https://doi.org/10.3390/axioms13010042.

Acknowledgments: The Guest Editor of this Special Issue would like to thank to all the authors who chose to submit papers and helped make this Special Issue a success, as well as to all the reviewers for their time, insightful feedback, and assistance in ensuring high standards of the published materials. Special gratitude is extended to the *Axioms* editors.

Conflicts of Interest: The author declares no conflicts of interest.

axioms

MDPI

Article

Coefficient Results concerning a New Class of Functions Associated with Gegenbauer Polynomials and Convolution in Terms of Subordination

Sunday Olufemi Olatunji [1], Matthew Olanrewaju Oluwayemi [2,3,*] and Georgia Irina Oros [4,*]

1 Department of Mathematical Sciences, Federal University of Technology, P.M.B. 704, Akure 340110, Nigeria
2 Quality Education Research Group, Landmark University, SDG 4, Omu-Aran 251103, Nigeria
3 Department of Mathematics, Landmark University, P.M.B. 1001, Omu-Aran 251103, Nigeria
4 Department of Mathematics and Computer Science, University of Oradea, 410087 Oradea, Romania
* Correspondence: oluwayemimatthew@gmail.com (M.O.O.); georgia_oros_ro@yahoo.co.uk (G.I.O.)

Abstract: Gegenbauer polynomials constitute a numerical tool that has attracted the interest of many function theorists in recent times mainly due to their real-life applications in many areas of the sciences and engineering. Their applications in geometric function theory (GFT) have also been considered by many researchers. In this paper, this powerful tool is associated with the prolific concepts of convolution and subordination. The main purpose of the research contained in this paper is to introduce and study a new subclass of analytic functions. This subclass is presented using an operator defined as the convolution of the generalized distribution and the error function and applying the principle of subordination. Investigations into this subclass are considered in connection to Carathéodory functions, the modified sigmoid function and Bell numbers to obtain coefficient estimates for the contained functions.

Keywords: analytic function; starlike function; convex function; univalent function; Gegenbauer polynomials; Bell numbers; sigmoid function

MSC: 30C45; 30C50

Citation: Olatunji, S.O.; Oluwayemi, M.O.; Oros, G.I. Coefficient Results concerning a New Class of Functions Associated Gegenbauer Polynomials and Convolution in Terms of Subordination. *Axioms* **2023**, *12*, 360. https://doi.org/10.3390/axioms12040360

Academic Editor: Hari Mohan Srivastava

Received: 21 February 2023
Revised: 5 April 2023
Accepted: 6 April 2023
Published: 8 April 2023

1. Introduction and Preliminaries

The beginning of univalent function theory is largely credited to P. Koebe's article published in 1907 [1]. Problems pertaining to the full class of univalent functions were the primary focus at first. Bieberbach, who published numerous significant papers on the theory of univalent functions in the early 1920s, was a key figure in the early development of geometric function theory. He conjectured his well-known bounds for a normalized univalent function's coefficients in 1916 [2] and established the bound for the second coefficient. It was not until 1984 [3] that the hypothesis was generally proven.

In a paper published in 1915 [4], Alexander intended to obtain sufficient conditions for a function to map the interior of the unit disc in a one-to-one manner. As a result, Alexander developed a number of classes of univalent functions as well as several tests that ensured the univalence of those classes, initiating new lines of research in GFT. Alexander first proposed the concepts of starlike functions, close-to-convex functions and functions of bounded turning, along with other ideas and theorems that were later rediscovered, often without awareness of Alexander's pioneering work. In a nice review paper [5], the authors analyze the content of Alexander's paper emphasizing his intuitive arguments and how those arguments were used by other researchers for further developments. Alexander describes [4] a star-shaped region as a set whose every point may be connected to point a via a linear segment made up only of points contained in the region. The center is designated as point a. The region is said to be convex when any point inside the region may be picked as the center. In an effort to guarantee the univalence of the mapping by controlling the shape of the boundary image, he proposed the idea of mapping the unit disc onto a starlike or convex region. By mandating that the boundary image is a starlike or a convex domain, univalence is achieved since overlapping or looping is avoided. Geometric characterization states that a mapping $w = w(z)$ is star-shaped if $\arg w(z)$ is a never-decreasing function of $\theta = \arg w(z)$ when z describes the unit circle in the counterclockwise direction, and it is a convex function if the argument of the normal vector of the image curve is a non-decreasing function of an increasing θ.

There are numerous intriguing uses for star-shaped bodies in various fields. For instance, star-shaped bodies were explored in the context of compressible fluid penetration in mechanics [6]. Computer simulations were extensively used in statistical mechanics to study models of fluids, liquid crystals, plastic crystals and other solid-phase systems made of hard convex bodies [7]. On the other hand, it has been demonstrated in [8] that hard star-shaped bodies can replace hard convex bodies in computer simulations of constant volume and constant pressure. As with other applications for star-shaped bodies, it has been determined in elasticity theory that the stress field is uniform when m is an odd integer for an m-pointed polygonal inclusion exposed to a uniform eigenstrain [9].

Many univalent function subclasses have captured the interest of GFT researchers. Such subclasses are defined using functions f belonging to the class $\mathcal{A}$ of holomorphic functions that have the following form:

$$f(z) = z + \sum_{n=2}^{\infty} a_n z^n, \quad z \in E, \tag{1}$$

where $E = \{z : |z| < 1\}$ with $f(0) = f'(0) - 1 = 0$. The class of starlike functions is comprised functions $f \in \mathcal{A}$ with the geometric representation $Re\frac{zf'(z)}{f(z)} > 0$, the class of convex functions contains functions $f \in \mathcal{A}$ with the geometric characterization given by $Re\left(1 + \frac{zf''(z)}{f'(z)}\right) > 0$ and the class of close-to-convex functions is characterized by $Re\frac{zf'(z)}{g(z)} > 0$, with g representing a starlike function.

Recently, Babalola [10] improved on a subclass of $\mathcal{A}$ called the class of starlike functions by introducing the class $\mathcal{L}_\lambda(\beta)$, which is defined as the class of functions f belonging to $\mathcal{A}$ that satisfies

$$Re\frac{z(f'(z))^\lambda(z)}{f(z)} > \beta, \tag{2}$$

where $\beta \in [0,1)$ and $\lambda \geq 1 \in \mathbb{R}$. Since then, many authors have used different approaches to study the class of functions introduced in [10].

Using an analytic function $F(z)$, the starlike and convex functions were investigated by authors such as [11–14] and extended to the class of $F-$starlike and $F-$convex functions denoted by FS^* and FK, respectively, which are represented by

$$Re\frac{F(z)f'(z)}{f(z)} > 0 \tag{3}$$

and

$$Re\left(1 + \frac{F(z)f''(z)}{f'(z)}\right) > 0, \tag{4}$$

respectively, with the condition $F(0) = 0$. By setting $F(z) = z$ in (3) and (4), the well-known starlike and convex functions are obtained [11,14].

Let

$$g(z) = z + \sum_{n=2}^{\infty} b_k z^n. \tag{5}$$

Then, the convolution of (1) and (5) gives

$$(f * g)(z) = z + \sum_{n=2}^{\infty} a_n b_n z^n. \tag{6}$$

For details, see [15,16].

A normalized Gegenbauer polynomial has the form

$$\mathcal{G}(z,m) = z + \sum_{n=2}^{\infty} c_{n-1}^{\beta}(m) z^n, \tag{7}$$

where $\beta > -\frac{1}{2}$. The first three coefficients of the forms are

$$c_0^{\beta}(m) = 1, \tag{8}$$

$$c_1^{\beta}(m) = 2\beta m, \tag{9}$$

$$c_2^{\beta}(m) = 2\beta(\beta+1)m^2 - \beta, \tag{10}$$

and the next coefficient is given by

$$c_3^{\beta}(m) = \frac{4\beta(\beta+1)(\beta+2)m^2}{3} - 2\beta(\beta+1)m. \tag{11}$$

In general, the *n-th* coefficient is defined by

$$c_n^{\beta}(m) = \frac{2m(n+\beta-1)c_{n-1}^{\beta}(m) - (n+2\beta-2)c_{n-2}^{\beta}(m)}{n}. \tag{12}$$

It originates from

$$q(z) = \int_{-1}^{1} \mathcal{G}(z,m) d\mu(m),$$

where

$$\mathcal{G}(z,m) = \frac{z}{(1-2mz+z^2)^{\beta}} \tag{13}$$

and μ is a probability measure on the interval $[-1,1]$. The collection of such measures on $[s,t]$ is denoted by $P_{[s,t]}$.

By substituting $\beta = \frac{1}{2}$ in $\mathcal{G}(z,m)$, the Legendre polynomial will be obtained, while by setting $\beta = 1$ in $\mathcal{G}(z,m)$, the famous Chebyshev polynomial will be obtained, which are both tools in the field. These recent results can be seen in [17,18].

Gegenbauer polynomials have been studied intensely and have proved to provide interesting results, as seen in early studies such as [19,20]. They have wide applications in queueing theory, as can be seen in [21], signal analysis, automatic control, scattering theory and many others. Applications in GFT include defining the subclasses of univalent functions [22] and bi-univalent functions [23]. Coefficient studies on the subclasses of bi-univalent functions can be seen in very recent papers, such as [24–27].

Let D denote the sum of the convergent series of the form

$$D = \sum_{n=0}^{\infty} a_n, \tag{14}$$

where $a_n \geq 0$ for all $n \in \mathbb{N}$. The probability mass function of the generalized discrete probability distribution defined using (14) is given by $p(n) = \frac{a_n}{D}, n = 0,1,2,3,\ldots$. Function $p(n)$ is the probability mass function because $p(n) \geq 0$ and $\sum_n p(n) = 1$.

Additionally, let $\psi(x) = \sum_{n=0}^{\infty} a_n x^n$. Then, since $D = \sum_{n=0}^{\infty} a_n$ is convergent, the series ψ is convergent for $|x| < 1$ and $x = 1$. The interest of the present investigation is the power series whose coefficients are probabilities of generalized distributions of the form

$$\mathcal{H}_{\psi}(z) = z + \sum_{n=2}^{\infty} \frac{a_{n-1}}{D} z^n. \tag{15}$$

Details can be found in [22,28,29].

The error function is a special function that occurs in probability, statistics, material science, partial differential equation, physics, chemistry, biology, mass flow and diffusion for transportation phenomena. It also occurs in quantum mechanics to eliminate the probability of observing a particle in a particular region. Barton et al. [30] introduced the function of the form

$$\mathrm{erf}(z) = \frac{2}{\sqrt{\pi}} \int_0^z e^{-t^2} dt = \frac{2}{\sqrt{\pi}} \sum_{n=0}^{\infty} \frac{(-1)^{n+1} z^{2n+1}}{n!(2n+1)}. \tag{16}$$

The properties and inequalities of error functions have also been considered by Alzer [31], Cartilz [32], Coman [33], Elbert [34] and many other researchers in the field.

Ramachandran et al. [35,36] modified (16) to

$$\mathrm{Erf}(z) = z + \sum_{n=2}^{\infty} \frac{(-1)^{n-1} z^n}{(n-1)!(2n-1)}, \tag{17}$$

which is analytic in the unit disk $U = z : |z| < 1$ and normalized by $\mathrm{Erf}(0) = 0$ and $\mathrm{Erf}'(0) = 1$.

The convolution of (15) and (17) generates the following function, which will be used to define the new subclass of functions that is investigated in this paper:

$$\mathcal{F}_{\leftarrow}(z) = \left(\mathcal{H}_{\psi} * \mathrm{Erf}\right)(z) = z + \sum_{n=2}^{\infty} \frac{(-1)^{n-1}}{(2n-1)(n-1)!} \frac{a_{n-1}}{D} z^n, \tag{18}$$

as a power series. See [16] for details.

Let $\mathcal{P}$ denote the class of the Carathéodory functions of the form

$$p(z) = 1 + \sum_{n=1}^{\infty} p_n z^n, \tag{19}$$

with the conditions $Re\ p(z) > 0$ and $p(0) = 1$.

The functions of the form

$$G(z) = \frac{1}{1+e^{-z}} = \frac{1}{2} + \frac{z}{4} - \frac{z^3}{48} + \frac{z^5}{480} - \frac{17z^7}{80640} + \dots,$$

referred to as sigmoid functions, are defined in [37] by the following modified form:

$$\gamma(z) = \frac{2}{1+e^{-z}} = 1 + \frac{z}{2} - \frac{z^3}{24} + \frac{z^5}{240} - \frac{17z^7}{40320} + \dots. \tag{20}$$

The sigmoid function has been repeatedly studied by many researchers because it has the following properties: it outputs real numbers between 0 and 1, maps a very large input domain to a small range of outputs, never loses information because it is a one-to-one function, increases monotonically and is also differentiable. The sigmoid function has useful applications in fields such as functional analysis, real analysis, algebra, topology, differential equations and many others. It has numerous methods of evaluation but, here, only the truncated series expansion is considered. See [38–44].

The function of the form

$$\mathcal{Q}(z) = e^{e^z - 1} = \sum_{n=0}^{\infty} B_n \frac{z^n}{n!} = 1 + z + z^2 + \frac{5}{6}z^3 + \frac{5}{8}z^4 + \dots, \qquad z \in \mathbb{E}, \tag{21}$$

was investigated by Kumar et al. [45]. This function is starlike with respect to one, and its coefficients generate the Bell numbers where $B_0 = 1, B_1 = 1, B_2 = 2, B_3 = 5, B_4 = 15$, $B_5 = 52$ and $B_6 = 203$ are the coefficients generated through binomial expansion. In recent times, some applications of the Beta function were considered in [46–48], while Olatunji and Altinkaya [49] used (21) to investigate the generalized distribution for the analytic function classes associated with error functions and Bell numbers. Further information can also be found in [49–51].

In the present work, the authors draw motivation from prior research in [15,17,29,49]. The aim of this paper is to consider applications of certain special functions in GFT. In particular, certain results are obtained in terms of subordination associated with Carathéodory functions, the modified sigmoid function and Bell numbers for the specific class of functions defined here and given in the next definition. The early coefficient bounds obtained are used to establish the famous Fekete–Szegö inequalities.

The following class is defined and studied in this paper.

Definition 1. *A function $f \in \mathcal{A}$ is said to be in the class $\mathcal{GS}^*_{\mathcal{F}\psi}(m, \beta)$, where $m \in [-1, 1]$ and $\beta > 1$, if the following subordination is satisfied*

$$Re \frac{\mathcal{G}\left(\mathcal{F}'_{\psi}\right)(z)}{\mathcal{F}_{\psi}(z)} \prec \sqrt{1+z} \tag{22}$$

with the condition $\mathcal{G}_{\psi}(0) = 0$. The function $\mathcal{F}_{\psi}(z)$, defined by (18), is a convolution of (7) and (17).

The class of functions $\mathcal{GS}^*_{\mathcal{F}_{\leftarrow}}(m, \beta)$, defined above, is investigated in the next section in relation to the Carathéodory function $p(z)$, the modified sigmoid function and Bell numbers by means of the subordination principle, and initial coefficient estimates are obtained. Furthermore, those results are used for investigating the Fekete–Szegö problem.

2. Main Results

The main aim of this work is to investigate the coefficient problems for the class of functions $\mathcal{GS}^*_{\mathcal{F}\psi}(m, \beta)$ defined in this study. The coefficient estimates are obtained using the Carathéodory function $p(z)$ defined by (19), the modified sigmoid function given by (20) and Bell numbers generated by the function given in (21) involving functions associated with Gegenbauer polynomials. The applications of Gegenbauer polynomials (7), the error function (17), a generalized distribution function (15), Carathéodory functions (19), the modified sigmoid function (20), Bell numbers (21) and some other functions in GFT have been considered by several authors in the field. In this study, the authors use combinations of all the functions mentioned above with the purpose of investigating the coefficients of the class of F-starlike functions $\mathcal{GS}^*_{\mathcal{F}\psi}(m, \beta)$ such that every function in the class satisfies the condition seen in (22). The Gegenbauer polynomials used in this work can be found to have some applications in queueing theory [21], signal analysis, automatic control, scattering theory and many other areas. Gengenbauer polynomials, also known as ultraspherical polynomials $C_n^{\alpha}(x)$, are orthogonal polynomials defined on the closed interval $[-1, 1]$. These polynomials are obtained as solutions of the Gengenbauer differential equation, which reduces to the Chebyshev differential equation for $\alpha = 1$.

First, we consider obtaining the coefficient bounds for the class of functions $\mathcal{GS}^*_{\mathcal{F}\psi}(m, \beta)$ associated with the Carathéodory functions given by (19).

Theorem 1. *Let $f(z)$ be defined by (1) and $p(z)$ by (19). Then, $f \in \mathcal{GS}^*_{\mathcal{F}\psi}(m,\beta)$ where $m \in [-1,1]$ and $\beta \geq 1$, if*

$$\left|\frac{a_1}{s}\right| \leq \left|\frac{3(4c_1^\beta(m) - p_1)}{4}\right| \tag{23}$$

and

$$\left|\frac{a_2}{s}\right| \leq \left|\frac{5\left[8p_2 - 7p_1^2 + 16c_1^\beta(m)p_1 + 32\left((c_1^\beta(m))^2 - c_2^\beta(m)\right)\right]}{32}\right|. \tag{24}$$

Proof. Let $f \in \mathcal{GS}^*_{\mathcal{F}\psi}(m,\beta)$ where $m \in [-1,1]$ and $\beta \geq 1$, then

$$\frac{\mathcal{G}\left(\mathcal{F}'_\psi\right)(z)}{\mathcal{F}_\psi(z)} = \sqrt{1+\omega(z)}. \tag{25}$$

The left-hand side of (25) gives

$$\frac{\mathcal{G}\left(\mathcal{F}'_\psi\right)(z)}{\mathcal{F}_\psi(z)} = 1 + \left(c_1^\beta(m) - \frac{a_1}{3s}\right)z + \left(c_2^\beta(m) - \frac{c_1^\beta(m)a_1}{3s} + \frac{a_2}{5s} - \frac{a_1^2}{9s^2}\right)z^2 + \ldots, \tag{26}$$

while the right-hand side gives

$$\sqrt{1 + \frac{p(z)-1}{p(z)+1}} = 1 + \frac{p_1}{4}z + \left(\frac{p_2}{4} - \frac{5p_1^2}{32}\right)z^2 + \ldots. \tag{27}$$

Comparing the coefficients of z and z^2 in (26) and (27), we obtain

$$\frac{a_1}{s} = \frac{3(4c_1^\beta(m) - p_1)}{4}$$

and

$$\frac{a_2}{s} = \frac{5\left[8p_2 - 7p_1^2 + 16c_1^\beta(m)p_1 + 32\left((c_1^\beta(m))^2 - c_2^\beta(m)\right)\right]}{32},$$

which completes the proof. □

The next two theorems are concerned with the investigation of certain coefficient problems for the class of functions $\mathcal{GS}^*_{\mathcal{F}\psi}(m,\beta)$ involving the sigmoid function given by (20).

Theorem 2. *Let $f(z)$ be defined by (1) and $\gamma(z)$ by (20). Then, $f \in \mathcal{GS}^*_{\mathcal{F}\psi}(m,\beta)$ where $m \in [-1,1]$ and $\beta \geq 1$ if the following condition holds true*

$$\left|\frac{a_2}{s} - \mu\frac{a_1^2}{s^2}\right| \leq \left|\frac{9(4c_1^\beta(m) - p_1)^2}{16}\left[\frac{5[8p_2 - 7p_1^2 + 16c_1^\beta(m)p_1 + 32((c_1^\beta(m))^2 - c_2^\beta(m))]}{18(4c_1^\beta(m) - p_1)^2} - \mu\right]\right|. \tag{28}$$

Proof. Let $f \in \mathcal{GS}^*_{\mathcal{F}\psi}(m,\beta)$ where $m \in [-1,1]$ $\beta \geq 1$ and $\mu \in \mathbb{R}$. Then

$$\frac{a_2}{2} - \mu\frac{a_1^2}{s^2} = \left[\frac{5[8p_2 - 7p_1^2 + 16c_1^\beta(m)p_1 + 32((c_1^\beta(m))^2 - c_2^\beta(m))]}{32} - \mu\left(\frac{3(4c_1^\beta(m) - p_1)}{4}\right)^2\right],$$

$$\frac{a_2}{2} - \mu\frac{a_1^2}{s^2} = \frac{9(4c_1^\beta(m) - p_1)^2}{16}\left[\frac{5[8p_2 - 7p_1^2 + 16c_1^\beta(m)p_1 + 32((c_1^\beta(m))^2 - c_2^\beta(m))]}{18(4c_1^\beta(m) - p_1)^2} - \mu\right],$$

which finally gives

$$\left|\frac{a_2}{2}-\mu\frac{a_1^2}{s^2}\right| \le \left|\frac{9(4c_1^{\beta}(m)-p_1)^2}{16}\left[\frac{5[8p_2-7p_1^2+16c_1^{\beta}(m)p_1+32((c_1^{\beta}(m))^2-c_2^{\beta}(m))]}{18(4c_1^{\beta}(m)-p_1)^2}-\mu\right]\right|.$$

□

Theorem 3. *Let $f(z)$ be defined by (1) and $\gamma(z)$ by (20). Then, $f \in \mathcal{GS}^*_{\mathcal{F}\psi}(m,\beta)$ where $m \in [-1,1]$ and $\beta \ge 1$, if*

$$\left|\frac{a_1}{s}\right| \le \left|\frac{3(8c_1^{\beta}(m)-1)}{8}\right| \tag{29}$$

and

$$\left|\frac{a_2}{s}\right| \le \left|\frac{5\left[256(c_1^{\beta}(m))^2-128c_2^{\beta}(m)-48c_1^{\beta}(m)-3\right]}{128}\right|. \tag{30}$$

Proof. Let $f \in \mathcal{GS}^*_{\mathcal{F}\psi}(m,\beta)$, where $m \in [-1,1]$ and $\beta \ge 1$. Then

$$\frac{\mathcal{G}\left(\mathcal{F}'_{\psi}\right)(z)}{\mathcal{F}_{\psi}(z)} = \sqrt{1+\omega(z)}.$$

The left-hand side of (25) gives

$$\frac{\mathcal{G}\left(\mathcal{F}'_{\psi}\right)(z)}{\mathcal{F}_{\psi}(z)} = 1+\left(c_1^{\beta}(m)-\frac{a_1}{3s}\right)z+\left(c_2^{\beta}(m)-\frac{c_1^{\beta}(m)a_1}{3s}+\frac{a_2}{5s}-\frac{a_1^2}{9s^2}\right)z^2+\dots, \tag{31}$$

while the right-hand side gives

$$\sqrt{1+\frac{\gamma(z)-1}{\gamma(z)+1}} = 1+\frac{1}{8}z-\frac{5}{128}z^2+\dots \tag{32}$$

Comparing the coefficients of z and z^2 in (26) and (32), we obtain

$$\frac{a_1}{s} = \frac{3(8c_1^{\beta}(m)-1)}{8}$$

and

$$\frac{a_2}{s} = \frac{5\left[256(c_1^{\beta}(m))^2-128c_2^{\beta}(m)-48c_1^{\beta}(m)-3\right]}{128},$$

which completes the proof. □

Theorems 4–6 involve the investigation of certain coefficient problems of the class $\mathcal{GS}^*_{\mathcal{F}\psi}(m,\beta)$ with respect to the Bell numbers (21).

Theorem 4. *Let $f(z)$ be defined by (1) and $\mathcal{Q}(z)$ by (21). Then, $f \in \mathcal{GS}^*_{\mathcal{F}\psi}(m,\beta)$ where $m \in [-1,1]$ and $\beta \ge 1$ if the following condition holds true*

$$\left|\frac{a_2}{s}-\mu\frac{a_1^2}{s^2}\right| \le \left|\frac{5\left[256(c_1^{\beta}(m))^2-128c_2^{\beta}(m)-48c_1^{\beta}(m)-3\right]}{36(8c_1^{\beta}(m)-1)^2}-\mu\right|. \tag{33}$$

Proof. Let $f \in \mathcal{GS}^*_{\mathcal{F}\psi}(m,\beta)$ where $m \in [-1,1]$ and $\beta \ge 1$ and $\mu \in \mathbb{R}$. Then

$$\frac{a_2}{s}-\mu\frac{a_1^2}{s^2} = \frac{5\left[256(c_1^{\beta}(m))^2-128c_2^{\beta}(m)-48c_1^{\beta}(m)-3\right]}{128}-\mu\left(\frac{3(8c_1^{\beta}(m)-1)}{8}\right)^2,$$

$$\frac{a_2}{2} - \mu\frac{a_1^2}{s^2} = \frac{9(8c_1^\beta(m)-1)^2}{64}\left(\frac{5\left[256(c_1^\beta(m))^2 - 128c_2^\beta(m) - 48c_1^\beta(m) - 3\right]}{36(8c_1^\beta(m)-1)^2} - \mu\right),$$

which finally gives:

$$\left|\frac{a_2}{s} - \mu\frac{a_1^2}{s^2}\right| \leq \left|\frac{5\left[256(c_1^\beta(m))^2 - 128c_2^\beta(m) - 48c_1^\beta(m) - 3\right]}{36(8c_1^\beta(m)-1)^2} - \mu\right|.$$

□

Theorem 5. *Let $f(z)$ be defined by (1) and $\mathcal{Q}(z)$ by (21). Then, $f \in \mathcal{GS}^*_{\mathcal{F}\psi}(m,\beta)$ where $m \in [-1,1]$ and $\beta \geq 1$, if*

$$\left|\frac{a_1}{s}\right| \leq \left|\frac{3(4c_1^\beta(m)-1)}{4}\right| \tag{34}$$

and

$$\left|\frac{a_2}{s}\right| \leq \left|\frac{5\left[5 + 16c_1^\beta(m) + 32\left(2(c_1^\beta(m))^2 - c_2^\beta(m)\right)\right]}{32}\right|. \tag{35}$$

Proof. Let $f \in \mathcal{GS}^*_{\mathcal{F}\psi}(m,\beta)$ where $m \in [-1,1]$ and $\beta \geq 1$. Then

$$\frac{\mathcal{G}\left(\mathcal{F}'_\psi\right)(z)}{\mathcal{F}_\psi(z)} = \sqrt{1+\omega(z)}.$$

The left-hand side of (25) gives

$$\frac{\mathcal{G}\left(\mathcal{F}'_\psi\right)(z)}{\mathcal{F}_\psi(z)} = 1 + \left(c_1^\beta(m) - \frac{a_1}{3s}\right)z + \left(c_2^\beta(m) - \frac{c_1^\beta(m)a_1}{3s} + \frac{a_2}{5s} - \frac{a_1^2}{9s^2}\right)z^2 + \ldots,$$

while the right-hand side gives

$$\sqrt{1 + \frac{\mathcal{Q}(z)-1}{\mathcal{Q}(z)+1}} = 1 + \frac{1}{4}z + \frac{3}{32}z^2 + \ldots. \tag{36}$$

When the coefficients of z and z^2 in (26) and (36), are compared, the following values are obtained:

$$\frac{a_1}{s} = \frac{3(4c_1^\beta(m)-1)}{4}$$

and

$$\frac{a_2}{s} = \frac{5\left[5 + 16c_1^\beta(m) + 32\left(2(c_1^\beta(m))^2 - c_2^\beta(m)\right)\right]}{32}.$$

Hence, the proof is completed. □

In Theorem 2, the coefficient estimates were established using the Carathéodory function $p(z)$ given by (19). We now consider in the next theorem the coefficient estimates for the class of functions $\mathcal{GS}^*_{\mathcal{F}\psi}(m,\beta)$ using the Bell numbers $\mathcal{Q}(z)$ as given by (21).

Theorem 6. *Let $f(z)$ be defined by (1) and $\mathcal{Q}(z)$ by (21). Then, $f \in \mathcal{GS}^*_{\mathcal{F}\psi}(m,\beta)$ where $m \in [-1,1]$ and $\beta \geq 1$ if the following condition holds true*

$$\left|\frac{a_2}{s} - \mu\frac{a_1^2}{s^2}\right| \leq \left|\frac{9(4c_1^\beta(m)-1)^2}{16}\left[\frac{5\left[5+16c_1^\beta(m)+32\left(2(c_1^\beta(m))^2-c_2^\beta(m)\right)\right]}{18(4c_1^\beta(m)-1)^2} - \mu\right]\right|. \quad (37)$$

Proof. Let $f \in \mathcal{GS}^*_{\mathcal{F}\psi}(m,\beta)$ where $m \in [-1,1]$, $\beta \geq 1$ and $\mu \in \mathbb{R}$. Then

$$\frac{a_2}{2} - \mu\frac{a_1^2}{s^2} = \left[\frac{5\left[5+16c_1^\beta(m)+32\left(2(c_1^\beta(m))^2-c_2^\beta(m)\right)\right]}{32} - \mu\left(\frac{3(4c_1^\beta(m)-1)}{4}\right)^2\right],$$

$$\frac{a_2}{2} - \mu\frac{a_1^2}{s^2} = \frac{9(4c_1^\beta(m)-1)^2}{16}\left[\frac{5\left[5+16c_1^\beta(m)+32\left(2(c_1^\beta(m))^2-c_2^\beta(m)\right)\right]}{18(4c_1^\beta(m)-p_1)^2} - \mu\right],$$

which finally gives

$$\left|\frac{a_2}{2} - \mu\frac{a_1^2}{s^2}\right| \leq \left|\frac{9(4c_1^\beta(m)-1)^2}{16}\left[\frac{5\left[5+16c_1^\beta(m)+32\left(2(c_1^\beta(m))^2-c_2^\beta(m)\right)\right]}{18(4c_1^\beta(m)-p_1)^2} - \mu\right]\right|.$$

□

3. Conclusions

The investigation presented in the paper concerns a new subclass of functions denoted by $\mathcal{GS}^*_{\mathcal{F}\psi}(m,\beta)$ introduced in Definition 1 by using an operator defined in (18) as the convolution of the generalized distribution and the error function using the concept of subordination. The new class is interesting due to the powerful tools in geometric function theory used for introducing it, namely convolution and subordination. The main aim of the research presented in this paper targets a topic of interest at this moment in GFT: coefficient-related studies. The first theorem proved in Section 2, Theorem 1, provides the coefficient estimates for functions that are part of the class $\mathcal{GS}^*_{\mathcal{F}\psi}(m,\beta)$ by involving the Carathéodory function $p(z)$ defined in (19). The next results, proved in Theorem 2 and Theorem 3, use the sigmoid function given by (20) for establishing further coefficient estimates regarding the class $\mathcal{GS}^*_{\mathcal{F}\psi}(m,\beta)$. Finally, the Bell numbers given by (21) are used in Theorems 4–6 to provide other forms of coefficient estimates concerning functions from the new class $\mathcal{GS}^*_{\mathcal{F}\psi}(m,\beta)$.

The initial results regarding the coefficient estimates obtained here can be used for further specific investigations regarding coefficients of the functions from class $\mathcal{GS}^*_{\mathcal{F}\psi}(m,\beta)$, such as estimations for Hankel determinants of different orders, Toeplitz determinants or the Fekete–Szegö problem.

Author Contributions: Conceptualization, S.O.O., M.O.O. and G.I.O.; methodology, S.O.O., M.O.O. and G.I.O.; software, M.O.O.; validation, S.O.O., M.O.O. and G.I.O.; formal analysis S.O.O. and M.O.O.; investigation S.O.O., M.O.O. and G.I.O.; resources S.O.O., M.O.O. and G.I.O. All authors have read and agreed to the published version of the manuscript.

Funding: This research received no external funding.

Institutional Review Board Statement: Not applicable.

Informed Consent Statement: Not applicable.

Data Availability Statement: Not applicable.

Conflicts of Interest: The authors declare no conflict of interest.

References

1. Koebe, P. Über die Uniformisierung beliebiger analytischer Kurven. *Nachr. Kgl. Ges. Wiss. Gött. Math-Phys. Kl.* **1907**, *1907*, 191–210.
2. Bieberbach, L. Über die koeffizienten derjenigen Potenzreihen, welche eine schlichte Abbildung des Einheitskreises vermitteln. *Sitzungsber. Preuss. Akad. Wiss. Phys.-Math. Kl.* **1916**, *138*, 940–955.
3. De Branges, L. A proof of the Bieberbach conjecture. *Acta Math.* **1985**, *154*, 137–152. [CrossRef]
4. Alexander, J.W. Functions which map the interior of the unit circle upon simple region. *Ann. Math.* **1915**, *17*, 12–22. [CrossRef]
5. Gluchoff, A.; Hartmann, F. On a "Much Underestimated" Paper of Alexander. *Arch. Hist. Exact Sci.* **2000**, *55*, 1–41. [CrossRef]
6. Gonor, A.L.; Poruchikov, V.B. The penetration of star-shaped bodies into a compressible fluid. *J. Appl. Math. Mech.* **1989**, *53*, 308–314. [CrossRef]
7. Frenkel, D. Computer simulation of hard-core models for liquid crystals. *Mol. Phys.* **1987**, *60*, 1–20. [CrossRef]
8. Wojciechowski, K.W. Hard star-shaped bodies and Monte Carlo simulations. *J. Chem. Phys.* **1991**, *94*, 4099–4100. [CrossRef]
9. Mura, T. The determination of the elastic field of a polygonal star shaped inclusion. *Mech. Res. Commun.* **1997**, *24*, 473–482. [CrossRef]
10. Babalola, K.O. On $\lambda-$pseudo-starlike functions. *J. Class. Anal.* **2013**, *3*, 137–147. [CrossRef]
11. Aghalary, R.; Arjomandinia, P. On a first order strong differential subordination and application to univalent functions. *Commun. Korean Math. Soc.* **2022**, *37*, 445–454.
12. Antonino, J.A. Strong differential subordination and applications to univalency conditions. *J. Korean Math. Soc.* **2006**, *43*, 311–322. [CrossRef]
13. Antonino, J.A.; Romaguera, S. Strong differential subordination to Briot-Bouquet differential equations. *J. Diff. Equ.* **1994**, *114*, 101–105. [CrossRef]
14. Olatunji, S.O.; Dutta, H.; Subclasses of multivalent functions of complex order associated with sigmoid function and Bernoulli lemniscate. *TWMS J. App. Eng. Math.* **2020**, *10*, 360–369.
15. Olatunji, S.O.; Gbolagade, A.M. On certain subclass of analytic functions associated with Gegenbauer polynomials. *J. Fract. Calc. Appl.* **2018**, *9*, 127–132.
16. Oladipo, A.T. Bounds for Probabilities of the Generalized Distribution Defined by Generalized Polylogarithm. *J. Math. Punjab Univ.* **2019**, *51*, 19–26.
17. Ahmad, I.; Shah, S.G.A.; Hussain, S.; Darus, M.; Ahmad, B. Fekete-Szegö Functional for Bi-univalent Functions Related with Gegenbauer Polynomials. *J. Math.* **2022**, *2022*, 2705203. [CrossRef]
18. Amourah, A.; Al Amoush, A.G.; Al-Kaseasbeh, M. Gegenbauer polynomials and bi-univalent functions. *Palest. J. Math.* **2021**, *10*, 625–632.
19. Szynal, J. An extension of typically real functions. *Ann. Univ. Mariae Curie-Sklodowska Sect A.* **1994** , *48*, 193–201.
20. Kiepiela, K.; Naraniecka, I.; Szynal, J. The Gegenbauer polynomials and typically real functions. *J. Comput. Appl. Math.* **2003**, *153*, 273–282. [CrossRef]
21. Bavinck, H.; Hooghiemstra, G.; De Waard, E. An application of Gegenbauer polynomials in queueing theory. *Int. J. Comput. Appl. Math.* **1993**, *49*, 1–10. [CrossRef]
22. Porwal, S. Generalized distribution and its geometric properties associated with univalent functions. *J. Complex. Anal.* **2018**, *2018*, 8654506. [CrossRef]
23. Swamy, S.R.; Yalçın, S. Coefficient bounds for regular and bi-univalent functions linked with Gegenbauer polynomials. *Probl. Anal. Issues Anal.* **2022**, *11*, 133–144. [CrossRef]
24. Amourah, A.; Frasin, B.A.; Abdeljawad, T. Fekete-Szegö inequality for analytic and biunivalent functions subordinate to Gegenbauer polynomials. *J. Funct. Spaces* **2021**, *2021*, 5574673. [CrossRef]
25. Amourah, A.; Alomari, M.; Yousef, F.; Alsoboh, A. Consolidation of a Certain Discrete Probability Distribution with a Subclass of Bi-Univalent Functions Involving Gegenbauer Polynomials. *Math. Probl. Eng.* **2022**, *2022*, 6354994. [CrossRef]
26. Çağlar, M.; Cotîrlă, L.-I.; Buyankara, M. Fekete–Szegö Inequalities for a New Subclass of Bi-Univalent Functions Associated with Gegenbauer Polynomials. *Symmetry* **2022**, *14*, 1572. [CrossRef]
27. Srivastava, H.M.; Kamalı, M.; Urdaletova, A. A study of the Fekete-Szegö functional and coefficient estimates for subclasses of analytic functions satisfying a certain subordination condition and associated with the Gegenbauer polynomials. *AIMS Math.* **2021**, *7*, 2568–2584. [CrossRef]
28. Oladipo, A.T. Analytic Univalent Functions defined by Generalized discrete probability distribution. *Eartline J. Math. Sci.* **2021**, *5*, 169–178. [CrossRef]
29. Oladipo, A.T. Generalized distribution associated with univalent functions in conical domain. *An. Univ. Oradea Fasc. Mat.* **2019**, *26*, 161–167.
30. Barton, D.E.; Abramovitz, M.; Stegun, I.A. Handbook of mathematical functions with formulas, graphs and mathematical tables. *J. R. Stat. Soc. Ser. A* **1965**, *128*, 593. [CrossRef]
31. Alzer, H. Error function inequalities. *Adv. Comput. Math.* **2010**, *33*, 349–379. [CrossRef]
32. Carlitz, L. The inverse of the error function. *Pac. J. Math.* **1963**, *13*, 459–470. [CrossRef]
33. Coman, D. The radius of srarlikeness for the error function. *Stud. Univ. Babes-Bolyai Math.* **1991**, *36*, 13–16.
34. Elbert, A.; Laforgia, A. The zeros of the complementary error function. *Numer. Algorithms* **2008**, *49*, 153–157. [CrossRef]

35. Ramachandran, C.; Vanitha, L.M; Kanias, S. Certain results on q-starlike and q-convex error functions. *Math. Slovaca* **2018**, *68*, 361–368. [CrossRef]
36. Ramachandran, C.; Dhanalakshmi, K.; Vanitha, L. Hankel determinant for a subclass of analytic functions associated with error functions bounded by conical regions. *Int. J. Math. Anal.* **2017**, *11*, 571–581. [CrossRef]
37. Fadipe-Joseph, O.A.; Moses, B.O.; Oluwayemi, M.O. Certain new classes of analytic functions defined by using sigmoid function. *Adv. Math. Sci. J.* **2016**, *5*, 83–89.
38. Ezeafulukwe, U.A.; Darus, M.; Fadipe-Joseph, O.A. The $q-$analogue of sigmoid function in the space of univalent $\lambda-$pseudo starlike function. *Int. J. Math. Comput. Sci.* **2020**, *15*, 621–626.
39. Fadipe-Joseph, O.A.; Oladipo, A.T.; Ezeafulukwe, U.A. Modified sigmoid function in univalent function theory. *Int. J. Math. Sci. Eng. App.* **2013**, *7*, 313–317.
40. Hamzat, J.O.; Oladipo, A.T.; Oros, G.I. Bi-Univalent Problems Involving Certain New Subclasses of Generalized Multiplier Transform on Analytic Functions Associated with Modified Sigmoid Function. *Symmetry* **2022**, *14*, 1479. [CrossRef]
41. Murugusundaramoorthy, G.; Janani, T. Sigmoid function in the space of univalent $\lambda-$pseudo starlike functions. *Int. J. Pure Appl. Math.* **2015**, *101*, 33–41. [CrossRef]
42. Murugusundaramoorthy, G.; Olatunji, S.O.; Fadipe-Joseph, O.A. Fekete-Szegö problems for analytic functions in the space of logistic sigmoid functions based on quasi-subordination. *Int. J. Nonlinear Anal. Appl.* **2018**, *9*, 55–68. [CrossRef]
43. Olatunji, S.O. Sigmoid function in the space of space of univalent $\lambda-$pseudo starlike function with Sakaguchi functions. *J. Progress. Res. Math.* **2016**, *7*, 1164–1172.
44. Olatunji, S.O. Fekete-Szegö inequalities on certain subclasses of analytic functions defined by $\lambda-$pseudo-$q-$difference operator associated with $s-$sigmoid function. *Bol. Soc. Mat. Mex.* **2022**, *28*, 55. [CrossRef]
45. Cho, N.E.; Kumar, S.; Kumar, V.; Ravichandran, V.; Srivastava, H.M. Starlike functions related to Bell numbers. *Symmetry* **2019**, *11*, 219. [CrossRef]
46. Goyal, R.; Agarwal, P.; Oros, G.I.; Jain, S. Extended Beta and Gamma Matrix Functions via 2-Parameter Mittag-Leffler Matrix Function. *Mathematics* **2022**, *10*, 892. [CrossRef]
47. Oluwayemi, M.O.; Olatunji, S.O.; Ogunlade, T.O. On certain properties of univalent functions associated with Beta function. *Abstr. Appl. Anal.* **2022**, *2022*, 8150057. [CrossRef]
48. Oluwayemi, M.O.; Olatunji, S.O.; Ogunlade, T.O. On certain subclass of univalent functions involving beta function. *Int. J. Math. Comput. Sci.* **2022**, *17*, 1715–1719.
49. Olatunji, S.O.; Altinkaya, S. Generalized distribution associated with quasi-subordination in terms of error functions and Bell numbers. *J. Jordan J. Math. Stat. (JJMS)* **2021**, *14*, 97–109.
50. Altinkaya, S.; Olatunji, S.O. Generalized distribution for analytic function classes associated with error functions and Bell numbers. *Bol. Soc. Mat. Mex.* **2020**, *26*, 377–384. [CrossRef]
51. Kumar, V.; Cho, N.E.; Ravichandran, V.; Srivastava, H.M. Sharp coefficient bounds for starlike functions associated with Bell numbers. *Math. Slovaca* **2019**, *69*, 1053–1064. [CrossRef]

axioms

MDPI

Article

Bell Distribution Series Defined on Subclasses of Bi-Univalent Functions That Are Subordinate to Horadam Polynomials

Ibtisam Aldawish [1], Basem Frasin [2,*] and Ala Amourah [3]

1 Department of Mathematics and Statistics, College of Science, IMSIU (Imam Mohammad Ibn Saud Islamic University), Riyadh 11564, Saudi Arabia
2 Faculty of Science, Department of Mathematics, Al al-Bayt University, Mafraq 25113, Jordan
3 Department of Mathematics, Faculty of Science and Technology, Irbid National University, Irbid 21110, Jordan
* Correspondence: bafrasin@yahoo.com or bafrasin@aabu.edu.jo

Abstract: Several different subclasses of the bi-univalent function class Σ were introduced and studied by many authors using distribution series like Pascal distribution, Poisson distribution, Borel distribution, the Mittag-Leffler-type Borel distribution, Miller–Ross-Type Poisson Distribution. In the present paper, by making use of the Bell distribution, we introduce and investigate a new family $\mathfrak{G}^{t}_{\Sigma}(x,p,q,\lambda,\beta,\gamma)$ of normalized bi-univalent functions in the open unit disk $\mathfrak{U}$, which are associated with the Horadam polynomials and estimate the second and the third coefficients in the Taylor-Maclaurin expansions of functions belonging to this class. Furthermore, we establish the Fekete–Szegö inequality for functions in the family $\mathfrak{G}^{t}_{\Sigma}(x,p,q,\lambda,\beta,\gamma)$. After specializing the parameters used in our main results, a number of new results are demonstrated to follow.

Keywords: fekete-Szegö problem; horadam polynomials; bi-univalent functions; bell distribution; analytic functions

MSC: 30C45

Citation: Aldawish, I.; Frasin, B.; Amourah, A. Bell Distribution Series Defined on Subclasses of Bi-Univalent Functions That Are Subordinate to Horadam Polynomials. *Axioms* **2023**, *12*, 362. https://doi.org/10.3390/axioms12040362

Academic Editor: Georgia Irina Oros

Received: 19 February 2023
Revised: 30 March 2023
Accepted: 7 April 2023
Published: 10 April 2023

1. Introduction and Preliminaries

Orthogonal polynomials [1] are commonly employed in mathematical model solving to find solutions to ordinary differential equations that satisfy model requirements. Orthogonal polynomials are important for contemporary mathematics and have a wide range of uses in physics and engineering. It is common knowledge that these polynomials play a key role in approximation theory-related concerns. They can be found in differential equation theory, mathematical statistics, interpolation, approximation theory, probability theory, and quantum mechanics. They are also used in signal processing, image processing, and data analysis, where they are used to model and analyze complex systems and data sets. Their applications to automated control, quantum physics, signal analysis, scattering theory, and axially symmetric potential theory are also widely known [2,3].

Two polynomials $\mathbb{S}_\rho$ and $\mathbb{S}_\sigma$, of order ρ and σ, respectively, are orthogonal if

$$\langle \mathbb{S}_\rho, \mathbb{S}_\sigma \rangle = \int_c^d \mathbb{S}_\rho(x)\mathbb{S}_\sigma(x)r(x)dx = 0, \qquad \text{for} \qquad \rho \neq \sigma, \tag{1}$$

where $r(x)$ is a non-negative function in the interval (c,d); therefore, all finite order polynomials $\mathbb{S}_\rho(x)$ have a well-defined integral.

Examples of well-known families of orthogonal polynomials include the Legendre polynomials, Hermite polynomials, Chebyshev polynomials, Jacobi polynomials, and Laguerre polynomials. Each family of orthogonal polynomials has its own weight function and interval, and they have many useful properties and applications.

Horadam polynomials are a family of polynomials defined by recurrence relations that generalize the Fibonacci and Lucas polynomials. They are named after Australian mathematician Murray S. Klamkin Horadam who introduced them in 1978.

Like the Fibonacci and Lucas polynomials, the Horadam polynomials have many interesting properties and connections to other areas of mathematics, including number theory, combinatorics, and algebraic geometry. They also satisfy various recurrence relations and identities, which can be used to derive closed-form expressions and study their properties.

Horadam polynomials have applications in various fields of science, including physics, engineering, and computer science. They have been used, for example, in modeling the behavior of certain physical systems, analyzing algorithms, and designing error-correcting codes.

The Horadam polynomials $h_n(x)$, which are provided by the recurrence relation as follows, were studied by Horzum and Kocer in 2009 [4].

$$h_n(x) = pxh_{n-1}(x) + qh_{n-2}(x), \quad (n \in \mathbb{N} \setminus \{1,2\}), \tag{2}$$

with

$$h_1(x) = a, h_2(x) = tx \text{ and } h_3(x) = ptx^2 + aq, \tag{3}$$

for some real constant a, t, p and q.

Remark 1. *For particular values of a, t, p and q, the Horadam polynomials $h_n(x)$ lead to various polynomials (see [4,5]), for example:*

1. *If $a = t = p = q = 1$, then we get the Fibonacci polynomials $F_n(x)$;*
2. *If $a = 2$ and $t = p = q = 1$, then we get the Lucas polynomials $L_n(x)$;*
3. *If $a = t = 1$, $p = 2$ and $q = -1$, then we get the Chebyshev polynomials $T_n(x)$ of the first kind;*
4. *If $a = 1$, $t = p = 2$ and $q = -1$, then we get the Chebyshev polynomials $U_n(x)$ of the second kind;*
5. *If $a = q = 1$ and $t = p = 2$, then we get the Pell polynomials $P_n(x)$;*
6. *If $a = t = p = 2$ and $q = 1$, then we get the Pell-Lucas polynomials $Q_n(x)$ of the first kind.*

Numerous fields in the mathematical, physical, statistical, and engineering sciences depend heavily on the Fibonacci, Lucas, Chebyshev, and families of orthogonal polynomials and other special polynomials as well as their generalizations. Numerous articles have examined these kinds of polynomials from a theoretical standpoint.

The generator of the Horadam polynomials $h_n(x)$ is as follows:

$$\Omega(x,\xi) = \sum_{n=1}^{\infty} h_n(x)\xi^{n-1} = \frac{a + (t - ap)x\xi}{1 - px\xi - q\xi^2}. \tag{4}$$

Let $\mathcal{A}$ be the class of functions f of the form

$$f(\xi) = \xi + a_2\xi^2 + a_3\xi^3 + \cdots, \tag{5}$$

that are analytic in the disk $\mathfrak{U} = \{\xi : |\xi| < 1\}$. Also, we represent by $\mathcal{S}$ the subclass of $\mathcal{A}$ comprising functions of the Equation (5) which are also univalent in $\mathfrak{U}$.

The subordination of analytic functions f and g is denoted by $f \prec g$ if, for all $\xi \in \mathfrak{U}$, there exists a Schwarz function ϖ with $\varpi(0) = 0$ and $|\varpi(\xi)| < 1$, such that

$$f(\xi) = g(\varpi(\xi)).$$

Moreover, if g is univalent in $\mathfrak{U}$, then

$$f(\xi) \prec g(\xi), \text{ if and only if, } f(0) = g(0)$$

and

$$f(\mathfrak{U}) \subset g(\mathfrak{U}).$$

According to the Koebe one-quarter theorem [6,7], every function $f \in \mathcal{S}$ has an inverse f^{-1} defined by

$$f^{-1}(f(\xi)) = \xi \qquad (\xi \in \mathfrak{U})$$

and

$$w = f(f^{-1}(w)) \qquad (|w| < r_0(f);\ r_0(f) \geq \frac{1}{4})$$

where

$$g(w) = f^{-1}(w) = w - a_2 w^2 + (-a_3 + 2a_2^2)w^3 - (a_4 + 5a_2^3 - 5a_3 a_2)w^4 + \cdots . \qquad (6)$$

A function $f \in \mathcal{S}$ is said to be bi-univalent in $\mathfrak{U}$ if both $f(\xi)$ and $f^{-1}(\xi)$ are univalent in $\mathfrak{U}$.

Let Σ denote the class of bi-univalent functions in $\mathfrak{U}$ given by (5). Examples in the class Σ are

$$f_1(\xi) = \frac{\xi}{1-\xi}, \qquad f_2(\xi) = \log \frac{1}{1-\xi},$$

and their inverses,

$$f_1^{-1}(w) = \frac{w}{1+w}, \qquad f_2^{-1}(w) = \frac{e^w - 1}{e^w}$$

are in the class Σ.

However, Σ does not include the well-known Koebe function. Additional typical instances of functions in $\mathfrak{U}$ include

$$\frac{2\xi - \xi^2}{2} \text{ and } \frac{\xi}{1-\xi^2}$$

are also not members of Σ. For interesting subclasses of functions in the class Σ, see ([8–10]).

Brannan and Taha [11] (see also [12]) introduced certain subclasses of the bi-univalent function class Σ similar to the familiar subclasses $\mathcal{S}^*(\alpha)$ and $\mathcal{K}(\alpha)$ of starlike and convex functions of order $\alpha (0 \leq \alpha < 1)$, respectively (see [13]). Thus, following Brannan and Taha [11] (see also [12]), a function $f \in \mathcal{A}$ is in the class $\mathcal{S}_\Sigma^*[\alpha]$ of strongly bi-starlike functions of order $\alpha (0 < \alpha \leq 1)$ if each of the following conditions is satisfied:

$$f \in \Sigma \text{ and } \left| \arg\left(\frac{\xi f'(\xi)}{f(\xi)} \right) \right| < \frac{\alpha\pi}{2} \qquad (0 < \alpha \leq 1,\ \xi \in \mathfrak{U})$$

and

$$\left| \arg\left(\frac{w g'(w)}{g(w)} \right) \right| < \frac{\alpha\pi}{2} \qquad (0 < \alpha \leq 1,\ w \in \mathfrak{U}),$$

where g is the extension of f^{-1} to $\mathfrak{U}$. The classes $\mathcal{S}_\Sigma^*(\alpha)$ and $\mathcal{K}_\Sigma(\alpha)$ of bi-starlike functions of order α and bi-convex functions of order α, corresponding (respectively) to the function classes $\mathcal{S}^*(\alpha)$ and $\mathcal{K}(\alpha)$, were also introduced analogously. For each of the function classes $\mathcal{S}_\Sigma^*(\alpha)$ and $\mathcal{K}_\Sigma(\alpha)$, they found non-sharp estimates on the first two Taylor–Maclaurin coefficients $|a_2|$ and $|a_3|$ (for details, see [11,12]). However, the coefficient problem for each of the succeeding Taylor–Maclaurin coefficients,

$$|a_n| \quad (n \in \mathbb{N} \setminus \{1, 2\})$$

is still an open problem (see [11–14]).

Several subclasses of the bi-univalent function class Σ were introduced, inspired by the ground-breaking work of Srivastava et al. [15], and non-sharp estimates on the first two coefficients $|a_2|$ and $|a_3|$ in the Taylor-Maclaurin series expansion (5) were obtained in ([16–28]).

Fekete and Szegö [29] proved that the estimate

$$\left|a_3 - \eta a_2^2\right| \leq 1 + 2e^{\left(\frac{-2\eta}{1-\eta}\right)}$$

holds for any normalized univalent function f and $\eta \in [0,1]$. This inequality is sharp for each η (see, [29]). Recently, many authors have obtained Fekete–Szegö inequalities for different classes of functions (see [30–34]).

In recent years, several studies have looked at crucial aspects of the geometric function theory including coefficient estimates, inclusion relations, and requirements for belonging to certain classes, using a variety of probability distributions, including the Poisson, Pascal, Borel, Mittag-Leffler-type Poisson distribution, etc. (see, [35–40]).

The Bell distribution, also known as the normal mixture distribution, is a probability distribution that arises in the context of statistical inference, signal processing, and other fields of science. The Bell distribution is a continuous probability distribution that is a mixture of normal distributions. In a Bell distribution, approximately 0.68 of the data falls within one standard deviation of the mean, 0.95 falls within two standard deviations, and 0.997 falls within three standard deviations.

The Bell distribution has a symmetric bell-shaped probability density function that resembles a normal distribution but with heavier tails. The mixing parameter p controls the degree of asymmetry of the distribution, with $p = 0.5$ corresponding to a perfectly symmetric distribution. The Bell distribution has applications in a wide range of fields, including finance, physics, engineering, and biology. It has been used, for example, to model the distribution of stock returns, the properties of noisy signals, and the behavior of biological systems. The Bell curve has many important applications in statistics, such as hypothesis testing, confidence intervals, and regression analysis. It is also used in fields such as finance, economics, and psychology, where it is used to model the behavior of complex systems and to make predictions based on empirical data.

In 2018, Castellares et al. [41] introduced the Bell distribution, it is improved from the Bell numbers [42].

When a discrete random variable X follows the Bell distribution, its probability density function can be expressed as

$$P(X = m) = \frac{\lambda^m e^{e^{(-\lambda^2)+1}} B_m}{m!}; \quad m = 1, 2, 3, \ldots, \tag{7}$$

where

$$B_m = \frac{1}{e} \sum_{k=0}^{\infty} \frac{k^m}{m!} \tag{8}$$

is the Bell numbers, $m \geq 2$, and $\lambda > 0$ .The Bell number B_m given in (8) is the mth moment of the Poisson distribution with parameter equal to 1. The first few Bell numbers are $B_2 = 2$, $B_3 = 5$, $B_4 = 15$ and $B_5 = 52$.

Now, we present the power series below, whose coefficients are from the Bell distribution.

$$\mathbb{B}(\lambda, \xi) = \xi + \sum_{n=2}^{\infty} \frac{\lambda^{n-1} e^{e^{(-\lambda^2)+1}} B_n}{(n-1)!} \xi^n, \qquad \xi \in \mathfrak{U}, \ \lambda > 0. \tag{9}$$

Consider the linear operator $\mathbb{P}_\lambda : \mathcal{A} \to \mathcal{A}$ defined by the convolution

$$\mathbb{P}_\lambda f(\xi) = \mathbb{B}(\lambda, \xi) * f(\xi) = \xi + \sum_{n=2}^{\infty} \frac{\lambda^{n-1} e^{e^{(-\lambda^2)+1}} B_n}{(n-1)!} a_n \xi^n, \qquad \xi \in \mathfrak{U}. \tag{10}$$

Recently, a large number of researchers have investigated bi-univalent functions connected to orthogonal polynomials, few to mention ([43–47]). As far as we are aware, there hasn't been any research on bi-univalent functions for Bell distribution subordinate to Horadam polynomials in the literature.

The rest of this article is organized as follows. In Section 2 we introduce a new subclass $\mathfrak{G}_{\Sigma}^{t}(x,p,q,\lambda,\beta,\gamma)$ of Σ involving the Bell distribution linked to Horadam polynomials, and deriving bounds for the second and the third coefficients in the Taylor-Maclaurin expansions. Section 3 deals with the estimation of Fekete–Szegö inequality for functions in the family $\mathfrak{G}_{\Sigma}^{t}(x,p,q,\lambda,\beta,\gamma)$. Relevant connections of some of the special cases of the main results are pointed out in Section 4. Section 5 closes up the paper with some conclusions.

2. Bounds of the Class $\mathfrak{G}_{\Sigma}^{t}(x,p,q,\lambda,\beta,\gamma)$

This section begins with a definition of a new subclass associated with the Bell distribution series.

Definition 1. *If the following subordinations are met, a function $f \in \Sigma$ given by (5) is said to belong to the class $\mathfrak{G}_{\Sigma}^{t}(x,p,q,\lambda,\beta,\gamma)$:*

$$(1-\gamma)\frac{\mathbb{P}_{\lambda}f(\xi)}{\xi}+\gamma(\mathbb{P}_{\lambda}f(\xi))'+\beta\xi(\mathbb{P}_{\lambda}f(\xi))''\prec\Omega(x,\xi)+1-a \tag{11}$$

and

$$(1-\gamma)\frac{\mathbb{P}_{\lambda}f(w)}{w}+\gamma(\mathbb{P}_{\lambda}f(w))'+\beta w(\mathbb{P}_{\lambda}f(w))''\prec\Omega(x,w)+1-a, \tag{12}$$

where $\xi, w \in \mathfrak{U}$, $\gamma,\beta \geq 0$, $x \in \mathbb{R}$, and the function $g = f^{-1}$ is given by (6).

Example 1. *For $\beta = 0$, we have, $\mathfrak{G}_{\Sigma}^{t}(x,p,q,\lambda,0,\gamma) = \mathfrak{G}_{\Sigma}^{t}(x,p,q,\lambda,\gamma)$, in which $\mathfrak{G}_{\Sigma}^{t}(x,p,q,\lambda,\gamma)$ indicates the group of functions $f \in \Sigma$ given by (5) and satisfying the criterion below.*

$$(1-\gamma)\frac{\mathbb{P}_{\lambda}f(\xi)}{\xi}+\gamma(\mathbb{P}_{\lambda}f(\xi))'\prec\Omega(x,\xi)+1-a \tag{13}$$

and

$$(1-\gamma)\frac{\mathbb{P}_{\lambda}f(w)}{w}+\gamma(\mathbb{P}_{\lambda}f(w))'\prec\Omega(x,w)+1-a, \tag{14}$$

where $\xi, w \in \mathfrak{U}$, $\gamma \geq 0$, $x \in \mathbb{R}$, and the function $g = f^{-1}$ is given by (6).

Example 2. *For $\beta = 0$ and $\gamma = 1$, we have, $\mathfrak{G}_{\Sigma}^{t}(x,p,q,\lambda,1) = \mathfrak{G}_{\Sigma}^{t}(x,p,q,\lambda)$, in which $\mathfrak{G}_{\Sigma}^{t}(x,p,q,\lambda)$ denotes the class of functions $f \in \Sigma$ given by (5) and satisfying the following condition*

$$(\mathbb{P}_{\lambda}f(\xi))'\prec\Omega(x,\xi)+1-a \tag{15}$$

and

$$(\mathbb{P}_{\lambda}f(w))'\prec\Omega(x,w)+1-a, \tag{16}$$

where $\xi, w \in \mathfrak{U}$, $x \in \mathbb{R}$, and the function $g = f^{-1}$ is given by (6).

Example 3. *For $\beta = 0$ and $\gamma = 0$, we have, $\mathfrak{G}_{\Sigma}^{t}(x,p,q,\lambda,0,0) = \mathfrak{G}_{\Sigma}^{t}(x,p,q,\lambda,0)$, in which $\mathfrak{G}_{\Sigma}^{t}(x,p,q,\lambda,0)$ indicates the group of functions $f \in \Sigma$ given by (5) and satisfying the criterion below.*

$$\frac{\mathbb{P}_{\lambda}f(\xi)}{\xi}\prec\Omega(x,\xi)+1-a \tag{17}$$

and

$$\frac{\mathbb{P}_{\lambda}f(w)}{w}\prec\Omega(x,w)+1-a, \tag{18}$$

where $\xi, w \in \mathfrak{U}$, $x \in \mathbb{R}$, and the function $g = f^{-1}$ is given by (6).

Example 4. *For $\lambda = 1$, we have, $\mathfrak{G}^t_\Sigma(x,p,q,1,\beta,\gamma) = \mathfrak{G}^t_\Sigma(x,p,q,\beta,\gamma)$, in which $\mathfrak{G}^t_\Sigma(x,p,q,\beta,\gamma)$ indicates the group of functions $f \in \Sigma$ given by (5) and satisfying the criterion below.*

$$(1-\gamma)\frac{\mathbb{P}_1 f(\xi)}{\xi} + \gamma(\mathbb{P}_1 f(\xi))' + \beta\xi(\mathbb{P}_1 f(\xi))'' \prec \Omega(x,\xi) + 1 - a \tag{19}$$

and

$$(1-\gamma)\frac{\mathbb{P}_1 f(w)}{w} + \gamma(\mathbb{P}_1 f(w))' + \beta w(\mathbb{P}_1 f(w))'' \prec \Omega(x,w) + 1 - a, \tag{20}$$

where $\xi, w \in \mathfrak{U}$, $\gamma \geq 0$, $x \in \mathbb{R}$, and the function $g = f^{-1}$ is given by (6).

First, we give the coefficient estimates for the class $\mathfrak{G}^t_\Sigma(x,p,q,\lambda,\beta,\gamma)$ given in Definition 1.

Theorem 1. *Let $f \in \Sigma$ given by (5) belongs to the class $\mathfrak{G}^t_\Sigma(x,p,q,\lambda,\beta,\gamma)$. Then*

$$|a_2| \leq \frac{tx\sqrt{2tx}}{\lambda e^{e^{\frac{1}{2}(1-\lambda^2)}}\sqrt{\left|\left[5(1+2\gamma+6\beta)(tx)^2 - 8e^{e^{(1-\lambda^2)}}(1+\gamma+2\beta)^2(ptx^2+aq)\right]\right|}},$$

and

$$|a_3| \leq \frac{t^2x^2}{4\lambda^2(1+\gamma+2\beta)^2 e^{2e^{(1-\lambda^2)}}} + \frac{2tx}{5\lambda^2(1+2\gamma+6\beta)e^{e^{(1-\lambda^2)}}}.$$

Proof. Let $f \in \mathfrak{G}^t_\Sigma(x,p,q,\lambda,\beta,\gamma)$. From Definition 1, we can write

$$(1-\gamma)\frac{\mathbb{P}_\lambda f(\xi)}{\xi} + \gamma(\mathbb{P}_\lambda f(\xi))' + \beta\xi(\mathbb{P}_\lambda f(\xi))'' = \Omega(x,\varkappa(\xi)) + 1 - a \tag{21}$$

and

$$(1-\gamma)\frac{\mathbb{P}_\lambda f(w)}{w} + \gamma(\mathbb{P}_\lambda f(w))' + \beta w(\mathbb{P}_\lambda f(w))'' = \Omega(x,\tau(w)) + 1 - a, \tag{22}$$

where the analytical functions $\varkappa$ and τ have the form

$$\varkappa(\xi) = c_1\xi + c_2\xi^2 + c_3\xi^3 + \cdots, \quad (\xi \in \mathfrak{U})$$

and

$$\tau(w) = d_1 w + d_2 w^2 + d_3 w^3 + \cdots, \quad (w \in \mathfrak{U}),$$

such that $\varkappa(0) = \tau(0) = 0$ and $|\varkappa(\xi)| < 1$, $|\tau(w)| < 1$ for all $\xi, w \in \mathfrak{U}$.

From the equalities (21) and (22), we get

$$(1-\gamma)\frac{\mathbb{P}_\lambda f(\xi)}{\xi} + \gamma(\mathbb{P}_\lambda f(\xi))' + \beta\xi(\mathbb{P}_\lambda f(\xi))'' = 1 + h_2(x)c_1\xi + \left[h_2(x)c_2 + h_3(x)c_1^2\right]\xi^2 + \cdots \tag{23}$$

and

$$(1-\gamma)\frac{\mathbb{P}_\lambda f(w)}{w} + \gamma(\mathbb{P}_\lambda f(w))' + \beta w(\mathbb{P}_\lambda f(w))'' = 1 + h_2(x)d_1 w + \left[h_2(x)d_2 + h_3(x)d_1^2\right]w^2 + \cdots. \tag{24}$$

It is common knowledge that if

$$|\varkappa(\xi)| = \left|c_1\xi + c_2\xi^2 + c_3\xi^3 + \cdots\right| < 1, \quad (\xi \in \mathfrak{U})$$

and

$$|\tau(w)| = \left|d_1 w + d_2 w^2 + d_3 w^3 + \cdots\right| < 1, \quad (w \in \mathfrak{U}),$$

then

$$|c_j| \le 1 \text{ and } |d_j| \le 1 \text{ for all } j \in \mathbb{N}. \tag{25}$$

Equating the coefficients of both sides in (23) and (24), we get

$$2\lambda(1+\gamma+2\beta)e^{e^{\left(1-\lambda^2\right)}}a_2 = h_2(x)c_1, \tag{26}$$

$$\frac{5}{2}\lambda^2(1+2\gamma+6\beta)e^{e^{\left(1-\lambda^2\right)}}a_3 = h_2(x)c_2 + h_3(x)c_1^2, \tag{27}$$

$$-2\lambda(1+\gamma+2\beta)e^{e^{\left(1-\lambda^2\right)}}a_2 = h_2(x)d_1, \tag{28}$$

and

$$\frac{5}{2}\lambda^2(1+2\gamma+6\beta)e^{e^{\left(1-\lambda^2\right)}}\left[2a_2^2 - a_3\right] = h_2(x)d_2 + h_3(x)d_1^2. \tag{29}$$

It follows from (26) and (28) that

$$c_1 = -d_1 \tag{30}$$

and

$$8\lambda^2(1+\gamma+2\beta)^2 e^{2e^{\left(1-\lambda^2\right)}}a_2^2 = [h_2(x)]^2\left(c_1^2 + d_1^2\right). \tag{31}$$

If we add (27) and (29), we get

$$5\lambda^2(1+2\gamma+6\beta)e^{e^{\left(1-\lambda^2\right)}}a_2^2 = h_2(x)(c_2+d_2) + h_3(x)\left(c_1^2 + d_1^2\right). \tag{32}$$

Replacing the value of $\left(c_1^2 + d_1^2\right)$ from (31) in the right hand side of (32), we have

$$\begin{aligned}&\left[5(1+2\gamma+6\beta) - 8(1+\gamma+2\beta)^2 e^{e^{\left(1-\lambda^2\right)}}\frac{h_3(x)}{[h_2(x)]^2}\right]\lambda^2 e^{e^{\left(1-\lambda^2\right)}}a_2^2 \\ &= h_2(x)(c_2+d_2).\end{aligned} \tag{33}$$

Using (3), (25) and (33), we find that

$$|a_2| \le \frac{tx\sqrt{2tx}}{\lambda e^{e^{\frac{1}{2}\left(1-\lambda^2\right)}}\sqrt{\left|\left[5(1+2\gamma+6\beta)[tx]^2 - 8e^{e^{\left(1-\lambda^2\right)}}(1+\gamma+2\beta)^2(ptx^2+aq)\right]\right|}}.$$

Moreover, if we subtract (29) from (27), we obtain

$$5\lambda^2(1+2\gamma+6\beta)e^{e^{\left(1-\lambda^2\right)}}\left(a_3 - a_2^2\right) = h_2(x)(c_2-d_2) + h_3(x)\left(c_1^2 - d_1^2\right). \tag{34}$$

Then, in view of (30) and (31), Equation (34) becomes

$$\begin{aligned}a_3 = &\frac{[h_2(x)]^2}{8\lambda^2(1+\gamma+2\beta)^2 e^{2e^{\left(1-\lambda^2\right)}}}\left(c_1^2 + d_1^2\right) \\ &+ \frac{h_2(x)}{5\lambda^2(1+2\gamma+6\beta)e^{e^{\left(1-\lambda^2\right)}}}(c_2 - d_2).\end{aligned}$$

By applying (3), we conclude that

$$|a_3| \leq \frac{t^2x^2}{4\lambda^2(1+\gamma+2\beta)^2 e^{2e^{(1-\lambda^2)}}} + \frac{2tx}{5\lambda^2(1+2\gamma+6\beta)e^{e^{(1-\lambda^2)}}}.$$

□

3. Fekete-Szegö Inequalities

Using the values of a_2^2 and a_3, we prove the functional $|a_3 - \eta a_2^2|$ for class functions $\mathfrak{G}_\Sigma^t(x, p, q, \lambda, \beta, \gamma)$.

Theorem 2. *Let $f \in \Sigma$ given by (5) belongs to the class $\mathfrak{G}_\Sigma^t(x, p, q, \lambda, \beta, \gamma)$. Then*

$$|a_3 - \eta a_2^2| \leq \begin{cases} \dfrac{2|tx|}{5\lambda^2(1+2\gamma+6\beta)e^{e^{(1-\lambda^2)}}}, & |\eta - 1| \leq \delta \\ \dfrac{2(tx)^3|1-\eta|}{\lambda^2 e^{e^{(1-\lambda^2)}}\left|\left[5(1+2\gamma+6\beta)t^2x^2 - 8(1+\gamma+2\beta)^2 e^{e^{(1-\lambda^2)}}(ptx^2+aq)\right]\right|}, & |\eta - 1| \geq \delta, \end{cases}$$

where

$$\delta = \left|1 - \frac{8(1+\gamma+2\beta)^2 e^{e^{(1-\lambda^2)}}(ptx^2+aq)}{5(1+2\gamma+6\beta)t^2x^2}\right|.$$

Proof. From (33) and (34)

$$\begin{aligned} &a_3 - \eta a_2^2 \\ &= (1-\eta)\frac{[h_2(x)]^3(c_2+d_2)}{\lambda^2 e^{e^{(1-\lambda^2)}}\left[5(1+2\gamma+6\beta)[h_2(x)]^2 - 8(1+\gamma+2\beta)^2 e^{e^{(1-\lambda^2)}} h_3(x)\right]} \\ &+ \frac{h_2(x)}{5\lambda^2(1+2\gamma+6\beta)e^{e^{(1-\lambda^2)}}}(c_2 - d_2) \\ &= h_2(x)\left[h(\eta) + \frac{1}{5\lambda^2(1+2\gamma+6\beta)e^{e^{(1-\lambda^2)}}}\right]c_2 \\ &+ h_2(x)\left[h(\eta) - \frac{1}{5\lambda^2(1+2\gamma+6\beta)e^{e^{(1-\lambda^2)}}}\right]d_2, \end{aligned}$$

where

$$\Upsilon(\eta) = \frac{[h_2(x)]^2(1-\eta)}{\lambda^2 e^{e^{(1-\lambda^2)}}\left[5(1+2\gamma+6\beta)[h_2(x)]^2 - 8(1+\gamma+2\beta)^2 e^{e^{(1-\lambda^2)}} h_3(x)\right]},$$

Then, in view of (3), we conclude that

$$\left|a_3 - \eta a_2^2\right| \leq \begin{cases} \dfrac{2|h_2(x)|}{5\lambda^2(1+2\gamma+6\beta)e^{e^{(1-\lambda^2)}}} & 0 \leq |\Upsilon(\eta)| \leq \dfrac{1}{5\lambda^2(1+2\gamma+6\beta)e^{e^{(1-\lambda^2)}}}, \\ 2|h_2(x)||\Upsilon(\eta)| & |\Upsilon(\eta)| \geq \dfrac{1}{5\lambda^2(1+2\gamma+6\beta)e^{e^{(1-\lambda^2)}}}. \end{cases}$$

□

4. Special Cases and Consequences

By specializing the parameters β, λ and γ in the above theorems, we obtain the following corollaries.

Corollary 1. *Let $f \in \Sigma$ given by (5) belongs to the class $\mathfrak{G}_{\Sigma}^{t}(x,p,q,\lambda,\gamma)$. Then*

$$|a_2| \leq \frac{tx\sqrt{2tx}}{\lambda e^{e^{\frac{1}{2}(1-\lambda^2)}}\sqrt{\left|\left[5(1+2\gamma)(tx)^2 - 8e^{e^{(1-\lambda^2)}}(1+\gamma)^2(ptx^2+aq)\right]\right|}},$$

$$|a_3| \leq \frac{t^2x^2}{4\lambda^2(1+\gamma)^2 e^{2e^{(1-\lambda^2)}}} + \frac{2tx}{5\lambda^2(1+2\gamma)e^{e^{(1-\lambda^2)}}},$$

and

$$|a_3 - \eta a_2^2| \leq \begin{cases} \frac{2|tx|}{5\lambda^2(1+2\gamma)e^{e^{(1-\lambda^2)}}}, & |\eta - 1| \leq \Phi \\ \frac{2(tx)^3|1-\eta|}{\lambda^2 e^{e^{(1-\lambda^2)}}\left|\left[5(1+2\gamma)t^2x^2 - 8(1+\gamma)^2 e^{e^{(1-\lambda^2)}}(ptx^2+aq)\right]\right|}, & |\eta - 1| \geq \Phi, \end{cases}$$

where

$$\Phi = \left|1 - \frac{8(1+\gamma)^2 e^{e^{(1-\lambda^2)}}(ptx^2+aq)}{5(1+2\gamma)t^2x^2}\right|.$$

Corollary 2. *Let $f \in \Sigma$ given by (5) belongs to the class $\mathfrak{G}_{\Sigma}^{t}(x,p,q,\lambda)$. Then*

$$|a_2| \leq \frac{tx\sqrt{2tx}}{\lambda e^{e^{\frac{1}{2}(1-\lambda^2)}}\sqrt{\left|\left[15(tx)^2 - 32e^{e^{(1-\lambda^2)}}(ptx^2+aq)\right]\right|}},$$

$$|a_3| \leq \frac{t^2x^2}{16\lambda^2 e^{2e^{(1-\lambda^2)}}} + \frac{2tx}{15\lambda^2 e^{e^{(1-\lambda^2)}}},$$

and

$$|a_3 - \eta a_2^2| \leq \begin{cases} \frac{2|tx|}{15\lambda^2 e^{e^{(1-\lambda^2)}}}, & |\eta - 1| \leq \left|1 - \frac{32e^{e^{(1-\lambda^2)}}(ptx^2+aq)}{15t^2x^2}\right| \\ \frac{2(tx)^3|1-\eta|}{\lambda^2 e^{e^{(1-\lambda^2)}}\left|\left[15t^2x^2 - 32e^{e^{(1-\lambda^2)}}(ptx^2+aq)\right]\right|}, & |\eta - 1| \geq \left|1 - \frac{32e^{e^{(1-\lambda^2)}}(ptx^2+aq)}{15t^2x^2}\right|. \end{cases}$$

Corollary 3. *Let $f \in \Sigma$ given by (5) belongs to the class $\mathfrak{G}_{\Sigma}^{t}(x,p,q,\lambda,0)$. Then*

$$|a_2| \leq \frac{tx\sqrt{2tx}}{\lambda e^{e^{\frac{1}{2}(1-\lambda^2)}}\sqrt{\left|\left[5(tx)^2 - 8e^{e^{(1-\lambda^2)}}(ptx^2+aq)\right]\right|}},$$

$$|a_3| \leq \frac{t^2x^2}{4\lambda^2 e^{2e^{(1-\lambda^2)}}} + \frac{2tx}{5\lambda^2 e^{e^{(1-\lambda^2)}}},$$

and

$$|a_3 - \eta a_2^2| \leq \begin{cases} \frac{2|tx|}{5\lambda^2 e^{e^{(1-\lambda^2)}}}, & |\eta - 1| < \Phi \\ \frac{2(tx)^3|1-\eta|}{\lambda^2 e^{e^{(1-\lambda^2)}}\left|\left[5t^2x^2 - 8e^{e^{(1-\lambda^2)}}(ptx^2+aq)\right]\right|}, & |\eta - 1| \geq \Phi, \end{cases}$$

where

$$\Phi = \left| 1 - \frac{8e^{e^{\left(1-\lambda^2\right)}}(ptx^2 + aq)}{5t^2x^2} \right|.$$

Corollary 4. *Let $f \in \Sigma$ given by (5) belongs to the class$\mathfrak{G}^t_\Sigma(x, p, q, \beta, \gamma)$. Then*

$$|a_2| \leq \frac{tx\sqrt{2tx}}{e\sqrt{\left|\left[5(1 + 2\gamma + 6\beta)(tx)^2 - 8e(1 + \gamma + 2\beta)^2(ptx^2 + aq)\right]\right|}},$$

$$|a_3| \leq \frac{t^2x^2}{4e^2(1 + \gamma + 2\beta)^2} + \frac{2tx}{5e(1 + 2\gamma + 6\beta)}.$$

and

$$\left|a_3 - \eta a_2^2\right| \leq \begin{cases} \frac{2|tx|}{5e(1+2\gamma+6\beta)}, & |\eta - 1| \leq \delta \\ \frac{2(tx)^3|1-\eta|}{e\left|\left[5(1+2\gamma+6\beta)t^2x^2 - 8e(1+\gamma+2\beta)^2(ptx^2+aq)\right]\right|}, & |\eta - 1| \geq \delta, \end{cases}$$

where

$$\delta = \left| 1 - \frac{8e(1 + \gamma + 2\beta)^2(ptx^2 + aq)}{5(1 + 2\gamma + 6\beta)t^2x^2} \right|.$$

5. Conclusions

In this study, we introduced a new class of normalized analytics and bi-univalent functions connected to the Bell distribution series denoted by $\mathfrak{G}^t_\Sigma(x, p, q, \lambda, \beta, \gamma)$. We have derived estimates for the Taylor-Maclaurin coefficients $|a_2|$ and $|a_3|$ and Fekete-Szegö functional problems. Additionally, by appropriately specializing the parameters β and γ, one may determine the outcomes for the subclasses$\mathfrak{G}^t_\Sigma(x, p, q, \lambda, \gamma)$, $\mathfrak{G}^t_\Sigma(x, p, q, \lambda)$, $\mathfrak{G}^t_\Sigma(x, p, q, \lambda, 0)$ and $\mathfrak{G}^t_\Sigma(x, p, q, \beta, \gamma)$ specified in Examples 1, 2, 3 and 4, respectively, and linked to the Bell distribution series. Making use of Bell distribution series (10) could inspire researchers to derive the estimates of the Taylor-Maclaurin coefficients $|a_2|$ and $|a_3|$ and Fekete-Szegö functional problems for functions belonging to new subclasses of bi-univalent functions defined by means of Horadam polynomials associated with this distribution series.

Author Contributions: Conceptualization, A.A. and B.F.; methodology, A.A.; validation, A.A., B.F. and I.A.; formal analysis, A.A.; investigation, A.A., B.F., and I.A.; writing-original draft preparation, B.F. and A.A., writing-review and editing, A.A., B.F., and I.A.; supervision, B.F. All authors have read and agreed to the published version of the manuscript.

Funding: This research received no external funding.

Institutional Review Board Statement: Not applicable.

Informed Consent Statement: Not applicable.

Data Availability Statement: Not applicable.

Conflicts of Interest: The authors declare no conflict of interest.

References

1. Legendre, A. *Recherches sur Laattraction des Sphéroides Homogénes*; Mémoires Présentes par Divers Savants a LaAcadémie des Sciences de LaInstitut de France; Academie Des Sciences (Paris): Paris, France, 1785; Volume 10, pp. 411–434.
2. Bateman, H. *Higher Transcendental Functions*; McGraw-Hill: New York, NY, USA, 1953.

3. Doman, B. *The Classical Orthogonal Polynomials*; World Scientific: Singapore, 2015.
4. Horzum, T.; Kocer, E.G. On some properties of Horadam polynomials. *Int. Math. Forum.* **2009**, *4*, 1243–1252.
5. Horadam, A.F.; Mahon, J.M. Pell and Pell-Lucas Polynomials. *Fibonacci Q.* **1985**, *23*, 7–20.
6. Miller, S.; Mocanu, P. *Differential Subordination: Theory and Applications*; CRC Press: New York, NY, USA, 2000.
7. Duren, P.L. *Univalent Functions, Grundlehren der Mathematischen Wissenschaften, Band 259*; Springer: New York, NY, USA; Berlin/Heidelberg, Germany; Tokyo, Japan, 1983.
8. Frasin, B.A.; Aouf, M.K. New subclasses of bi-univalent functions. *Appl. Math. Lett.* **2011**, *24*, 1569–1573. [CrossRef]
9. Illafe, M.; Yousef, F.; Mohd, M.H.; Supramaniam, S. Initial Coefficients Estimates and Problem for a General Subclass of Bi-Univalent Functions Defined by Subordination. *Axioms* **2023**, *12*, 235. [CrossRef]
10. Murugusundaramoorthy, G. Subclasses of starlike and convex functions involving Poisson distribution series. *Afr. Mat.* **2017**, *28*, 1357–1366. [CrossRef]
11. Brannan, D.A.; Taha, T.S. On some classes of bi-univalent functions. In Proceedings of the International Conference on Mathematical Analysis and Its Applications, Kuwait, 18–21 February 1985; KFAS Proceedings Series; Pergamon Press (Elsevier Science Limited): Oxford, UK, 1988; Volume 3, pp. 53–60.
12. Taha, T.S. Topics in Univalent Function Theory. Ph.D. Thesis, University of London, London, UK, 1981.
13. Brannan, D.A.; Clunie, J.; Kirwan, W.E. Coefficient estimates for a class of starlike functions. *Canad. J. Math.* **1970**, *22*, 476–485. [CrossRef]
14. Lewin, M. On a coefficient problem for bi-univalent functions. *Proc. Am. Math. Soc.* **1967**, *18*, 63–68. [CrossRef]
15. Srivastava, H.M.; Mishra, A.K.; Gochhayat, P. Certain subclasses of analytic and bi-univalent functions. *Appl. Math. Lett.* **2010**, *23*, 1188–1192. [CrossRef]
16. Murugusundaramoorthy, G.; Magesh, N.; Prameela, V. Coefficient bounds for certain subclasses of bi-univalent function. *Abst. Appl. Anal.* **2013**, *2013*, 573017. [CrossRef]
17. Alsoboh, A.; Darus, M. On subclasses of harmonic univalent functions defined by Jackson (p,q)-derivative. *J. Anal.* **2019**, *10*, 123–130.
18. Al-Hawary, T.; Amourah, A.; Alsoboh, A.; Alsalhi, O. A new comprehensive subclass of analytic bi-univalent functions related to gegenbauer polynomials. *Symmetry* **2023**, *15*, 576. [CrossRef]
19. Amourah, A.; Aldawish, I.; Alhindi, K.R.; Frasin, B.A. An Application of Rabotnov Functions on Certain Subclasses of Bi-Univalent Functions. *Axioms* **2022**, *11*, 680. [CrossRef]
20. Amourah, A.; Alomari, M.; Yousef, F.; Alsoboh, A. Consolidation of a certain discrete probability distribution with a subclass of bi-univalent functions involving Gegenbauer polynomials. *Math. Probl. Eng.* **2022**, *2022*, 6354994. [CrossRef]
21. Peng, Z.; Murugusundaramoorthy, G.; Janani, T. Coefficient estimate of bi-univalent functions of complex order associated with the Hohlov operator. *J. Complex Anal.* **2014**, *2014*, 693908.
22. Srivastava, H.M.; Altınkaya, Ş; Yalçın, S. Certain subclasses of bi-univalent functions associated with the Horadam polynomials. *Iran. J. Sci. Technol. Trans. Sci.* **2019**, *43*, 1873–1879. [CrossRef]
23. Yousef, F.; Al-Hawary, T.; Murugusundaramoorthy, G. Fekete-Szegö functional problems for some subclasses of bi-univalent functions defined by Frasin differential operator. *Afr. Mat.* **2019**, *30*, 495–503. [CrossRef]
24. Frasin, B.A.; Swamy, S.R.; Nirmala, J. Some special families of holomorphic and Al-Oboudi type bi-univalent functions related to k-Fibonacci numbers involving modified Sigmoid activation function. *Afr. Mat.* **2021**, *32*, 631–643. [CrossRef]
25. Amourah, A.; Frasin, B.A.; Murugusundaramoorthy, G.; Al-Hawary, T. Bi-Bazilevič functions of order $\vartheta + i\delta$ associated with (p,q)-Lucas polynomials. *AIMS Math.* **2021**, *6*, 4296–4305. [CrossRef]
26. Guney, H.O.; Murugusundaramoorthy, G.; Sokol, J. Subclasses of bi-univalent functions related to shell-like curves connected with Fibonacci numbers. *Acta Univ. Sapientiae Math.* **2018**, *10*, 70–84. [CrossRef]
27. Altınkaya, S.; Yalcin, S. On the (p,q)-Lucas polynomial coefficient bounds of the bi-univalent function class. *Bol. Soc. Mat. Mex.* **2018**, *25*, 567–575. [CrossRef]
28. Bulut, S. Coefficient estimates for a class of analytic and bi-univalent functions. *Novi. Sad. J. Math.* **2013**, *43*, 59–65.
29. Fekete, M.; Szegö, G. Eine Bemerkung Ãber ungerade schlichte Funktionen. *J. Lond. Math. Soc.* **1933**, *1*, 85–89. [CrossRef]
30. Bukhari, S.Z.H.; Mohsan, R.; Nazir, M. Some generalizations of the class of analytic functions with respect to k-symmetric points. *Hacet. J. Math. Stat.* **2016**, *45*, 1–14.
31. Abirami, C.; Magesh, N.; Yamini, J. Initial bounds for certain classes of bi-univalent functions defined by Horadam Polynomial. *Abst. Appl. Anal.* **2020**, *2020*, 7391058. [CrossRef]
32. Magesh, N.; Yamini, J. Fekete-Szegö problem and second Hankel determinant for a class of bi-univalent functions. *Tbilisi Math. J.* **2018**, *11*, 141–157. [CrossRef]
33. Alsoboh, A.; Darus, M. On Fekete–Szegö Problems for Certain Subclasses of Analytic Functions Defined by Differential Operator Involving q-Ruscheweyh Operator. *J. Funct. Spaces* **2020**, *2020*, 8459405. [CrossRef]
34. Al-Hawary, T.; Frasin, B.A.; Darus, M. Fekete–Szegö problem for certain classes of analytic functions defined by Dziok-Srivastava operator. *Acta Math. Vietnam.* **2014**, *39*, 185–192. [CrossRef]
35. Wanas, A.K.; Khuttar, J.A. Applications of Borel distribution series on analytic functions. *Earthline J. Math. Sci.* **2020**, *4*, 71–82. [CrossRef]

36. Frasin, B. A.; Gharaibeh, M. M. Subclass of analytic functions associated with Poisson distribution series. *Afr. Matematika* **2020**, *31*, 1167–1173. [CrossRef]
37. Frasin, B. A. Subclasses of analytic functions associated with Pascal distribution series. *Adv. Theory Nonlinear Anal. Appl.* **2020**, *4*, 92–99. [CrossRef]
38. Amourah, A.; Frasin, B.A.; Ahmad, M.; Yousef, F. Exploiting the Pascal Distribution Series and Gegenbauer Polynomials to Construct and Study a New Subclass of Analytic Bi-Univalent Functions. *Symmetry* **2022**, *14*, 147. [CrossRef]
39. Khan, M.G.; Ahmad, B.; Khan, N.; Mashwani, W.K.; Arjika, S.; Khan, B.; Chinram, R. Applications of Mittag-Leffer type Poisson distribution to a subclass of analytic functions involving conic-type regions. *J. Funct. Spaces* **2021**, *2021*, 4343163. [CrossRef]
40. Srivastava, H.M.; Wanas, A.K.; Murugusundaramoorthy, G. A certain family of bi-univalent functions associated with the Pascal distribution series based upon the Horadam polynomials. *Surv. Math. Appl.* **2021**, *16*, 193–205.
41. Castellares, F.; Ferrari, S.L.; Lemonte, A.J. On the Bell distribution and its associated regression model for count data. *Appl. Math. Model.* **2018**, *56*, 172–185. [CrossRef]
42. Bell, E.T. Exponential numbers. *Am. Math. Mon.* **1934**, *41*, 411–419. [CrossRef]
43. Yousef, F.; Alroud, S.; Illafe, M. New subclasses of analytic and bi-univalent functions endowed with coefficient estimate problems. *Anal. Math. Phys.* **2021**, *11*, 1–12. [CrossRef]
44. Amourah, A.; Alsoboh, A.; Ogilat, O.; Gharib, G.M.; Saadeh, R.; Soudi, M.A. A Generalization of Gegenbauer Polynomials and Bi-Univalent Functions. *Axioms* **2023**, *12*, 128. [CrossRef]
45. Alsoboh, A.; Amourah, A.; Darus, M.; Sharefeen, R.I.A. Applications of Neutrosophic q-Poisson distribution Series for Subclass of Analytic Functions and Bi-Univalent Functions. *Mathematics* **2023**, *11*, 868. [CrossRef]
46. Kumar, V.; Cho, N.E.; Ravichandran, V.; Srivastava, H.M. Sharp coefficient bounds for starlike functions associated with the Bell numbers. *Math. Slovaca* **2019**, *69*, 1053–1064. [CrossRef]
47. Amourah, A.; Frasin, B.A.; Abdeljawad, T. Fekete-Szegö inequality for analytic and bi-univalent functions subordinate to Gegenbauer polynomials. *J. Funct. Spaces* **2021**, *2021*, 5574673.

axioms

MDPI

Article

New Criteria for Convex-Exponent Product of Log-Harmonic Functions

Rasoul Aghalary [1], Ali Ebadian [1], Nak Eun Cho [2,*] and Mehri Alizadeh [3]

1 Department of Mathematics, Faculty of Science, Urmia University, Urmia 57561-51818, Iran; r.aghalary@urmia.ac.ir (R.A.); a.ebadian@urmia.ac.ir (A.E.)
2 Department of Applied Mathematics, College of Natural Sciences, Pukyong National University, Busan 48513, Republic of Korea
3 Department of Mathematics, Faculty of Science, Payame Noor University, Tehran 19556-43183, Iran; a.alizadeh@pnu.ac.ir
* Correspondence: necho@pknu.ac.kr

Abstract: In this study, we consider different types of convex-exponent products of elements of a certain class of log-harmonic mapping and then find sufficient conditions for them to be starlike log-harmonic functions. For instance, we show that, if f is a spirallike function, then choosing a suitable value of γ, the log-harmonic mapping $F(z) = f(z)|f(z)|^{2\gamma}$ is α-*spiralike* of order ρ. Our results generalize earlier work in the literature.

Keywords: product; log-harmonic function; convex-exponent combination; starlike and spirallike functions

MSC: 30C45; 30C80

Citation: Aghalary, R.; Ebadian, A.; Cho, N.E.; Alizadeh, M. New Criteria for Convex-Exponent Product of Log-Harmonic Functions. *Axioms* **2023**, *12*, 409. https://doi.org/10.3390/axioms12050409

Academic Editor: Georgia Irina Oros

Received: 3 April 2023
Revised: 20 April 2023
Accepted: 20 April 2023
Published: 22 April 2023

1. Introduction

Let E be the open unit disk $E = \{z \in \mathbb{C} : |z| < 1\}$ and $\mathcal{H}(E)$ denote the linear space of all analytic functions defined on E. Additionally, let $\mathcal{A}$ be a subclass consisting of $f \in \mathcal{H}(E)$ such that $f(0) = f'(0) - 1 = 0$.

A C^2-function defined in E is said to be harmonic if $\Delta f = 0$, and a log-harmonic function f is a solution of the nonlinear elliptic partial differential equation

$$\frac{\overline{f}_{\overline{z}}}{\overline{f}} = a\frac{f_z}{f}, \tag{1}$$

where the second dilation function $a \in \mathcal{H}(E)$ is such that $|a(z)| < 1$ for all $z \in E$. In the above formula, $\overline{f}_{\overline{z}}$ means $\overline{(f_{\overline{z}})}$. Observe that f is log-harmonic if $\log f$ is harmonic. The authors in [1] have proven that, if f is a non-constant log-harmonic mapping that vanishes only at $z = 0$, then f should be in the form

$$f(z) = z^m|z|^{2m\beta}h(z)\overline{g}(z), \tag{2}$$

where m is a nonnegative integer, $\mathrm{Re}\beta > -\frac{1}{2}$, while h and g are analytic functions in $\mathcal{H}(E)$ satisfying $g(0) = 1$ and $h(0) \neq 0$. The exponent β in (2) depends only on $a(0)$ and is given by

$$\beta = \overline{a}(0)\frac{1 + a(0)}{1 - |a(0)|^2}. \tag{3}$$

We remark that $f(0) \neq 0$ if and only if $m = 0$ and that a univalent log-harmonic mapping in E vanishes at the origin if and only if $m = 1$, that is, f has the form

$$f(z) = z|z|^{2\beta}h(z)\overline{g}(z),$$

where $\mathrm{Re}\beta > -\frac{1}{2}$ and $0 \notin hg(E)$.

Recently, the class of log-harmonic functions has been extensively studied by many authors; for instance, see [1–10].

The Jacobian of log-harmonic function f is given by

$$J_f(z) = |f_z|^2(1 - |a(z)|^2) \tag{4}$$

and is positive. Therefore, all non-constant log-harmonic mappings are sense-preserving in the unit disk E. Let B denote the class of functions $a \in \mathcal{H}(E)$ with $|a(z)| < 1$ and B_0 denote $a \in B$ such that $a(0) = 0$.

It is easy to see that, if $f(z) = zh(z)\overline{g(z)}$, then the functions h and g, and the dilation a satisfy

$$\frac{zg'(z)}{g(z)} = a(z)\left(1 + \frac{zh'(z)}{h(z)}\right). \tag{5}$$

Definition 1. *(See [2].) Let $f = z|z|^{2\beta}h(z)\overline{g(z)}$ be a univalent log-harmonic mapping. We say that f is a starlike log-harmonic mapping of order α if*

$$\frac{\partial \arg f(re^{i\theta})}{\partial\theta} = \mathrm{Re}\frac{zf_z - \overline{z}f_{\overline{z}}}{f} > \alpha, \qquad 0 \leq \alpha < 1$$

for all $z \in E$. Denote by $ST_{LH}(\alpha)$ the class of all starlike log-harmonic mappings.

By taking $\beta = 0$ and $g(z) = 1$ in Definition 1, we obtain the class of starlike analytic functions in $\mathcal{A}$, which we denote by $S^*(\alpha)$.

The following lemma shows the relationship of the classes $ST_{LH}(\alpha)$ and $S^*(\alpha)$.

Lemma 1. *(See [2].) Let $f(z) = z|z|^{2\beta}h(z)\overline{g(z)}$ be a log-harmonic mapping on E, $0 \notin hg(E)$. Then, $f \in ST_{LH}(\alpha)$ if and only if $\varphi(z) = \frac{zh(z)}{g(z)} \in S^*(\alpha)$.*

In [2], the authors studied the class of $\alpha - spirallike$ functions and proved that, if $f(z) = z|z|^{2\beta}h(z)\overline{g(z)}$ is a log-harmonic mapping on E, $0 \notin hg(E)$, then f is $\alpha - spirallike$ if

$$\mathrm{Re}\left(e^{-i\alpha}\frac{zf_z - \overline{z}f_{\overline{z}}}{f}\right) > 0, \qquad 0 \leq \alpha < 1$$

for all $z \in E$. We remark that a simply connected domain Ω in $\mathbb{C}$ containing the origin is said to be $\alpha - spirallike$, $-\frac{\pi}{2} < \alpha < \frac{\pi}{2}$ if $w\exp(-te^{i\alpha}) \in \Omega$ for all $t \geq 0$ whenever $w \in \Omega$ and that f is an $\alpha - spirallike$ function, if $f(E)$ is an α-*spiralike* domain. Motivated by this, we define the class of $\alpha - spirallike$ log-harmonic mappings of order ρ as follows:

Definition 2. *Let $f(z) = z|z|^{2\beta}h(z)\overline{g(z)}$ be a univalent log harmonic mapping on E, with $0 \notin hg(E)$. Then, we say that f is an $\alpha - spirallike$ log-harmonic mapping of order ρ $(0 \leq \rho < 1)$ if*

$$\mathrm{Re}\left(e^{-i\alpha}\frac{zf_z - \overline{z}f_{\overline{z}}}{f(z)}\right) > \rho\cos\alpha \qquad (z \in E)$$

for some real $\alpha(|\alpha| < \frac{\pi}{2})$. The class of these functions is denoted by $S^{\alpha}_{LH}(\rho)$. Furthermore, we define $S^{\alpha}_{LH}(1) = \bigcap_{0\leq\rho<1} S^{\alpha}_{LH}(\rho)$.

Additionally, we denote by $S^{\alpha}(\rho)$ the subclass of all $f \in \mathcal{A}$ such that f is α-*spiralike* of order ρ and $S^{\alpha}(1) = \bigcap_{0\leq\rho<1} S^{\alpha}(\rho)$.

Lemma 2. *([2]) If $f(z) = z|z|^{2\beta}h(z)\overline{g(z)}$ is log-harmonic on E and $0 \notin hg(E)$, with $\mathrm{Re}\beta > -\frac{1}{2}$, then $f \in S^{\alpha}_{LH}(\rho)$ if and only if $\psi(z) = \frac{zh(z)}{g(z)^{e^{2i\alpha}}} \in S^{\alpha}(\rho)$.*

In the celebrated paper [11], the authors introduce a new way of studying harmonic functions in Geometric Function Theory. Additionally, many authors investigated the linear combinations of harmonic functions in a plane; see, for example, [12–14]. In Section 2 of this paper, taking the convex-exponent product combination of two elements, a specified class of new log-harmonic functions is constructed. Indeed, we show that, if $f(z) = zh(z)\bar{g}(z)$ is spirallike log-harmonic of order ρ, then by choosing suitable parameters of α and γ, the function $F(z) = f(z)|f(z|^{2\gamma}$ is log-harmonic spirallike of order α. Additionally, in Section 3, we provide some examples that are constructed from Section 2.

2. Main Results

Theorem 1. *Let $f(z) = zh(z)\overline{g(z)} \in ST_{LH}(\rho), (0 \le \rho < 1)$ with respect to $a \in B_0$, $\phi \in S^*(\gamma), (0 \le \gamma < 1)$ and α, β be real numbers with $\alpha + \beta = 1$. Then, $F(z) = f(z)^{\alpha}K(z)^{\beta}$ is starlike log-harmonic mapping of order $\alpha\rho + \beta\gamma$ with respect to a, where*

$$K(z) = \phi(z)\exp\left\{2\mathrm{Re}\int_0^z \frac{a(s)}{1-a(s)}\frac{\phi'(s)}{\phi(s)}ds\right\}.$$

Proof. By definition of F, we have

$$\frac{F_z}{F} = \alpha\frac{f_z}{f} + \beta\frac{K_z}{K} \quad and \quad \frac{F_{\bar{z}}}{F} = \alpha\frac{f_{\bar{z}}}{f} + \beta\frac{K_{\bar{z}}}{K}. \tag{6}$$

Additionally direct computations show that

$$\frac{K_z}{K} = \frac{1}{1-a(z)}\frac{\phi'(z)}{\phi(z)}, \quad and \quad \frac{\overline{K_{\bar{z}}}}{\overline{K}} = \frac{a(z)}{1-a(z)}\frac{\phi'(z)}{\phi(z)}. \tag{7}$$

Now, in view of Equations (6) and (7),

$$\hat{a}(z) = \frac{\frac{\overline{F_{\bar{z}}}}{\overline{F}}}{\frac{F_z}{F}} = \frac{\alpha\frac{\overline{f_{\bar{z}}}}{\overline{f}} + \beta\frac{\overline{K_{\bar{z}}}}{\overline{K}}}{\alpha\frac{f_z}{f} + \beta\frac{K_z}{K}} = a(z)\frac{\alpha\frac{f_z}{f} + \beta\frac{K_z}{K}}{\alpha\frac{f_z}{f} + \beta\frac{K_z}{K}} = a(z).$$

On the other hand,

$$\begin{aligned}\mathrm{Re}\frac{zF_z - \bar{z}F_{\bar{z}}}{F} &= \mathrm{Re}\left(\alpha\frac{zf_z}{f} + \beta\frac{zK_z}{K}\right) - \mathrm{Re}\left(\alpha\frac{\overline{zf_{\bar{z}}}}{\overline{f}} + \beta\frac{\overline{zK_{\bar{z}}}}{\overline{K}}\right)\\ &= \alpha\mathrm{Re}\left(\frac{zf_z}{f} - \frac{\overline{zf_{\bar{z}}}}{\overline{f}}\right) + \beta\mathrm{Re}\left(\frac{zK_z}{K} - \frac{\overline{zK_{\bar{z}}}}{\overline{K}}\right)\\ &> \alpha\rho + \beta\gamma.\end{aligned}$$

The above relation shows that F is a log-harmonic starlike function of order $\alpha\rho + \beta\gamma$, and the proof is complete. □

Theorem 2. *Let $f(z) = zh(z)\overline{g(z)} \in S^{\beta}_{LH}(\rho)$ with respect to $a \in B_0$ and γ be a constant with $\mathrm{Re}\gamma > -\frac{1}{2}$. Then, $F(z) = f(z)|f(z)|^{2\gamma}$ is an α − spirallike log-harmonic mapping of order ρ with respect to*

$$\hat{a}(z) = \frac{(1+\bar{\gamma})a(z) + \bar{\gamma}}{1+\gamma+\gamma a(z)},$$

where $|\beta| < \frac{\pi}{2}$ and $\alpha = \tan^{-1}\left(\frac{\tan\beta + 2\mathrm{Im}\gamma}{1+2\mathrm{Re}\gamma}\right)$.

Proof. By definition of F, we have

$$F(z) = f(z)|f(z)|^{2\gamma} = z^{1+\gamma}\bar{z}^{\gamma} H(z)\overline{G(z)},$$

where

$$H(z) = h^{1+\gamma}(z)g^{\gamma}(z) \qquad \text{and} \qquad G(z) = h^{\bar{\gamma}}(z)g^{1+\bar{\gamma}}(z).$$

With a straightforward calculation and using Equation (5),

$$\frac{zF_z}{F} = (1+\gamma)\left(1+\frac{zh'(z)}{h(z)}\right) + \gamma\frac{zg'(z)}{g(z)} = \left(1+\frac{zh'(z)}{h(z)}\right)((1+\gamma)+\gamma a(z)),$$

and

$$\frac{\bar{z}F_{\bar{z}}}{F} = \gamma\left(1+\overline{\frac{zh'(z)}{h(z)}}\right) + (1+\gamma)\overline{\frac{zg'(z)}{g(z)}} = \left(1+\overline{\frac{zh'(z)}{h(z)}}\right)(\gamma+(1+\gamma)\overline{a(z)}).$$

If we consider

$$\hat{a}(z) = \frac{\overline{\left(\frac{\bar{z}F_{\bar{z}}(z)}{F(z)}\right)}}{\frac{zF_z(z)}{F(z)}},$$

then

$$\hat{a}(z) = \frac{\gamma+(1+\gamma)a(z)}{(1+\gamma)+\gamma a(z)}.$$

Now, in view of $|a(z)| < 1$, it easy to see that $|\hat{a}(z)| < 1$ provided that $\left|\frac{\overline{\gamma}}{1+\overline{\gamma}}\right| < 1$, which evidently holds $|\gamma|^2 < |1+\overline{\gamma}|^2$ since $\mathrm{Re}\gamma > -\frac{1}{2}$, and this means that F is a log-harmonic function.

Additionally, by putting

$$\psi(z) = \frac{zH(z)}{G(z)^{e^{2i\alpha}}},$$

we have

$$\psi(z) = \frac{zH(z)}{G(z)^{e^{2i\alpha}}} = \frac{zh(z)^{1+\gamma}g(z)^{\gamma}}{(h^{\bar{\gamma}}(z)g^{1+\bar{\gamma}}(z))^{e^{2i\alpha}}}.$$

Then, we obtain

$$\begin{aligned}
e^{-i\alpha}\frac{z\psi'(z)}{\psi(z)} &= e^{-i\alpha} + [(1+\gamma)e^{-i\alpha} - \overline{\gamma}e^{i\alpha}]\frac{zh'(z)}{h(z)} - [(1+\overline{\gamma})e^{i\alpha} - \gamma e^{-i\alpha}]\frac{zg'(z)}{g(z)} \\
&= (-\gamma e^{-i\alpha} + \bar{\gamma}e^{i\alpha}) + [(1+\gamma)e^{-i\alpha} - \overline{\gamma}e^{i\alpha}]\left(1+\frac{zh'(z)}{h(z)}\right) \\
&- [(1+\overline{\gamma})e^{i\alpha} - \gamma e^{-i\alpha}]\frac{zg'(z)}{g(z)}.
\end{aligned}$$

The condition on α ensures that

$$(1+\gamma)e^{-i\alpha} - \overline{\gamma}e^{i\alpha} = \frac{\cos\alpha}{\cos\beta}e^{-i\beta} \quad \text{and} \quad (1+\overline{\gamma})e^{i\alpha} - \gamma e^{-i\alpha} = \frac{\cos\alpha}{\cos\beta}e^{i\beta},$$

because by letting $\gamma = \gamma_1 + i\gamma_2$, the first equality holds true if and only if

$$\cos\beta\cos\alpha - i(1+2\gamma_1)\sin\alpha\cos\beta + i2\gamma_2\cos\beta\cos\alpha = \cos\alpha\cos\beta - i\cos\alpha\sin\beta$$

or, equivalently, after simplification

$$2\gamma_2\cot\beta - (1+2\gamma_1)\tan\alpha\cot\beta = -1$$

or

$$\alpha = \tan^{-1}\left(\frac{\tan\beta + 2\text{Im}\gamma}{1 + 2\text{Re}\gamma}\right).$$

Thus, by hypothesis,

$$\text{Re}\{e^{-i\alpha}\frac{z\psi'(z)}{\psi(z)}\} = \frac{\cos\alpha}{\cos\beta}\text{Re}\left(e^{-i\beta}(1 + \frac{zh'(z)}{h(z)}) - e^{i\beta}\frac{zg'(z)}{g(z)}\right) > \rho\cos\alpha$$

and it follows that F is an α-spirallike log-harmonic mapping of order ρ in which the dilation is $\hat{a}(z)$. □

Theorem 3. *Let $f_k(z) = zh_k(z)\overline{g_k}(z) \in S^{\beta}_{LH}(\rho)$ with $k = 1,2$ and with respect to the same $a \in B_0$ and γ be a constant with $\text{Re}\gamma > -\frac{1}{2}$. Moreover, let*

$$F_1(z) = f_1(z)|f_1(z)|^{2\gamma} \quad \textit{and} \quad F_2(z) = f_2(z)|f_2(z)|^{2\gamma}.$$

Then, $F(z) = F_1^{\lambda}(z)F_2^{1-\lambda}(z)$ is an α-spirallike log-harmonic mapping of order ρ with respect to

$$\hat{a}(z) = \frac{(1+\overline{\gamma})a(z) + \overline{\gamma}}{1 + \gamma + \gamma a(z)},$$

where $|\beta| < \frac{\pi}{2}$ and $\alpha = \tan^{-1}\left(\frac{\tan\beta + 2\text{Im}\gamma}{1+2\text{Re}\gamma}\right)$.

Proof. According to the definitions of F_1 and F_2, we have

$$\begin{aligned} F_1^{\lambda}(z) &= (f_1(z)|f_1(z)|^{2\gamma})^{\lambda} \\ &= \left(z|z|^{2\gamma}h_1^{1+\gamma}(z)g_1^{\gamma}(z)\overline{h_1^{\overline{\gamma}}(z)g_1^{1+\overline{\gamma}}(z))}\right)^{\lambda} \end{aligned}$$

and

$$\begin{aligned} F_2^{1-\lambda}(z) &= (f_2(z)|f_2(z)|^{2\gamma})^{1-\lambda} \\ &= \left(z|z|^{2\gamma}h_2^{1+\gamma}(z)g_2^{\gamma}(z)\overline{h_2^{\overline{\gamma}}(z)g_2^{1+\overline{\gamma}}(z))}\right)^{1-\lambda}. \end{aligned}$$

Putting the values of F_1^{λ} and $F_2^{1-\lambda}$ on F, we obtain

$$\begin{aligned} F(z) &= \left(z|z|^{2\gamma}h_1^{1+\gamma}(z)g_1^{\gamma}(z)\overline{h_1^{\overline{\gamma}}(z)g_1^{1+\overline{\gamma}}(z))}\right)^{\lambda}\left(z|z|^{2\gamma}h_2^{1+\gamma}(z)g_2^{\gamma}(z)\overline{h_2^{\overline{\gamma}}(z)g_2^{1+\overline{\gamma}}(z))}\right)^{1-\lambda} \\ &= z|z|^{2\gamma}H(z)\overline{G(z)}, \end{aligned}$$

where

$$H(z) = h_1(z)^{\lambda(1+\gamma)}g_1(z)^{\lambda\gamma}h_2(z)^{(1-\lambda)(1+\gamma)}g_2(z)^{(1-\lambda)\gamma} \tag{8}$$

and

$$G(z) = h_1(z)^{\lambda\overline{\gamma}}g_1(z)^{\lambda(1+\overline{\gamma})}h_2(z)^{(1-\lambda)\overline{\gamma}}g_2(z)^{(1-\lambda)(1+\overline{\gamma})}. \tag{9}$$

Now, we show that the second dilation of F i.e., $\mu(z)$ satisfies the condition $|\mu(z)| < 1$. For this, since

$$\mu(z) = \frac{\frac{\overline{F_{\overline{z}}(z)}}{\overline{F(z)}}}{\frac{F_z(z)}{F(z)}},$$

we have

$$
\begin{aligned}
\mu(z) &= \frac{\lambda \frac{\overline{F_{1\bar{z}}(z)}}{\overline{F_1(z)}} + (1-\lambda)\frac{\overline{F_{2\bar{z}}(z)}}{\overline{F_2(z)}}}{\lambda \frac{F_{1z}(z)}{F_1(z)} + (1-\lambda)\frac{F_{2z}(z)}{F_2(z)}} \\
&= \frac{\lambda[\overline{\gamma}(1+\frac{zh_1'}{h_1}) + (1+\overline{\gamma})\frac{zg_1'}{g_1}] + (1-\lambda)[\overline{\gamma}(1+\frac{zh_2'}{h_2}) + (1+\overline{\gamma})\frac{zg_2'}{g_2}]}{\lambda[(1+\gamma)(1+\frac{zh_1'}{h_1}) + \gamma\frac{zg_1'}{g_1}] + (1-\lambda)[(1+\gamma)(1+\frac{zh_2'}{h_2}) + \gamma\frac{zg_2'}{g_2}]} \\
&= \frac{\lambda(1+\frac{zh_1'}{h_1})[\overline{\gamma} + (1+\overline{\gamma})a(z)] + (1-\lambda)(1+\frac{zh_2'}{h_2})[\overline{\gamma} + (1+\overline{\gamma})a(z)]}{\lambda(1+\frac{zh_1'}{h_1})[(1+\gamma) + \gamma a(z)] + (1-\lambda)(1+\frac{zh_2'}{h_2})[(1+\gamma) + \gamma a(z)]} \qquad (10) \\
&= \frac{[\lambda(1+\frac{zh_1'}{h_1}) + (1-\lambda)(1+\frac{zh_2'}{h_2})][\overline{\gamma} + (1+\overline{\gamma})a(z)]}{[\lambda(1+\frac{zh_1'}{h_1}) + (1-\lambda)(1+\frac{zh_2'}{h_2})][(1+\gamma) + \gamma a(z)]} \\
&= \frac{[\overline{\gamma} + (1+\overline{\gamma})a(z)]}{[(1+\gamma) + \gamma a(z)]} \\
&= \frac{(1+\overline{\gamma})}{(1+\gamma)} \frac{a(z) + \frac{\overline{\gamma}}{1+\overline{\gamma}}}{1 + \frac{a(z)\gamma}{1+\gamma}},
\end{aligned}
$$

and the condition $\mathrm{Re}\gamma > -\frac{1}{2}$ ensures that $|\mu(z)| < 1$ in E, which implies that F is a locally univalent log-harmonic mapping. Now, to prove

$$F(z) = F_1^{\lambda}(z)F_2^{1-\lambda}(z) \in S_{LH}^{\alpha}(\rho),$$

we have to show that $\psi(z) = \frac{zH(z)}{G(z)^{e^{2i\alpha}}} \in S^{\alpha}(\rho)$. However, a direct calculation shows that

$$\psi(z) = \frac{zH(z)}{G(z)^{e^{2i\alpha}}} = \frac{[zh_1^{\lambda(1+\gamma)}(z)g_1^{\lambda\gamma}(z)h_2^{(1-\lambda)(1+\gamma)}(z)g_2^{(1-\lambda)\gamma}(z)]}{[h_1^{\lambda\overline{\gamma}}(z)g_1^{\lambda(1+\overline{\gamma})}(z)h_2^{(1-\lambda)\overline{\gamma}}(z)g_2^{(1-\lambda)(1+\overline{\gamma})}(z)]^{e^{2i\alpha}}}.$$

Now,

$$
\begin{aligned}
& e^{-i\alpha}\frac{z\psi'(z)}{\psi(z)} \\
&= e^{-i\alpha}\left[1 + \lambda(((1+\gamma) - e^{2i\alpha}\overline{\gamma})\frac{zh_1'(z)}{h_1(z)} - ((1+\overline{\gamma})e^{2i\alpha} - \gamma)\frac{zg_1'(z)}{g_1(z)})\right] \\
&+ e^{-i\alpha}\left[(1-\lambda)(((1+\gamma) - e^{2i\alpha}\overline{\gamma})\frac{zh_2'(z)}{h_2(z)} - ((1+\overline{\gamma})e^{2i\alpha} - \gamma)\frac{zg_2'(z)}{g_2(z)})\right] \\
&= -\gamma e^{-i\alpha} + e^{i\alpha}\overline{\gamma} \\
&+ \lambda\left[((1+\gamma)e^{-i\alpha} - e^{i\alpha}\overline{\gamma})(1 + \frac{zh_1'(z)}{h_1(z)}) - ((1+\overline{\gamma})e^{i\alpha} - \gamma e^{-i\alpha})\frac{zg_1'(z)}{g_1(z)}\right] \\
&+ (1-\lambda)\left[((1+\gamma)e^{-i\alpha} - e^{i\alpha}\overline{\gamma})(1 + \frac{zh_2'(z)}{h_2(z)}) - ((1+\overline{\gamma})e^{i\alpha} - \gamma e^{-i\alpha})\frac{zg_2'(z)}{g_2(z)}\right].
\end{aligned}
$$

By hypothesis, we know that

$$(1+\gamma)e^{-i\alpha} - \overline{\gamma}e^{i\alpha} = \frac{\cos\alpha}{\cos\beta}e^{-i\beta} \quad \text{and} \quad (1+\overline{\gamma})e^{i\alpha} - \gamma e^{-i\alpha} = \frac{\cos\alpha}{\cos\beta}e^{i\beta},$$

so

$$\begin{aligned}\mathrm{Re}\{e^{-i\alpha}\frac{z\psi'(z)}{\psi(z)}\}\\ &= \lambda\frac{\cos\alpha}{\cos\beta}\mathrm{Re}\left(e^{-i\beta}(1+\frac{zh_1'(z)}{h_1(z)}) - e^{i\beta}\frac{zg_1'(z)}{g_1(z)}\right)\\ &+(1-\lambda)\frac{\cos\alpha}{\cos\beta}\mathrm{Re}\left(e^{-i\beta}(1+\frac{zh_2'(z)}{h_2(z)}) - e^{i\beta}\frac{zg_1'(z)}{g_1(z)}\right)\\ &> \rho\cos\alpha\end{aligned}$$

and the proof is completed. □

Theorem 4. *Let $f_k(z) = zh_k(z)\overline{g}_k(z) \in S^{\beta}_{LH}(\rho)$ with respect to $a_k \in B_0 (k = 1,2)$. Moreover, suppose that* $\mathrm{Re}\gamma > -\frac{1}{2}$,

$$F_1(z) = f_1(z)|f_1(z)|^{2\gamma} \text{ and } F_2(z) = f_2(z)|f_2(z)|^{2\gamma}.$$

If

$$\mathrm{Re}\left[(1-a_1(z)\overline{a}_2(z))\left(1+\frac{zh_1'(z)}{h_1(z)}\right)\overline{\left(1+\frac{zh_2'(z)}{h_2(z)}\right)}\right] \geq 0 \qquad (\textit{for any } z \in E),$$

then

$$F(z) = F_1^{\lambda}(z)F_2^{1-\lambda}(z) \in S^{\alpha}_{LH}(\rho),$$

where $|\beta| < \frac{\pi}{2}, 0 \leq \lambda \leq 1$ *and* $\alpha = \tan^{-1}\left(\frac{\tan\beta + 2Im\gamma}{1+2Re\gamma}\right)$.

Proof. Using the same argument as in Theorem 3, we have

$$F(z) = z|z|^{2\gamma}H(z)\overline{G(z)},$$

where $H(z)$ and $G(z)$ are defined by Equations (8) and (9). Now, we show that the second dilation of F, i.e., $\mu(z)$, satisfies the condition $|\mu(z)| < 1$. For this, since

$$\mu(z) = \frac{\frac{\overline{F_{\overline{z}}(z)}}{\overline{F(z)}}}{\frac{F_z(z)}{F(z)}},$$

using a similar argument to the relation Equation (10) of Theorem 3, we have

$$|\mu(z)| = \left|\frac{\lambda(1+\frac{zh_1'}{h_1})[\overline{\gamma}+(1+\overline{\gamma})a_1(z)] + (1-\lambda)(1+\frac{zh_2'}{h_2})[\overline{\gamma}+(1+\overline{\gamma})a_2(z)]}{\lambda(1+\frac{zh_1'}{h_1})[(1+\gamma)+\gamma a_1(z)] + (1-\lambda)(1+\frac{zh_2'}{h_2})[(1+\gamma)+\gamma a_2(z)]}\right|.$$

However, by hypothesis, we obtain

$$\begin{aligned}&\left|\lambda(1+\frac{zh_1'}{h_1})[(1+\gamma)+\gamma a_1(z)] + (1-\lambda)(1+\frac{zh_2'}{h_2})[(1+\gamma)+\gamma a_2(z)]\right|^2\\ &-\left|\lambda(1+\frac{zh_1'}{h_1})[\overline{\gamma}+(1+\overline{\gamma})a_1(z)] + (1-\lambda)(1+\frac{zh_2'}{h_2})[\overline{\gamma}+(1+\overline{\gamma})a_2(z)]\right|^2\\ &= (2\mathrm{Re}\gamma+1)\left(\lambda^2\left|1+\frac{zh_1'}{h_1}\right|^2(1-|a_1|^2) + (1-\lambda)^2\left|1+\frac{zh_2'}{h_2}\right|^2(1-|a_2|^2)\right)\\ &+ (2\mathrm{Re}\gamma+1)\left(2\lambda(1-\lambda)\mathrm{Re}[(1-a_1\overline{a}_2)(1+\frac{zh_1'}{h_1})\overline{(1+\frac{zh_2'}{h_2})}]\right) > 0.\end{aligned}$$

Therefore, $|\mu(z)| < 1$ in E, which implies that F is a locally univalent mapping. Moreover, by following a similar proof to that in Theorem 3, we observe that

$$F(z) = F_1^{\lambda}(z)F_2^{1-\lambda}(z) \in S_{LH}^{\alpha}(\rho),$$

and the proof is completed. □

Theorem 5. *Let $f_k(z) = zh_k(z)\overline{g}_k(z)$ be univalent log-harmonic functions with respect to $a_k \in B_0 (k = 1, 2)$ and $\mathrm{Re}\gamma > -\frac{1}{2}$. Moreover, suppose that $zh_k g_k = \phi_k(z)$, where*

$$\phi_k(z) = zexp\left\{2\int_0^z \frac{a_k(t)}{t(1-a_k(t))}dt\right\}$$

and

$$F_1(z) = f_1(z)|f_1(z)|^{2\gamma} \quad and \quad F_2(z) = f_2(z)|f_2(z)|^{2\gamma}.$$

Then,

$$F(z) = F_1^{\lambda}(z)F_2^{1-\lambda}(z) \in S_{LH}^{\alpha}(1)$$

where $0 \leq \lambda \leq 1$ and $\alpha = \tan^{-1}\left(\frac{2\mathrm{Im}\gamma}{1+2\mathrm{Re}\gamma}\right)$.

Proof. Since $zh_k g_k = \phi_k(z)$, by definition of $a_k(z)$ and $\phi_k(z)$, we obtain

$$1 + \frac{zh_k'(z)}{h_k(z)} = \frac{1}{1-a_k(z)} \quad (k = 1, 2).$$

Let

$$\mu(z) = \frac{\frac{\overline{F_{\overline{z}}(z)}}{\overline{F(z)}}}{\frac{F_z(z)}{F(z)}}.$$

Using a similar argument to the relation in Equation (10) of Theorem 3, we obtain

$$|\mu(z)| = \left|\frac{\lambda(1-a_2(z))[\overline{\gamma} + (1+\overline{\gamma})a_1(z)] + (1-\lambda)((1-a_1(z))[\overline{\gamma} + (1+\overline{\gamma})a_2(z)]}{\lambda(1-a_2(z))[(1+\gamma) + \gamma a_1(z)] + (1-\lambda)(1-a_1(z))[(1+\gamma) + \gamma a_2(z)]}\right|.$$

Now, $|\mu(z)| < 1$ is equivalent to

$$\begin{aligned}
\psi(\lambda) :=& |\lambda(1-a_2(z))[(1+\gamma) + \gamma a_1(z)] + (1-\lambda)(1-a_1(z))[(1+\gamma) + \gamma a_2(z)]|^2 \\
&- |\lambda(1-a_2(z))[\overline{\gamma} + (1+\overline{\gamma})a_1(z)] + (1-\lambda)((1-a_1(z))[\overline{\gamma} + (1+\overline{\gamma})a_2(z)]|^2 \\
=& (2\mathrm{Re}\gamma + 1)[\lambda^2|1-a_2(z)|^2(1-|a_1(z)|^2) \\
&+ 2\lambda(1-\lambda)\mathrm{Re}[(1-a_2(z))(1-\overline{a_1(z)})(1-a_1(z)\overline{a_2(z)})] \\
&+ (1-\lambda)^2|1-a_1(z)|^2(1-|a_2(z)|^2)] > 0.
\end{aligned}$$

However, by taking the derivative of $\psi(\lambda)$, we have

$$\begin{aligned}
\psi'(\lambda) =& 2(2\mathrm{Re}\gamma + 1) \\
&\left[\mathrm{Re}[(1-a_2(z))(1-a_1(z))(1-a_1(z)\overline{a_2(z)})] - |1-a_1(z)|^2(1-|a_2(z)|^2)\right],
\end{aligned}$$

which shows that ψ is a continuous monotonic function of λ in the interval $[0, 1]$. Since

$$\psi(0) = (2\mathrm{Re}\gamma + 1)|1-a_2(z)|^2(1-|a_1(z)|^2) > 0$$

and

$$\psi(1) = (2\text{Re}\gamma + 1)|1 - a_1(z)|^2(1 - |a_2(z)|^2) > 0,$$

we deduce that $\psi(\lambda) > 0$ for all $\lambda \in [0,1]$, which implies that F is a locally univalent mapping. Now, to prove

$$F = F_1^\lambda F_2^{1-\lambda} \in S_{LH}^\alpha \tag{11}$$

we have to show that $\psi(z) = \frac{zH(z)}{G(z)^{e^{2i\alpha}}} \in S^\alpha(1)$, where $H(z)$ and $G(z)$ are defined by Equations (8) and (9). A direct computation such as that in Theorem 3 shows that

$$\frac{(1+\gamma)e^{-i\alpha} - \overline{\gamma}e^{i\alpha}}{\cos\alpha} = \frac{(1+\overline{\gamma})e^{i\alpha} - \gamma e^{-i\alpha}}{\cos\alpha} = 1.$$

Additionally, we note that

$$1 + \frac{zh_1'}{h_1} - \frac{zg_1'}{g_1} = 1 + \frac{zh_2'}{h_2} - \frac{zg_2'}{g_2} = 1.$$

Using these relation and the same argument as that made in Theorem 3, we obtain $\psi(z) = \frac{zH(z)}{G(z)^{e^{2i\alpha}}} \in S^\alpha(1)$, and the proof is complete. □

Theorem 6. *Let $f_k(z) = zh_k(z)\overline{g}_k(z)(k = 1,2)$ be log-harmonic functions with respect to $a_k \in B_0$. Moreover, suppose that $zh_k g_k = z$ and*

$$F_1(z) = f_1(z)|f_1(z)|^{2\gamma} \quad \text{and} \quad F_2(z) = f_2(z)|f_2(z)|^{2\gamma}.$$

Then,

$$F(z) = F_1^\lambda(z)F_2^{1-\lambda}(z) \in S_{LH}^\alpha(1),$$

where $0 \le \lambda \le 1$ and $\alpha = \tan^{-1}\left(\frac{2\text{Im}\gamma}{(1+2\text{Re}\gamma)}\right)$.

Proof. Since $zh_k g_k = z$, by definition of $a_k(z)$, we obtain

$$1 + \frac{zh_k'(z)}{h_k(z)} = \frac{1}{1 + a_k(z)} \quad (k = 1,2).$$

Using the same argument as that in Theorem 5, we obtain our result, but we omit the details. □

3. Examples

We provide several examples in this section.

Example 1. *Let $\text{Re}\gamma > -\frac{1}{2}$ and*

$$f(z) = z\frac{(1+z)^{[\cos\beta(1-\rho)e^{i\beta}-1]}}{(1-z)^{(1-\rho)\cos\beta e^{i\beta}}}(1+\overline{z})^{[(1-\rho)\cos\beta e^{i\beta} - e^{2i\beta}]}(1-\overline{z})^{(1-\rho)\cos\beta e^{i\beta}}.$$

Then, it is easy to see that f is a β-spirallike log-harmonic mapping of order ρ with respect to $a(z) = -ze^{-2i\beta}$. Now, Theorem 2 implies that the function $F(z) = f(z)|f(z)|^{2\gamma}$ is a α-spirallike log-harmonic mapping of order ρ with respect to

$$\hat{a}(z) = \frac{-(1+\bar{\gamma})ze^{-2i\beta} + \bar{\gamma}}{(1+\gamma) - \gamma e^{-2i\beta}z},$$

where

$$\alpha = \tan^{-1}\left(\frac{\tan\beta + 2\mathrm{Im}\gamma}{1 + 2\mathrm{Re}\gamma}\right).$$

The image in Example 1 is shown in Figure 1.

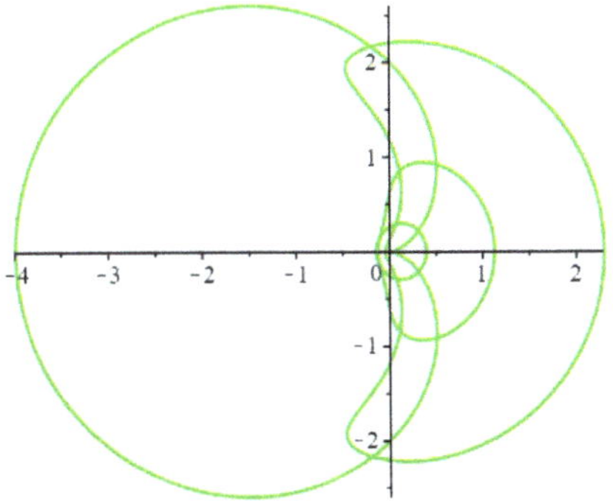

Figure 1. Image of $F(z)$ for $\beta = 0.5$, $\rho = 1$, and $\gamma = 0.25$ in Example 1.

Example 2. *Let* $\mathrm{Re}\gamma > -\frac{1}{2}, 0 < a < 1$, f_1 *be the function defined in Example 1 and*

$$f_2(z) = z\frac{(1+z)^{[\cos\beta\frac{(1+a-2\rho)}{1+a}e^{i\beta}-1]}}{(1-az)^{\frac{(1+a-2\rho)}{1+a}\cos\beta e^{i\beta}}}(1+\overline{z})^{[\frac{(1+a-2\rho)}{1+a}\cos\beta e^{i\beta}-e^{2i\beta}]}(1-a\overline{z})^{\frac{(1+a-2\rho)}{a(1+a)}\cos\beta e^{i\beta}}.$$

Then, it is easy to see that f_1 *and* f_2 *are* β*-spirallike log-harmonic mappings of order* ρ *with respect to* $a_2(z) = a_1(z) = -ze^{-2i\beta}$. *Additionally, suppose that*

$$F_1(z) = f_1(z)|f_1(z)|^{2\gamma} \text{ and } F_2(z) = f_2(z)|f_2(z)|^{2\gamma}.$$

Then, Theorem 3 shows that

$$F(z) = F_1^{\lambda}(z)F_2^{1-\lambda}(z) \in S_{LH}^{\alpha}(\rho),$$

where $0 \leq \lambda \leq 1$ *and* $\alpha = \tan^{-1}\left(\frac{\tan\beta + 2\mathrm{Im}\gamma}{(1+2\mathrm{Re}\gamma)}\right)$.

Example 3. *Let* $\mathrm{Re}\gamma > -\frac{1}{2}$,

$$f_1(z) = \frac{z}{|1+z|}\sqrt{\frac{1-\overline{z}}{1-z}}$$

and

$$f_2(z) = \frac{z}{1-z}e^{\mathrm{Re}\frac{1}{1-z}}.$$

Firstly, we show that f_1 *and* f_2 *are log-harmonic starlike functions of order* $1/2$ *with respect to* $a_1(z) = z$ *and* $a_2(z) = \frac{z}{2-z}$, *respectively. A direct computation shows that*

$$\frac{z(f_1)_z}{f_1} = \frac{1}{1-z^2}, \quad \overline{\left(\frac{\overline{z}(f_1)_{\overline{z}}}{f_1}\right)} = \frac{-z}{1-z^2}$$

$$\frac{z(f_2)_z}{f_2} = \frac{2-z}{2(1-z^2)}, \quad \overline{\left(\frac{\overline{z}(f_2)_{\overline{z}}}{f_2}\right)} = \frac{z}{2(1-z^2)}.$$

Therefore, we obtain

$$\overline{\left(\frac{\bar{z}(f_1)_{\bar{z}}}{f_1}\right)} = a_1(z)\frac{z(f_1)_z}{f_1} \quad \text{and} \quad \overline{\left(\frac{\bar{z}(f_2)_{\bar{z}}}{f_2}\right)} = a_2(z)\frac{z(f_2)_z}{f_2},$$

and this means that f_1 *and* f_2 *are locally univalent log-harmonic functions. Additionally,*

$$Re\frac{z(f_1)_z - \bar{z}(f_1)_{\bar{z}}}{f_1} = Re\left(\frac{1}{1-z^2} + \frac{z}{1-z^2}\right) = Re\frac{1}{1-z} > \frac{1}{2},$$

and

$$Re\frac{z(f_2)_z - \bar{z}(f_2)_{\bar{z}}}{f_2} = Re\left(\frac{2-z}{2(1-z^2)} - \frac{z}{2(1-z^2)}\right) = Re\frac{1}{1+z} > \frac{1}{2}.$$

Hence, f_1 *and* f_2 *are starlike log-harmonic functions of order* $1/2$. *Additionally, let*

$$F_1(z) = f_1(z)|f_1(z)|^{2\gamma} \text{ and } F_2(z) = f_2(z)|f_2(z)|^{2\gamma}.$$

Since for $z = re^{i\theta}$,

$$\begin{aligned}
&\mathrm{Re}(1-a_1\bar{a}_2)(1+\frac{zh_1'}{h_1})\overline{(1+\frac{zh_2'}{h_2})} \\
&= (1-|z|^2)\mathrm{Re}\frac{1}{(1-\bar{z})^2}\frac{1}{1-z^2} = \frac{1-|z|^2}{|1-z|^2}\mathrm{Re}\frac{1}{(1-\bar{z})(1+z)} \\
&= \frac{1-r^2}{|1-re^i\theta|^2}(1-r^2) > 0.
\end{aligned}$$

Theorem 4 implies that

$$F(z) = F_1^{\lambda}(z)F_2^{1-\lambda}(z) \in S_{LH}^{\alpha}(\frac{1}{2}),$$

where $0 \le \lambda \le 1$ *and* $\alpha = \tan^{-1}\left(\frac{2\mathrm{Im}\gamma}{1+2\mathrm{Re}\gamma}\right)$.

The images in Example 2–4 are shown in Figures 2–4.

Example 4. *Let* $\mathrm{Re}\gamma > \frac{1}{2}$, $a_1(z) = z$, *and* $h_1(z) = g_1(z) = \frac{1}{1-z}$. *Moreover, let* $a_2(z) = -z$ *and* $h_2(z) = g_2(z) = \frac{1}{1+z}$. *Then, it is easy to verify that all conditions of Theorem 5 are satisfied. Hence, according to Theorem 5, by taking*

$$F_1(z) = \frac{z|z|^{2\gamma}}{(1-z)^{1+2\gamma}(1-\bar{z})^{1+2\gamma}}$$

and

$$F_2(z) = \frac{z|z|^{2\gamma}}{(1+z)^{1+2\gamma}(1+\bar{z})^{1+2\gamma}},$$

we have

$$F(z) = F_1^{\lambda}(z)F_2^{1-\lambda}(z) \in S_{LH}^{\alpha}(1),$$

where $0 \le \lambda \le 1$ *and* $\alpha = \tan^{-1}\left(\frac{2\mathrm{Im}\gamma}{1-\rho+2\mathrm{Re}\gamma}\right)$.

Example 5. *Let* $\mathrm{Re}\gamma > -\frac{1}{2}$, $a_1(z) = -z$ *and* $h_1(z) = \frac{1}{1-z}, g(z) = 1-z$. *Moreover, let* $a_2(z) = z$ *and* $h_2(z) = \frac{1}{1+z}$, $g_2(z) = 1+z$. *Then, it is easy to verify that all conditions of Theorem 6 are satisfied. Hence, according to Theorem 6, by taking*

$$F_1(z) = \frac{z|z|^{2\gamma}(1-\bar{z})}{(1-z)} \qquad and \qquad F_2(z) = \frac{z|z|^{2\gamma}(1+\bar{z})}{(1+z)},$$

we have

$$F(z) = F_1^{\lambda}(z) F_2^{1-\lambda}(z) \in S_{LH}^{\alpha}(1),$$

where $0 \leq \lambda \leq 1$ *and* $\alpha = \tan^{-1}\left(\frac{2\mathrm{Im}\gamma}{1-\rho+2\mathrm{Re}\gamma}\right)$.

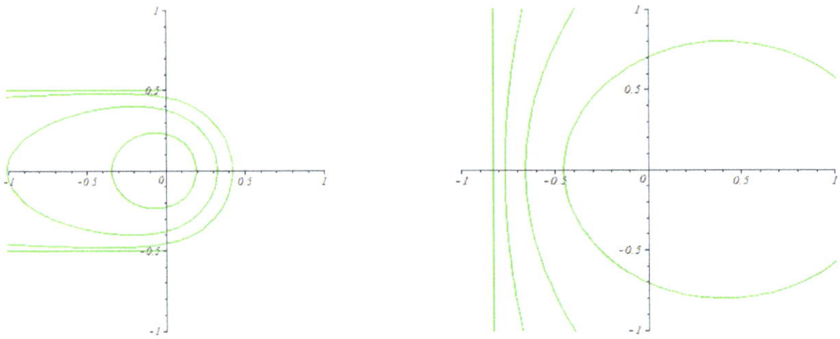

Figure 2. Images of $f_1(z)$ and $f_2(z)$ in Example 3.

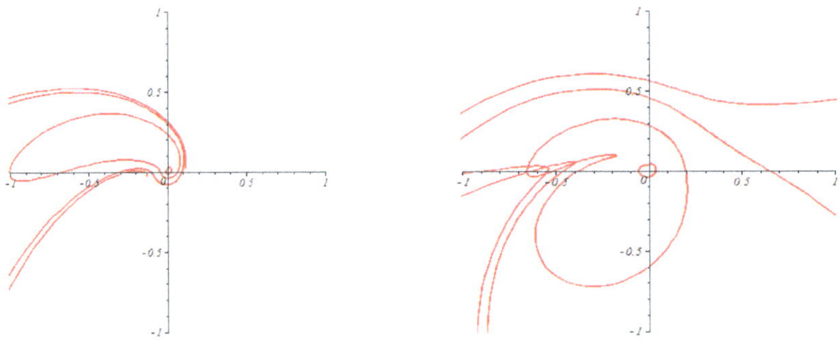

Figure 3. Images of $F_1(z)$ and $F_2(z)$ for $\gamma = 1 + i$ in Example 3.

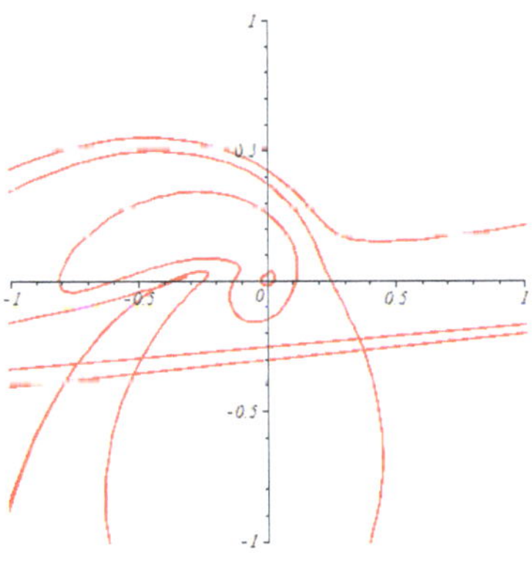

Figure 4. Image of $F(z)$ for $\gamma = 1 + i$ and $\lambda = 0.5$ in Example 3.

4. Conclusions

In this paper, we have shown that, if $f(z) = zh(z)\bar{g}(z)$ is spirallike log-harmonic of order ρ, then by choosing suitable parameters of α and γ, the function $F(z) = f(z)|f(z|^{2\gamma}$ is log-harmonic spirallike of order α. Moreover, we provide some examples for the obtained results.

Author Contributions: Conceptualization: R.A. and A.E.; original draft preparation: R.A.; writing—review and editing: A.E. and N.E.C.; investigation: M.A. All authors read and approved the final manuscript.

Funding: The third author was supported by the Basic Science Research Program through the National Research Foundation of the Republic of Korea (NRF) funded by the Ministry of Education, Science and Technology (grant No. 2019R1I1A3A01050861).

Data Availability Statement: Not applicable.

Acknowledgments: The authors thank the anonymous referees for their invaluable comments in improving the first draft of this paper.

Conflicts of Interest: The authors declare no conflict of interest.

References

1. Abdulhadi, Z.; Bshouty, D. Univalent functions in $H \cdot \overline{H(D)}$. *Trans. Am. Math. Soc.* **1988**, *305*, 841–849.
2. Abdulhadi, Z.; Hengartner, W. Spirallike log-harmonic mappings. *Complex Var. Theory Appl.* **1987**, *9*, 121–130.
3. Abdulhadi, Z. Close-to-starlike logharmonic mappings. *Internat. J. Math. Math. Sci.* **1996**, *19*, 563–574. [CrossRef]
4. Aydogan, M.; Polatŏlu, Y. A certain class of starlike log-harmonic mappings. *J. Comput. Appl. Math.* **2014**, *270*, 506–509. [CrossRef]
5. Aydogan, M. Some results on a starlike log-harmonic mapping of order alpha. *J. Comput. Appl. Math.* **2014**, *256*, 77–82. [CrossRef]
6. Abdulhadi, Z.; Ali, R.M. Univalent log-harmonic mapping in the plane. *J. Abstr. Appl.* **2012**, *2012*, 721943.
7. Abdulhadi, Z.; Alareefi, N.M.; Ali, R.M. On the convex-exponent product of log-harmonic mappings. *J. Inequal. Appl.* **2014**, *2014*, 485. [CrossRef]
8. Li, P.; Ponnusamy, S; Wang, X. Some properties of planar p-harmonic and log-p-harmonic mappings. *Bull. Malays. Math. Sci. Soc.* **2013**, *36*, 595–609.
9. Liu, Z.; Ponnusamy, S. Some properties of univalent log-harmonic mappings. *Filomat* **2018**, *32*, 5275–5288. [CrossRef]
10. Seoudy, T.; Aouf, M.K. Fekete-Szeg problem for certain subclass of analytic functions with complex order defined by q-analogue of Ruscheweyh operator. *Constr. Math. Anal.* **2020**, *3*, 36–44.
11. Clunie, J.; Sheil-Small, T. Harmonic univalent functions. *Ann. Acad. Sci. Fenn. Ser. A. I Math.* **1984**, *9*, 3–25. [CrossRef]
12. Sun, Y.; Jiang, Y.; Wang, Z. On the convex combinations of slanted half-plane harmonic mappings. *Houst. J. Math. Anal. Appl.* **2015**, *6*, 46–50.
13. Sun, Y.; Rasila, A.; Jiang, Y. Linear combinations of harmonic quasiconformal mappings convex in one direction. *J. Kodai Math. Appl.* **2016**, *39*, 1323–1334. [CrossRef]
14. Wang, Z.G.; Liu, Z.H.; Li, Y.C. On the linear combinations of harmonic univalent mappings. *J. Math. Anal. Appl.* **2013**, *400*, 452–459. [CrossRef]

axioms

MDPI

Article

A q-Analog of the Class of Completely Convex Functions and Lidstone Series

Maryam Al-Towailb [1,*] and Zeinab S. I. Mansour [2]

1 Department of Computer Science and Engineering, College of Applied Studies and Community Service, King Saud University, Riyadh 11451, Saudi Arabia
2 Department of Mathematics, Faculty of Science, Cairo University, Giza 12613, Egypt; zsmansour@cu.edu.eg
* Correspondence: mtowaileb@ksu.edu.sa

Abstract: This paper introduces a q-analog of the class of completely convex functions. We prove specific properties, including that q-completely convex functions have convergent q-Lidstone series expansions. We also provide a sufficient and necessary condition for a real function to have an absolutely convergent q-Lidstone series expansion.

Keywords: quantum calculus; q-series; q-Lidstone polynomials; completely convex functions

MSC: 05A30; 41A58; 39A70; 40A05

Citation: Al-Towailb, M.; Mansour, Z.S.I. A q-Analog of the Class of Completely Convex Functions and Lidstone Series. *Axioms* **2023**, *12*, 412. https://doi.org/10.3390/axioms12050412

Academic Editors: Ivanka Stamova, Gheorghe Oros and Georgia Irina Oros

Received: 14 February 2023
Revised: 8 March 2023
Accepted: 19 March 2023
Published: 24 April 2023

1. Introduction

In 1929, Lidstone [1] introduced a generalization of Taylor's theorem that approximates an entire function f in a neighborhood of two points instead of one. That is

$$f(x) = \sum_{n=0}^{\infty} \left[f^{(2n)}(1)\Lambda_n(x) + f^{(2n)}(0)\Lambda_n(1-x) \right], \tag{1}$$

where $\Lambda_n(x)$ is a unique polynomial of degree $2n+1$, and called a Lidstone polynomial. In [2], Whittaker proved that an entire function of an exponential type of less than π has a convergent Lidstone series expansion in any compact set of the complex plane. Buckholtz and Shaw [3] provided some conditions for (1) to hold. Other authors worked on this problem (see, e.g., [4–10]). They presented different sufficient and necessary conditions for the representation of functions by this series. We mention, in particular, the result of Widder [10]. He proved that if f is a real-valued function satisfying

$$(-1)^k f^{(2k)}(x) \geq 0 \quad (k \in \mathbb{N}_0) \tag{2}$$

in an interval of length greater than π, then it has a Lidstone series expansion (1) (such a function is known as completely convex). Furthermore, he defined the class of minimal completely convex functions, and then he proved that a real-valued function $f(x)$ could be expanded in an absolutely convergent Lidstone series if and only if it is the difference of two minimal completely convex functions.

Recently, the Lidstone expansion theorem was generalized in quantum calculus (as can be seen in [11–17]). The quantum calculus (Jackson calculus or q-calculus [18]) is an extension of the traditional calculus, and it has been used by many researchers in different branches of science and engineering (as can be seen in, e.g., [19–24]). It has a lot of applications in different mathematical areas such as orthogonal polynomials, number theory, hypergeometric functions, theory of finite differences, gamma function theory, Sobolev spaces, Bernoulli and Euler polynomials, operator theory, and quantum mechanics. For the basic definitions and notations applicable in the q-calculus, see Section 2.

In [11], Ismail and Mansour proved the following q-analog of the Lidstone expansion theorem.

Theorem 1. *Assume that the function $f(z)$ is an entire function of q^{-1}-exponential growth of order 1 and a finite type α less than ξ_1, or it is an entire function of q^{-1}-exponential growth of an order of less than 1. Then, $f(z)$ has a convergent q-Lidstone representation*

$$f(z) = \sum_{n=0}^{\infty} \left[D_{q^{-1}}^{2n} f(1) A_n(z) - D_{q^{-1}}^{2n} f(0) B_n(z) \right], \tag{3}$$

where $(A_n)_n$ and $(B_n)_n$ are the q-Lidstone polynomials defined, respectively, by the generating functions

$$\frac{E_q(zw) - E_q(-zw)}{E_q(w) - E_q(-w)} = \sum_{n=0}^{\infty} A_n(z) w^{2n}, \tag{4}$$

$$\frac{E_q(zw)E_q(-w) - E_q(-zw)E_q(w)}{E_q(w) - E_q(-w)} = \sum_{n=0}^{\infty} B_n(z) \frac{w^n}{[n]_q!}. \tag{5}$$

Moreover, $A_0(z) = z$, $B_0(z) = 1 - z$, and for $n \in \mathbb{N}$, $A_n(z)$ and $B_n(z)$ satisfy the q-difference equation

$$D_{q^{-1}}^2 y_n(z) = y_{n-1}(z) \quad \text{with} \quad y_n(0) = y_n(1) = 0. \tag{6}$$

In [16], AL-Towailb and Mansour proved that the condition

$$D_{q^{-1}}^n f(0) = o(\xi_1^n) \quad \text{as } n \to \infty \tag{7}$$

is both sufficient and necessary for expanding an entire function $f(z)$ in the q-Lidstone series

$$f(1)A_0(z) - f(0)B_0(z) + D_{q^{-1}}^2 f(1) A_1(z) - D_{q^{-1}}^2 f(0) B_1(z) + \ldots,$$

and we noted that Condition (7) is insufficient for the convergence of the following arrangement of the q-Lidstone series:

$$\sum_{n=0}^{\infty} D_{q^{-1}}^{2n} f(1) A_n(z) - \sum_{n=0}^{\infty} D_{q^{-1}}^{2n} f(0) B_n(z),$$

and not necessary for the convergence of (3). This paper aimed to obtain a sufficient and necessary condition for a real-valued function to have an absolutely convergent q-Lidstone series expansion (3). To achieve this aim, we introduced generalizations for the class of completely convex functions (2) on a closed interval of form $[0, a]$ $(a > 0)$, and the class of minimal completely convex functions on the interval $[0, 1]$. This paper is organized as follows. The following section gives the essential notions and basic definitions of q-calculus. Section 3 contains some properties and basic results on q-Lidstone polynomials, which we need in our investigation. In Section 4, we define a q-analog of the class of completely convex functions for the difference operator $D_{q^{-1}}$. Then, we study the relation of this class to a problem of the representation of functions by the q-Lidstone series. In Section 5, we provide a necessary and sufficient condition for a real function to have an absolutely convergent q-Lidstone series expansion.

2. Preliminaries

In this section, we recall some definitions, notations, and results in the q-calculus, which we need in our investigations (see [25]).

Throughout this paper, q is a positive number less than one, and we use the following standard notations:

$$\mathbb{N} := \{1, 2, 3, \ldots\}, \quad \mathbb{N}_0 := \{0, 1, 2, \ldots\} = \mathbb{N} \cup \{0\}.$$

The sets A_q and A_q^* are defined by $A_q := \{q^n : n \in \mathbb{N}_0\}$ and $A_q^* := A_q \cup \{0\}$. For $a \in \mathbb{C}, n \in \mathbb{N}_0$,

$$(a;q)_\infty = \prod_{j=0}^{\infty}(1 - aq^j), \quad (a;q)_n := \frac{(a;q)_\infty}{(aq^n;q)_\infty},$$

and the q-numbers $[n]_q$ and q-factorial $[n]_q!$ are defined by

$$[n]_q = \frac{1-q^n}{1-q}, \quad [n]_q! = \prod_{k=1}^{n}[k]_q.$$

Let $\mu \in \mathbb{C}$. A set $A \subset \mathbb{C}$ is called μ-geometric set if $\mu z \in A$ for any $z \in A$. If f is a function defined on a q-geometric set A, then Jackson's q-difference operator is defined by

$$D_q f(z) = \begin{cases} \dfrac{f(z) - f(qz)}{(1-q)z}, & z \in A - \{0\}; \\ f'(0), & z = 0, \end{cases} \tag{8}$$

provided that f is differentiable at zero. Furthermore, Jackson [26] introduced the following q-integrals for a function f defined on a q-geometric set A:

$$\int_a^b f(t)\,d_qt := \int_0^b f(t)d_qt - \int_0^a f(t)\,d_qt \quad (a,b \in \mathbb{R}),$$

where

$$\int_0^z f(t)\,d_qt := (1-q)\sum_{n=0}^{\infty} zq^n f(zq^n),$$

provided that the series converges at $z = a$ and $z = b$.

Jackson's q-trigonometric functions $\mathrm{Sin}_q z$ and $\mathrm{Cos}_q z$ are defined by

$$\begin{aligned} \mathrm{Sin}_q z &:= \sum_{n=0}^{\infty}(-1)^n \frac{q^{n(2n+1)}}{(q;q)_{2n+1}}(z(1-q))^{2n+1}, \\ \mathrm{Cos}_q z &:= \sum_{n=0}^{\infty}(-1)^n \frac{q^{n(2n-1)}}{(q;q)_{2n}}(z(1-q))^{2n}, \end{aligned} \tag{9}$$

where $E_q(\cdot)$ is one of Jackson's q-exponential function defined by

$$E_q(z) = \sum_{n=0}^{\infty} q^{\frac{n(n-1)}{2}} \frac{(z(1-q))^n}{(q;q)_n} = (-z(1-q);q)_\infty \quad (z \in \mathbb{C}). \tag{10}$$

We use $\{\xi_k\}_{k\in\mathbb{N}}$ to denote the positive zeros of $\mathrm{Sin}_q z$ arranged in increasing order of magnitude. One can verify that $\mathrm{Sin}_q z$ has no zeroes on $|z| < q^{-3/2}$, i.e., the first positive zeros $\xi_1 > q^{-3/2}$.

Lemma 1. *For any $x \in [0,1]$, we have*

$$\mathrm{Sin}_q \xi_1 x \leq \xi_1 x. \tag{11}$$

Proof. Let $f(x) = \xi_1 x - \mathrm{Sin}_q \xi_1 x$, $x \in [0,1]$. Then, $D_{q^{-1}} f(x) = \xi_1(1 - \mathrm{Cos}_q \xi_1 x) \geq 0$. Therefore, by using (8), we obtain

$$f(x) \leq f(\frac{x}{q}) \quad (x \in [0,1]),$$

which implies $f(x) \geq \lim_{n\to\infty} f(q^n x) = 0$. Then, Inequality (11) holds. □

3. Some Results on q-Lidstone Polynomials

We start this section by recalling some properties of the q-Lidstone polynomials $A_n(x)$ and $B_n(x)$ from [14,16,17], for which we need to prove the main results.

Proposition 1 ([16]). *Let $\{\xi_k\}_{k\in\mathbb{N}}$ be the sequence of the positive zeros of $\mathrm{Sin}_q(x)$ and $m \in \mathbb{N}_0$. Then,*

$$(-1)^{n-1}A_n(x) = \frac{2\mathrm{Sin}_q(\xi_1 x)}{\xi_1^{2n+1}\mathrm{Sin}_q'(\xi_1)} + \mathcal{O}(\xi_2^{-(2n+1)}); \tag{12}$$

$$(-1)^{n-1}B_n(x) = \frac{\mathrm{Sin}_q(\xi_1 x)\mathrm{Cos}_q(\xi_1)}{(1-q)(\xi_1)^{2n+1}\mathrm{Sin}_q'(\xi_1)} + \mathcal{O}(\xi_1^{-2n}(2n)^{-m}), \tag{13}$$

for a sufficiently large n.

Proposition 2 ([17]). *If $f \in C_q^{2n}([0,1])$, then*

$$f(x) = \sum_{m=0}^{n-1}\left[D_{q^{-1}}^{2m} f(1)A_m(x) - D_{q^{-1}}^{2m} f(0)B_m(x)\right] + \int_0^1 G_n(x,qt)D_{q^{-1}}^{2n} f(q^2 t)\,d_q t, \tag{14}$$

where

$$G(x,t) = G_1(x,t) = \begin{cases} -qt(1-x), & 0 \le t < x \le 1; \\ -qx(1-t), & 0 \le x < t \le 1, \end{cases} \tag{15}$$

$$G_n(x,qt) = \int_0^1 G(x,qy)\,G_{n-1}(qy,qt)\,d_q y \quad (n \in \mathbb{N}). \tag{16}$$

Moreover,

$$\int_0^1 G_n(x,qt)\,d_q t = A_n(x) - B_n(x) \quad (n \in \mathbb{N}). \tag{17}$$

Remark 1 ([14]). *For $x \in [0,1]$ and $n \in \mathbb{N}_0$, we have*

$$(-1)^n A_n(x) \ge 0 \quad \text{and} \quad (-1)^{n-1}B_n(x) \ge 0. \tag{18}$$

Proposition 3. *Let ξ_1 be the smallest positive zero of $\mathrm{Sin}_q(x)$. Then, there exist some constants M_1 and M_2 and a positive integer n_0 such that the following inequalities hold*

$$0 \le (-1)^n A_n(x) \le \frac{M_1}{\xi_1^{2n}}; \tag{19}$$

$$0 \le (-1)^{n-1}B_n(x) \le \frac{M_2}{\xi_1^{2n}}, \tag{20}$$

for all $x \in [0,1]$ and $n \ge n_0$.

Proof. From (12), there is a positive real number C_1 and $n_0 \in \mathbb{N}$ such that

$$\left|(-1)^{n-1}A_n(x) - 2\frac{\mathrm{Sin}_q(\xi_1 x)}{\xi_1^{2n+1}\mathrm{Sin}_q'(\xi_1)}\right| \le \frac{C_1}{\xi_2^{2n}}, \tag{21}$$

for all $x \in [0,1]$ and $n \ge n_0$. Consequently,

$$0 \le (-1)^n A_n(x) \le \frac{C_1}{\xi_2^{2n}} - 2\frac{\mathrm{Sin}_q(\xi_1 x)}{\xi_1^{2n+1}\mathrm{Sin}_q'(\xi_1)}. \tag{22}$$

Note that $\xi_1 < \xi_2$ and $\mathrm{Sin}_q(\xi_1 x)$ is bounded on $[0,1]$. Then, from (22), we obtain

$$\begin{aligned} 0 \le (-1)^n A_n(x) &\le \frac{C_1}{\xi_1^{2n}} + \frac{2}{\xi_1^{2n+1}} \left| \frac{\mathrm{Sin}_q(\xi_1 x)}{\mathrm{Sin}_q'(\xi_1)} \right| \\ &\le \frac{C_1}{\xi_1^{2n}} + \frac{C_2}{\xi_1^{2n}} = \frac{M_1}{\xi_1^{2n}}. \end{aligned} \tag{23}$$

Similarly, we obtain (20) from (13). □

Proposition 4. *There exists a constant M such that*

$$0 \le \int_0^1 (-1)^n G_n(x, qt)\, d_q t \le \frac{M}{\xi_1^{2n}}.$$

Proof. The proof follows immediately from Equation (17) and Proposition 3. □

Proposition 5. *For any fixed point $x_0 \in (0,1)$ and sufficiently large n, there exist some constants M_1 and M_2 such that*

$$(-1)^n A_n(x_0) \ge \frac{M_1}{\xi_1^{2n}}; \tag{24}$$

$$(-1)^{n-1} B_n(x_0) \ge \frac{M_2}{\xi_1^{2n}}. \tag{25}$$

Proof. From (12), we obtain

$$(-1)^n A_n(x)\xi_1^{2n+1} = L(x) + \mathcal{O}\Big(\big(\frac{\xi_1}{\xi_2}\big)^{2n+1}\Big) \quad (n \to \infty),$$

where $L(x) = \frac{-2\mathrm{Sin}_q(\xi_1 x)}{\mathrm{Sin}_q'(\xi_1)}$. Notice, for any fixed $x_0 \in (0,1)$, $L(x_0) > 0$ and

$$\lim_{n\to\infty} (-1)^n A_n(x_0)\xi_1^{2n+1} = L(x_0).$$

This implies that the sequence $(-1)^n A_n(x_0)\xi_1^{2n+1}$ is bounded below by a positive number. I.e., (24) holds. Similarly, we obtain the Inequality (25) from (13). □

Now, using the previous results, we prove the following theorem.

Theorem 2. *If the series*

$$S = a_0 A_0(x) + b_0 B_0(x) + a_1 A_1(x) + b_1 B_1(x) + \dots \tag{26}$$

converges for a single value $x_0 \subset (0,1)$, then the series $\sum_{n=0}^{\infty} (-1)^n \left[\frac{a_n + b_n}{\xi_1^{2n}}\right]$ is absolutely convergent.

Proof. Since the series (26) converges for $x_0 \in (0,1)$, we have

$$\lim_{n\to\infty} a_n A_n(x_0) = 0, \quad \lim_{n\to\infty} b_n B_n(x_0) = 0$$

Then, from the inequalities (24) and (25), we obtain

$$a_n = \mathcal{O}(\xi_1^{2n}) \quad \text{and} \quad b_n = \mathcal{O}(\xi_1^{2n}). \tag{27}$$

From (12), (13), and (27), we conclude that the series

$$S_1 = \sum_{n=0}^{\infty}\left\{a_n\left[A_n(x_0) + \frac{2(-1)^n \mathrm{Sin}_q(\xi_1 x_0)}{\xi_1^{2n+1}\mathrm{Sin}_q'(\xi_1)}\right] + b_n\left[B_n(x_0) + \frac{(-1)^n \mathrm{Cos}_q\xi_1 \mathrm{Sin}_q(\xi_1 x_0)}{(1-q)\xi_1^{2n+1}\mathrm{Sin}_q'(\xi_1)}\right]\right\}$$

converges absolutely. This implies that $S_1 - S$ is also convergent. Notice that

$$\begin{aligned} S_1 - S &= \sum_{n=0}^{\infty}\left[\frac{2\mathrm{Sin}_q(\xi_1 x_0)}{\xi_1 \mathrm{Sin}_q'(\xi_1)}\frac{(-1)^n}{\xi_1^{2n}}a_n + \frac{\mathrm{Cos}_q\xi_1\mathrm{Sin}_q(\xi_1 x_0)}{(1-q)\xi_1\mathrm{Sin}_q'(\xi_1)}\frac{(-1)^n}{\xi_1^{2n}}b_n\right] \\ &> \frac{2\mathrm{Sin}_q(\xi_1 x_0)}{\xi_1\mathrm{Sin}_q'(\xi_1)}\sum_{n=0}^{\infty}\left[\frac{(-1)^n}{\xi_1^{2n}}a_n + \frac{(-1)^n}{\xi_1^{2n}}b_n\right]. \end{aligned}$$

Therefore, we obtain the result. □

4. A q-Analog of Completely Convex Function

In this section, by $C_q^{\infty}[0,a]$, we mean the space of all functions defined on $[0,a]$ such that $D_{q^{-1}}^n f(x)$ is defined and continuous at zero.

Definition 1. *A real-valued function f, defined on the interval $[0,a]$ $(a > 0)$, is said to be a q-completely convex function if $f \in C_q^{\infty}[0,a]$ and*

$$(-1)^n D_{q^{-1}}^{2n} f(aq^k) \geq 0 \quad (\textit{for all } \{n,k\} \subset \mathbb{N}_0). \tag{28}$$

Example 1. *The functions $f(x) = Sin_q\xi_1 x$, defined in (9), are q-completely convex on the interval $[0,1]$. Indeed, one can verify that*

$$(-1)^n D_{q^{-1}}^{2n} f(x) = (-1)^n D_{q^{-1}}^{2n} Sin_q\xi_1 x = \xi_1^{2n}\, Sin_q(\xi_1\, x) > 0, \tag{29}$$

for all $x \in [0,1]$ and $n \in \mathbb{N}_0$.

In the following, we prove certain properties of q-completely convex functions.

Proposition 6. *If a function $f \in C_q^{\infty}[0,a]$ is q-completely convex, then*

$$(-1)^n D_{q^{-1}}^{2n} f(0) \geq 0 \quad (n \in \mathbb{N}_0). \tag{30}$$

Proof. The proof follows directly by taking the limit as $k \to \infty$ in (28) and using that $D_{q^{-1}}^{2n} f$ is continuous at zero for all $n \in \mathbb{N}_0$. □

Proposition 7. *Let $f \in C_q^{\infty}(0,1)$ be a q-completely convex function on $[0,1]$. Then, for a sufficiently large n, we have*

$$D_{q^{-1}}^{2n} f(0) = \mathcal{O}(\xi_1^{2n}); \tag{31}$$

$$D_{q^{-1}}^{2n} f(1) = \mathcal{O}(\xi_1^{2n}). \tag{32}$$

Proof. From Proposition 1 and Inequality (28), every term of (14) is non-negative. Therefore,

$$0 \leq A_n(x)\, D_{q^{-1}}^{2n} f(0) \leq f(x); \tag{33}$$

$$0 \leq (-B_n(x)) D_{q^{-1}}^{2n} f(1) \leq f(x) \quad (x \in [0,1];\ n \in \mathbb{N}_0). \tag{34}$$

Thus, by using (24) and (33), we obtain

$$0 \leq (-1)^n D^{2n}_{q^{-1}} f(0) \leq \frac{f(x_0)}{(-1)^n A_n(x_0)} \leq K\xi_1^{2n} \quad (n \to \infty),$$

for some constant $K > 0$ and $x_0 \in (0,1)$. Then, we have (31). Similarly, we obtain the asymptotic behavior in (32). □

Proposition 8. *Let f be a q-completely convex function on $[0,1]$. Then, there exists a positive constant C such that for all $x \in A_q$*

$$0 \leq (-1)^n D^{2n}_{q^{-1}} f(x) \leq C\left(\frac{\xi_1}{x}\right)^{2n}, \tag{35}$$

where ξ_1 is the smallest positive zero of $\mathrm{Sin}_q(x)$.

Proof. If f is q-completely convex on $[0,1]$, then it is q-completely convex on $[0,x]$ for all $x \in A_q$. Consequently, the function $\widetilde{f}(t) := f(xt)$ is q-completely convex on $[0,1]$. Therefore, from Proposition (7), we have

$$0 \leq (-1)^n D^{2n}_{q^{-1}} \widetilde{f}(1) = (-1)^n x^{2n} D^{2n}_{q^{-1}} f(x) = \mathcal{O}(\xi_1^{2n}),$$

which is nothing else but (35). □

Lemma 2. *Let $f(x)$ and $-D^2_{q^{-1}} f(x)$ be non-negative on A_q^*, and continuous at 0. Assume that there exists a number $x_0 \in A_q$ such that $f(x_0) \leq \alpha$ ($\alpha \in \mathbb{R}$). Then,*

$$f(x) \leq \frac{(1+q)\alpha}{(1-q)x_0}, \quad \text{for all} \quad x \in A_q^*.$$

Proof. First, let $x \in A_q^*$ and $x \geq x_0$. Then, by using the assumption $D^2_{q^{-1}} f(x) \leq 0$, we have

$$\int_{x_0}^{x} D_q^2 f(\frac{t}{q^2})\, d_q t \leq 0.$$

Therefore, $D_q f(x) \leq D_q f(x_0)$, and

$$\int_{x_0}^{x} D_q f(t)\, d_q t \leq (x - x_0) D_q f(x_0) \quad (x \in A_q^*,\ x_0 \leq x). \tag{36}$$

Since $f(x) \geq 0$ on A_q^*, from (8) and Inequality (36), we obtain

$$f(x) \leq f(x_0) + \frac{(x - x_0)}{(1-q)x_0} f(x_0) = \frac{x - x_0 q}{(1-q)x_0} f(x_0) < \frac{\alpha}{(1-q)x_0}, \tag{37}$$

for all $x \in A_q^*$ and $x_0 \leq x$. Similarly, if $x \in A_q^*$ and $x < x_0$, then

$$f(x) \leq \frac{x_0 - x}{(1-q)x_0} f(qx_0) < \frac{f(qx_0)}{(1-q)x_0}. \tag{38}$$

On the other hand, since $D^2_{q^{-1}} f(x) \leq 0$, we have

$$(1+q)f(qx) \geq qf(x) + f(q^2 x) \quad (x \in A_q^*).$$

Therefore, from the condition $f(x) \geq 0$, we obtain

$$(1+q)f(qx) \geq qf(\frac{x}{q}) + f(qx) > f(qx) \quad (x \in A_q^*). \tag{39}$$

So, from the inequalities (38) and (39), we obtain

$$f(x) < \frac{(1+q)\alpha}{(1-q)x_0} \quad (x \in A_q^*,\ x < x_0). \tag{40}$$

Hence, the relations (37) and (40) yield the required result. □

Corollary 1. *If $f \in C_q^\infty[0,1]$ is a q-completely convex function, then there exists a positive constant M such that*

$$0 \leq (-1)^n D_{q^{-1}}^{2n} f(x) \leq M\xi_1^{2n} \quad (n \in \mathbb{N}_0,\ x \in A_q^*). \tag{41}$$

Proof. The proof follows from Proposition 8 and Lemma 2 by taking $x_0 = 1$ and $M = \frac{1+q}{1-q}C$. □

Lemma 3. *If $f \in C_q^\infty[0,1]$ is a q-completely convex function on $[0,1]$, then there exists a constant $K > 0$ such that*

$$|D_{q^{-1}}^n f(x)| \leq K\xi_1^n \ (x \in A_q^*), \tag{42}$$

where ξ_1 is the smallest positive zero of $\mathrm{Sin}_q(z)$.

Proof. From Corollary 1, it suffices to prove (42) when n is an odd integer. We set $g(x) = (-1)^n D_{q^{-1}}^{2n} f(x)$. Since $f(x)$ is a q-completely convex on $0 \leq x \leq 1$, again from Corollary 1, there exists the constant $M > 0$ (independent of n) such that for all $x \in A_q^*$

$$\begin{aligned} 0 &\leq g(x) \leq M\xi_1^{2n}, \\ 0 &\leq -D_{q^{-1}}^2 g(x) \leq M\xi_1^{2n+2}. \end{aligned} \tag{43}$$

Therefore, for every $x \in A_q^* - \{1\}$, we have

$$0 \leq \int_{qx}^{q^2} -D_{q^{-1}}^2 g(t)\, d_q t \leq Mq(q-x)\xi_1^{2n+2}.$$

So, by using the fundamental theorem of the q-calculus, we obtain

$$0 \leq (-1)^n D_{q^{-1}}^{2n+1} f(x) - (-1)^n D_{q^{-1}}^{2n+1} f(1) \leq M\xi_1^{2n+2},$$

and hence,

$$(-1)^n D_{q^{-1}}^{2n+1} f(1) \leq (-1)^n D_{q^{-1}}^{2n+1} f(x) \leq (-1)^n D_{q^{-1}}^{2n+1} f(1) + M\xi_1^{2n+2},$$

for all $x \in A_q^* - \{1\}$. Consequently,

$$|D_{q^{-1}}^{2n+1} f(x)| \leq |D_{q^{-1}}^{2n+1} f(1)| + M\xi_1^{2n+2}. \tag{44}$$

On the other hand, since $D_{q^{-1}}^2 g(x) < 0$, one can verify that for all $x \in A_q^*$

$$(1+q)g(\frac{x}{q}) \geq g(x) + qg(\frac{x}{q^2}),$$

and then

$$qg(\frac{x}{q}) \leq (1+q)g(x) - g(qx) \quad (x \in A_q^*).$$

Thus, if $x = 1$, we obtain

$$\left|(D_{q^{-1}}^{2n} f)(\frac{1}{q})\right| = (-1)^n (D_{q^{-1}}^{2n} f)(\frac{1}{q}) \leq \frac{(1+q)}{q} \left|D_{q^{-1}}^{2n} f(1)\right|. \quad (45)$$

Hence, from (8), (43) and (45), we have

$$\left|D_{q^{-1}}^{2n+1} f(1)\right| = |D_{q^{-1}} g(1)| \leq \frac{|g(1)| + |g(1/q)|}{1/q - 1} \leq \frac{2q+1}{q} M \xi_1^{2n}. \quad (46)$$

However, $\xi_1 > q^{-3/2}$, this implies

$$\left|D_{q^{-1}}^{2n+1} f(1)\right| \leq \sqrt{q}(2q+1) M \xi_1^{2n+1}. \quad (47)$$

By substituting (47) in (44), we obtain

$$|D_{q^{-1}}^{2n+1} f(x)| \leq \sqrt{q}(2q+1) M \xi_1^{2n+1} + M \xi_1^{2n+2} \leq M_1 M \xi_1^{2n+1},$$

for all $n \in \mathbb{N}$ and $x \in A_q^*$, where $M_1 = \sqrt{q}(2q+1) + q^{-3/2}$.

Since $D_{q^{-1}}^{2n+1} f(x)$ is continuous at zero, then we obtain $D_{q^{-1}}^{2n+1} f(x) = \mathcal{O}(\xi_1^{2n+1})$ for a sufficiently large n. This completes the proof. □

Theorem 3. *Let $f \in C_q^\infty[0,1]$ be a q-completely convex on $[0,1]$. If f is analytic at zero, then the following q-Lidstone series expansion holds for all $x \in [0,1]$.*

$$f(x) = \sum_{n=0}^{\infty} \left[D_{q^{-1}}^{2n} f(1) A_n(x) - D_{q^{-1}}^{2n} f(0) B_n(x)\right]. \quad (48)$$

Moreover, $f(x)$ is the restriction of an entire function of q^{-1}-exponential growth of order 1 and a finite type less than ξ_1 and the expansion (48) holds for all x on the entire complex plane.

Proof. Since f is analytic at 0, there exists $0 < c < 1$ and the open interval $\Omega_c = (-c, c)$ such that $f(x)$ has the Maclaurin series expansion

$$f(x) = \sum_{n=0}^{\infty} \frac{f^{(n)}(0)}{n!} x^n = \sum_{n=0}^{\infty} q^{\frac{n(n-1)}{2}} \frac{D_{q^{-1}}^n f(0)}{[n]_q!} x^n \quad (x \in \Omega_c). \quad (49)$$

From Lemma 3, there exists a constant K such that

$$\left|f(x)\right| \leq \sum_{n=0}^{\infty} \left|q^{\frac{n(n-1)}{2}} \frac{D_{q^{-1}}^n f(0)}{[n]_q!} x^n\right| \leq K \sum_{n=0}^{\infty} q^{\frac{n(n-1)}{2}} \frac{(\xi_1 x)^n}{[n]_q!} = K\, E_q(\xi_1 x), \quad (50)$$

where $E_q(.)$ is Jackson's q-exponential function defined in (10). Notice that, by the known properties of $E_q(.)$ (see [11]), $E_q(x)$ is an entire function that has a q^{-1}-exponential growth of order 1, and it converges everywhere in the complex plane. Therefore, $f(x)$ is the restriction of an entire function of q^{-1}-exponential growth of order 1 and a finite type less than ξ_1. So, according to Theorem 1, we obtain the result. □

5. A q-Analog of Minimal Completely Convex Function

Definition 2. *A real-valued function $f \in C_q^\infty[0,1]$ is a minimal q-completely convex on $[0,1]$ if it is q-completely convex in the interval $[0,1]$, and if the function $g(x) = f(x) - \epsilon\, Sin_q \xi_1 x$ is not q-completely convex for any $\epsilon > 0$.*

For example, the function $f(x) = \text{Sin}_q x$ is a minimal q-completely convex in $0 \le x \le 1$ while the function $f(x) = \text{Sin}_q \xi_1 x$ is not because for any $0 < \epsilon < 1$ and $x \in (0,1)$,

$$(-1)^n D_{q^{-1}}^{2n} (\text{Sin}_q \xi_1 x - \epsilon\, \text{Sin}_q \xi_1 x) = (1-\epsilon)\xi_1^{2n} \text{Sin}_q(\xi_1 x) > 0.$$

Theorem 4. *Let $n \in \mathbb{N}_0$, $(a_n)_n$ and $(b_n)_n$ be two sequences of non-negative integers. Assume that the series*

$$\sum_{n=0}^{\infty} \Big[(-1)^n a_n\, A_n(x) - (-1)^n b_n\, B_n(x)\Big]$$

converges to a function $f(x)$, $0 \le x \le 1$. Then, $f(x)$ is a minimal q-completely convex on the interval $[0,1]$.

Proof. From the assumption, we have

$$f(x) = \sum_{n=0}^{\infty} \Big[(-1)^n a_n\, A_n(x) - (-1)^n b_n\, B_n(x)\Big],\ 0 \le x \le 1. \tag{51}$$

Taking the q^{-1}-derivative for (51) $2k$ times and using (6), we obtain

$$\begin{aligned}(-1)^k D_{q^{-1}}^{2k} f(x) &= \sum_{n=k}^{\infty} (-1)^{n-k} a_n\, A_{n-k}(x) - (-1)^{n-k} b_n\, B_{n-k}(x) \\ &= \sum_{m=0}^{\infty} (-1)^m a_{m+k}\, A_m(x) - (-1)^m b_{m+k}\, B_m(x).\end{aligned} \tag{52}$$

From Proposition 5, since $(a_n)_n$ and $(b_n)_n$ are positive sequences, the right-hand side of Equation (52) is non-negative, and $f(x)$ is q-completely convex in $[0,1]$. On the other hand, from Proposition 3 and Equation (52), there exists a constant $M > 0$ such that

$$(-1)^k D_{q^{-1}}^{2k} f(x) \le M \sum_{m=0}^{\infty} \Big[a_{m+k} + b_{m+k}\Big]\, \xi_1^{-2m} = M\xi_1^{2k} \sum_{n=k}^{\infty} \frac{a_n + b_n}{\xi_1^{2n}}. \tag{53}$$

According to Theorem 2, the power series $T_k = \sum_{n=k}^{\infty} \frac{a_n+b_n}{\xi_1^{2n}}$ converges to zero as $k \to \infty$. Hence, for given $\epsilon > 0$ and $x_0 \in A_q$, there exists an integer $k_0 \in \mathbb{N}$ such that

$$MT_k - \epsilon\, \text{Sin}_q(\xi_1 x_0) < 0\ (k \ge k_0).$$

This implies from (53) that the function

$$(-1)^k D_{q^{-1}}^{2k} \Big(f(x) - \epsilon\, \text{Sin}_q(\xi_1 x)\Big) = (-1)^k D_{q^{-1}}^{2k} f(x) - \epsilon\, \xi_1^{2k}\, \text{Sin}_q(\xi_1 x)$$

is negative at x_0. Therefore, the function f is a minimal q-completely convex in $[0,1]$. □

Theorem 5. *If $f(x)$ is a minimal q-completely convex function on $[0,1]$, then it can be expanded into a convergent q-Lidstone series:*

$$f(x) = f(1)A_0(x) - f(0)B_0(x) + D_{q^{-1}}^2 f(1)A_1(x) - D_{q^{-1}}^2 f(0)B_1(x) + \dots. \tag{54}$$

Proof. We denote by $S_n(x)$ the nth partial sum of the series (54). Then, from the hypothesis on $f(x)$ and Equation (14), we obtain

$$S_n(x) < f(x) \quad (0 \le x \le 1,\ n \in \mathbb{N}_0).$$

Moreover, for each x, $S_n(x)$ is a non-decreasing function of n. Thus, $\lim_{n\to\infty} S_n(x)$ exists and tends towards some function. To prove the result, we prove that

$$\lim_{n\to\infty} S_n(x) = f(x) \quad (x \in [0,1]).$$

Suppose the contrary, and assume that for some $x_0 \in [0,1]$

$$f(x_0) - \lim_{n\to\infty} S_n(x_0) = \triangle > 0.$$

Then, by using Equation (14), we have

$$f(x_0) - S_{2n}(x_0) = \int_0^1 G_n(x_0, qt) D_{q^{-1}}^{2n} f(q^2 t)\, d_q t \geq \triangle \qquad (n \in \mathbb{N}). \tag{55}$$

Since $f(x)$ is a minimal q-completely convex function on $[0,1]$, then $f(x) - \epsilon\, \mathrm{Sin}_q \xi_1 x$ is not q-completely convex in $0 \leq x \leq 1$ for any $\epsilon > 0$. That is, there exists $n_0 \in \mathbb{N}$ and $t_0 \in A_q$,

$$(-1)^{n_0} D_{q^{-1}}^{2n_0} f(t_0) - \epsilon\, \xi_1^{2n_0}\, \mathrm{Sin}_q(\xi_1 t_0) < 0.$$

From Inequality (11), we have

$$(-1)^{n_0} D_{q^{-1}}^{2n_0} f(t_0) < \epsilon\, \xi_1^{2n_0+1}\, t_0.$$

By applying Lemma 2 on the function $g(x) = (-1)^{n_0} D_{q^{-1}}^{2n_0} f(x)$, we obtain

$$(-1)^{n_0} D_{q^{-1}}^{2n_0} f(t) \leq \frac{1+q}{1-q}\, \epsilon\, \xi_1^{2n_0+1} \quad (t \in A_q).$$

Therefore, by choosing $\epsilon < \frac{1-q}{(1+q)\xi_1 M} \triangle$, where M is the constant of Proposition 4, we obtain

$$0 \leq \int_0^1 G_{n_0}(x_0, qt) D_{q^{-1}}^{2n_0} f(q^2 t)\, d_q t < \triangle,$$

which contradicts Inequality (55), and then the result is proved. □

The following theorem is the main result of this section.

Theorem 6. *A real function $f(x)$ can be represented by an absolutely convergent q-Lidstone series if and only if it is the difference of two minimal q-completely convex functions on $[0,1]$.*

Proof. First, assume that $f(x) = g(x) - h(x)$, where $g(x)$ and $h(x)$ are both minimal q-completely convex functions on $[0,1]$. According to Theorem 5, we have

$$g(x) = \sum_{n=0}^{\infty} \left[D_{q^{-1}}^{2n} g(1) A_n(x) - D_{q^{-1}}^{2n} g(0) B_n(x) \right], \tag{56}$$

$$h(x) = \sum_{n=0}^{\infty} \left[D_{q^{-1}}^{2n} h(1) A_n(x) - D_{q^{-1}}^{2n} h(0) B_n(x) \right]. \tag{57}$$

Notice that each series only has positive terms. Thus, by subtracting (57) from (56), we obtain an absolutely convergent q-Lidstone series whose sum is $f(x)$.

Conversely, assume that $f(x)$ can be represented by an absolutely convergent q-Lidstone series

$$f(x) = \sum_{n=0}^{\infty} \left[D_{q^{-1}}^{2n} f(1) A_n(x) - D_{q^{-1}}^{2n} f(0) B_n(x) \right]. \tag{58}$$

Set $a_n = D^{2n}_{q^{-1}} f(1)$, $b_n = D^{2n}_{q^{-1}} f(0)$, and

$$g(x) = \sum_{n=0}^{\infty} \Big[(-1)^n\{|a_n| - (-1)^n a_n\}\, A_n(x) + (-1)^{n+1}\{|b_n| - (-1)^n b_n\}\, B_n(x)\Big], \quad (59)$$

$$h(x) = \sum_{n=0}^{\infty} \Big[(-1)^n |a_n|\, A_n(x) + (-1)^{n+1}|b_n|\, B_n(x)\Big]. \quad (60)$$

Since series in (58) is absolutely convergent, then the two series in (59) and (60) both converge. Furthermore, note that every term of these series is positive. Hence, by using Theorem 4, $g(x)$ and $h(x)$ are minimal q-completely convex functions on $[0,1]$. Since $f(x) = h(x) - g(x)$, the proof is complete. □

6. Conclusions

We introduced the class of q-completely convex functions in the interval $[0, a]$, with the functions satisfying the inequality

$$(-1)^n D^{2n}_{q^{-1}} f(aq^k) \geq 0 \quad (\{n, k\} \subset \mathbb{N}_0)).$$

This class of functions is a generalization of the class of completely convex functions introduced by Widder [10]. First, we presented some properties of a q-completely convex function, and then we proved that such a function could be expanded in a convergent q-Lidstone series:

$$f(x) = \sum_{n=0}^{\infty} \Big[D^{2n}_{q^{-1}} f(1) A_n(x) - D^{2n}_{q^{-1}} f(0) B_n(x)\Big].$$

Furthermore, we obtained a necessary and sufficient condition for a function $f(x)$ to have an absolutely convergent q-Lidstone series expansion by introducing the class of minimal q-completely convex functions.

Author Contributions: M.A.-T. and Z.S.I.M. equally and significantly contributed to writing this article. All authors have read and agreed to the published version of the manuscript.

Funding: Research Center of the Female Scientific and Medical Colleges, Deanship of Scientific Research, King Saud University.

Institutional Review Board Statement: Not applicable.

Informed Consent Statement: Not applicable.

Data Availability Statement: Not applicable.

Acknowledgments: This research project was supported by a grant from the "Research Center of the Female Scientific and Medical Colleges", Deanship of Scientific Research, King Saud University. The authors would like to thank the editor and the referees for their helpful comments and suggestions that improved this article.

Conflicts of Interest: The authors declare no conflicts of interest.

References

1. Lidstone, G. Notes on the extension of Aitken's theorem (for polynomial interpolation) to the Everett types. *Proc. Edinb. Math. Soc.* **1929**, *2*, 16–19. [CrossRef]
2. Whittaker, J.M. On Lidstone' series and two-point expansions of analytic functions. *Proc. Lond. Math. Soc.* **1934**, *2*, 451–469. [CrossRef]
3. Buckholtz, J.D.; Shaw, J.K. On functions expandable in Lidstone series. *J. Math. Anal. Appl.* **1974**, *47*, 626–632. [CrossRef]
4. Boas, R.P. Representation of functions by Lidstone series. *Duke Math. J.* **1943**, *10*, 239–245.
5. Boas, R.P.; Buck, R.C. *Polynomial Expansions of Analytic Functions*, 2nd ed.; Springer: Berlin, Germany, 1964.
6. Golightly, G.O. Coefficients in sine series expansions of special entire functions. *Huston J. Math.* **1988**, *14*, 365–410.
7. Leeming, D.; Sharma, A. A generalization of the class of completely convex functions. *Symp. Inequalities* **1972**, *3*, 177–199.

8. Portisky, H. On certain polynomial and other approximations to analytic functions. *Proc. Natl. Acad. Sci. USA* **1930**, *16*, 83–85. [CrossRef]
9. Schoenberg, I. On certain two-point expansions of integral functions of exponential type. *Bull. Am. Math. Soc.* **1936**, *42*, 284–288. [CrossRef]
10. Widder, D. Completely convex functions and Lidstone series. *Trans. Am. Math. Soc.* **1942**, *51*, 387–398. [CrossRef]
11. Ismail, M.; Mansour, Z.S. q-analogs of Lidstone expansion theorem, two point Taylor expansion theorem, and Bernoulli polynomials. *Anal. Appl.* **2018**, *17*, 1–47. [CrossRef]
12. AL-Towailb, M. A generalization of the q-Lidstone series. *AIMS Math. J.* **2022**, *7*, 9339–9352. [CrossRef]
13. AL-Towailb, M.; Mansour, Z.S. The q-Lidstone series involving q-Bernoulli and q-Euler polynomials generated by the third Jackson q-Bessel function. *Khayyam J. Math.* 2022, *accepted.*
14. Mansour, Z.S.; AL-Towailb, M. The Complementary q-Lidstone Interpolating Polynomials and Applications. *Math. Comput. Appl.* **2020**, *25*, 34. [CrossRef]
15. Al-Towailb, M. A q-Difference Equation and Fourier Series Expansions of q-Lidstone Polynomials. *Symmetry* **2022**, *14*, 782. [CrossRef]
16. AL-Towailb, M.; Mansour, Z.S. Conditional expanding of functions by q-Lidstone series. *Axiom* **2023**, *12*, 22. [CrossRef]
17. Mansour, Z.S.; AL-Towailb, M. q-Lidstone polynomials and existence results for q-boundary value problems. *Bound Value Probl.* **2017**, *2017*, 178. [CrossRef]
18. Jackson, F.H. On q-functions and a certain difference operator. *Trans. Roy. Soc. Edinb.* **1908**, *46*, 64–72. [CrossRef]
19. Ayman Mursaleen, M.; Serra-Capizzano, S. Statistical Convergence via q-Calculus and a Korovkin's Type Approximation Theorem. *Axioms* **2022**, *11*, 70. [CrossRef]
20. Kac, V.; Cheung, P. *Quantum Calculus*; Universitext; Springer: New York, NY, USA, 2002.
21. Hadid, S.B.; Ibrahim, R.W.; Shaher, M. Multivalent functions and differential operator extended by the quantum calculus. *Fractal Fract.* **2022**, *6*, 354. [CrossRef]
22. Ali, I.; Malghani, Y.A.K.; Hussain, S.M.; Khan, N.; Ro, J.-S. Generalization of k-Uniformly Starlike and Convex Functions Using q-Difference Operator. *Fractal Fract.* **2022**, *6*, 216. [CrossRef]
23. Aldawish, I.; Ibrahim, R.W. Solvability of a new q-differential equation related to q-differential inequality of a special type of analytic functions. *Fractal Fract.* **2021**, *5*, 228. [CrossRef]
24. Vivas-Cortez, M.; Aamir Ali, M.; Kashuri, A.; Bashir Sial, I.; Zhang, Z. Some New Newton's Type Integral Inequalities for Co-Ordinated Convex Functions in Quantum Calculus. *Symmetry* **2020**, *12*, 1476. [CrossRef]
25. Gasper, G.; Rahman, M. *Basic Hypergeometric Series*, 2nd ed.; Cambridge University Press: Cambridge, UK, 2004.
26. Jackson, F.H. On q-definite integrals. *Quart. J. Pure Appl. Math.* **1910**, *41*, 193–203.

axioms

MDPI

Article

Applications Laguerre Polynomials for Families of Bi-Univalent Functions Defined with (p, q)-Wanas Operator

Abbas Kareem Wanas [1], **Fethiye Müge Sakar** [2] and **Alina Alb Lupaş** [3,*]

[1] Department of Mathematics, College of Science, University of Al-Qadisiyah, Al Diwaniyah 58001, Iraq
[2] Department of Management, Faculty of Economics and Administrative Sciences, Dicle University, Diyarbakir 21280, Turkey
[3] Department of Mathematics and Computer Science, University of Oradea, 1 Universitatii Street, 410087 Oradea, Romania
* Correspondence: dalb@uoradea.ro or alblupas@gmail.com

Abstract: In current manuscript, using Laguerre polynomials and $(p-q)$-Wanas operator, we identify upper bounds $|a_2|$ and $|a_3|$ which are first two Taylor-Maclaurin coefficients for a specific bi-univalent functions classes $\mathcal{W}_\Sigma(\eta, \delta, \lambda, \sigma, \theta, \alpha, \beta, p, q; h)$ and $\mathcal{K}_\Sigma(\xi, \rho, \sigma, \theta, \alpha, \beta, p, q; h)$ which cover the convex and starlike functions. Also, we discuss Fekete-Szegö type inequality for defined class.

Keywords: bi-univalent function; Fekete-Szegö problem; coefficient bound; Laguerre polynomial; (p, q)-Wanas operator; subordination

MSC: 30C45; 30C80

Citation: Wanas, A.K.; Sakar, F.M.; Alb Lupaş, A. Applications Laguerre Polynomials for Families of Bi-Univalent Functions Defined with (p, q)-Wanas Operator. *Axioms* **2023**, *12*, 430. https://doi.org/10.3390/axioms12050430

Academic Editors: Georgia Irina Oros and Nhon Nguyen-Thanh

Received: 25 February 2023
Revised: 13 March 2023
Accepted: 25 April 2023
Published: 26 April 2023

1. Introduction

Denote by $\mathcal{A}$ function collections that have the style:

$$f(z) = z + \sum_{n=2}^{\infty} a_n z^n, \quad z \in \mathbb{D}, \tag{1}$$

holomorphic in $\mathbb{D} = \{z : |z| < 1\}$ in the complex plane $\mathbb{C}$.

Further, present by $\mathcal{S}$ the sub-set of $\mathcal{A}$ including of univalent functions in $\mathbb{D}$ fullfiling (1). Taking account the Koebe $\frac{1}{4}$ theorem (see [1]), each $f \in \mathcal{S}$ has an inverse f^{-1} with the properties $f^{-1}(f(z)) = z$, for $z \in \mathbb{D}$ and $f(f^{-1}(w)) = w$, with $|w| < r_0(f)$, where $r_0(f) \geq \frac{1}{4}$. If f is of the style (1), then

$$f^{-1}(w) = w - a_2 w^2 + \left(2a_2^2 - a_3\right) w^3 - \left(5a_2^3 - 5a_2 a_3 + a_4\right) w^4 + \cdots, \quad |w| < r_0(f). \tag{2}$$

When f and f^{-1} are univalent functions, $f \in \mathcal{A}$ is bi-univalent in $\mathbb{D}$. The set of bi-univalent functions can be expressed by Σ. The work on bi-univalent functions have been brightened by Srivastava et al. [2] in recent years. The following functions can be examplified for functions in the set of bi-univalent.

$$\frac{z}{1-z}, \quad -\log(1-z) \qquad \text{and} \qquad \frac{1}{2}\log\left(\frac{1+z}{1-z}\right).$$

Although Koebe function is not an element of bi-univalent set of functions, the Σ is not null set.

Later, such studies continued by Ali et al. [3], Bulut et al. [4], Srivastava et al. [5] and others (see, for example, [6–18]). However, non decisive predictions of the $|a_2|$ and $|a_3|$

coefficients in given by (1) were declared in different studies. Generalized inequalities on Taylor-Maclaurin coefficients

$$|a_n| \qquad (n \in \mathbb{N};\ n \geqq 3)$$

for $f \in \Sigma$ has not been totally solved yet for several subfamilies of the Σ.

$|a_3 - \mu a_2^2|$ of the Fekete-Szegö function for $f \in \mathcal{S}$ is well-known in the Geometric Function Theory.

Its origin lies in the refutation of the Littlewood-Paley conjecture by Fekete-Szegö [19]. In that case, the coefficients of odd (single-valued) univalent functions are bounded by unity.

Functions have received much attention since then, especially in the investigation of many subclasses of the single-valued function family.

This topic has become very interesting for Geometric Function Theorists (see for example [20–25]).

The generator function for Laguerre polynomial $L_n^{\gamma}(\tau)$ is the polynomial answer $\phi(\tau)$ of the differential equation ([26])

$$\tau\phi'' + (1 + \gamma - \tau)\phi' + n\phi = 0,$$

where $\gamma > -1$ and n is non-negative integers.

The generating function of generator function for Laguerre polynomial $L_n^{\gamma}(\tau)$ is expressed as below:

$$H_{\gamma}(\tau, z) = \sum_{n=0}^{\infty} L_n^{\gamma}(\tau)z^n = \frac{e^{-\frac{\tau z}{1-z}}}{(1-z)^{\gamma+1}}, \tag{3}$$

where $\tau \in \mathbb{R}$ and $z \in \mathbb{D}$. The generator function for Laguerre polynomial can also be expressed given below:

$$L_{n+1}^{\gamma}(\tau) = \frac{2n+1+\gamma-\tau}{n+1}L_n^{\gamma}(\tau) - \frac{n+\gamma}{n+1}L_{n-1}^{\gamma}(\tau) \quad (n \geq 1),$$

with the initial terms

$$L_0^{\gamma}(\tau) = 1, \quad L_1^{\gamma}(\tau) = 1 + \gamma - \tau \quad \text{and} \quad L_2^{\gamma}(\tau) = \frac{\tau^2}{2} - (\gamma+2)\tau + \frac{(\gamma+1)(\gamma+2)}{2}. \tag{4}$$

Simply, when $\gamma = 0$ the generator function for Laguerre polynomial leads to the simply Laguerre polynomial, $L_n^0(\tau) = L_n(\tau)$.

Let f and g be holomorphic in $\mathbb{D}$, it is clear that f is subordinate to g, if there occurs a holomorphic function w in $\mathbb{D}$ such that $w(0) = 0$, and $|w(z)| < 1$, for $z \in \mathbb{D}$ so that $f(z) = g(w(z))$. This subordination is indicated by $f \prec g$. Moreover, if g is univalent in $\mathbb{D}$, then we have the balance (see [27]), given by $f(z) \prec g(z) \iff f(\mathbb{D}) \subset g(\mathbb{D})$ *and* $f(0) = g(0)$.

The (p,q)-derivative operator or (p,q)-difference operator $(0 < q < p \leq 1)$, for a function f is stated by

$$D_{p,q}f(z) = \frac{f(pz) - f(qz)}{(p-q)z} \qquad (z \in \mathbb{D}^* = \mathbb{D} \setminus \{0\}),$$

and

$$D_{p,q}f(0) = f'(0).$$

More information on the subject of (p,q)-calculus are founded in [28–33].

For $f \in \mathcal{A}$, we conclude that

$$D_{p,q}f(z) = 1 + \sum_{n=2}^{\infty} [n]_{p,q}a_n z^{n-1},$$

where the (p,q)-bracket number or twin-basic $[n]_{p,q}$ is showed by

$$[n]_{p,q} = \frac{p^n - q^n}{p-q} = p^{n-1} + p^{n-2}q + p^{n-3}q^2 + \cdots + pq^{n-2} + q^{n-1} \quad (p \neq q),$$

which is a native generator number for q, namely is, we get (see [34,35])

$$\lim_{p \to 1^-} [n]_{p,q} = [n]_q = \frac{1-q^n}{1-q}.$$

Obviously, the impression $[n]_{p,q}$ is symmetric, namely,

$$[n]_{p,q} = [n]_{q,p}.$$

Wanas and Cotîrlă [36] presented $W^{\sigma,\theta}_{\alpha,\beta,p,q} : \mathcal{A} \longrightarrow \mathcal{A}$ known as $(p-q)$-Wanas operator showed by

$$W^{\sigma,\theta}_{\alpha,\beta,p,q} f(z) = z + \sum_{n=2}^{\infty} \left(\frac{[\Psi_n(\sigma,\alpha,\beta)]_{p,q}}{[\Psi_1(\sigma,\alpha,\beta)]_{p,q}} \right)^{\theta} a_n z^n = z + \sum_{n=2}^{\infty} \frac{[\Psi_n(\sigma,\alpha,\beta)]^{\theta}_{p,q}}{[\Psi_1(\sigma,\alpha,\beta)]^{\theta}_{p,q}} a_n z^n,$$

where

$$\Psi_n(\sigma,\alpha,\beta) = \sum_{\tau=1}^{\sigma} \binom{\sigma}{\tau} (-1)^{\tau+1} (\alpha^{\tau} + n\beta^{\tau}), \ \Psi_1(\sigma,\alpha,\beta) = \sum_{\tau=1}^{\sigma} \binom{\sigma}{\tau} (-1)^{\tau+1} (\alpha^{\tau} + \beta^{\tau}),$$

and

$$\alpha \in \mathbb{R}, \beta \in \mathbb{R}^+_0 \text{ with } \alpha + \beta > 0, n-1 \in \mathbb{N}, \sigma \in \mathbb{N}, \theta \in \mathbb{N}_0, 0 < q < p \leq 1 \text{ and } z \in \mathbb{D}.$$

Remark 1. *The operator $W^{\sigma,\theta}_{\alpha,\beta,p,q}$ is a generalized form of several operators given in previous researches for some values of parameters which are mentioned below.*

1. *For $p = \sigma = \beta = 1$, $\theta = -\nu$, $\Re(\nu) > 1$ and $\alpha \in \mathbb{C} \setminus \mathbb{Z}^-_0$, the operator $W^{\sigma,\theta}_{\alpha,\beta,p,q}$ decreases to the q-Srivastava Attiya operator $J^{\nu}_{q,\alpha}$ [37].*
2. *For $p = \sigma = \beta = 1$, $\theta = -1$ and $\alpha > -1$, the operator $W^{\sigma,\theta}_{\alpha,\beta,p,q}$ decreases to the q-Bernardi operator [38].*
3. *For $p = \sigma = \alpha = \beta = 1$ and $\theta = -1$, the operator $W^{\sigma,\theta}_{\alpha,\beta,p,q}$ decreases to the q-Libera operator [38].*
4. *For $\alpha = 0$ and $p = \sigma = \beta = 1$, the operator $W^{\sigma,\theta}_{\alpha,\beta,p,q}$ decreases to the q-Sălăgean operator [39].*
5. *For $q \longrightarrow 1^-$ and $p = \sigma = 1$, the operator $W^{\sigma,\theta}_{\alpha,\beta,p,q}$ decreases to the operator $I^{\theta}_{\alpha,\beta}$ was presented and studied by Swamy [40].*
6. *For $q \longrightarrow 1^-$, $p = \sigma = \beta = 1$, $\theta = -\nu$, $\Re(\nu) > 1$ and $s \in \mathbb{C} \setminus \mathbb{Z}^-_0$, the operator $W^{\sigma,\theta}_{\alpha,\beta,p,q}$ decreases to the operator J^{ν}_{α} was presented by Srivastava and Attiya [41]. The operator J^{ν}_{s} is well-known as Srivastava-Attiya operator by researchers.*
7. *For $q \longrightarrow 1^-$, $p = \sigma = \beta = 1$ and $\alpha > -1$, the operator $W^{\sigma,\theta}_{\alpha,\beta,p,q}$, decreases to the operator I^{θ}_{α} was presented by Cho and Srivastava [42].*
8. *For $q \longrightarrow 1^-$, $p = \sigma = \alpha = \beta = 1$, the operator $W^{\sigma,\theta}_{\alpha,\beta,p,q}$ decreases to the operator I^{θ} was presented by Uralegaddi and Somanatha [43].*
9. *For $q \longrightarrow 1^-$, $p = \sigma = \alpha = \beta = 1$, $\theta = -\xi$ and $\xi > 0$, the operator $W^{\sigma,\theta}_{\alpha,\beta,p,q}$ decreases to the operator I^{ξ} was presented by Jung et al. [44]. The operator I^{ξ} is the Jung-Kim-Srivastava integral operator.*
10. *For $q \longrightarrow 1^-$, $p = \sigma = \beta = 1$, $\theta = -1$ and $\alpha > -1$, the operator $W^{\sigma,\theta}_{\alpha,\beta,p,q}$ decreases to the Bernardi operator [45].*

11. *For $q \longrightarrow 1^-$, $\alpha = 0$, $p = \sigma = \beta = 1$ and $\theta = -1$, the operator $W^{\sigma,\theta}_{\alpha,\beta,p,q}$ decreases to the Alexander operator [46].*
12. *For $q \longrightarrow 1^-$, $p = \sigma = 1$, $\alpha = 1 - \beta$ and $t \geq 0$, the operator $W^{\sigma,\theta}_{\alpha,\beta,p,q}$ decreases to the operator D^{θ}_{β} was presented by Al-Oboudi [19].*
13. *For $q \longrightarrow 1^-$, $p = \sigma = 1$, $\alpha = 0$ and $\beta = 1$, the operator $W^{\sigma,\theta}_{\alpha,\beta,p,q}$ decreases to the operator S^{θ} was presented by Sălăgean [47].*

2. Main Results

Firstly, We start to present the classes $\mathcal{W}_{\Sigma}(\eta,\delta,\lambda,\sigma,\theta,\alpha,\beta,p,q;h)$ and $\mathcal{K}_{\Sigma}(\xi,\rho,\sigma,\theta,\alpha,\beta,p,q;h)$ given below:

Definition 1. *Suppose that $0 \leq \eta \leq 1$, $0 \leq \lambda \leq 1$, $0 \leq \delta \leq 1$ and h is analytic in $\mathbb{D}$, $h(0) = 1$. $f \in \Sigma$ is in the class $\mathcal{W}_{\Sigma}(\eta,\delta,\lambda,\sigma,\theta,\alpha,\beta,p,q;h)$ if it provides the subordinations:*

$$\left(\frac{z\left(W^{\sigma,\theta}_{\alpha,\beta,p,q}f(z)\right)'}{W^{\sigma,\theta}_{\alpha,\beta,p,q}f(z)}\right)^{\eta}\left[(1-\delta)\frac{z\left(W^{\sigma,\theta}_{\alpha,\beta,p,q}f(z)\right)'}{W^{\sigma,\theta}_{\alpha,\beta,p,q}f(z)}+\delta\left(1+\frac{z\left(W^{\sigma,\theta}_{\alpha,\beta,p,q}f(z)\right)''}{\left(W^{\sigma,\theta}_{\alpha,\beta,p,q}f(z)\right)'}\right)\right]^{\lambda} \prec h(z)$$

and

$$\left(\frac{w\left(W^{\sigma,\theta}_{\alpha,\beta,p,q}f^{-1}(w)\right)'}{W^{\sigma,\theta}_{\alpha,\beta,p,q}f^{-1}(w)}\right)^{\eta}\left[(1-\delta)\frac{w\left(W^{\sigma,\theta}_{\alpha,\beta,p,q}f^{-1}(w)\right)'}{W^{\sigma,\theta}_{\alpha,\beta,p,q}f^{-1}(w)}+\delta\left(1+\frac{w\left(W^{\sigma,\theta}_{\alpha,\beta,p,q}f^{-1}(w)\right)''}{\left(W^{\sigma,\theta}_{\alpha,\beta,p,q}f^{-1}(w)\right)'}\right)\right]^{\lambda} \prec h(w),$$

where f^{-1} is given by (2).

Definition 2. *Suppose that $0 \leq \xi \leq 1$, $0 \leq \rho < 1$ and h is analytic in $\mathbb{D}$, $h(0) = 1$. $f \in \Sigma$ is in the class $\mathcal{K}_{\Sigma}(\xi,\rho,\sigma,\theta,\alpha,\beta,p,q;h)$ if it provides the subordinations:*

$$(1-\xi)\frac{z\left(W^{\sigma,\theta}_{\alpha,\beta,p,q}f(z)\right)'}{(1-\rho)W^{\sigma,\theta}_{\alpha,\beta,p,q}f(z)+\rho z\left(W^{\sigma,\theta}_{\alpha,\beta,p,q}f(z)\right)'}$$
$$+\xi\left(\frac{\left(W^{\sigma,\theta}_{\alpha,\beta,p,q}f(z)\right)'+z\left(W^{\sigma,\theta}_{\alpha,\beta,p,q}f(z)\right)''}{\left(W^{\sigma,\theta}_{\alpha,\beta,p,q}f(z)\right)'+\rho z\left(W^{\sigma,\theta}_{\alpha,\beta,p,q}f(z)\right)''}\right) \prec h(z)$$

and

$$(1-\xi)\frac{w\left(W^{\sigma,\theta}_{\alpha,\beta,p,q}f^{-1}(w)\right)'}{(1-\rho)W^{\sigma,\theta}_{\alpha,\beta,p,q}f^{-1}(w)+\rho w\left(W^{\sigma,\theta}_{\alpha,\beta,p,q}f^{-1}(w)\right)'}$$
$$+\xi\left(\frac{\left(W^{\sigma,\theta}_{\alpha,\beta,p,q}f^{-1}(w)\right)'+w\left(W^{\sigma,\theta}_{\alpha,\beta,p,q}f^{-1}(w)\right)''}{\left(W^{\sigma,\theta}_{\alpha,\beta,p,q}f^{-1}(w)\right)'+\rho w\left(W^{\sigma,\theta}_{\alpha,\beta,p,q}f^{-1}(w)\right)''}\right) \prec h(w),$$

where f^{-1} is given by (2).

Theorem 1. *Suppose that $0 \leq \eta \leq 1$, $0 \leq \lambda \leq 1$ and $0 \leq \delta \leq 1$. If $f \in \Sigma$ of the style* (1) *be an element of class $\mathcal{W}_{\Sigma}(\eta,\delta,\lambda,\sigma,\theta,\alpha,\beta,p,q;h)$, with $h(z) = 1 + e_1 z + e_2 z^2 + \cdots$, then*

$$|a_2| \leq \frac{(\eta+\lambda(\delta+1))[\Psi_2(\sigma,\alpha,\beta)]^{\theta}_{p,q}|e_1|}{[\Psi_1(\sigma,\alpha,\beta)]^{\theta}_{p,q}} = \frac{|e_1|}{\Omega}$$

and

$$|a_3| \le \min\left\{\max\left\{\left|\frac{e_1}{\Delta}\right|, \left|\frac{e_2}{\Delta} - \frac{\varphi e_1^2}{\Omega^2\Delta}\right|\right\}, \max\left\{\left|\frac{e_1}{\Delta}\right|, \left|\frac{e_2}{\Delta} - \frac{(2\Delta+\varphi)e_1^2}{\Omega^2\Delta}\right|\right\}\right\}, \tag{5}$$

where

$$\begin{aligned}
\Omega &= \frac{(\eta+\lambda(\delta+1))[\Psi_2(\sigma,\alpha,\beta)]_{p,q}^{\theta}}{[\Psi_1(\sigma,\alpha,\beta)]_{p,q}^{\theta}}, \\
\Delta &= \frac{2(\eta+\lambda(2\delta+1))[\Psi_3(\sigma,\alpha,\beta)]_{p,q}^{\theta}}{[\Psi_1(\sigma,\alpha,\beta)]_{p,q}^{\theta}}, \\
\varphi &= \frac{[\eta(\eta-1)+\lambda(\delta+1)(2\eta+(\lambda-1)(\delta+1))-2(\eta+\lambda(3\delta+1))][\Psi_2(\sigma,\alpha,\beta)]_{p,q}^{2\theta}}{2[\Psi_1(\sigma,\alpha,\beta)]_{p,q}^{2\theta}}.
\end{aligned} \tag{6}$$

Proof. Assume that $f \in \mathcal{W}_\Sigma(\eta,\delta,\lambda,\sigma,\theta,\alpha,\beta,p,q;e_1;e_2)$. Then there consists two holomorphic functions $\phi,\psi : \mathbb{D} \longrightarrow \mathbb{D}$ showed by

$$\phi(z) = r_1 z + r_2 z^2 + r_3 z^3 + \cdots \quad (z \in \mathbb{D}) \tag{7}$$

and

$$\psi(w) = s_1 w + s_2 w^2 + s_3 w^3 + \cdots \quad (w \in \mathbb{D}), \tag{8}$$

with $\phi(0) = \psi(0) = 0$, $|\phi(z)| < 1$, $|\psi(w)| < 1$, $z,w \in \mathbb{D}$ so that

$$\begin{aligned}
&\left(\frac{z\left(W_{\alpha,\beta,p,q}^{\sigma,\theta}f(z)\right)'}{W_{\alpha,\beta,p,q}^{\sigma,\theta}f(z)}\right)^{\eta}\left[(1-\delta)\frac{z\left(W_{\alpha,\beta,p,q}^{\sigma,\theta}f(z)\right)'}{W_{\alpha,\beta,p,q}^{\sigma,\theta}f(z)} + \delta\left(1+\frac{z\left(W_{\alpha,\beta,p,q}^{\sigma,\theta}f(z)\right)''}{\left(W_{\alpha,\beta,p,q}^{\sigma,\theta}f(z)\right)'}\right)\right]^{\lambda} \\
&= 1 + e_1\phi(z) + e_2\phi^2(z) + \cdots
\end{aligned} \tag{9}$$

and

$$\begin{aligned}
&\left(\frac{w\left(W_{\alpha,\beta,p,q}^{\sigma,\theta}f^{-1}(w)\right)'}{W_{\alpha,\beta,p,q}^{\sigma,\theta}f^{-1}(w)}\right)^{\eta}\left[(1-\delta)\frac{w\left(W_{\alpha,\beta,p,q}^{\sigma,\theta}f^{-1}(w)\right)'}{W_{\alpha,\beta,p,q}^{\sigma,\theta}f^{-1}(w)} + \delta\left(1+\frac{w\left(W_{\alpha,\beta,p,q}^{\sigma,\theta}f^{-1}(w)\right)''}{\left(W_{\alpha,\beta,p,q}^{\sigma,\theta}f^{-1}(w)\right)'}\right)\right]^{\lambda} \\
&= 1 + e_1\psi(w) + e_2\psi^2(w) + \cdots.
\end{aligned} \tag{10}$$

Unification of (7), (8), (9) and (10), yield

$$\begin{aligned}
&\left(\frac{z\left(W_{\alpha,\beta,p,q}^{\sigma,\theta}f(z)\right)'}{W_{\alpha,\beta,p,q}^{\sigma,\theta}f(z)}\right)^{\eta}\left[(1-\delta)\frac{z\left(W_{\alpha,\beta,p,q}^{\sigma,\theta}f(z)\right)'}{W_{\alpha,\beta,p,q}^{\sigma,\theta}f(z)} + \delta\left(1+\frac{z\left(W_{\alpha,\beta,p,q}^{\sigma,\theta}f(z)\right)''}{\left(W_{\alpha,\beta,p,q}^{\sigma,\theta}f(z)\right)'}\right)\right]^{\lambda} \\
&= 1 + e_1 r_1 z + \left[e_1 r_2 + e_2 r_1^2\right] z^2 + \cdots
\end{aligned} \tag{11}$$

and

$$\begin{aligned}
&\left(\frac{w\left(W_{\alpha,\beta,p,q}^{\sigma,\theta}f^{-1}(w)\right)'}{W_{\alpha,\beta,p,q}^{\sigma,\theta}f^{-1}(w)}\right)^{\eta}\left[(1-\delta)\frac{w\left(W_{\alpha,\beta,p,q}^{\sigma,\theta}f^{-1}(w)\right)'}{W_{\alpha,\beta,p,q}^{\sigma,\theta}f^{-1}(w)} + \delta\left(1+\frac{w\left(W_{\alpha,\beta,p,q}^{\sigma,\theta}f^{-1}(w)\right)''}{\left(W_{\alpha,\beta,p,q}^{\sigma,\theta}f^{-1}(w)\right)'}\right)\right]^{\lambda} \\
&= 1 + e_1 s_1 w + \left[e_1 s_2 + e_2 s_1^2\right] w^2 + \cdots.
\end{aligned} \tag{12}$$

It is clear that if $|\phi(z)| < 1$ and $|\psi(w)| < 1$, $z,w \in \mathbb{D}$, we obtain

$$|r_j| \le 1 \quad \text{and} \quad |s_j| \le 1 \ (j \in \mathbb{N}).$$

Taking into account (11) and (12), after simplifying, we find that

$$\frac{(\eta+\lambda(\delta+1))[\Psi_2(\sigma,\alpha,\beta)]^{\theta}_{p,q}}{[\Psi_1(\sigma,\alpha,\beta)]^{\theta}_{p,q}}a_2=e_1r_1, \tag{13}$$

$$\begin{aligned}&\frac{2(\eta+\lambda(2\delta+1))[\Psi_3(\sigma,\alpha,\beta)]^{\theta}_{p,q}}{[\Psi_1(\sigma,\alpha,\beta)]^{\theta}_{p,q}}a_3\\&+\frac{[\eta(\eta-1)+\lambda(\delta+1)(2\eta+(\lambda-1)(\delta+1))-2(\eta+\lambda(3\delta+1))][\Psi_2(\sigma,\alpha,\beta)]^{2\theta}_{p,q}}{2[\Psi_1(\sigma,\alpha,\beta)]^{2\theta}_{p,q}}a_2^2\\&=e_1r_2+e_2r_1^2,\end{aligned} \tag{14}$$

$$-\frac{(\eta+\lambda(\delta+1))[\Psi_2(\sigma,\alpha,\beta)]^{\theta}_{p,q}}{[\Psi_1(\sigma,\alpha,\beta)]^{\theta}_{p,q}}a_2=e_1s_1 \tag{15}$$

and

$$\begin{aligned}&\frac{2(\eta+\lambda(2\delta+1))[\Psi_3(\sigma,\alpha,\beta)]^{\theta}_{p,q}}{[\Psi_1(\sigma,\alpha,\beta)]^{\theta}_{p,q}}\left(2a_2^2-a_3\right)\\&+\frac{[\eta(\eta-1)+\lambda(\delta+1)(2\eta+(\lambda-1)(\delta+1))-2(\eta+\lambda(3\delta+1))][\Psi_2(\sigma,\alpha,\beta)]^{2\theta}_{p,q}}{2[\Psi_1(\sigma,\alpha,\beta)]^{2\theta}_{p,q}}a_2^2\\&=e_1s_2+e_2s_1^2.\end{aligned} \tag{16}$$

If we implement notation (6), then (13) and (14) becomes

$$\Omega a_2=e_1r_1,\quad \Delta a_3+\varphi a_2^2=e_1r_2+e_2r_1^2. \tag{17}$$

This gives

$$\frac{\Delta}{e_1}a_3=r_2+\left(\frac{e_2}{e_1}-\frac{\varphi e_1}{\Omega^2}\right)r_1^2, \tag{18}$$

and on using the given certain result ([48], p. 10):

$$|r_2-\mu r_1^2|\le\max\{1,|\mu|\} \tag{19}$$

for every $\mu\in\mathbb{C}$, we get

$$\left|\frac{\Delta}{e_1}\right||a_3|\le\max\left\{1,\left|\frac{e_2}{e_1}-\frac{\varphi e_1}{\Omega^2}\right|\right\}. \tag{20}$$

In the same way, (15) and (16) becomes

$$-\Omega a_2=e_1s_1,\quad \Delta(2a_2^2-a_3)+\varphi a_2^2=e_1s_2+e_2s_1^2. \tag{21}$$

This gives

$$-\frac{\Delta}{e_1}a_3=s_2+\left(\frac{e_2}{e_1}-\frac{(2\Delta+\varphi)e_1}{\Omega^2}\right)s_1^2. \tag{22}$$

Applying (19), we obtain

$$\left|\frac{\Delta}{e_1}\right||a_3|\le\max\left\{1,\left|\frac{e_2}{e_1}-\frac{(2\Delta+\varphi)e_1}{\Omega^2}\right|\right\}. \tag{23}$$

Inequality (5) follows from (20) and (23). □

If we take the generating function $L_n^{\gamma}(\tau)$ given by (3) common generalized Laguerre polynomials as $h(z)$, then from the equalities given(4), we get $e_1=1+\gamma-\tau$ and $e_2=\frac{\tau^2}{2}-(\gamma+2)\tau+\frac{(\gamma+1)(\gamma+2)}{2}$. We obtain following corollary from Theorem 1.

Corollary 1. *If $f \in \Sigma$ given by style* (1) *is in the family $\mathcal{W}_\Sigma(\eta,\delta,\lambda,\sigma,\theta,\alpha,\beta,p,q;H_\gamma(\tau,z))$, then*

$$|a_2| \le \frac{(\eta+\lambda(\delta+1))[\Psi_2(\sigma,\alpha,\beta)]^{\theta}_{p,q}|1+\gamma-\tau|}{[\Psi_1(\sigma,\alpha,\beta)]^{\theta}_{p,q}} = \frac{|1+\gamma-\tau|}{\Omega}$$

and

$$\begin{aligned}|a_3| \;\le\; & \min\left\{\max\left\{\left|\frac{1+\gamma-\tau}{\Delta}\right|,\left|\frac{\frac{\tau^2}{2}-(\gamma+2)\tau+\frac{(\gamma+1)(\gamma+2)}{2}}{\Delta}-\frac{\varphi(1+\gamma-\tau)^2}{\Omega^2\Delta}\right|\right\},\right.\\ & \left.\max\left\{\left|\frac{1+\gamma-\tau}{\Delta}\right|,\left|\frac{\frac{\tau^2}{2}-(\gamma+2)\tau+\frac{(\gamma+1)(\gamma+2)}{2}}{\Delta}-\frac{(2\Delta+\varphi)(1+\gamma-\tau)^2}{\Omega^2\Delta}\right|\right\}\right\},\end{aligned}$$

for all η,λ,δ so that $0\le\eta\le1$, $0\le\lambda\le1$ and $0\le\delta\le1$, where Ω,Δ,φ are given by (6) *and $H_\gamma(\tau,z)$ is given by* (3).

Theorem 2. *Suppose that $0\le\xi\le1$ and $0\le\rho<1$. If $f\in\Sigma$ of the style* (1) *be an element of the class $\mathcal{K}_\Sigma(\xi,\rho,\sigma,\theta,\alpha,\beta,p,q;h)$, with $h(z)=1+e_1z+e_2z^2+\cdots$, then*

$$|a_2| \le \frac{(\xi+1)(1-\rho)[\Psi_2(\sigma,\alpha,\beta)]^{\theta}_{p,q}|e_1|}{[\Psi_1(\sigma,\alpha,\beta)]^{\theta}_{p,q}} = \frac{|e_1|}{\Upsilon}$$

and

$$|a_3| \le \min\left\{\max\left\{\left|\frac{e_1}{\Phi}\right|,\left|\frac{e_2}{\Phi}-\frac{\chi e_1^2}{\Upsilon^2\Phi}\right|\right\},\max\left\{\left|\frac{e_1}{\Phi}\right|,\left|\frac{e_2}{\Phi}-\frac{(2\Phi+\chi)e_1^2}{\Upsilon^2\Phi}\right|\right\}\right\}, \tag{24}$$

where

$$\begin{aligned}\Upsilon &= \frac{(\xi+1)(1-\rho)[\Psi_2(\sigma,\alpha,\beta)]^{\theta}_{p,q}}{[\Psi_1(\sigma,\alpha,\beta)]^{\theta}_{p,q}},\\ \Phi &= \frac{2(2\xi+1)(1-\rho)[\Psi_3(\sigma,\alpha,\beta)]^{\theta}_{p,q}}{[\Psi_1(\sigma,\alpha,\beta)]^{\theta}_{p,q}},\\ \chi &= \frac{(2\xi+1)(\rho^2-1)[\Psi_2(\sigma,\alpha,\beta)]^{2\theta}_{p,q}}{[\Psi_1(\sigma,\alpha,\beta)]^{2\theta}_{p,q}}.\end{aligned} \tag{25}$$

Proof. Assume that $f\in\mathcal{K}_\Sigma(\xi,\rho,\sigma,\theta,\alpha,\beta,p,q;e_1;e_2)$. Then there consists two holomorphic functions $\phi,\psi:\mathbb{D}\longrightarrow\mathbb{D}$ such that

$$\begin{aligned}&(1-\xi)\frac{z\left(W^{\sigma,\theta}_{\alpha,\beta,p,q}f(z)\right)'}{(1-\rho)W^{\sigma,\theta}_{\alpha,\beta,p,q}f(z)+\rho z\left(W^{\sigma,\theta}_{\alpha,\beta,p,q}f(z)\right)'}+\xi\left(\frac{\left(W^{\sigma,\theta}_{\alpha,\beta,p,q}f(z)\right)'+z\left(W^{\sigma,\theta}_{\alpha,\beta,p,q}f(z)\right)''}{\left(W^{\sigma,\theta}_{\alpha,\beta,p,q}f(z)\right)'+\rho z\left(W^{\sigma,\theta}_{\alpha,\beta,p,q}f(z)\right)''}\right)\\ &=1+e_1\phi(z)+e_2\phi^2(z)+\cdots\end{aligned} \tag{26}$$

and

$$\begin{aligned}&(1-\xi)\frac{w\left(W^{\sigma,\theta}_{\alpha,\beta,p,q}f^{-1}(w)\right)'}{(1-\rho)W^{\sigma,\theta}_{\alpha,\beta,p,q}f^{-1}(w)+\rho w\left(W^{\sigma,\theta}_{\alpha,\beta,p,q}f^{-1}(w)\right)'}+\xi\left(\frac{\left(W^{\sigma,\theta}_{\alpha,\beta,p,q}f^{-1}(w)\right)'+w\left(W^{\sigma,\theta}_{\alpha,\beta,p,q}f^{-1}(w)\right)''}{\left(W^{\sigma,\theta}_{\alpha,\beta,p,q}f^{-1}(w)\right)'+\rho w\left(W^{\sigma,\theta}_{\alpha,\beta,p,q}f^{-1}(w)\right)''}\right)\\ &=1+e_1\psi(w)+e_2\psi^2(w)+\cdots,\end{aligned} \tag{27}$$

where ϕ and ψ given by the style (7) and (8). Unification of (26) and (27), serve

$$(1-\xi)\frac{z\left(W^{\sigma,\theta}_{\alpha,\beta,p,q}f(z)\right)'}{(1-\rho)W^{\sigma,\theta}_{\alpha,\beta,p,q}f(z)+\rho z\left(W^{\sigma,\theta}_{\alpha,\beta,p,q}f(z)\right)'}+\xi\left(\frac{\left(W^{\sigma,\theta}_{\alpha,\beta,p,q}f(z)\right)'+z\left(W^{\sigma,\theta}_{\alpha,\beta,p,q}f(z)\right)''}{\left(W^{\sigma,\theta}_{\alpha,\beta,p,q}f(z)\right)'+\rho z\left(W^{\sigma,\theta}_{\alpha,\beta,p,q}f(z)\right)''}\right)$$
$$=1+e_1r_1z+\left[e_1r_2+e_2r_1^2\right]z^2+\cdots \tag{28}$$

and

$$(1-\xi)\frac{w\left(W^{\sigma,\theta}_{\alpha,\beta,p,q}f^{-1}(w)\right)'}{(1-\rho)W^{\sigma,\theta}_{\alpha,\beta,p,q}f^{-1}(w)+\rho w\left(W^{\sigma,\theta}_{\alpha,\beta,p,q}f^{-1}(w)\right)'}+\xi\left(\frac{\left(W^{\sigma,\theta}_{\alpha,\beta,p,q}f^{-1}(w)\right)'+w\left(W^{\sigma,\theta}_{\alpha,\beta,p,q}f^{-1}(w)\right)''}{\left(W^{\sigma,\theta}_{\alpha,\beta,p,q}f^{-1}(w)\right)'+\rho w\left(W^{\sigma,\theta}_{\alpha,\beta,p,q}f^{-1}(w)\right)''}\right)$$
$$=1+e_1s_1w+\left[e_1s_2+e_2s_1^2\right]w^2+\cdots. \tag{29}$$

It is clear that if $|\phi(z)|<1$ and $|\psi(w)|<1$, $z,w\in\mathbb{D}$, we obtain

$$|r_j|\leq 1 \quad\text{and}\quad |s_j|\leq 1\ (j\subset\mathbb{N}).$$

Taking into account (28) and (29), after simplifying, we find that

$$\frac{(\xi+1)(1-\rho)[\Psi_2(\sigma,\alpha,\beta)]^{\theta}_{p,q}}{[\Psi_1(\sigma,\alpha,\beta)]^{\theta}_{p,q}}a_2=e_1r_1, \tag{30}$$

$$\frac{2(2\xi+1)(1-\rho)[\Psi_3(\sigma,\alpha,\beta)]^{\theta}_{p,q}}{[\Psi_1(\sigma,\alpha,\beta)]^{\theta}_{p,q}}a_3+\frac{(2\xi+1)(\rho^2-1)[\Psi_2(\sigma,\alpha,\beta)]^{2\theta}_{p,q}}{[\Psi_1(\sigma,\alpha,\beta)]^{2\theta}_{p,q}}a_2^2=e_1r_2+e_2r_1^2, \tag{31}$$

$$-\frac{(\xi+1)(1-\rho)[\Psi_2(\sigma,\alpha,\beta)]^{\theta}_{p,q}}{[\Psi_1(\sigma,\alpha,\beta)]^{\theta}_{p,q}}a_2=e_1s_1 \tag{32}$$

and

$$\frac{2(2\xi+1)(1-\rho)[\Psi_3(\sigma,\alpha,\beta)]^{\theta}_{p,q}}{[\Psi_1(\sigma,\alpha,\beta)]^{\theta}_{p,q}}\left(2a_2^2-a_3\right)+\frac{(2\xi+1)(\rho^2-1)[\Psi_2(\sigma,\alpha,\beta)]^{2\theta}_{p,q}}{[\Psi_1(\sigma,\alpha,\beta)]^{2\theta}_{p,q}}a_2^2$$
$$=e_1s_2+e_2s_1^2. \tag{33}$$

If we implement notation (25), then (30) and (31) becomes

$$\Upsilon a_2=e_1r_1,\quad \Phi a_3+\chi a_2^2=e_1r_2+e_2r_1^2. \tag{34}$$

This gives

$$\frac{\Phi}{c_1}a_3=r_2+\left(\frac{e_2}{c_1}-\frac{\chi e_1}{\Upsilon^2}\right)r_1^2, \tag{35}$$

and on using the given certain result ([48], p. 10):

$$|r_2-\mu r_1^2|\leq\max\{1,|\mu|\} \tag{36}$$

for every $\mu\in\mathbb{C}$, we get

$$\left|\frac{\Phi}{e_1}\right||a_3|\leq\max\left\{1,\left|\frac{e_2}{e_1}-\frac{\chi e_1}{\Upsilon^2}\right|\right\}. \tag{37}$$

In the same way, (32) and (33) becomes

$$-\Upsilon a_2=e_1s_1,\quad \Phi(2a_2^2-a_3)+\chi a_2^2=e_1s_2+e_2s_1^2. \tag{38}$$

This gives

$$-\frac{\Phi}{e_1}a_3 = s_2 + \left(\frac{e_2}{e_1} - \frac{(2\Phi+\chi)e_1}{\Upsilon^2}\right)s_1^2. \quad (39)$$

Applying (36), we obtain

$$\left|\frac{\Phi}{e_1}\right||a_3| \le \max\left\{1, \left|\frac{e_2}{e_1} - \frac{(2\Phi+\chi)e_1}{\Upsilon^2}\right|\right\}. \quad (40)$$

Inequality (24) follows from (37) and (40). □

If we take the generating function $L_n^{\gamma}(\tau)$ given by (3) common generalized Laguerre polynomials as $h(z)$, then from the equalities given(4), we get $e_1 = 1+\gamma-\tau$ and $e_2 = \frac{\tau^2}{2} - (\gamma+2)\tau + \frac{(\gamma+1)(\gamma+2)}{2}$. We obtain following corollary from Theorem 2.

Corollary 2. *If $f \in \Sigma$ of the style* (1) *be an element of the class $\mathcal{K}_\Sigma(\xi,\rho,\sigma,\theta,\alpha,\beta,p,q;H_\gamma(\tau,z))$, then*

$$|a_2| \le \frac{(\xi+1)(1-\rho)[\Psi_2(\sigma,\alpha,\beta)]_{p,q}^{\theta}|1+\gamma-\tau|}{[\Psi_1(\sigma,\alpha,\beta)]_{p,q}^{\theta}} = \frac{|1+\gamma-\tau|}{\Upsilon}$$

and

$$\begin{aligned}|a_3| \le \min\Bigg\{&\max\left\{\left|\frac{1+\gamma-\tau}{\Phi}\right|, \left|\frac{\frac{\tau^2}{2}-(\gamma+2)\tau+\frac{(\gamma+1)(\gamma+2)}{2}}{\Phi} - \frac{\chi(1+\gamma-\tau)^2}{\Upsilon^2\Phi}\right|\right\},\\ &\max\left\{\left|\frac{1+\gamma-\tau}{\Phi}\right|, \left|\frac{\frac{\tau^2}{2}-(\gamma+2)\tau+\frac{(\gamma+1)(\gamma+2)}{2}}{\Phi} - \frac{(2\Phi+\chi)(1+\gamma-\tau)^2}{\Upsilon^2\Phi}\right|\right\}\Bigg\},\end{aligned}$$

for all ξ,ρ so that $0 \le \xi \le 1$ and $0 \le \rho < 1$, where Υ,Φ,χ are introduced by (25) *and $H_\gamma(\tau,z)$ is given by* (3).

We investigate the "Fekete-Szegö Inequalities" for the families $\mathcal{W}_\Sigma(\eta,\delta,\lambda,\sigma,\theta,\alpha,\beta,p,q;h)$ and $\mathcal{K}_\Sigma(\xi,\rho,\sigma,\theta,\alpha,\beta,p,q;h)$ in next theorems.

Theorem 3. *If $f \in \Sigma$ of the style* (1) *be an element of family $\mathcal{W}_\Sigma(\eta,\delta,\lambda,\sigma,\theta,\alpha,\beta,p,q;h)$, then*

$$\left|a_3 - \zeta a_2^2\right| \le \frac{|e_1|}{\Delta}\min\left\{\max\left\{1, \left|\frac{e_2}{e_1} + \frac{(\zeta\Delta-\varphi)e_1}{\Omega^2}\right|\right\}, \max\left\{1, \left|\frac{e_2}{e_1} - \frac{(2\Delta+\varphi-\zeta\Delta)e_1}{\Omega^2}\right|\right\}\right\},$$

for all $\zeta,\eta,\lambda,\delta$ such that $\zeta \in \mathbb{R}$, $0 \le \eta \le 1$, $0 \le \lambda \le 1$ and $0 \le \delta \le 1$, where Ω,Δ,φ are given by (6) *and e_1, e_2, a_2 and a_3 as defined in Theorem 1.*

Proof. We implement the impressions from the Theorem 1's proof. From (17) and from (18), we get

$$a_3 - \zeta a_2^2 = \frac{e_1}{\Delta}\left(r_2 + \left(\frac{e_2}{e_1} + \frac{(\zeta\Delta-\varphi)e_1}{\Omega^2}\right)r_1^2\right)$$

by using the certain result $|r_2 - \mu r_1^2| \le \max\{1,|\mu|\}$, we get

$$|a_3 - \zeta a_2^2| \le \frac{|e_1|}{\Delta}\max\left\{1, \left|\frac{e_2}{e_1} + \frac{(\zeta\Delta-\varphi)e_1}{\Omega^2}\right|\right\}.$$

In the same way, from (21) and from (22), we get

$$a_3 - \zeta a_2^2 = -\frac{e_1}{\Delta}\left(s_2 + \left(\frac{e_2}{e_1} - \frac{(2\Delta+\varphi-\zeta\Delta)e_1}{\Omega^2}\right)s_1^2\right)$$

and on using $|s_2 - \mu s_1^2| \leq \max\{1, |\mu|\}$, we get

$$|a_3 - \zeta a_2^2| \leq \frac{|e_1|}{\Delta} \max\left\{1, \left|\frac{e_2}{e_1} - \frac{(2\Delta + \varphi - \zeta\Delta)e_1}{\Omega^2}\right|\right\}.$$

□

Corollary 3. *If $f \in \Sigma$ of the style (1) be an element of $\mathcal{W}_\Sigma(\eta, \delta, \lambda, \sigma, \theta, \alpha, \beta, p, q; H_\gamma(\tau, z))$, then*

$$\begin{aligned} &\left|a_3 - \zeta a_2^2\right| \\ \leq\; &\frac{|1+\gamma-\tau|}{\Delta} \min\left\{\max\left\{1, \left|\frac{\frac{\tau^2}{2} - (\gamma+2)\tau + \frac{(\gamma+1)(\gamma+2)}{2}}{1+\gamma-\tau} + \frac{(\zeta\Delta - \varphi)(1+\gamma-\tau)}{\Omega^2}\right|\right\},\right. \\ &\left.\max\left\{1, \left|\frac{\frac{\tau^2}{2} - (\gamma+2)\tau + \frac{(\gamma+1)(\gamma+2)}{2}}{1+\gamma-\tau} - \frac{(2\Delta + \varphi - \zeta\Delta)(1+\gamma-\tau)}{\Omega^2}\right|\right\}\right\}, \end{aligned}$$

for each $\zeta, \eta, \lambda, \delta$ such that $\zeta \in \mathbb{R}$, $0 \leq \eta \leq 1$, $0 \leq \lambda \leq 1$ and $0 \leq \delta \leq 1$, where Ω, Δ, φ are given by (6) and $H_\gamma(\tau, z)$ is presented by (3).

Theorem 4. *If $f \in \Sigma$ of the style (1) is in the family $\mathcal{K}_\Sigma(\xi, \rho, \sigma, 0, \alpha, \beta, p, q; h)$, then*

$$\left|a_3 - \zeta a_2^2\right| \leq \frac{|e_1|}{\Phi} \min\left\{\max\left\{1, \left|\frac{e_2}{e_1} + \frac{(\zeta\Phi - \chi)e_1}{\Upsilon^2}\right|\right\}, \max\left\{1, \left|\frac{e_2}{e_1} - \frac{(2\Phi + \chi - \zeta\Phi)e_1}{\Upsilon^2}\right|\right\}\right\},$$

for all ζ, ξ, ρ such that $\zeta \in \mathbb{R}$, $0 \leq \xi \leq 1$ and $0 \leq \rho < 1$, where Υ, Φ, χ are given by (25) and e_1, e_2, a_2 and a_3 as defined in Theorem 2.

Proof. We implement the impressions from the Theorem 2's proof. From (34) and from (35), we get

$$a_3 - \zeta a_2^2 = \frac{e_1}{\Phi}\left(r_2 + \left(\frac{e_2}{e_1} + \frac{(\zeta\Phi - \chi)e_1}{\Upsilon^2}\right) r_1^2\right)$$

by using the certain result $|r_2 - \mu r_1^2| \leq \max\{1, |\mu|\}$, we get

$$|a_3 - \zeta a_2^2| \leq \frac{|e_1|}{\Phi} \max\left\{1, \left|\frac{e_2}{e_1} + \frac{(\zeta\Phi - \chi)e_1}{\Upsilon^2}\right|\right\}.$$

In the same way, from (38) and from (39), we get

$$a_3 - \zeta a_2^2 = -\frac{e_1}{\Phi}\left(s_2 + \left(\frac{e_2}{e_1} - \frac{(2\Phi + \chi - \zeta\Phi)e_1}{\Upsilon^2}\right) s_1^2\right)$$

and on using $|s_2 - \mu s_1^2| \leq \max\{1, |\mu|\}$, we get

$$|a_3 - \zeta a_2^2| \leq \frac{|e_1|}{\Phi} \max\left\{1, \left|\frac{e_2}{e_1} - \frac{(2\Phi + \chi - \zeta\Phi)e_1}{\Upsilon^2}\right|\right\}.$$

□

Corollary 4. *If $f \in \Sigma$ of the style* (1) *be an element of $\mathcal{K}_{\Sigma}(\xi, \rho, \sigma, \theta, \alpha, \beta, p, q; H_{\gamma}(\tau, z))$, then*

$$\left|a_3 - \zeta a_2^2\right| \le \frac{|1+\gamma-\tau|}{\Phi} \min\left\{ \max\left\{1, \left| \frac{\frac{\tau^2}{2} - (\gamma+2)\tau + \frac{(\gamma+1)(\gamma+2)}{2}}{1+\gamma-\tau} + \frac{(\zeta\Phi - \chi)(1+\gamma-\tau)}{\Upsilon^2} \right| \right\}, \max\left\{1, \left| \frac{\frac{\tau^2}{2} - (\gamma+2)\tau + \frac{(\gamma+1)(\gamma+2)}{2}}{1+\gamma-\tau} - \frac{(2\Phi + \chi - \zeta\Phi)(1+\gamma-\tau)}{\Upsilon^2} \right| \right\} \right\},$$

for each ζ, ξ, ρ such that $\zeta \in \mathbb{R}$, $0 \le \xi \le 1$ and $0 \le \rho < 1$, where Υ, Φ, χ are given by (25) *and $H_{\gamma}(\tau, z)$ is presented by* (3).

3. Conclusions

The main aim of this study was to constitute a new classes $\mathcal{W}_{\Sigma}(\eta, \delta, \lambda, \sigma, \theta, \alpha, \beta, p, q; h)$ and $\mathcal{K}_{\Sigma}(\xi, \rho, \sigma, \theta, \alpha, \beta, p, q; h)$ of bi-univalent functions described through $(p-q)$-Wanas operator and also utilization of the generator function for Laguerre polynomial $L_n^{\gamma}(\tau)$, presented by the equalities in (4) and the producing function $H_{\gamma}(\tau, z)$ given by (3). The initial Taylor-Maclaurin coefficient estimates for functions of these freshly presented bi-univalent function classes $\mathcal{W}_{\Sigma}(\eta, \delta, \lambda, \sigma, \theta, \alpha, \beta, p, q; h)$ and $\mathcal{K}_{\Sigma}(\xi, \rho, \sigma, \theta, \alpha, \beta, p, q; h)$ were produced and the well-known Fekete-Szegö inequalities were examined.

Author Contributions: Conceptualization, A.K.W. and F.M.S.; methodology, A.K.W. and F.M.S.; software, A.A.L.; validation, A.A.L. and A.K.W.; formal analysis, A.K.W. and F.M.S.; investigation, A.K.W. and F.M.S.; resources, F.M.S.; data curation, A.K.W.; writing—original draft preparation, F.M.S.; writing—review and editing, A.A.L. and F.M.S.; visualization, A.K.W.; supervision, F.M.S.; project administration, F.M.S.; funding acquisition, A.A.L. All authors have read and agreed to the published version of the manuscript.

Funding: This research was funded by the University of Oradea.

Data Availability Statement: Not applicable.

Conflicts of Interest: The authors declare no conflict of interest.

References

1. Duren, P.L. *Univalent Functions, Grundlehren der Mathematischen Wissenschaften, Band 259*; Springer: New York, NY, USA; Berlin/Heidelberg, Germany; Tokyo, Japan, 1983.
2. Srivastava, H.M.; Mishra, A.K.; Gochhayat, P. Certain subclasses of analytic and bi-univalent functions. *Appl. Math. Lett.* **2010**, *23*, 1188–1192. [CrossRef]
3. Ali, R.M.; Lee, S.K.; Ravichandran, V.; Supramaniam, S. Coefficient estimates for bi-univalent Ma-Minda starlike and convex functions. *Appl. Math. Lett.* **2012**, *25*, 344–351. [CrossRef]
4. Bulut, S.; Magesh, N.; Abirami, C. A comprehensive class of analytic bi-univalent functions by means of Chebyshev polynomials. *J. Fract. Calc. Appl.* **2017**, *8*, 32–39.
5. Srivastava, H.M.; Wanas, A.K.; Srivastava, R. Applications of the q-Srivastava-Attiya operator involving a certain family of bi-univalent functions associated with the Horadam polynomials. *Symmetry* **2021**, *13*, 1230. [CrossRef]
6. Akgül, A. (P,Q)-Lucas polynomial coefficient inequalities of the bi-univalent function class. *Turk. J. Math.* **2019**, *43*, 2170–2176. [CrossRef]
7. Al-Amoush, A.G. Coefficient estimates for a new subclasses of λ-pseudo biunivalent functions with respect to symmetrical points associated with the Horadam Polynomials. *Turk. J. Math.* **2019**, *43*, 2865–2875. [CrossRef]
8. Al-Shbeil, I.; Wanas, A.K.; Saliu, A.; Cătaş, A. Applications of beta negative binomial distribution and Laguerre polynomials on Ozaki bi-close-to-convex functions. *Axioms* **2022**, *11*, 451. [CrossRef]
9. Altınkaya, Ş. Inclusion properties of Lucas polynomials for bi-univalent functions introduced through the q-analogue of the Noor integral operator. *Turk. J. Math.* **2019**, *43*, 620–629. [CrossRef]
10. Amourah, A.; Frasin, B.A.; Murugusundaramoorthy, G.; Al-Hawary, T. Bi-Bazilevič functions of order $\vartheta + i\delta$ associated with (p,q)-Lucas polynomials. *AIMS Math.* **2021**, *6*, 4296–4305. [CrossRef]
11. Cotîrlă, L.I. New classes of analytic and bi-univalent functions. *AIMS Math.* **2021**, *6*, 10642–10651. [CrossRef]
12. Cotîrlă, L.-I.; Wanas, A.K. Applications of Laguerre polynomials for BazileviÄ and θ-pseudo-starlike bi-univalent functions associated with Sakaguchi-type functions. *Symmetry* **2023**, *15*, 406. [CrossRef]

13. Khan, B.; Srivastava, H.M.; Tahir, M.; Darus, M.; Ahmad, Q.Z.; Khan, N. Applications of a certain q-integral operator to the subclasses of analytic and bi-univalent functions. *AIMS Math.* **2021**, *6*, 1024–1039. [CrossRef]
14. Juma, A.R.S.; Al-Fayadh, A.; Vijayalakshmi, S.P.; Sudharsan, T.V. Upper bound on the third hnkel determinant of the class of univalent functions using an operator. *Afr. Mat.* **2022**, *33*, 56. [CrossRef]
15. Páll-Szabó, A.O.; Wanas, A.K. Coefficient estimates for some new classes of bi- Bazilevic functions of Ma-Minda type involving the Salagean integro-differential operator. *Quaest. Math.* **2021**, *44*, 495–502.
16. Sakar, F.M.; Akgül, A. Based on a family of bi-univalent functions introduced through the Faber polynomial expansions and Noor integral operator. *AIMS Math.* **2022**, *7*, 5146–5155. [CrossRef]
17. Shahab, N.H.; Juma, A.R.S. Coefficient bounds for certain subclasses for meromorphic functions involving quasi subordination. *AIP Conf. Proc.* **2022**, *2400*, 030001.
18. Srivastava, H.M.; Motamednezhad, A.; Adegani, E.A. Faber polynomial coefficient estimates for bi-univalent functions defined by using differential subordination and a certain fractional derivative operator. *Mathematics* **2020**, *8*, 172. [CrossRef]
19. Al-Oboudi, F.M. On univalent functions defined by a generalized Sălăgean operator. *Int. J. Math. Math. Sci.* **2004**, *27*, 1429–1436. [CrossRef]
20. Srivastava, H.M.; Hussain, S.; Raziq, A.; Raza, M. The Fekete-Szegö functional for a subclass of analytic functions associated with quasi-subordination. *Carpathian J. Math.* **2018**, **34**, 103–113. [CrossRef]
21. Srivastava, H.M.; Mishra, A.K.; Das, M.K. The Fekete-Szegö problem for a subclass of close-to-convex functions. *Complex Var. Theory Appl.* **2001**, *44*, 145–163. [CrossRef]
22. Srivastava, H.M.; Shaba, T.G.; Murugusundaramoorthy, G.; Wanas, A.K.; Oros, G.I. The Fekete-Szegö functional and the Hankel determinant for a certain class of analytic functions involving the Hohlov operator. *AIMS Math.* **2022**, **8**, 340–360. [CrossRef]
23. Srivastava, H.M.; Sakar, F.M.; Güney, H.Ö. Some general coefficient estimates for a new class of analytic and bi-univalent functions defined by a linear combination. *Filomat* **2018**, *32*, 1313–1322. [CrossRef]
24. Wanas, A.K.; Cotîrlă, L.-I. Applications of $(M-N)$-Lucas polynomials on a certain family of bi-univalent functions. *Mathematics* **2022**, *10*, 595. [CrossRef]
25. Wanas, A.K.; Lupaş, A.A. Applications of Laguerre polynomials on a new family of bi-prestarlike functions. *Symmetry* **2022**, *14*, 645. [CrossRef]
26. Lebedev, N.N. *Special Functions and Their Applications*; Translated from the revised Russian edition (Moscow, 1963) by Richard A. Silverman; Prentice-Hall: Englewood Cliffs, NJ, USA, 1965.
27. Miller, S.S.; Mocanu, P.T. *Differential Subordinations: Theory and Applications, Series on Monographs and Textbooks in Pure and Applied Mathematics*; Marcel Dekker Inc.: New York, NY, USA; Basel, Switzerland, 2000; Volume 225.
28. Çağlar, M.; Aslan, S. Fekete-Szegö inequalities for subclasses of bi-univalent functions satisfying subordinate conditions. *AIP Conf. Proc.* **2016**, *1726*, 020078. [CrossRef]
29. Jagannathan, R.; Rao, K.S. Two-parameter quantum algebras, twin-basic numbers, and associated generalized hypergeometric series. *arXiv* **2006**, arXiv:math/0602613.
30. Srivastava, H.M. Some generalizations and basic (or q-) extensions of the Bernoulli, Euler and Genocchi polynomials. *Appl.Math. Inf. Sci.* **2011**, *5*, 390–444.
31. Srivastava, H.M.; Choi, J. *Zeta and q-Zeta Functions and Associated Series and Integrals*; Elsevier: Amsterdam, The Netherlands, 2012.
32. Srivastava, H.M.; Raza, N.; AbuJarad, E.S.A.; Srivastava, G.; AbuJarad, M.H. Fekete-Szegö inequality for classes of (p,q)-starlike and (p,q)-convex functions. *Rev. Real Acad. Cienc. Exactas Físicas Y Nat. Ser. A Matemáticas (RACSAM)* **2019**, *113*, 3563–3584. [CrossRef]
33. Victor, K.; Pokman, C. *Quantum Calculus*; Springer: New York, NY, USA, 2002.
34. Corcino, R.B. On p,q-binomial coefficients. *Integers* **2008**, *8*, A29.
35. Sadjang, P.N. On the fundamental theorem of (p,q)-calculus and some (p,q)-Taylor formulas. *arXiv* **2013**, arXiv:1309.3934.
36. Wanas, A.K.; Cotîrlă, L.-I. Initial coefficient estimates and Fekete- Szegö inequalities for new families of bi-univalent functions governed by $(p-q)$-Wanas operator. *Symmetry* **2021**, *13*, 2118. [CrossRef]
37. Shah, S.A.; Noor, K.I. Study on the q-analogue of a certain family of linear operators. *Turk. J. Math.* **2019**, *43*, 2707–2714. [CrossRef]
38. Noor, K.I.; Riaz, S.; Noor, M.A. On q-Bernardi integral operator. *TWMS J. Pure Appl. Math.* **2017**, *8*, 3–11.
39. Govindaraj, M.; Sivasubramanian, S. On a class of analytic functions related to conic domains involving q-calculus. *Anal. Math.* **2017**, *43*, 475–487. [CrossRef]
40. Swamy, S.R. Inclusion properties of certain subclasses of analytic functions. *Int. Math. Forum* **2012**, *7*, 1751–1760.
41. Srivastava, H.M.; Attiya, A.A. An integral operator associated with the Hurwitz-Lerch Zeta function and differential subordination. *Integral Transform. Spec. Funct.* **2007**, *18*, 207–216. [CrossRef]
42. Cho, N.E.; Srivastava, H.M. Argument estimates of certain analytic functions defined by a class of multiplier transformations. *Math. Comput. Model.* **2003**, *37*, 39–49. [CrossRef]
43. Uralegaddi, B.A.; Somanatha, C. Certain classes of univalent functions. In *Current Topics in Analytic Function Theory*; Srivastava, H.M., Own, S., Eds.; World Scientific: Singapore, 1992; pp. 371–374.
44. Jung, I.B.; Kim, Y.C.; Srivastava, H.M. The Hardy space of analytic functions associated with certain one-parameter families of integral operators. *J. Math. Anal. Appl.* **1993**, *176*, 138–147. [CrossRef]
45. Bernardi, S.D. Convex and starlike univalent functions. *Trans. Am. Math. Soc.* **1969**, *135*, 429–446. [CrossRef]

46. Alexander, J.W. Functions which map the interior of the unit circle upon simple region. *Ann. Math.* **1915**, *17*, 12–22. [CrossRef]
47. Sălăgean, G.S. *Subclasses of Univalent Functions*; Lecture Notes in Mathematics; Springer: Berlin, Germany, 1983; Volume 1013, pp. 362–372.
48. Keogh, F.R.; Merkes, E.P. A coefficient inequality for certain classes of analytic functions. *Proc. Am. Math. Soc.* **1969**, *20*, 8–12. [CrossRef]

axioms

Article

Coefficient Estimation Utilizing the Faber Polynomial for a Subfamily of Bi-Univalent Functions

Abdullah Alsoboh [1,*], Ala Amourah [2,*], Fethiye Müge Sakar [3,*], Osama Ogilat [4], Gharib Mousa Gharib [5] and Nasser Zomot [5]

1 Department of Mathematics, Al-Leith University College, Umm Al-Qura University, Mecca 24382, Saudi Arabia
2 Department of Mathematics, Faculty of Science and Technology, Irbid National University, Irbid 21110, Jordan
3 Department of Management, Faculty of Economics and Administrative Sciences, Dicle University, Diyarbakir 21280, Turkey
4 Department of Basic Sciences, Faculty of Arts and Science, Al-Ahliyya Amman University, Amman 19328, Jordan; o.oqilat@ammanu.edu.jo
5 Department of Mathematics, Faculty of Science, Zarqa University, Zarqa 13110, Jordan; ggharib@zu.edu.jo (G.M.G.); nzomot@zu.edu.jo (N.Z.)
* Correspondence: amsoboh@uqu.edu.sa (A.A.); dr.alm@inu.edu.jo (A.A.); muge.sakar@dicle.edu.tr (F.M.S.)

Abstract: The paper introduces a new family of analytic bi-univalent functions that are injective and possess analytic inverses, by employing a q-analogue of the derivative operator. Moreover, the article establishes the upper bounds of the Taylor–Maclaurin coefficients of these functions, which can aid in approximating the accuracy of approximations using a finite number of terms. The upper bounds are obtained by approximating analytic functions using Faber polynomial expansions. These bounds apply to both the initial few coefficients and all coefficients in the series, making them general and early, respectively.

Keywords: analytic function; univalent functions; bi-univalent functions; Faber polynomial; q-derivative operator; quantum calculus

MSC: 30C45; 30C50

Citation: Alsoboh, A.; Amourah, A.; Sakar, F.M.; Ogilat, O.; Gharib, M.G.; Zomot, N. Coefficient Estimation Utilizing the Faber Polynomial for a Subfamily of Bi-Univalent Functions. *Axioms* **2023**, *12*, 512. https://doi.org/10.3390/axioms12060512

Academic Editor: Georgia Irina Oros

Received: 9 April 2023
Revised: 18 May 2023
Accepted: 19 May 2023
Published: 24 May 2023

1. Introduction

A Faber polynomial is a sequence of polynomials used to approximate an analytic function on a compact set. It is named after the German mathematician Georg Faber, who introduced the Faber polynomials in 1903 [1]. The Faber polynomial of degree n for a given analytic function f is defined as the unique polynomial $P_n(z)$ of degree n that interpolates f at its first $n+1$ distinct zeros, counting multiplicities, on the compact set. The sequence of Faber polynomials is known to converge uniformly to f on the compact set, and the convergence rate is related to the smoothness of f. Faber polynomial expansions are often used to obtain upper bounds on the Taylor–Maclaurin coefficients of analytic functions.

Q-calculus is a branch of mathematics that generalizes and extends calculus by introducing a new parameter q, which is a complex number or a variable. Jackson [2] pioneered and systematically developed the application of q-calculus. It has applications in various fields of mathematics and physics, such as number theory, combinatorics, quantum mechanics, and statistical mechanics. In q-calculus, basic concepts, such as derivatives, integrals, and functions, are modified to incorporate the parameter q. For instance, the q-derivative is defined as the difference quotient involving q-analogs of the usual derivatives. Similarly, the q-integral is defined as the q-analog of the Riemann integral. Q-calculus also includes q-special functions, such as q-binomial coefficients, q-factorials, and q-hypergeometric functions, which play significant roles in various areas of mathematics and physics. Overall,

q-calculus provides a powerful tool for studying and solving problems involving discrete and quantum systems.

Fractional calculus operators have found extensive use in the description and resolution of problems in applied sciences, as well as in geometric functions, as noted in [3]. Fractional q-calculus is an extension of ordinary fractional calculus and has been applied in a range of areas, including optimal control problems, solving q-difference and q-integral equations, and ordinary fractional calculus. To learn more about this topic, one can refer to [4] and recent papers, such as [5–7].

2. Preliminaries

Let $\mathbf{A}$ denote the set of analytic functions that can be expressed in the following form

$$\Phi(\eta) = \eta + \sum_{\Bbbk=2}^{\infty} \varrho_{\Bbbk}\eta^{\Bbbk}, \quad (\varrho_{\Bbbk} \in \mathbb{C}), \tag{1}$$

and are defined in the open unit disk $\nabla = \{\eta \in \mathbb{C} : |\eta| < 1\}$. Within $\mathbf{A}$, there is a subfamily $\mathcal{S}$ that consists of univalent functions in ∇. Additionally, let P denote the subclass of analytic functions in ∇ that satisfy the inequality $Re(\varphi(\eta)) > 0$ and are of the form

$$\varphi(\eta) = 1 + \sum_{\Bbbk=1}^{\infty} \varphi_{\Bbbk}\eta^{\Bbbk}, \tag{2}$$

where $|\varphi_{\Bbbk}| < 2$. Caratheodory's Lemma (refer to [8]).

In the context of analytic functions defined in the open unit disk ∇, we can define a relationship between two of such functions, Φ_1 and Φ_2, known as "subordination". We note that Φ_1 is subordinate to Φ_2, denoted by $\Phi_1 \prec \Phi_2$ $(\eta \in \nabla)$, if there exists a Schwarz function:

$$\psi(\eta) = \sum_{\Bbbk=1}^{\infty} m_{\Bbbk}\eta^{\Bbbk}, \qquad \text{with } \psi(0) = 0 \text{ and } \psi(1) = 1,$$

such that

$$\Phi_1(\eta) = \Phi_2(\psi(\eta)), \quad \text{for } (\eta \in \nabla).$$

In other words, Φ_1 can be expressed as a composition of Φ_2 with a certain conformal mapping $\psi(\eta)$, where $\psi(\eta)$ maps the unit disk to itself and satisfies certain conditions. This notion of subordination is described in [9].

Koebe's one-quarter theorem, named after Paul Koebe, is a result of the complex analysis, which states that if a biholomorphic mapping f maps the unit disk ∇ onto a domain D in the complex plane, then the image of each tangent disk to ∇ under f contains a disk of radius $\frac{1}{4}$ of the radius of the tangent disk. In other words, if $z_0 \in \nabla$ and $r > 0$ is such that the disk $B(z_0, r)$ is tangent to ∇ at some point, then $f(B(z_0, r))$ contains a disk of radius $\frac{1}{4}r$.

It is a well-known fact that, as per Koebe's theorem, for any $\Phi \in \mathcal{S}$, the image of the open unit disk under Φ satisfies $\Phi(\nabla) \geq \frac{1}{4}$. Moreover, every univalent function Φ has an inverse function Φ^{-1}, which is defined by the following properties:

1. For $\eta \in \nabla$, $\Phi^{-1}(\Phi(\eta)) = \eta$.
2. For $\rho \in \mathbb{D}(0, r_0)$, where $r_0 \geq \frac{1}{4}$ is a positive constant. Then, $\Phi(\Phi^{-1}(\rho)) = \rho$. Here, $\mathbb{D}(0, r_0)$ denotes the open disk centered at the origin with radius r_0.

The inverse function Φ^{-1} can be expressed as a power series of the form:

$$h(\rho) = \Phi^{-1}(\rho) = \rho - \varrho_2\rho^2 + (2\varrho_2^2 - \varrho_3)\rho^3 - (5\varrho_2^3 - 5\varrho_2\varrho_3 + \varrho_4)\rho^4 + \dots. \tag{3}$$

Here, $\varrho_{\Bbbk}$'s are the Taylor coefficients of Φ in the power series expansion of $\Phi(\eta)$, which is given by (1), and $h(\rho)$ is the inverse function evaluated at ρ.

Netanyahu [10] improved this bound to $|\varrho_2| \leq \frac{4}{3}$. On the other hand, Brannan and Clunie [11] improved Lewin's [12] result and they showed that $|\varrho_2| \leq \sqrt{2}$.

Some examples of functions in the class Σ are

$$\Phi_1(\varrho) = \frac{\eta}{1-\eta}, \quad \Phi_2(\varrho) = -\log(1-\eta) \quad \text{and} \quad \Phi_3(\varrho) = \frac{1}{2}\log\left(\frac{1+\eta}{1-\eta}\right).$$

The inverse functions that correspond to these:

$$\Phi_1^{-1}(\rho) = \frac{\rho}{1+\rho}, \quad \Phi_2^{-1}(\rho) = \frac{e^{2\rho}-1}{e^{2\rho}+1} \quad \text{and} \quad \Phi_3^{-1}(\rho) = \frac{e^{\rho}-1}{e^{\rho}}.$$

are also univalent functions. Thus, the functions $\Phi_1(\varrho), \Phi_2(\varrho)$, and $\Phi_3(\varrho)$ are bi-univalent functions.

However, it is well-known that the Koebe function of the form

$$\Phi(\eta) = \frac{\varrho}{(1-\varrho)^2},$$

is not in the class Σ. For more details, we refer to [13].

We emphasize that, as in the class $\mathcal{S}$ of normalized univalent functions, the convex combination of two functions of class Σ need not be bi-univalent. For example, the functions

$$\varphi_1(\eta) = \frac{\eta}{1-\eta} \quad \text{and} \quad \varphi_2(\eta) = \frac{\eta}{1+i\eta}$$

are bi-univalent but their sum $\varphi_1 + \varphi_2$ is not even univalent, as its derivative vanishes at $\frac{1}{2}(1+i)$. However, the class Σ is preserved under a number of elementary transformations.

Several subclasses of bi-univalent functions have been investigated and introduced by various authors, including Srivastava [13]. The class of bi-univalent functions in ∇ given by (1) is denoted by Σ. Other different subclasses of Σ have also been studied by many authors (see, for example, [14–35].

The significance of Faber polynomials in geometric function theory was demonstrated by Schiffer [36]. However, there are only a few articles in the literature that use the Faber polynomial expansion to determine the early and general coefficient bounds $|\varrho_{\Bbbk}|$ for bi-univalent functions. Consequently, very little is known about the general coefficient bounds $\varrho_{\Bbbk}$ for $\Bbbk \geq 4$, due to the unpredictable nature of the coefficients of both Φ and Φ^{-1} when bi-univalency is required (see, for instance, [37–44]).

The coefficient of $h(\rho) = \Phi^{-1}(\rho)$ of the form (3), can be expressed using the Faber polynomial expansion as:

$$h(\rho) = \Phi^{-1}(\rho) = \rho + \sum_{\pounds=2}^{\infty} \frac{1}{\pounds} K_{\pounds-1}^{-\pounds}(\varrho_2, \varrho_3, \varrho_4, \ldots)\rho^{\pounds},$$

where

$$\begin{aligned} K_{\pounds-1}^{-\pounds} = {} & \frac{(-\pounds)!}{(-2\pounds+1)!(\pounds-1)!}\varrho_2^{\pounds-1} + \frac{(-\pounds)!}{[2(-\pounds+1)]!(\pounds-3)!}\varrho_2^{\pounds-3}\varrho_3 \\ & + \frac{(-\pounds)!}{(-2\pounds+3)!(\pounds-4)!}\varrho_2^{\pounds-4}\varrho_4 + \frac{(-\pounds)!}{[2(-\pounds+2)]!(\pounds-5)!}\varrho_2^{\pounds-5}[\varrho_5 + (-\pounds+2)\varrho_3^2] \\ & + \frac{(-\pounds)!}{(-2\pounds+5)!(\pounds-6)!}\varrho_2^{\pounds-6}[\varrho_6 + (-2\pounds+5)\varrho_3\varrho_4] + \sum_{\aleph\geq 7}^{\infty} \varrho_2^{\pounds-\aleph} V_{\aleph}, \end{aligned} \tag{4}$$

where $V_{\aleph}$ denotes a function such that $7 \leq \aleph \leq \pounds$. It can be expressed as a homogeneous polynomial of degree $\aleph$ in the variables $\varrho_2, \varrho_3, \ldots, \varrho_{\pounds}$. All of the pertinent details can be found in [41].

In particular, the first three terms of $K_{\pounds-1}^{-\pounds}$ are given below:

$$\frac{1}{2}K_1^{-2} = -\varrho_2$$

$$\frac{1}{3}K_2^{-3} = 2\varrho_2^2 - \varrho_3$$

$$\frac{1}{4}K_3^{-4} = -(5\varrho_2^3 - 5\varrho_2\varrho_3 + \varrho_4).$$

In general, for any $\pounds \in \mathbb{N}$, an expansion of the Faber polynomial is given by [45],

$$K_{\kappa-1}^{\pounds} = \pounds\varrho_\kappa + \frac{\pounds(\pounds-1)}{2}E_\kappa^2 + \frac{\pounds!}{(\pounds-3)!(3)!}E_\kappa^3 + \ldots + \frac{\pounds!}{(\pounds-\kappa+1)!(\kappa-1)!}E_{\kappa-1}^{\kappa-1} \tag{5}$$

where $E_{\kappa-1}^{\pounds} = E_{\kappa-1}^{\pounds}(\varrho_2, \varrho_3, \ldots)$, and by [45],

$$E_{\kappa-1}^{\pounds}(\varrho_2, \varrho_3, \ldots, \varrho_\kappa) = \sum_{\kappa=2}^{\infty} \frac{m!(\varrho_2)^{\mu_2}(\varrho_3)^{\mu_3}\ldots(\varrho_\kappa)^{\mu_{\kappa-1}}}{\mu_1!\,\mu_2!\,\ldots\,\mu_{\kappa-1}!}, \qquad (\pounds \leq \kappa),$$

while $\varrho_1 = 1$, the sum is taken over all nonnegative integers $\mu_1\,\mu_2\,\ldots\,\mu_\kappa$, satisfying

$$\mu_1 + \mu_2 + \ldots + \mu_\kappa = m$$

$$\mu_1 + 2\mu_2 + \ldots + (\kappa-1)\mu_{\kappa-1} = \kappa - 1.$$

Evidently,

$$E_{\kappa-1}^{\kappa-1}(\varrho_2, \varrho_3, \ldots, \varrho_\kappa) = \varrho_2^{\kappa-1},$$

or, equivalently, by [46]

$$E_\kappa^{\pounds}(\varrho_2, \varrho_3, \ldots, \varrho_\kappa) = \sum_{\kappa=2}^{\infty} \frac{m!(\varrho_2)^{\mu_2}(\varrho_3)^{\mu_3}\ldots(\varrho_\kappa)^{\mu_\kappa}}{\mu_1!\,\mu_2!\,\ldots\,\mu_\kappa!}, \qquad (\pounds \leq \kappa),$$

while $\varrho_1 = 1$, the sum is taken over all nonnegative integers $\mu_1\,\mu_2\,\ldots\,\mu_\kappa$, satisfying

$$\mu_1 + \mu_2 + \ldots + \mu_\kappa = m$$

$$\mu_1 + 2\mu_2 + \ldots + (\kappa-1)\mu_{\kappa-1} + (\kappa)\mu_\kappa = \kappa.$$

It is clear that

$$E_\kappa^\kappa(\varrho_2, \varrho_3, \ldots, \varrho_\kappa) = E_1^\kappa$$

where the first and last polynomials are

$$E_\kappa^\kappa = \varrho_1^\kappa \text{ and } E_\kappa^1 = \varrho_\kappa.$$

The concept of q-calculus was first introduced by Jackson in a systematic way, and it has since been studied by many mathematicians [47–50]. In this article, we introduce some key concepts and definitions of q-calculus, assuming $0 < q < 1$. Some of these concepts include:

Definition 1. *The* $[\varkappa]_q$ *denotes the basic (or* $q-$*) number, where* $0 < q < 1$ *is defined as follows:*

$$[\varkappa]_q = \begin{cases} (1-q^{\varkappa})(1-q)^{-1} & , \ \varkappa \in \mathbb{C}\backslash\{0\} \\ 0 & , \ \varkappa = 0 \\ q^{\Bbbk-1} + q^{\Bbbk-2} + \cdots + q^2 + q + 1 = \sum_{i=0}^{\Bbbk-1} q^i & , \ \varkappa = \Bbbk \in \mathbb{N}. \end{cases}$$

It is obvious from Definition 1 that $\lim_{q\to1^-}[\Bbbk]_q = \lim_{q\to1^-}\frac{1-q^{\Bbbk}}{1-q} = \Bbbk.$

Definition 2 ([51])**.** *The q-difference operator (or q-derivative) of a function f is defined by*

$$\partial_q(\Phi(\eta)) = \begin{cases} \frac{\Phi(\eta)-\Phi(q\eta)}{\eta-q\eta} & \eta \in \mathbb{C}\backslash\{0\} \\ 1 & \eta = 0. \end{cases}$$

We note that $\lim_{q\to1^-}\partial_q\Phi(\eta) = \Phi'(\eta)$ *if* Φ *is differentiable for all* $\eta \in \mathbb{C}$.

One can easily see that

$$\partial_q\left\{\sum_{\Bbbk=2}^{\infty}\varrho_{\Bbbk}\eta^{\Bbbk}\right\} = \sum_{\Bbbk=2}^{\infty}[\Bbbk]_q\varrho_{\Bbbk}\eta^{\Bbbk-1}, \qquad (\Bbbk \in \mathbb{N}, \eta \in \nabla), \tag{6}$$

and

$$\partial_q^{\kappa}\left\{\sum_{\Bbbk=2}^{\infty}\varrho_{\Bbbk}\eta^{\Bbbk}\right\} = \partial_q\left(\partial_q^{\kappa-1}\left\{\sum_{\Bbbk=2}^{\infty}\varrho_{\Bbbk}\eta^{\Bbbk}\right\}\right) = \varrho_{\Bbbk}[\Bbbk]_q!, \qquad (\Bbbk \in \mathbb{N}). \tag{7}$$

In 2019, Alsoboh and Darus [48] introduced the q-derivative operator $\Upsilon^{(\ell)}_{q,\mu,\beta,\gamma,\delta} : \mathbf{A} \to \mathbf{A}$, as:

$$\Upsilon^{(\ell)}_{q,\mu,\beta,\gamma,\delta}\Phi(\eta) = z + \sum_{\Bbbk=2}^{\infty}\Omega^{\ell}_{\Bbbk}\varrho_{\Bbbk}\eta^{\Bbbk}, \tag{8}$$

where

$$\Omega^{\ell}_{\Bbbk} = \Big[(\gamma-\delta)(\beta-\mu)([\Bbbk]_q - 1) + 1\Big]^{\ell}, \tag{9}$$

and $(\mu, \beta, \gamma, \delta \geq 0, \gamma > \delta, \beta > \mu, \ell \in \mathbb{N}_0, \eta \in \nabla)$.

Lemma 1 ([52])**.** *Let the Schwarz function* $\omega(\eta)$ *be given by*

$$\omega(\eta) = \omega_1\eta + \omega_2\eta^2 + \omega_3\eta^3 + \ldots + \omega_{\Bbbk}\eta^{\Bbbk} + \ldots \qquad (\eta \in \nabla);$$

then

$$|\omega_1| \leq 1,$$
$$|\omega_2| \leq 1 - |\omega_1|^2, \tag{10}$$
$$|\omega_2 - t\omega_1^2| \leq 1 + (|t| - 1)|\omega_1|^2.$$

3. Class $D^{\ell}_{\Sigma_q}(\chi,\delta,\gamma,\mu;\varphi)$

In this section, we define and study a new subclass of bi-univalent functions in an open unit disk that has symmetry, using the derivative operator $\Upsilon^{(\ell)}_{q,\mu,\beta,\gamma,\delta}\Phi(\eta)$ of the form (8) and the principle of subordination, as follows:

Definition 3. *For $\mu,\beta,\gamma,\delta \geq 0$, $\gamma > \delta, \beta > \mu$ and $k \in \mathbb{N}_0$, a bi-univalent function Φ of the form (1) is in the class $D^{\ell}_{\Sigma_q}(\chi,\delta,\gamma,\mu;\varphi)$ if it satisfies the following subordination conditions:*

$$(1-\chi)\frac{\Upsilon^{(\ell)}_{q,\mu,\beta,\gamma,\delta}\Phi(\eta)}{\eta} + \chi\partial_q\Upsilon^{(\ell)}_{q,\mu,\beta,\gamma,\delta}\Phi(\eta) \prec \varphi(\eta), \quad (\eta \in \nabla; \chi \geq 1), \tag{11}$$

and

$$(1-\chi)\frac{\Upsilon^{(\ell)}_{q,\mu,\beta,\gamma,\delta}h(\rho)}{\rho} + \chi\partial_q\Upsilon^{(\ell)}_{q,\mu,\beta,\gamma,\delta}h(\rho) \prec \varphi(\rho), \quad (\rho \in \nabla; \chi \geq 1), \tag{12}$$

where $h(\rho)$ and $\Upsilon^{(\ell)}_{q,\mu,\beta,\gamma,\delta}\Phi(\eta)$ are defined by (3) and (8), respectively.

Example 1. *A bi-univalent function f of the form (1) is referred to as being in the class $D^{0}_{\Sigma_q}(\chi,\delta,\gamma,\mu;\varphi)= D_{\Sigma}(q;\chi,\varphi)$, if the following conditions of subordination are met:*

$$(1-\chi)\frac{\Phi(\eta)}{\eta} + \chi\partial_q\Phi(\eta) \prec \varphi(\eta), \quad (\eta \in \nabla),$$

and

$$(1-\chi)\frac{h(\rho)}{\rho} + \chi\partial_q h(\rho) \prec \varphi(\rho), \quad (\rho \in \nabla),$$

where $h(\rho)$ is defined by (3). This class was introduced by Altınkaya and Yalçın [37].

Example 2. *A bi-univalent function f of the form (1) is referred to as being in the class $\lim_{q\to 1^-} D^{0}_{\Sigma_q}$ $(\chi,\delta,\gamma,\mu;\varphi) = R_{\sigma}(\chi,\varphi)$, if the following conditions of subordination are met:*

$$(1-\chi)\frac{\Phi(\eta)}{\eta} + \chi(\Phi(\eta))' \prec \varphi(\eta), \quad (\eta \in \nabla),$$

and

$$(1-\chi)\frac{h(\rho)}{\rho} + \chi(h(\rho))' \prec \varphi(\rho), \quad (\rho \in \nabla),$$

where $h(\rho)$ is defined by (3). This class was introduced by Kumar et al. [53].

4. Coefficient Bounds of the Class $D^{\ell}_{\Sigma_q}(\chi,\delta,\gamma,\mu;\varphi)$

The following theorem provides an estimate of the bounds of the coefficients for functions of class $D^{\ell}_{\Sigma_q}(\chi,\delta,\gamma,\mu;\varphi)$. The theorem provides an estimate of the coefficients $\varrho_{\Bbbk}$ for $\Bbbk \geq \ell+2$ in terms of the parameters χ,δ,γ,μ, and φ, as well as the maximum value of $|\varphi'(t)|$ on the interval $[0,1]$. The proof of the theorem uses a method similar to those employed by various authors, including Hussien et al. [54] and Altınkaya and Yalçın ([55,56]).

Theorem 1. *Let Φ be given by (1). For $\chi \geq 1$, $0 \leq \alpha < 1$, $(\mu,\beta,\gamma,\delta \geq 0)$, $\gamma > \delta, \beta > \mu$ and $k \in \mathbb{N}_0$. If $\Phi \in D^{\ell}_{\Sigma_q}(\chi,\delta,\gamma,\mu;\varphi)$ and $\varrho_m = 0$; $m = 2,\ldots,\Bbbk-1$, then*

$$|\varrho_{\Bbbk}| \leq \frac{2(1-q)}{\left|1+(q-q^{\Bbbk})\chi\right|\left|\Omega^{\ell}_{\Bbbk}\right|}; \qquad (\Bbbk = 4,5,6,\ldots). \tag{13}$$

Proof. Since $\Phi \in D^{\ell}_{\Sigma_q}(\chi, \delta, \gamma, \mu; \varphi)$ of form (1), we have:

$$(1-\chi)\frac{\Upsilon^{(\ell)}_{q,\mu,\beta,\gamma,\delta}\Phi(\eta)}{\eta} + \chi D_q \Upsilon^{(\ell)}_{q,\mu,\beta,\gamma,\delta}\Phi(\eta) = 1 + \sum_{\Bbbk=1}^{\infty}\Big(1-\chi(1-[\Bbbk]_q)\Big)\Omega^{\ell}_{\Bbbk}\varrho_{\Bbbk}\eta^{\Bbbk-1} \tag{14}$$

and for $h = \Phi^{-1}$, we have

$$\begin{aligned}(1-\chi)\frac{\Upsilon^{(\ell)}_{q,\mu,\beta,\gamma,\delta}h(\rho)}{\rho} + \chi D_q \Upsilon^{(\ell)}_{q,\mu,\beta,\gamma,\delta}h(\rho) &= 1 + \sum_{\Bbbk=1}^{\infty}\Big(1-\chi(1-[\Bbbk]_q)\Big)\Omega^{\ell}_{\Bbbk}b_{\Bbbk}\rho^{\Bbbk-1} \\ = 1 + \sum_{\Bbbk=1}^{\infty}\Big(1-\chi(1-[\Bbbk]_q)\Big)\Omega^{\ell}_{\Bbbk}\left(\frac{1}{\Bbbk}K^{-\Bbbk}_{\Bbbk-1}(\varrho_2, \varrho_3, \ldots, \varrho_{\Bbbk})\right)\rho^{\Bbbk-1},\end{aligned} \tag{15}$$

where $\Omega^{\ell}_{\Bbbk}$ and $K^{-\Bbbk}_{\Bbbk-1}$ are given by (4) and (9), respectively.

Since $\Phi, \Phi^{-1} \in D^{\ell}_{\Sigma_q}(\chi, \delta, \gamma, \mu; \varphi)$. Then, by using the definition of subordination, two Schwartz functions exist,

$$u(\eta) = \sum_{\Bbbk=1}^{\infty}\gimel_{\Bbbk}\eta^{\Bbbk} \quad \text{and} \quad v(\rho) = \sum_{\Bbbk=1}^{\infty}\daleth_{\Bbbk}\rho^{\Bbbk},$$

which are analytic in ∇, such that

$$\varphi(u(\eta)) = (1-\chi)\frac{\Upsilon^{(\ell)}_{q,\mu,\beta,\gamma,\delta}\Phi(\eta)}{\eta} + \chi D_q \Upsilon^{(\ell)}_{q,\mu,\beta,\gamma,\delta}\Phi(\eta), \quad (\eta \in \nabla) \tag{16}$$

$$\varphi(v(\rho)) = (1-\chi)\frac{\Upsilon^{(\ell)}_{q,\mu,\beta,\gamma,\delta}h(\rho)}{\rho} + \chi D_q \Upsilon^{(\ell)}_{q,\mu,\beta,\gamma,\delta}h(\rho), \quad (\rho \in \nabla), \tag{17}$$

where

$$\varphi(u(\eta)) = 1 + \sum_{\Bbbk=1}^{\infty}\sum_{\ell=1}^{\Bbbk}\varphi_k E^{\ell}_{\Bbbk}(\gimel_1, \gimel_2, \ldots, \gimel_{\Bbbk})\eta^{\Bbbk}. \tag{18}$$

and

$$\varphi(v(\rho)) = 1 + \sum_{\Bbbk=1}^{\infty}\sum_{\ell=1}^{\Bbbk}\varphi_k E^{\ell}_{\Bbbk}(\daleth_1, \daleth_2, \ldots, \daleth_{\Bbbk})\rho^{\Bbbk}. \tag{19}$$

From (14), (16), and (18), we have

$$\Big(1-\chi(1-[\Bbbk]_q)\Big)\Omega^{\ell}_{\Bbbk}\varrho_{\Bbbk} = \sum_{\ell=1}^{\Bbbk-1}\varphi_k E^{\ell}_{n-1}(\gimel_1, \gimel_2, \ldots, \gimel_{n-1}) \qquad (n \geq 2), \tag{20}$$

Similarly, from (15), (17), and (19), we have

$$\Big(1-\chi(1-[\Bbbk]_q)\Big)\Omega^{\ell}_{\Bbbk}b_{\Bbbk} = \sum_{\ell=1}^{\Bbbk-1}\varphi_k E^{\ell}_{\Bbbk-1}(\daleth_1, \daleth_2, \ldots, \daleth_{\Bbbk-1}) \quad (\Bbbk \geq 2), \tag{21}$$

by the given assumption

$$\varrho_m = 0, \quad (2 \leq m \leq \Bbbk - 1),$$

which is equivalent to

$$\gimel_m = \daleth_m = 0; \quad (1 \leq m \leq \Bbbk - 2),$$

and from Equations (20) and (21), we have $b_{\Bbbk} = -\varrho_{\Bbbk}$ and so

$$\begin{cases} \left(1-\chi(1-[\Bbbk]_q)\right)\Omega_{\Bbbk}^{\ell}\varrho_{\Bbbk} = \varphi_1 \beth_{\Bbbk-1}, \\ \left(1-\chi(1-[\Bbbk]_q)\right)\Omega_{\Bbbk}^{\ell}\varrho_{\Bbbk} = -\varphi_1 \daleth_{\Bbbk-1}. \end{cases} \tag{22}$$

Taking the absolute value for Equation (22), we obtain

$$\begin{aligned} |\varrho_{\Bbbk}| &\leq \frac{|\varphi_1||\beth_{\Bbbk-1}|}{\left(1-\chi(1-[\Bbbk]_q)\right)\Omega_{\Bbbk}^{\ell}} \\ &= \frac{|\varphi_1||\daleth_{\Bbbk-1}|}{\left(1-\chi(1-[\Bbbk]_q)\right)\Omega_{\Bbbk}^{\ell}}, \qquad (n \geq 4). \end{aligned} \tag{23}$$

Using Caratheodory's Lemma, we obtain

$$|\varrho_{\Bbbk}| \leq \frac{2(1-q)}{\left|1-q+(q-q^{\Bbbk})\chi\right|\left|\Omega_{\Bbbk}^{\ell}\right|}.$$

This completes the proof of the theorem. □

In the next theorem, we estimate the initial coefficients of the functions from the indicated class $D_{\Sigma_q}^{\ell}(\chi,\delta,\gamma,\mu;\varphi)$.

Theorem 2. *For $\chi \geq 1$, $0 \leq \alpha < 1$, $(\mu,\beta,\gamma,\delta \geq 0)$, $\gamma > \delta, \beta > \mu$ and $k \in \Bbbk_0$, if $\Phi \in D_{\Sigma_q}^{\ell}(\chi,\delta,\gamma,\mu;\varphi)$ where $\Phi(\eta)$ is given by (1), then we have the following consequence*

$$|\varrho_2| \leq min\left\{\frac{2}{(1+\chi q)\Omega_2^{\ell}}, \frac{2}{\sqrt{(1+\chi(q^2+q))\Omega_3^{\ell}}}\right\},$$

$$|\varrho_3| \leq min\left\{\frac{4}{(1+\chi(2+q)\Omega_2^{\ell})^2} + \frac{2}{(1+\chi(q^2+q))\Omega_3^{\ell}}, \frac{6}{(1+\chi(q^2+q))\Omega_3^{\ell}}\right\},$$

and

$$|2\varrho_2^2 - \varrho_3| \leq \frac{4}{|(1+\chi([3]_q-1))\Omega_3^{\ell}|}.$$

Proof. Replacing $\Bbbk$ by 2 and 3 in (20) and (21), respectively, we obtain:

$$(1-\chi(1-[2]_q))\Omega_2^{\ell}\varrho_2 = \varphi_1 \beth_1, \tag{24}$$

$$(1-\chi(1-[3]_q))\Omega_3^{\ell}\varrho_3 = \varphi_1 \beth_2 + \varphi_2 c_1^2, \tag{25}$$

$$(1-\chi(1-[2]_q))\Omega_2^{\ell}\varrho_2 = -\varphi_1 \daleth_1, \tag{26}$$

and

$$\left(1-\chi(1-[3]_q)\right)\Omega_3^{\ell}(2\varrho_2^2-\varrho_3) = \varphi_1 \daleth_2 + \varphi_2 d_1^2. \tag{27}$$

From (24) and (26), we have $\daleth_1 = -\gimel_1$ and

$$|\varrho_2| = \frac{|\varphi_1 \gimel_1|}{\Big|1-\chi(1-[2]_q)\Big|\Omega_2^{\ell}} = \frac{|\varphi_1 \daleth_1|}{\Big|1-\chi(1-[2]_q)\Big|\Omega_2^{\ell}} \leq \frac{2}{1+\chi(1+[2]_q)\Omega_2^{\ell}}. \tag{28}$$

Now, by adding (25) and (27)

$$2\Big(1-\chi(1-[3]_q)\Big)\Omega_3^{\ell}\varrho_2^2 = \varphi_1(\gimel_2+\daleth_1)+\varphi_2(c_1^2+d_1^2),$$

or, equivalently,

$$|\varrho_2| \leq \frac{2}{\sqrt{\Big(1+\chi(q^2+q)\Big)\Omega_3^{\ell}}}. \tag{29}$$

Next, in order to find the bounds of $|\varrho_3|$, subtract (25) from (27), we have

$$2\Big(1+\chi([3]_q-1)\Big)\Omega_3^{\ell}(\varrho_3-\varrho_2^2) = \varphi_1(\gimel_2-\daleth_2)+\varphi_2(c_1^2-d_1^2), \tag{30}$$

or

$$2\Big(1+\chi([3]_q-1)\Big)\Omega_3^{\ell}(\varrho_3-\varrho_2^2) \leq \varphi_2(\gimel_2-\daleth_2),$$

$$|\varrho_3| \leq \varrho_2^2 + \frac{|\varphi_2(\gimel_2-\daleth_2)|}{2\Big|\Big(1+\chi([3]_q-1)\Big)\Omega_3^{\ell}\Big|}. \tag{31}$$

Equivalent to

$$|\varrho_3| \leq \varrho_2^2 + \frac{|\varphi_2(\gimel_2-\daleth_2)|}{2\Big|\Big(1+\chi(q^2+q)\Big)\Omega_3^{\ell}\Big|},$$

Substituting the value ϱ_2 from (29) and (30) into (31), one obtains

$$|\varrho_3| \leq \frac{4}{(1+\chi(2+q)\Omega_2^{\ell})^2} + \frac{2}{\Big(1+\chi(q^2+q)\Big)\Omega_3^{\ell}},$$

and

$$|\varrho_3| \leq \frac{6}{\Big(1+\chi(q^2+q)\Big)\Omega_3^{\ell}}.$$

Finally, from (30), by applying the Caratheodory Lemma, we obtain

$$|2\varrho_2^2-\varrho_3| = \frac{|\varphi_1\daleth_2+\varphi_2 d_1^2|}{\Big|(1-\chi(1-[3]_q))\Omega_3^{\ell}\Big|} < \frac{4}{\Big|(1+\chi([3]_q-1))\Omega_3^{\ell}\Big|}. \tag{32}$$

This completes the proof of Theorem 2. □

5. Corollaries

The following corollaries, which roughly match Examples 1 and 2, are produced by Theorems 1 and 2.

By putting $\ell = 0$ in Theorem 1, we obtain the following corollary.

Corollary 1 ([37])**.** *Let $\chi \geq 1$. A bi-univalent function Φ given by (1) belongs to the class $D_\Sigma(q,\chi;\varphi)$ $(\chi \geq 1)$. If $\varrho_m = 0$; $m = 2,\ldots,\Bbbk-1$. Then*

$$|\varrho_{\Bbbk}| \leq \frac{2(1-q)}{1-q+(q-q^{\Bbbk})\chi} \qquad (n \geq 4).$$

Applying the limit $q \to 1^-$ in Theorem 1 and considering the case when $\ell = 0$, we obtain the following corollary.

Corollary 2 ([37]). *Let* $\chi \geq 1$. *A bi-univalent function* Φ *given by (1) belongs to the class* $R_\sigma(\chi, \varphi)(\chi \geq 1)$. *If* $\varrho_m = 0$; $m = 2, \ldots, \Bbbk - 1$. *Then*

$$|\varrho_\Bbbk| \leq \frac{2}{1 + \chi(\Bbbk - 1)} \qquad (n \geq 4).$$

For $k = 0$ in Theorem 2, we obtain the following corollary.

Corollary 3 ([37]). *Let* $\chi \geq 1$. *A bi-univalent function* Φ *given by (1) belongs to the class* $D_\Sigma(q; \chi, \varphi)$. *Then*

(1) $|\varrho_2| \leq \frac{2}{1+q\chi}$,

(2) $|\varrho_3| \leq \frac{4}{(1+q\chi)^2} + \frac{2}{1+(q^2+q)\chi}$,

(3) $|2\varrho_2^2 - \varrho_3| \leq \frac{4}{1+(q^2+q)\chi}$.

For $k = 0$ and $q \to 1^-$ in Theorem 2, we obtain the following corollary.

Corollary 4. *A bi-univalent function* Φ *given by (1) belongs to the class* $R_\sigma(\chi, \varphi)(\chi \geq 1)$. *Then*

(1) $|\varrho_2| \leq \frac{2}{1+\chi}$,

(2) $|\varrho_3| \leq \frac{4}{(1+3\chi)^2} + \frac{2}{1+2\chi}$.

6. Conclusions

This article investigated a novel subclass of bi-univalent functions, $D^\ell\Sigma q(\chi, \delta, \gamma, \mu; \varphi)$, on the symmetry disk ∇. For functions belonging to each of these three classes of bi-univalent functions, we calculated estimates for the upper bound of the Taylor–Maclaurin coefficients of these functions in the aforementioned subset. By concentrating on the variables employed in our primary findings, several additional novel findings were made.

The study of bi-univalent functions is an important and active area of research in complex analysis and its applications. The investigation of this subclass provides deeper insights into the theory and applications of bi-univalent functions. The results obtained in this article can be generalized in the future using post-quantum calculus and other q-analogs of the fractional derivative operator. Additionally, further analysis can be conducted to explore additional subclasses and their characteristics.

Overall, this article contributes to the ongoing research in the field of complex analysis by providing a detailed study of three important subclasses of bi-univalent functions. Further research can be conducted to investigate more subclasses and their properties to enhance our understanding of the theory and applications of bi-univalent functions.

Author Contributions: Conceptualization, A.A. (Abdullah Alsoboh) and A.A. (Ala Amourah); methodology, A.A. (Ala Amourah); validation, A.A. (Ala Amourah), A.A. (Abdullah Alsoboh), O.O., G.M.G. and N.Z.; formal analysis, A.A. (Ala Amourah); investigation, F.M.S., A.A. (Abdullah Alsoboh); writing—original draft preparation, A.A. (Abdullah Alsoboh) and A.A. (Ala Amourah); writing—review and editing, A.A. (Ala Amourah) and O.O.; supervision, A.A. (Abdullah Alsoboh) and F.M.S. All authors have read and agreed to the published version of the manuscript.

Funding: The authors would like to thank the Deanship of Scientific Research at Umm Al-Qura University for supporting this work under grant code: (23UQU4320576DSR003).

Institutional Review Board Statement: Not applicable.

Informed Consent Statement: Not applicable.

Data Availability Statement: No data were used to support this study.

Conflicts of Interest: The authors declare that there are no conflict of interest.

References

1. Faber, G. Über polynomische entwickelungen. *Math. Ann.* **1903**, *57*, 389–408. [CrossRef]
2. Jackson, F.H. On $q-$definite integrals. *Q. J. Pure Appl. Math.* **1910**, *41*, 193–203.
3. Purohit, S.D.; Raina, R.K. Certain subclasses of analytic functions associated with fractional $q-$calculus operators. *Fract. Differ. Equ. Introd. Fract. Deriv.* **2011**, *109*, 55–70. [CrossRef]
4. Podlubny, I. Fractional differential equations, to methods of their solution and some of their applications. *Math. Scand.* **1998**, *340*.
5. Gasper, G.; Rahman, M. *Basic Hypergeometric Series*; Cambridge University Press: Cambridge, UK, 2004; Volume 96.
6. Al-Salam, W.A. Some fractional $q-$integrals and $q-$derivatives. *Proc. Edinb. Math. Soc.* **1966**, *15*, 135–140. [CrossRef]
7. Agarwal, R.P. Certain fractional $q-$integrals and $q-$derivatives. *Proc. Camb. Philos.* **1969**, *66*, 365–370. [CrossRef]
8. Duren, P.L. *Univalent Functions*; Spriger Science & Business Media: Berlin/Heidelberg, Germany, 2001; Volume 259.
9. Miller, S.S.; Mocanu, P.T. *Differential Subordinations: Theory and Applications*; CRC Press: Boca Raton, FL, USA, 2000.
10. Netanyahu, E. The minimal distance of the image boundary from the origin and the second coefficient of a univalent function in $|z| < 1$. *Arch. Ration. Mech. Anal.* **1969**, 32, 100–112.
11. Brannan, D.A.; Taha, T.S. On some classes of bi-univalent functions. In *Mathematical Analysis and Its Applications*; Pergamon; Elsevier: Amsterdam, The Netherlands, 1988; pp. 53–60.
12. Lewin, M. On a coefficient problem for bi-univalent functions. *Proc. Am. Math. Soc.* **1967**, *18*, 63–68. [CrossRef]
13. Srivastava, H.M.; Mishra, A.K.; Gochhayat, P. Certain subclasses of analytic and bi-univalent functions. *Appl. Math. Lett. Int. J. Rapid Publ.* **2010**, *23*, 1188–1192. [CrossRef]
14. Akgül, A.; Sakar, F.M. A new characterization of (P,Q)-Lucas polynomial coefficients of the bi-univalent function class associated with q-analog of Noor integral operator. *Afr. Mat.* **2022**, *33*, 87. [CrossRef]
15. Illafe, M.; Amourah, A.; Haji Mohd, M. Coefficient estimates and Fekete–Szegö functional inequalities for a certain subclass of analytic and bi-univalent functions. *Axioms* **2022**, *11*, 147. [CrossRef]
16. Illafe, M.; Yousef, F.; Haji Mohd, M.; Supramaniam, S. Initial Coefficients Estimates and Fekete–Szegö Inequality Problem for a General Subclass of Bi-Univalent Functions Defined by Subordination. *Axioms* **2023**, *12*, 235. [CrossRef]
17. Yousef, F., Amourah, A., Frasin, B. A., Bulboaca, T. An avant-Garde construction for subclasses of analytic bi-univalent functions. *Axioms* **2022**, *11*, 267. [CrossRef]
18. Al-Hawary, T.; Aldawish, I.; Frasin, B.A.; Alkam, O.; Yousef, F. Necessary and Sufficient Conditions for Normalized Wright Functions to be in Certain Classes of Analytic Functions. Mathematics. *Mathematics* **2022**, *10*, 4693. [CrossRef]
19. AlAmoush, A. G., Wanas, A. K. Coefficient estimates for a new subclass of bi-close-to-convex functions associated with the Horadam polynomials. *Int. J. Open Probl. Complex Anal.* **2022**, *14*, 16–26.
20. Al-Kaseasbeh, M. Construction of Differential Operators. *Int. J. Open Probl. Complex Anal.* **2021**, *13*, 29–43.
21. Alamoush, A.G. On subclass of analytic bi-close-to-convex functions. *Int. J. Open Probl. Complex Anal.* **2021**, *13*, 10–18.
22. Aldweby, H.; Darus, M. On a subclass of bi-univalent functions associated with the q-derivative operator. *J. Math. Comput. Sci.* **2019**, *19*, 58–64. [CrossRef]
23. Porwal, S.; Darus, M. On a new subclass of bi-univalent functions. *J. Egypt. Math. Soc.* **2013**, *21*, 190–193. [CrossRef]
24. Amourah, A.; Frasin, B.A.; Seoudy, T.M. An Application of Miller–Ross-Type Poisson Distribution on Certain Subclasses of Bi-Univalent Functions Subordinate to Gegenbauer Polynomials. *Mathematics* **2022**, *10*, 2462. [CrossRef]
25. Shammaky, A.E.; Frasin, B.A.; Seoudy, T.M. Subclass of Analytic Functions Related with Pascal Distribution Series. *J. Math.* **2022**, *2022*, 8355285. [CrossRef]
26. Seoudy, T.; Aouf, M. Admissible classes of multivalent functions associated with an integral operator. *Ann. Univ. Mariae-Curie-Sklodowska Sect. Math.* **2019**, *73*, 57–73. [CrossRef]
27. Seoudy, T. Convolution Results and Fekete–Szegö Inequalities for Certain Classes of Symmetric-Starlike and Symmetric-Convex Functions. *J. Math.* **2022**, *2022*, 57–73. [CrossRef]
28. Sunthrayuth, P.; Iqbal, N.; Naeem, M.; Jawarneh, Y.; ; Samura, S.K. The Sharp Upper Bounds of the Hankel Determinant on Logarithmic Coefficients for Certain Analytic Functions Connected with Eight-Shaped Domains. *J. Funct. Spaces* **2022**, 2229960. [CrossRef]
29. Alsoboh, A.; Amourah, A.; Darus, M.; Rudder, C.A. Studying the Harmonic Functions Associated with Quantum Calculus. *Mathematics* **2023**, *11*, 2220. [CrossRef]
30. Amourah, A.; Alomari, M.; Yousef, F.; Alsoboh, A. Consolidation of a Certain Discrete Probability Distribution with a Subclass of Bi-Univalent Functions Involving Gegenbauer Polynomials. *Math. Probl. Eng.* **2022**, *2022*, 6354994. [CrossRef]
31. Amourah, A.; Alsoboh, A.; Ogilat, O.; Gharib, G.M.; Saadeh, R.; Al Soudi, M. A Generalization of Gegenbauer Polynomials and Bi-Univalent Functions. *Axioms* **2023**, *12*, 128. [CrossRef]
32. Alsoboh, A.; Amourah, A.; Darus, M.; Sharefeen, R.I.A. Applications of Neutrosophic $q-$Poisson distribution Series for Subclass of Analytic Functions and Bi-Univalent Functions. *Mathematics* **2023**, *11*, 868. [CrossRef]

33. Alsoboh, A.; Amourah, A.; Darus, M.; Rudder, C. A. Investigating New Subclasses of Bi-Univalent Functions Associated with q-Pascal Distribution Series Using the Subordination Principle. *Symmetry* **2023**, *15*, 1109. [CrossRef]
34. Al-Hawary, T.; Amourah, A.; Alsoboh, A.; Alsalhi, O. A New Comprehensive Subclass of Analytic Bi-Univalent Functions Related to Gegenbauer Polynomials. *Symmetry* **2023**, *15*, 576. [CrossRef]
35. Sakar, F.M.; Akgül, A. Based on a family of bi-univalent functions introduced through the Faber polynomial expansions and Noor integral operator. *AIMS Math.* **2022**, *7*, 5146–5155. [CrossRef]
36. Schiffer, M. A method of variation within the family of simple functions. *Proc. Lond. Math. Soc.* **1938**, *2*, 432–449. [CrossRef]
37. Altınkaya, Ş.; Yalçın, S. Faber polynomial coefficient estimates for certain classes of bi-univalent functions defined by using the Jackson (p, q)-derivative operator. *J. Nonlinear Sci. Appl.* **2017**, *10*, 3067–3074. [CrossRef]
38. Alsoboh, A.; Darus, M. On subclasses of harmonic univalent functions defined by Jackson (p, q)-derivative. *J. Anal.* **2019**, *10*, 123–130.
39. Amourah, A.; Frasin, B.A.; Al-Hawary, T. Coefficient Estimates for a Subclass of Bi-univalent Functions Associated with Symmetric q-derivative Operator by Means of the Gegenbauer Polynomials. *Kyungpook Math. J.* **2022**, *62*, 257–269.
40. Jahangiri, J.M.; Hamidi, S.G. Coefficient estimates for certain classes of bi-univalent functions. *Int. J. Math. Math. Sci.* **2013**, *2013*, 190560. [CrossRef]
41. Airault, H.; Bouali, A. Differential calculus on the Faber polynomials. *Bull. Des Sci. Math.* **2006**, *130*, 179–222. [CrossRef]
42. Al-Refai, O. Integral Operators Preserving Univalence. *Malays. J. Math. Sci.* **2014**, *8*, 163–172.
43. Al-Refai, O.; Darus, M. General Univalence Criterion Associated with the n-th Derivative. *Abstr. Appl. Anal.* **2012**, *2012*, 307526. [CrossRef]
44. Khandaqji, M.; M; Burqan, A. Results on sequential conformable fractional derivatives with applications. *J. Comput. Anal.* **2021**, *29*, 1115–1125.
45. Airault, H. Symmetric sums associated to the factorizations of Grunsky coefficients. In Proceedings of the Groups and Symmetries, Montreal, QC, Canada, April 2007.
46. Airault, H. Remarks on Faber polynomials. *Int. Math. Forum* **2008**, *3*, 449–456.
47. Aldweby, H.; Darus, M. Some subordination results on q-analogue of Ruscheweyh differential operator. *Abstr. Appl. Anal.* **2014**, *2014*, 958563. [CrossRef]
48. Alsoboh, A.; Darus, M. New Subclass of Analytic Functions Defined by q-Differential Operator with Respect to k-Symmetric Points. *Int. J. Math. Comput. Sci.* **2019**, *14*, 761–773.
49. Alsoboh, A.; Darus, M. On Fekete-Szego problem associated with q- derivative operator. *J. Phys. Conf. Ser.* **2019**, *1212*, 012003. [CrossRef]
50. Elhaddad, S.; Aldweby, H.; Darus, M. Some properties on a class of harmonic univalent functions defined by q-analogue of Ruscheweyh operator. *J. Math. Anal.* **2018**, *9*, 28–35.
51. Jackson, F.H. On q-functions and a certain difference operator. *Earth Environ. Sci. Trans. R. Soc. Edinb.* **1909**, *46*, 253–281. [CrossRef]
52. Keogh F.R.; Merkes, E.P. A coefficient inequality for certain classes of analytic functions. *Proc. Am. Soc.* **1969**, *20*, 8–12. [CrossRef]
53. Kumar, S.S.; Kumar, V.; Ravichandran, V. Estimates for the initial coefficients of bi-univalent functions. *arXiv* **2012**, arXiv:1203.5480.
54. Hussain, S.; Khan, S.; Zaighum, M.A.; Darus, M.; Shareef, Z. Coefficients bounds for certain subclass of biunivalent functions associated with Ruscheweyh-Differential operator. *J. Complex Anal.* **2017**, *2017*, 1–9. [CrossRef]
55. Altınkaya, Ş.; Yalçın, S. Faber polynomial coefficient bounds for a subclass of bi-univalent functions. *Comptes Rendus Math.* **2015**, *353*, 1075–1080. [CrossRef]
56. Bulut, S. Faber polynomial coefficient estimates for a comprehensive subclass of analytic bi-univalent functions. *Comptes Rendus Math.* **2014**, *352*, 479–484. [CrossRef]

axioms

MDPI

Article

Geometric Properties of Generalized Integral Operators Related to The Miller–Ross Function

Sercan Kazımoğlu [1], Erhan Deniz [1,*] and Luminita-Ioana Cotirla [2]

[1] Department of Mathematics, Faculty of Science and Letters, Kafkas University, Campus, 36100 Kars, Turkey; srcnkzmglu@gmail.com or sercan@kafkas.edu.tr
[2] Department of Mathematics, Technical University of Cluj-Napoca, 400114 Cluj-Napoca, Romania; luminita.cotirla@math.utcluj.ro
* Correspondence: edeniz36@gmail.com or edeniz@kafkas.edu.tr

Abstract: It is very well-known that the special functions and integral operators play a vital role in the research of applied and mathematical sciences. In this paper, our aim is to present sufficient conditions for the families of integral operators containing the normalized forms of the Miller–Ross functions such that they can be univalent in the open unit disk. Moreover, we find the convexity order of these operators. In proof of results, we use some differential inequalities related with Miller–Ross functions and well-known lemmas. The various results, which are established in this paper, are presumably new, and their importance is illustrated by several interesting consequences and examples.

Keywords: analytic functions; Miller–Ross functions; univalence; convexity; special functions; univalent functions; integral operators

MSC: 30C45; 33C10

Citation: Kazımoğlu, S.; Deniz, E.; Cotirla, L.-I. Geometric Properties of Generalized Integral Operators Related to The Miller–Ross Function. *Axioms* **2023**, *12*, 563. https://doi.org/10.3390/axioms12060563

Academic Editor: Georgia Irina Oros

Received: 16 May 2023
Revised: 31 May 2023
Accepted: 1 June 2023
Published: 7 June 2023

1. Introduction

Special functions are mathematical functions that lack a precise formal definition, yet they hold significant importance in various fields such as mathematical analysis, physics, functional analysis, and other branches of applied science. Despite their lack of a rigid definition, these functions are widely utilized due to their valuable properties and widespread applicability. Many elementary functions, such as exponential, trigonometric, and hyperbolic functions, are also treated as special functions. The theory of special functions has earned the attention of many researchers throughout the nineteenth century and has been involved in many emerging fields. Indeed, numerous special functions, including the generalized hypergeometric functions, have emerged as a result of solving specific differential equations. These functions have proven to be instrumental in addressing complex mathematical problems, showcasing their remarkable utility in various domains. The geometric properties such as univalence and convexity of special functions and their integral operators are important in complex analysis. Several researchers have dedicated their efforts to investigating integral operators that incorporate special functions such as the Bessel, Lommel, Struve, Wright, and Mittag–Leffler functions. These studies have focused on examining the geometric properties of these operators within various classes of univalent functions. By exploring the interplay between these integral operators and special functions, researchers have deepened our understanding of the behavior and characteristics of univalent functions in different contexts. It is noteworthy that contemporary researchers in the field are actively pursuing the development of novel theoretical methodologies and techniques that combine observational results with various practical applications. Therefore, the primary objective of this paper is to investigate the criteria for univalence and convexity of integral operators that employ Miller–Ross functions.

Let $\mathcal{A}$ denote the class of analytic functions $\hbar$ of the form

$$\hbar(\rho) = \rho + \sum_{v=2}^{\infty} a_v \rho^v$$

in the open unit disk $\mathbb{D} = \{\rho : |\rho| < 1, \rho \in \mathbb{C}\}$ and satisfy the standard normalization condition:

$$\hbar(0) = 0, \hbar'(0) = 1.$$

We denote by $\mathcal{S}$ the subclass of $\mathcal{A}$ which are also univalent in $\mathbb{D}$. A function $\hbar \in \mathcal{S}$ is convex of order $\delta (0 \leq \delta < 1)$ if the following condition holds:

$$\Re\left(1 + \frac{\rho \hbar''(\rho)}{\hbar'(\rho)}\right) > \delta.$$

For $n \in \mathbb{N} := \{1, 2, 3, \ldots\}$, define

$$\mathcal{A}^n := \{(\hbar_1, \hbar_2, \cdots, \hbar_n) : \hbar_v \in \mathcal{A}, v = 1, 2, \ldots, n\}.$$

For $\hbar_v \in \mathcal{A}$ $(v = 1, 2, \ldots, n)$, the parameters $\eta_v, \zeta_v \in \mathbb{C}$ $(v = 1, 2, \ldots, n)$ and $\gamma \in \mathbb{C}$, we define the following three integral operators:

$$\mathcal{J}_{\eta_1,\eta_2,\ldots,\eta_n;\zeta_1,\zeta_2,\ldots,\zeta_n;n;\gamma} : \mathcal{A}^n \longrightarrow \mathcal{A},$$

$$\mathcal{K}_{\eta_1,\eta_2,\ldots,\eta_n;\zeta_1,\zeta_2,\ldots,\zeta_n;n} : \mathcal{A}^n \longrightarrow \mathcal{A}$$

and

$$\mathcal{L}_{\eta_1,\eta_2,\ldots,\eta_n;\zeta_1,\zeta_2,\ldots,\zeta_n;n;\gamma} : \mathcal{A}^n \longrightarrow \mathcal{A}$$

by

$$\mathcal{J}_{\eta_1,\eta_2,\ldots,\eta_n;\zeta_1,\zeta_2,\ldots,\zeta_n;n;\gamma}[\hbar_1, \hbar_2, \ldots, \hbar_n](\rho) := \left[\gamma \int_0^\rho t^{\gamma-1} \prod_{v=1}^{n} (\hbar_v'(t))^{\eta_v} \left(\frac{\hbar_v(t)}{t}\right)^{\zeta_v} dt\right]^{1/\gamma}, \tag{1}$$

$$\mathcal{K}_{\eta_1,\eta_2,\ldots,\eta_n;\zeta_1,\zeta_2,\ldots,\zeta_n;n}[\hbar_1, \hbar_2, \ldots, \hbar_n](\rho) := \left[\left(1 + \sum_{v=1}^{n} \eta_v\right) \int_0^\rho \prod_{v=1}^{n} (\hbar_v(t))^{\eta_v} \left(e^{\hbar_v(t)}\right)^{\zeta_v} dt\right]^{1/\left(1+\sum_{v=1}^{n} \eta_v\right)} \tag{2}$$

and

$$\mathcal{L}_{\eta_1,\eta_2,\ldots,\eta_n;\zeta_1,\zeta_2,\ldots,\zeta_n;n;\gamma}[\hbar_1, \hbar_2, \ldots, \hbar_n](\rho) := \left[\gamma \int_0^\rho t^{\gamma-1} \prod_{v=1}^{n} (\hbar_v'(t))^{\eta_v} \left(e^{\hbar_v(t)}\right)^{\zeta_v} dt\right]^{1/\gamma}. \tag{3}$$

Here, we need to note that, many authors have studied the integral operators (1), (2) and (3) for some specific parameters as follows:

(1) $\mathcal{J}_{0,0,\ldots,0;\zeta_1,\zeta_2,\ldots,\zeta_n;n;\gamma}[\hbar_1, \hbar_2, \ldots, \hbar_n] \equiv \mathcal{F}_{1/\zeta_1,1/\zeta_2,\ldots,1/\zeta_n;\gamma}$ (Seenivasagan and Breaz [1]; see also [2,3]);
(2) $\mathcal{J}_{\eta_1,\eta_2,\ldots,\eta_n;0,0,\ldots,0;n;\gamma}[\hbar_1, \hbar_2, \ldots, \hbar_n] \equiv \mathcal{L}_{\eta_1,\eta_2,\ldots,\eta_n;0,0,\ldots,0;n;\gamma}[\hbar_1, \hbar_2, \ldots, \hbar_n] \equiv \mathcal{H}_{\eta_1,\eta_2,\ldots,\eta_n;\gamma}$ (Breaz and Breaz [4]);
(3) $\mathcal{J}_{\eta_1,\eta_2,\ldots,\eta_n;0,0,\ldots,0;n;1}[\hbar_1, \hbar_2, \ldots, \hbar_n] \equiv \mathcal{L}_{\eta_1,\eta_2,\ldots,\eta_n;0,0,\ldots,0;n;1}[\hbar_1, \hbar_2, \ldots, \hbar_n] \equiv \mathcal{H}_{\eta_1,\eta_2,\ldots,\eta_n}$ (Breaz et al. [5]);
(4) $\mathcal{J}_{\eta;0;1;1}[\hbar] \equiv \mathcal{H}_\eta$ (Kim and Merkes [6]; see also Pfaltzgraff [7]);
(5) $\mathcal{L}_{0;\zeta;1;\gamma}[\hbar] \equiv \mathcal{Q}_\zeta$ (Pescar [8]);
(6) $\mathcal{K}_{\eta,\eta,\ldots,\eta;0,0,\ldots,0;n}[\hbar_1, \hbar_2, \ldots, \hbar_n] \equiv \mathcal{G}_{n,\eta}[\hbar_1, \hbar_2, \ldots, \hbar_n]$ (Breaz and Breaz [9]; see also [10]);
(7) $\mathcal{K}_{\eta;0;1}[\hbar] \equiv \mathcal{G}_{1,\eta}[\hbar]$ (Moldoveanu and Pascu [11]).

Furthermore, the specific integral operators via an obvious parametric changes of the classical Bessel function $J_\nu(\rho)$ of order ν and of the first kind by Deniz et al. [12]

were introduced and they worked on the univalence condition of the related integral operators. In addition, the starlikeness, convexity and uniform convexity of integral operators containing these equivalent forms of $J_\nu(\rho)$ were discussed by Raza et al. [13] and Deniz [14]. Recently, some sufficient conditions for univalence of various linear fractional derivative operators containing the normalized forms of the similar parametric variation of $J_\nu(\rho)$ were investigated by Al-Khrasani et al. [15]. Moreover, the theory of derivatives and integrals of an arbitrary complex or real order has been utilized not only in complex analysis, but also in the mathematical analysis and modeling of real-world problems in applied sciences (see, for example, [16,17]).

Inspired by the studies mentioned above, in the present paper, we work on some mappings and univalence and convexity conditions for the integral operators given by (1), (2) and (3), related to the following Miller–Ross function $E_{\xi,\varrho}$, defined by

$$E_{\xi,\varrho}(\rho) = \rho^{\xi} e^{\varrho\rho} \gamma^*(\xi, \varrho\rho),$$

where γ^* is the incomplete gamma function (see [18]).

$E_{\xi,\varrho}(\rho)$ a solution of the following ordinary differential equation

$$Dy - \varrho y = \frac{\rho^{\xi-1}}{\Gamma(\xi)}, \xi > 0.$$

With the help of the gamma function we obtain the following series form of $E_{\xi,\varrho}(\rho)$:

$$E_{\xi,\varrho}(\rho) = \rho^{\xi} \sum_{v=0}^{\infty} \frac{(\varrho\rho)^v}{\Gamma(\xi + v + 1)},$$

where $\varrho, \rho \in \mathbb{C}$.

The function $E_{\xi,\varrho}(\rho)$ does not belong to the class $\mathcal{A}$. The normalization form of the function $E_{\xi,\varrho}$ is written as

$$\mathbb{E}_{\xi,\varrho}(\rho) = \Gamma(\xi + 1)\rho^{1-\xi} E_{\xi,\varrho}(\rho) = \sum_{v=0}^{\infty} \frac{\varrho^v \Gamma(\xi + 1)}{\Gamma(\xi + v + 1)} \rho^{v+1}, \tag{4}$$

where $\xi > -1$ and $\varrho > 0$.

Recently, Eker and Ece [19] and Şeker et al. [20] studied geometric and characteristic properties of this function, respectively. Also, some problems as partial sums, coefficient inequalities, inclusion relations and neighborhoods for Miller-Ross function were studied by Kazımoğlu [21,22].

We note that by choosing particular values for ξ and ϱ, we obtain the following functions

$$\mathbb{E}_{1,1/2}(\rho) = 2e^{\rho/2} - 2, \mathbb{E}_{3,1}(\rho) = \frac{6e^{\rho} - 3\rho^2 - 6\rho - 6}{\rho^2}$$

and

$$\mathbb{E}_{\frac{1}{2},1}(\rho) = \frac{1}{2} e^{\rho/5} \sqrt{5\pi} \sqrt{\rho} \mathrm{Erf} \sqrt{\frac{\rho}{5}}, \mathbb{E}_{2,1/2}(\rho) = \frac{4\left(2e^{\rho/2} - \rho - 2\right)}{\rho},$$

where $\mathrm{Erf}\sqrt{\rho}$ is the error function.

Let $\xi_v > -1$ for $v = 1, 2, \ldots, n$ and $\varrho > 0$. Consider the functions $\mathbb{E}_{\xi_v,\varrho}$ defined by

$$\mathbb{E}_{\xi_v,\varrho}(\rho) = \Gamma(\xi_v + 1)\rho^{1-\xi_v} E_{\xi_v,\varrho}(\rho).$$

Using the functions $\mathbb{E}_{\xi_v,\varrho}$ and the integral operators given by (1), (2) and (3), we define $\mathcal{J}^{\xi_1,\xi_2,\ldots,\xi_n;\varrho}_{\eta_1,\eta_2,\ldots,\eta_n;\zeta_1,\zeta_2,\ldots,\zeta_n;n;\gamma}$, $\mathcal{K}^{\xi_1,\xi_2,\ldots,\xi_n;\varrho}_{\eta_1,\eta_2,\ldots,\eta_n;\zeta_1,\zeta_2,\ldots,\zeta_n;n}$ and $\mathcal{L}^{\xi_1,\xi_2,\ldots,\xi_n;\varrho}_{\eta_1,\eta_2,\ldots,\eta_n;\zeta_1,\zeta_2,\ldots,\zeta_n;n;\gamma}: \mathbb{D} \longrightarrow \mathbb{C}$ as follows:

$$\begin{aligned}\mathcal{J}^{\xi_1,\xi_2,\ldots,\xi_n;\varrho}_{\eta_1,\eta_2,\ldots,\eta_n;\zeta_1,\zeta_2,\ldots,\zeta_n;n;\gamma}(\rho) := \quad & \mathcal{J}_{\eta_1,\eta_2,\ldots,\eta_n;\zeta_1,\zeta_2,\ldots,\zeta_n;n;\gamma}\left[\mathbb{E}_{\xi_1,\varrho}, \mathbb{E}_{\xi_2,\varrho}, \ldots, \mathbb{E}_{\xi_n,\varrho}\right](\rho) \\ = \quad & \left[\gamma \int_0^\rho t^{\gamma-1} \prod_{v=1}^{n} \left(\mathbb{E}'_{\xi_v,\varrho}(t)\right)^{\eta_v} \left(\frac{\mathbb{E}_{\xi_v,\varrho}(t)}{t}\right)^{\zeta_v} dt\right]^{1/\gamma}, \quad (5)\end{aligned}$$

$$\begin{aligned}\mathcal{K}^{\xi_1,\xi_2,\ldots,\xi_n;\varrho}_{\eta_1,\eta_2,\ldots,\eta_n;\zeta_1,\zeta_2,\ldots,\zeta_n;n}(\rho) := \quad & \mathcal{K}_{\eta_1,\eta_2,\ldots,\eta_n;\zeta_1,\zeta_2,\ldots,\zeta_n;n}\left[\mathbb{E}_{\xi_1,\varrho}, \mathbb{E}_{\xi_2,\varrho}, \ldots, \mathbb{E}_{\xi_n,\varrho}\right](\rho) \\ = \quad & \left[\left(1 + \sum_{v=1}^{n} \eta_v\right) \int_0^\rho \prod_{v=1}^{n} \left(\mathbb{E}_{\xi_v,\varrho}(t)\right)^{\eta_v} \left(e^{\mathbb{E}_{\xi_v,\varrho}(t)}\right)^{\zeta_v} dt\right]^{1/\left(1+\sum_{v=1}^{n} \eta_v\right)} \quad (6)\end{aligned}$$

and

$$\begin{aligned}\mathcal{L}^{\xi_1,\xi_2,\ldots,\xi_n;\varrho}_{\eta_1,\eta_2,\ldots,\eta_n;\zeta_1,\zeta_2,\ldots,\zeta_n;n;\gamma}(\rho) := \quad & \mathcal{L}_{\eta_1,\eta_2,\ldots,\eta_n;\zeta_1,\zeta_2,\ldots,\zeta_n;n;\gamma}\left[\mathbb{E}_{\xi_1,\varrho}, \mathbb{E}_{\xi_2,\varrho}, \ldots, \mathbb{E}_{\xi_n,\varrho}\right](\rho) \\ = \quad & \left[\gamma \int_0^z t^{\gamma-1} \prod_{v=1}^{n} \left(\mathbb{E}'_{\xi_v,\varrho}(t)\right)^{\eta_v} \left(e^{\mathbb{E}_{\xi_v,\varrho}(t)}\right)^{\zeta_v} dt\right]^{1/\gamma}. \quad (7)\end{aligned}$$

An extensive literature in geometric function theory dealing with the geometric properties of the integral operators using different types of special functions can be found. In 2010, some integral operators containing Bessel functions were studied by Baricz and Frasin [2]. They obtained some sufficient conditions for univalence of these operators. The convexity and strongly convexity of the integral operators given in [2] were investigated by Arif and Raza [23] and Frasin [24]. Deniz [14] and Deniz et al. [12] gave convexity and univalence conditions for integral operators involving generalized Bessel Functions, respectively. Between 2018 and 2020, Mahmood et al. [25], Mahmood and his co-authors [26] and Din and Yalçın [27] investigated the certain geometric properties such as univalence, convexity, strongly starlikeness and strongly convexity of integral operators involving Struve functions. Recently, Din and Yalçın [28] obtained some sufficients condidions on starlikeness, convexity and uniformly close-to-convexity of the modified Lommel function. Park et al. [29] investigated univalence and convexity conditions for certain integral operators involving the Lommel function. Srivastava and his co-authors [30] studied sufficient conditions for univalence of certain integral operators involving the normalized Mittag–Leffler functions. Oros [31] studied geometric properties of certain classes of univalent functions using the classical Bernardi and Libera integral operators and the confluent (or Kummer) hypergeometric function. Very recently, Raza et al. [32] obtained the necessary conditions for the univalence of integral operators containing the generalized Bessel function. Studies on this subject are still ongoing.

Motivated by the these works, we obtain some sufficient conditions for the operators (5), (6) and (7), in order to be univalent in $\mathbb{D}$. Moreover, we determine the order of the convexity of these integral operators. By using Mathematica (version 8.0), we give some graphics that support the main results.

2. A Set of Lemmas

The following lemmas will be required in our current research.

Lemma 1 (see Pescar [33])**.** *Let α and β be complex number such that*

$$\Re(\alpha) > 0 \text{ and } |\beta| \leqq 1 (\beta \neq -1).$$

If the function $h \in \mathcal{A}$ satisfies the following inequality:

$$\left|\beta|\rho|^{2\alpha} + \left(1 - |\rho|^{2\alpha}\right)\frac{\rho h''(\rho)}{\alpha h'(\rho)}\right| \leqq 1$$

for all $\rho \in \mathbb{D}$, then the function $F_\alpha \in \mathcal{A}$ defined by

$$F_\alpha(\rho) = \left(\alpha \int_0^\rho t^{\alpha-1} h'(t)dt\right))^{1/\alpha} \tag{8}$$

is in the class $\mathcal{S}$.

Lemma 2 (see Pascu [34]). *Let $\varpi \in \mathbb{C}$ such that $\Re(\varpi) > 0$. If $h \in \mathcal{A}$ satisfies the following inequality:*

$$\left(\frac{1 - |\rho|^{2\Re(\varpi)}}{\Re(\varpi)}\right)\left|\frac{\rho h''(\rho)}{h'(\rho)}\right| \leqq 1$$

for all $\rho \in \mathbb{D}$. Then, for all $\alpha \in \mathbb{C}$ such that

$$\Re(\alpha) \geqq \Re(\varpi),$$

the function F_α defined by (8) is in the class $\mathcal{S}$.

Lemma 3. *Let $\xi > -1$ and $\varrho > 0$. Then, for $\forall \rho \in \mathbb{D}$, the function $\mathbb{E}_{\xi,\varrho}$ defined by (4) provides the following inequalities:*

$$\left|\mathbb{E}'_{\xi,\varrho}(\rho) - \frac{\mathbb{E}_{\xi,\varrho}(\rho)}{\rho}\right| \leqq \frac{\varrho(\xi+1)}{(\xi-\varrho+1)^2}(\varrho - 1 < \xi), \tag{9}$$

$$\left|\frac{\rho\mathbb{E}'_{\xi,\varrho}(\rho)}{\mathbb{E}_{\xi,\varrho}(\rho)} - 1\right| \leqq \frac{\varrho(\xi+1)}{(\xi-\varrho+1)(\xi-2\varrho+1)}(2\varrho - 1 < \xi), \tag{10}$$

$$\left|\rho\mathbb{E}'_{\xi,\varrho}(\rho)\right| \leqq \left(\frac{\xi+1}{\xi-\varrho+1}\right)^2 (\varrho - 1 < \xi), \tag{11}$$

$$\left|\frac{\rho\mathbb{E}'_{\xi,\varrho}(\rho)}{\mathbb{E}_{\xi,\varrho}(\rho)}\right| \leqq \frac{(\xi+1)^2}{(\xi-\varrho+1)(\xi-2\varrho+1)}(2\varrho - 1 < \xi) \tag{12}$$

and

$$\left|\frac{\rho\mathbb{E}''_{\xi,\varrho}(\rho)}{\mathbb{E}'_{\xi,\varrho}(\rho)}\right| \leqq \frac{(\xi-\varrho+1)^3 + 2\varrho(\xi+1)^2}{(\xi-\varrho+1)^2 + (\varrho-1)^2 - (2\xi\varrho+1)}\left(\left(2+\sqrt{2}\right)\varrho - 1 < \xi\right). \tag{13}$$

Proof. The inequalities (9) and (10) were proved by Eker and Ece [19]. On the other hand, by using the triangle inequality and the following inequality (see [19])

$$\frac{\Gamma(\xi+1)}{\Gamma(\xi+v)} \leq \frac{1}{(\xi+1)^{v-1}}, \tag{14}$$

we have

$$\left|\frac{\mathbb{E}_{\xi,\varrho}(\rho)}{\rho}\right| \leq \frac{\xi-2\varrho+1}{\xi-\varrho+1}(2\varrho - 1 < \xi) \tag{15}$$

and

$$
\begin{aligned}
\left|\rho\mathbb{E}'_{\xi,\varrho}(\rho)\right| &= \left|\rho+\sum_{v=2}^{\infty}\frac{v\Gamma(\xi+1)\varrho^{v-1}}{\Gamma(\xi+v)}\rho^{v}\right| \\
&\leq 1+\sum_{v=2}^{\infty}\frac{v\Gamma(\xi+1)\varrho^{v-1}}{\Gamma(\xi+v)} \\
&\leq 1+\sum_{v=2}^{\infty}v\left(\frac{\varrho}{\xi+1}\right)^{v-1}=\left(\frac{\xi+1}{\xi-\varrho+1}\right)^{2}(\varrho-1<\xi).
\end{aligned} \tag{16}
$$

Thus, from (15) and (16), we obtain

$$
\left|\frac{\rho\mathbb{E}'_{\xi,\varrho}(\rho)}{\mathbb{E}_{\xi,\varrho}(\rho)}\right| \leq \frac{(\xi+1)^2}{(\xi-\varrho+1)(\xi-2\varrho+1)}(2\varrho-1<\xi).
$$

Using the inequality (14), it follows that

$$
\begin{aligned}
\left|\rho\mathbb{E}''_{\xi,\varrho}(\rho)\right| &= \left|\sum_{v=2}^{\infty}\frac{v(v-1)\Gamma(\xi+1)\varrho^{v-1}}{\Gamma(\xi+v)}\rho^{v-1}\right| \\
&\leq \sum_{v=2}^{\infty}\frac{v(v-1)\Gamma(\xi+1)\varrho^{v-1}}{\Gamma(\xi+v)} \\
&\leq 1+\sum_{v=2}^{\infty}v(v-1)\left(\frac{\varrho}{\xi+1}\right)^{v-1}=\frac{(\xi-\varrho+1)^3+2\varrho(\xi+1)^2}{(\xi-\varrho+1)^3}
\end{aligned} \tag{17}
$$

for $\varrho-1<\xi$. Finally, applying reverse triangle inequality, we conclude that

$$
\begin{aligned}
\left|\mathbb{E}'_{\xi,\varrho}(\rho)\right| &= \left|1+\sum_{v=2}^{\infty}\frac{v\Gamma(\xi+1)\varrho^{v-1}}{\Gamma(\xi+v)}\rho^{v-1}\right| \\
&\geq 1-\sum_{v=2}^{\infty}\frac{v\Gamma(\xi+1)\varrho^{v-1}}{\Gamma(\xi+v)} \\
&\geq 1-\sum_{v=2}^{\infty}v\left(\frac{\varrho}{\xi+1}\right)^{v-1}=\frac{(\xi-\varrho+1)^2-2\xi\varrho-2\varrho+\varrho^2}{(\xi-\varrho+1)^2}
\end{aligned} \tag{18}
$$

for $\left(2+\sqrt{2}\right)\varrho-1<\xi$. Next, by combining the inequalities (17) with (18), we can easily see that

$$
\left|\frac{\rho\mathbb{E}''_{\xi,\varrho}(\rho)}{\mathbb{E}'_{\xi,\varrho}(\rho)}\right| \leq \frac{(\xi-\varrho+1)^3+2\varrho(\xi+1)^2}{(\xi-\varrho+1)^2+(\varrho-1)^2-(2\xi\varrho+1)}\left(\left(2+\sqrt{2}\right)\varrho-1<\xi\right).
$$

This completes the proof. □

3. Univalence and Convexity Conditions for the Integral Operator in (5)

Firstly, we take into account the integral operator defined by (5).

Theorem 1. *Let $v=1,2,\ldots,n$, $\xi_v>-1$, $\varrho>0$ and $\left(2+\sqrt{2}\right)\varrho-1<\xi_v$. Also, let γ,β,η_v and ζ_v be in $\mathbb{C}$ such that*

$$
\Re(\gamma)>0, |\beta|\leq 1(\beta\neq -1).
$$

Assume that these numbers satisfy the following inequality:

$$|\beta| + \frac{1}{|\gamma|}\left(\frac{(\xi-\varrho+1)^3+2\varrho(\xi+1)^2}{(\xi-\varrho+1)^2+(\varrho-1)^2-(2\xi\varrho+1)}\sum_{v=1}^{n}|\eta_v| + \frac{\varrho(\xi+1)}{(\xi-\varrho+1)(\xi-2\varrho+1)}\sum_{v=1}^{n}|\zeta_v|\right) \leqq 1,$$

where $\xi = \min\{\xi_1, \xi_2, \ldots, \xi_n\}$*. Then the function* $\mathcal{J}^{\xi_1,\xi_2,\ldots,\xi_n;\varrho}_{\eta_1,\eta_2,\ldots,\eta_n;\zeta_1,\zeta_2,\ldots,\zeta_n;n;\gamma}$ *defined by (5) is in the class* $\mathcal{S}$.

Proof. Let us define the function φ as follows:

$$\varphi(\rho) = \mathcal{J}^{\xi_1,\xi_2,\ldots,\xi_n;\varrho}_{\eta_1,\eta_2,\ldots,\eta_n;\zeta_1,\zeta_2,\ldots,\zeta_n;n;1}(\rho) = \int_0^{\rho}\prod_{v=1}^{n}\left(\mathbb{E}'_{\xi_v,\varrho}(t)\right)^{\eta_v}\left(\frac{\mathbb{E}_{\xi_v,\varrho}(t)}{t}\right)^{\zeta_v}dt. \tag{19}$$

First of all, we observe that $\varphi(\rho) = \varphi'(\rho) - 1 = 0$, since $\mathbb{E}_{\xi_v,\varrho} \in \mathcal{A}$ for all $v = 1, 2, \ldots, n$. However, we also have

$$\varphi'(\rho) = \prod_{v=1}^{n}\left(\mathbb{E}'_{\xi_v,\varrho}(\rho)\right)^{\eta_v}\left(\frac{\mathbb{E}_{\xi_v,\varrho}(\rho)}{\rho}\right)^{\zeta_v}. \tag{20}$$

Taking the logarithmic derivative of both sides of (20), we get

$$\frac{\rho\varphi''(\rho)}{\varphi'(\rho)} = \sum_{v=1}^{n}\eta_v\frac{\rho\mathbb{E}''_{\xi_v,\varrho}(\rho)}{\mathbb{E}'_{\xi_v,\varrho}(\rho)} + \sum_{v=1}^{n}\zeta_v\left(\frac{\rho\mathbb{E}'_{\xi_v,\varrho}(\rho)}{\mathbb{E}_{\xi_v,\varrho}(\rho)} - 1\right) \tag{21}$$

and, from (10) and (13), we have

$$\begin{aligned}\left|\frac{\rho\varphi''(\rho)}{\varphi'(\rho)}\right| &\leqq \sum_{v=1}^{n}\left(|\eta_v|\left|\frac{\rho\mathbb{E}''_{\xi_v,\varrho}(\rho)}{\mathbb{E}'_{\xi_v,\varrho}(\rho)}\right| + |\zeta_v|\left|\frac{\rho\mathbb{E}'_{\xi_v,\varrho}(\rho)}{\mathbb{E}_{\xi_v,\varrho}(\rho)} - 1\right|\right)\\ &\leqq \sum_{v=1}^{n}\left(|\eta_v|\frac{(\xi_v-\varrho+1)^3+2\varrho(\xi_v+1)^2}{(\xi_v-\varrho+1)^2+(\varrho-1)^2-(2\xi_v\varrho+1)} + |\zeta_v|\frac{\varrho(\xi_v+1)}{(\xi_v-\varrho+1)(\xi_v-2\varrho+1)}\right)\\ &\leqq \sum_{v=1}^{n}\left(|\eta_v|\frac{(\xi-\varrho+1)^3+2\varrho(\xi+1)^2}{(\xi-\varrho+1)^2+(\varrho-1)^2-(2\xi\varrho+1)} + |\zeta_v|\frac{\varrho(\xi+1)}{(\xi-\varrho+1)(\xi-2\varrho+1)}\right),\end{aligned} \tag{22}$$

$$\left(\rho \in \mathbb{D}; \left(2+\sqrt{2}\right)\varrho - 1 < \xi, \xi_v < \varrho_0, (v = 1, 2, \ldots, n)\right)$$

where $\varrho_0 = \frac{1}{3}\left[-3+\varrho\left(7+\frac{49}{(370-3\sqrt{2139})^{1/3}}+\left(370-3\sqrt{2139}\right)^{1/3}\right)\right]$. Here, we have also used the fact that the functions

$$\Theta_1, \Theta_2 : \left(\left(2+\sqrt{2}\right)\varrho - 1, \varrho_0\right) \longrightarrow \mathbb{R},$$

defined by

$$\Theta_1(x) = \frac{(x-\varrho+1)^3+2\varrho(x+1)^2}{(x-\varrho+1)^2+(\varrho-1)^2-(2x\varrho+1)} \text{ and } \Theta_2(x) = \frac{\varrho(x+1)}{(x-\varrho+1)(x-2\varrho+1)},$$

are decreasing and, consequently, we have

$$\frac{(\xi_v-\varrho+1)^3+2\varrho(\xi_v+1)^2}{(\xi_v-\varrho+1)^2+(\varrho-1)^2-(2\xi_v\varrho+1)} < \frac{(\xi-\varrho+1)^3+2\varrho(\xi+1)^2}{(\xi-\varrho+1)^2+(\varrho-1)^2-(2\xi\varrho+1)} \tag{23}$$

and

$$\frac{\varrho(\xi_v+1)}{(\xi_v-\varrho+1)(\xi_v-2\varrho+1)} < \frac{\varrho(\xi+1)}{(\xi-\varrho+1)(\xi-2\varrho+1)}.$$

Therefore, from hypothesis of theorem we obtain

$$\begin{aligned}&\left|\beta|\rho|^{2\gamma}+\left(1-|\rho|^{2\gamma}\right)\frac{\rho\varphi''(\rho)}{\gamma\varphi'(\rho)}\right|\\&\leqq|\beta|+\frac{1}{|\gamma|}\left(\frac{(\xi-\varrho+1)^3+2\varrho(\xi+1)^2}{(\xi-\varrho+1)^2+(\varrho-1)^2-(2\xi\varrho+1)}\sum_{v=1}^{n}|\eta_v|+\frac{\varrho(\xi+1)}{(\xi-\varrho+1)(\xi-2\varrho+1)}\sum_{v=1}^{n}|\zeta_v|\right)\\&\leqq 1,\end{aligned}$$

which imply that the function $\mathcal{J}^{\xi_1,\xi_2,\ldots,\xi_n;\varrho}_{\eta_1,\eta_2,\ldots,\eta_n;\zeta_1,\zeta_2,\ldots,\zeta_n;n;\gamma}\in\mathcal{S}$ by Lemma 1. □

Theorem 2. *Let the parameters* $\varrho,\gamma,\eta_v,\xi_v$ *and* ζ_v $(v=1,2,\ldots,n)$ *be as in Theorem 1. Suppose that* $\xi=\min\{\xi_1,\xi_2,\ldots,\xi_n\}$ *and that the following inequality holds true:*

$$\Re(\gamma)\geqq\sum_{v=1}^{n}|\eta_v|\frac{(\xi-\varrho+1)^3+2\varrho(\xi+1)^2}{(\xi-\varrho+1)^2+(\varrho-1)^2-(2\xi\varrho+1)}+\sum_{v=1}^{n}|\zeta_v|\frac{\varrho(\xi+1)}{(\xi-\varrho+1)(\xi-2\varrho+1)}.$$

Then the function $\mathcal{J}^{\xi_1,\xi_2,\ldots,\xi_n;\varrho}_{\eta_1,\eta_2,\ldots,\eta_n;\zeta_1,\zeta_2,\ldots,\zeta_n;n;\gamma}$ *defined by (5) is in the class* $\mathcal{S}$.

Proof. Let us consider the function φ as in (19). From (22) and hypothesis of theorem, we get

$$\begin{aligned}&\frac{1-|\rho|^{2\Re(\gamma)}}{\Re(\gamma)}\left|\frac{\rho\varphi''(\rho)}{\varphi'(\rho)}\right|\\&\leq\frac{1-|\rho|^{2\Re(\gamma)}}{\Re(\gamma)}\sum_{v=1}^{n}\left(|\eta_v|\frac{(\xi_v-\varrho+1)^3+2\varrho(\xi_v+1)^2}{(\xi_v-\varrho+1)^2+(\varrho-1)^2-(2\xi_v\varrho+1)}+|\zeta_v|\frac{\varrho(\xi_v+1)}{(\xi_v-\varrho+1)(\xi_v-2\varrho+1)}\right)\\&\leq\frac{1}{\Re(\gamma)}\sum_{v=1}^{n}\left(|\eta_v|\frac{(\xi-\varrho+1)^3+2\varrho(\xi+1)^2}{(\xi-\varrho+1)^2+(\varrho-1)^2-(2\xi\varrho+1)}+|\zeta_v|\frac{\varrho(\xi+1)}{(\xi-\varrho+1)(\xi-2\varrho+1)}\right)\\&\leq 1.\end{aligned}\tag{24}$$

By Lemma 2, the inequality (24) imply that the function $\mathcal{J}^{\xi_1,\xi_2,\ldots,\xi_n;\varrho}_{\eta_1,\eta_2,\ldots,\eta_n;\zeta_1,\zeta_2,\ldots,\zeta_n;n;\gamma}\in\mathcal{S}$. □

Theorem 3. *Let the parameters* ϱ,η_v,ξ_v *and* ζ_v $(v=1,2,\ldots,n)$ *be as in Theorem 1. Suppose that* $\xi=\min\{\xi_1,\xi_2,\ldots,\xi_n\}$ *and that the following inequality holds true:*

$$0<\sum_{v=1}^{n}\left(|\eta_v|\frac{(\xi-\varrho+1)^3+2\varrho(\xi+1)^2}{(\xi-\varrho+1)^2+(\varrho-1)^2-(2\xi\varrho+1)}+|\zeta_v|\frac{\varrho(\xi+1)}{(\xi-\varrho+1)(\xi-2\varrho+1)}\right)\leqq 1.$$

Then the function $\mathcal{J}^{\xi_1,\xi_2,\ldots,\xi_n;\varrho}_{\eta_1,\eta_2,\ldots,\eta_n;\zeta_1,\zeta_2,\ldots,\zeta_n;n;1}$ *defined by (5) with* $\gamma=1$ *is convex of order* δ *given by*

$$\delta=1-\sum_{v=1}^{n}\left(|\eta_v|\frac{(\xi-\varrho+1)^3+2\varrho(\xi+1)^2}{(\xi-\varrho+1)^2+(\varrho-1)^2-(2\xi\varrho+1)}+|\zeta_v|\frac{\varrho(\xi+1)}{(\xi-\varrho+1)(\xi-2\varrho+1)}\right).$$

Proof. The inequality (22) and hypothesis of theorem show that

$$\begin{aligned}\left|\frac{\rho\varphi''(\rho)}{\varphi'(\rho)}\right|&\leqq\sum_{v=1}^{n}|\eta_v|\frac{(\xi-\varrho+1)^3+2\varrho(\xi+1)^2}{(\xi-\varrho+1)^2+(\varrho-1)^2-(2\xi\varrho+1)}+\sum_{v=1}^{n}|\zeta_v|\frac{\varrho(\xi+1)}{(\xi-\varrho+1)(\xi-2\varrho+1)}\\&=1-\delta.\end{aligned}$$

As a result, the function φ is convex of order

$$\delta=1-\sum_{v=1}^{n}\left(|\eta_v|\frac{(\xi-\varrho+1)^3+2\varrho(\xi+1)^2}{(\xi-\varrho+1)^2+(\varrho-1)^2-(2\xi\varrho+1)}+|\zeta_v|\frac{\varrho(\xi+1)}{(\xi-\varrho+1)(\xi-2\varrho+1)}\right).$$

□

In Theorem 1 with $n=1,\xi_1=1$ and $\varrho=1/2$, we can write the following corollary.

Corollary 1. *Let γ, β, η and ζ be in $\mathbb{C}$ such that $\Re(\gamma) > 0$ and $|\beta| \leq 1 (\beta \neq -1)$. If the inequality*

$$|\beta| + \frac{1}{|\gamma|}\left(\frac{59}{4}|\eta| + \frac{2}{3}|\zeta|\right) \leqq 1$$

holds true, then the function

$$\left[\gamma \int_0^\rho t^{-\zeta+\gamma-1}\left(e^{t/2}\right)^\eta \left(2e^{t/2} - 2\right)^\zeta dt\right]^{1/\gamma}$$

is in the class $\mathcal{S}$.

Example 1.

$$f_1(\rho) = \int_0^\rho t^{-1}\left(e^{t/200}\right)\left(2e^{t/2} - 2\right)dt \in \mathcal{S}.$$

Normally, it is almost impossible to find the geometric properties (univalent, convex, starlike, etc.) of a complex function and especially integral operators with classical methods. However, from Corollary 1 (also from Figure 1) with $\gamma = \zeta = 1$ and $\eta = 0.01$, we can see that the function f_1 belongs to the class $\mathcal{S}$.

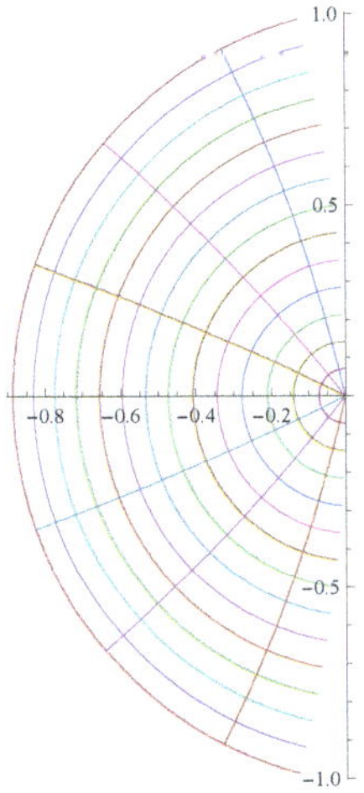

Figure 1. Image of $\mathbb{D}$ under f_1.

Setting $n = 1, \xi_1 = 3$ and $\varrho = 1$ in the Theorem 1, we can get result below.

Corollary 2. *Let γ, β, η and ζ be in $\mathbb{C}$ such that $\Re(\gamma) > 0$ and $|\beta| \leq 1 (\beta \neq -1)$. If the inequality*

$$|\beta| + \frac{1}{|\gamma|}\left(\frac{59}{2}|\eta| + \frac{2}{3}|\zeta|\right) \leqq 1$$

holds, then the function

$$\left[6^\eta 3^\zeta \gamma \int_0^\rho t^{-3\eta-3\zeta+\gamma-1}\left(te^t - 2e^t + t + 2\right)^\eta \left(2e^t - t^2 - 2t - 2\right)^\zeta dt\right]^{1/\gamma}$$

is in the class $\mathcal{S}$.

From Theorem 3 with $n = 1, \xi_1 = 1$ and $\varrho = 1/2$, we can get result below.

Corollary 3. *Let η and ζ be complex numbers such that*

$$\frac{59}{4}|\eta| + \frac{2}{3}|\zeta| \leqq 1.$$

Then the function

$$\int_0^\rho t^{-\zeta}\left(e^{t/2}\right)^\eta \left(2e^{t/2} - 2\right)^\zeta dt$$

is convex of order δ given by

$$\delta = 1 - \frac{59}{4}|\eta| - \frac{2}{3}|\zeta|.$$

Let $n = 1, \xi_1 = 3$ and $\varrho = 1$ in the Theorem 3, then we get following result.

Corollary 4. *Let η and ζ be complex numbers such that*

$$0 < \frac{59}{2}|\eta| + \frac{2}{3}|\zeta| \leqq 1.$$

Then the function

$$6^\eta 3^\zeta \int_0^\rho t^{-3\eta-3\zeta}\left(te^t - 2e^t + t + 2\right)^\eta \left(2e^t - t^2 - 2t - 2\right)^\zeta dt$$

is convex of order δ given by

$$\delta = 1 - \frac{59}{2}|\eta| - \frac{2}{3}|\zeta|.$$

4. Univalence and Convexity Conditions for the Integral Operator in (6)

In this section, we investigate the univalence and convexity properties for the integral operator defined by (6).

Theorem 4. *Let $v = 1, 2, \ldots, n$, $\xi_v > -1$, $\varrho > 0$ and $2\varrho - 1 < \xi_v$. Also, let β, η_v and ζ_v be in $\mathbb{C}$ such that*

$$|\beta| \leq 1 (\beta \neq -1) \text{ and } \Re\left(1 + \sum_{v=1}^{n} \eta_v\right) > 0.$$

Assume that these numbers satisfy the following inequality:

$$|\beta| + \frac{1}{|1 + \sum_{v=1}^{n} \eta_v|} \sum_{v=1}^{n} \left[|\eta_v| \frac{(\xi+1)^2}{(\xi - \varrho + 1)(\xi - 2\varrho + 1)} + |\zeta_v| \left(\frac{\xi + 1}{\xi - \varrho + 1} \right)^2 \right] \leqq 1,$$

where $\xi = \min\{\xi_1, \xi_2, \ldots, \xi_n\}$. Then the function $\mathcal{K}^{\xi_1,\xi_2,\ldots,\xi_n;\varrho}_{\eta_1,\eta_2,\ldots,\eta_n;\zeta_1,\zeta_2,\ldots,\zeta_n;n}$ defined by (6) is in the class $\mathcal{S}$.

Proof. Let us define the functions ψ by

$$\psi(\rho) = \int_0^\rho \prod_{v=1}^{n} \left(\mathbb{E}_{\xi_v,\varrho_v}(t)\right)^{\eta_v} \left(e^{\mathbb{E}_{\xi_v,\varrho_v}(t)}\right)^{\zeta_v} dt. \tag{25}$$

Then $\psi(0) = \psi'(0) - 1 = 0$. Differentiating both sides of (25) logarithmically, we get

$$\frac{\rho\psi''(\rho)}{\psi'(\rho)} = \sum_{v=1}^{n} \eta_v \left(\frac{\rho \mathbb{E}'_{\xi_v,\varrho}(\rho)}{\mathbb{E}_{\xi_v,\varrho}(\rho)} \right) + \sum_{v=1}^{n} \zeta_v \left(\rho \mathbb{E}'_{\xi_v,\varrho}(\rho) \right)$$

and, from (11) and (12) in Lemma 3, we obtain

$$\begin{aligned}\left|\frac{\rho\psi''(\rho)}{\psi'(\rho)}\right| &\leqq \sum_{v=1}^{n}\left(|\eta_v|\left|\frac{\rho\mathbb{E}'_{\xi_v,\varrho}(\rho)}{\mathbb{E}_{\xi_v,\varrho}(\rho)}\right| + |\zeta_v|\left|\rho\mathbb{E}'_{\xi_v,\varrho}(\rho)\right|\right)\\ &\leqq \sum_{v=1}^{n}\left[|\eta_v|\frac{(\xi_v+1)^2}{(\xi_v-\varrho+1)(\xi_v-2\varrho+1)} + |\zeta_v|\left(\frac{\xi_v+1}{\xi_v-\varrho+1}\right)^2\right]\\ &\leqq \sum_{v=1}^{n}\left[|\eta_v|\frac{(\xi+1)^2}{(\xi-\varrho+1)(\xi-2\varrho+1)} + |\zeta_v|\left(\frac{\xi+1}{\xi-\varrho+1}\right)^2\right].\end{aligned} \tag{26}$$

$$(\rho\in\mathbb{D};\xi,\xi_v > 2\varrho-1,(v=1,2,\ldots,n)).$$

Here, since the functions

$$\Theta_3,\Theta_4 : (2\varrho-1,\infty)\longrightarrow\mathbb{R},$$

defined by

$$\Theta_3(x) = \frac{(x+1)^2}{(x-\varrho+1)(x-2\varrho+1)} \text{ and } \Theta_4(x) = \left(\frac{x+1}{x-\varrho+1}\right)^2,$$

are decreasing, the inequalities

$$\frac{(\xi_v+1)^2}{(\xi_v-\varrho+1)(\xi_v-2\varrho+1)} < \frac{(\xi+1)^2}{(\xi-\varrho+1)(\xi-2\varrho+1)}$$

and

$$\left(\frac{\xi_v+1}{\xi_v-\varrho+1}\right)^2 < \left(\frac{\xi+1}{\xi-\varrho+1}\right)^2 \tag{27}$$

holds. Thus, we have

$$\begin{aligned}&\left|\beta|\rho|^{2(1+\sum_{v=1}^{n}\eta_v)} + \left(1-|\rho|^{2(1+\sum_{v=1}^{n}\eta_v)}\right)\frac{\rho\psi''(\rho)}{(1+\sum_{v=1}^{n}\eta_v)\psi'(\rho)}\right|\\ &\leq |\beta| + \left|\frac{\rho\psi''(\rho)}{(1+\sum_{v=1}^{n}\eta_v)\psi'(\rho)}\right|\\ &\leq |\beta| + \frac{1}{|1+\sum_{v=1}^{n}\eta_v|}\sum_{v=1}^{n}\left[|\eta_v|\frac{(\xi+1)^2}{(\xi-\varrho+1)(\xi-2\varrho+1)} + |\zeta_v|\left(\frac{\xi+1}{\xi-\varrho+1}\right)^2\right]\\ &\leq 1.\end{aligned} \tag{28}$$

Using Lemma 1 with

$$\alpha = 1 + \sum_{v=1}^{n}\eta_v,$$

the inequality (28) imply that the function $\mathcal{K}^{\xi_1,\xi_2,\ldots,\xi_n;\varrho}_{\eta_1,\eta_2,\ldots,\eta_n;\zeta_1,\zeta_2,\ldots,\zeta_n;n} \in \mathcal{S}$. □

Theorem 5. *Let the parameters ϱ, η_v, ξ_v and ζ_v $(v=1,2,\ldots,n)$ be as in Theorem 4. Suppose that $\xi = \min\{\xi_1,\xi_2,\ldots,\xi_n\}$ and that the following inequality holds true:*

$$\sum_{v=1}^{n}\left[|\eta_v|\frac{(\xi+1)^2}{(\xi-\varrho+1)(\xi-2\varrho+1)} + |\zeta_v|\left(\frac{\xi+1}{\xi-\varrho+1}\right)^2\right] \leqq 1.$$

Then the function $\mathcal{K}^{\xi_1,\xi_2,\ldots,\xi_n;\varrho}_{\eta_1,\eta_2,\ldots,\eta_n;\zeta_1,\zeta_2,\ldots,\zeta_n;n}$ defined by (6) is in the normalized univalent function class $\mathcal{S}$.

Proof. Let us consider the function ψ as in (25). Therefore, from (26) and hypothesis of theorem we can easily see that

$$\begin{aligned}&\left(1-|\rho|^2\right)\left|\frac{\rho\psi''(\rho)}{\psi'(\rho)}\right| \\ &\leqq \sum_{v=1}^{n}\left[|\eta_v|\frac{(\xi+1)^2}{(\xi-\varrho+1)(\xi-2\varrho+1)}+|\zeta_v|\left(\frac{\xi+1}{\xi-\varrho+1}\right)^2\right] \\ &\leq 1.\end{aligned} \tag{29}$$

By Lemma 2, with $\varpi = 1$ and $\alpha = 1 + \sum_{v=1}^{n} \eta_v$, the inequality (29) imply that the function $\mathcal{K}^{\xi_1,\xi_2,\ldots,\xi_n;\varrho}_{\eta_1,\eta_2,\ldots,\eta_n;\zeta_1,\zeta_2,\ldots,\zeta_n;n} \in \mathcal{S}$. □

Theorem 6. *Let $v = 1,2,\ldots,n$, $\xi_v > -1$, $\varrho > 0$ and $2\varrho - 1 < \xi_v$. Also, let η_v and ζ_v be in $\mathbb{C}$ such that*

$$\Re\left(1+\sum_{v=1}^{n}\eta_v\right) > 0.$$

Moreover, suppose that the following inequality holds true:

$$0 < \sum_{v=1}^{n}\left[|\eta_v|\frac{(\xi+1)^2}{(\xi-\varrho+1)(\xi-2\varrho+1)}+|\zeta_v|\left(\frac{\xi+1}{\xi-\varrho+1}\right)^2\right] \leqq 1,$$

where $\xi = \min\{\xi_1,\xi_2,\ldots,\xi_n\}$. Then the function $\mathcal{K}^{\xi_1,\xi_2,\ldots,\xi_n;\varrho}_{\eta_1,\eta_2,\ldots,\eta_n;\zeta_1,\zeta_2,\ldots,\zeta_n;n}$ defined by (6), is convex of order δ given by

$$\delta = 1-\sum_{v=1}^{n}\left[|\eta_v|\frac{(\xi+1)^2}{(\xi-\varrho+1)(\xi-2\varrho+1)}+|\zeta_v|\left(\frac{\xi+1}{\xi-\varrho+1}\right)^2\right].$$

Proof. By using (26) we conclude that

$$\begin{aligned}\left|\frac{\rho\psi''(\rho)}{\psi'(\rho)}\right| &\leqq \sum_{v=1}^{n}\left[|\eta_v|\left|\frac{\rho\mathbb{E}'_{\xi_v,\varrho}(\rho)}{\mathbb{E}_{\xi_v,\varrho}(\rho)}\right|+|\zeta_v|\left|z\mathbb{E}'_{\xi_v,\varrho}(\rho)\right|\right] \\ &\leqq \sum_{v=1}^{n}\left[|\eta_v|\frac{(\xi+1)^2}{(\xi-\varrho+1)(\xi-2\varrho+1)}+|\zeta_v|\left(\frac{\xi+1}{\xi-\varrho+1}\right)^2\right] \\ &= 1-\delta.\end{aligned}$$

This show that, the function ψ is convex of order

$$\delta = 1-\sum_{v=1}^{n}\left[|\eta_v|\frac{(\xi+1)^2}{(\xi-\varrho+1)(\xi-2\varrho+1)}+|\zeta_v|\left(\frac{\xi+1}{\xi-\varrho+1}\right)^2\right].$$

□

From Theorem 4 with $n = 1, \xi_1 = 2$ and $\varrho = 1/2$, we can get the following result.

Corollary 5. *Let β, η and ζ be in $\mathbb{C}$ such that $\Re(1+\eta) > 0$ and $|\beta| \leq 1 (\beta \neq -1)$. If these numbers satisfy the inequality:*

$$|\beta| + \frac{1}{|1+\eta|}\left(\frac{9}{5}|\eta| + \frac{36}{25}|\zeta|\right) \leqq 1,$$

then the function

$$\left[2^{\eta}(1+\eta)\int_0^{\rho}\left(\frac{4\left(2e^{t/2}-t-2\right)}{t}\right)^{\eta}e^{\frac{4\zeta\left(2e^{t/2}-t-2\right)}{t}}dt\right]^{1/(1+\eta)} \tag{30}$$

is in the class $\mathcal{S}$.

Example 2. *From Corollary 5 with* $\eta=1$ *and* $\zeta=1/8$, *we have*

$$\hbar_2(\rho)=4\left[\int_0^{\rho}\left(\frac{2e^{t/2}-t-2}{t}\right)e^{\frac{2e^{t/2}-t-2}{2t}}dt\right]^{1/2}\in\mathcal{S}.$$

In reality, by a simple calculation, we get

$$1+\frac{\rho\hbar_2''(\rho)}{\hbar_2'(\rho)}+\frac{\rho\hbar_2'(\rho)}{\hbar_2(\rho)}=1+\frac{2e^{\rho}(\rho-2)+e^{\rho/2}(\rho^2-4\rho+8)+2\rho-4}{2\rho(2e^{\rho/2}-\rho-2)}=g(\rho).$$

It also holds true that $\Re(g(\rho))>0$ *for all* $\rho\in\mathbb{D}$ *(see Figure 2). Therefore,* $\hbar_2$ *is a* $1/2-$*convex function [[35], Vol. I, p. 142]. Thus it follows from [[35], Vol. I, p. 142] that* $\hbar_2$ *belongs to the class* $\mathcal{S}$.

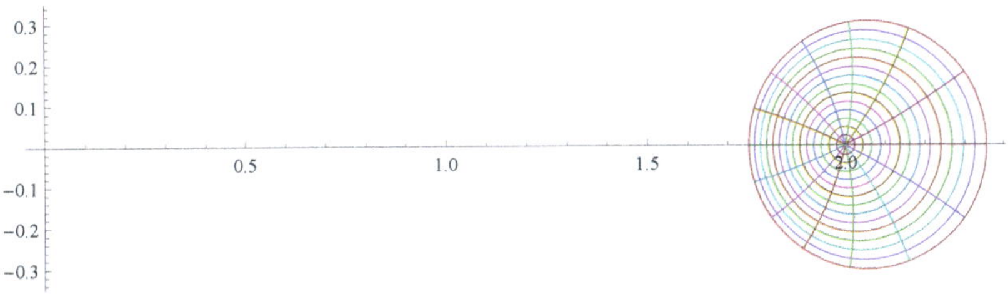

Figure 2. Image of $\mathbb{D}$ under g.

From Theorem 4 with $n=1,\xi_1=3$ and $\varrho=1$, we can get result below.

Corollary 6. *Let* β, η *and* ζ *be in* $\mathbb{C}$ *such that* $\Re(1+\eta)>0$ *and* $|\beta|\leq 1(\beta\neq -1)$. *If these numbers satisfy the follwing inequality*

$$|\beta|+\frac{1}{|1+\eta|}\left(\frac{8}{3}|\eta|+\frac{16}{9}|\zeta|\right)\leqq 1,$$

then the function

$$\left[3^{\eta}(1+\eta)\int_0^{\rho}\left(\frac{2e^{t}-t^2-2t-2}{t^2}\right)^{\eta}e^{\zeta\left(\frac{6e^{t}-3t^2-6t-6}{t^2}\right)}dt\right]^{1/(1+\eta)} \tag{31}$$

is in the class $\mathcal{S}$.

From Theorem 6 with $n=1,\xi_1=2$ and $\varrho=1/2$, we can get the following result.

Corollary 7. *Let* η *and* ζ *be a complex numbers such that*

$$\Re(1+\eta)>0 \text{ and } 0<\frac{9}{5}|\eta|+\frac{36}{25}|\zeta|\leqq 1.$$

Then the function defined by (30) is convex of order δ given by

$$\delta = 1 - \frac{9}{5}|\eta| - \frac{36}{25}|\zeta|.$$

From Theorem 6 with $n = 1, \xi_1 = 3$ and $\varrho = 1$, we can get the following result.

Corollary 8. *Let η and ζ be a complex numbers such that*

$$\Re(1+\eta) > 0 \text{ and } 0 < \frac{8}{3}|\eta| + \frac{16}{9}|\zeta| \leqq 1.$$

Then the function defined by (31) is convex of order δ given by

$$\delta = 1 - \frac{8}{3}|\eta| - \frac{16}{9}|\zeta|.$$

5. Univalence and Convexity Conditions for the Integral Operator in (7)

In this section, we derive the univalence and convexity results for the integral operator defined by (7).

Theorem 7. *Let $v = 1, 2, \ldots, n$, $\xi_v > -1$, $\varrho > 0$ and $\left(2+\sqrt{2}\right)\varrho - 1 < \xi_v$. Also, let γ, β, η_v and ζ_v be in $\mathbb{C}$ such that*

$$\Re(\gamma) > 0, |\beta| \leq 1 (\beta \neq -1).$$

Assume that these numbers satisfy the following inequality:

$$|\beta| + \frac{1}{|\gamma|}\left\{\sum_{v=1}^{n}|\eta_v|\frac{(\xi-\varrho+1)^3 + 2\varrho(\xi+1)^2}{(\xi-\varrho+1)^2 + (\varrho-1)^2 - (2\xi\varrho+1)} + \sum_{v=1}^{n}|\zeta_v|\left(\frac{\xi+1}{\xi-\varrho+1}\right)^2\right\} \leqq 1,$$

where $\xi = \min\{\xi_1, \xi_2, \ldots, \xi_n\}$. Then the function $\mathcal{L}^{\xi_1,\xi_2,\ldots,\xi_n;\varrho}_{\eta_1,\eta_2,\ldots,\eta_n;\zeta_1,\zeta_2,\ldots,\zeta_n;n;\gamma}$ defined by (7) is in the class $\mathcal{S}$.

Proof. Let us define the function ϕ by

$$\phi(\rho) := \mathcal{L}^{\xi_1,\xi_2,\ldots,\xi_n;\varrho}_{\eta_1,\eta_2,\ldots,\eta_n;\zeta_1,\zeta_2,\ldots,\zeta_n;n;1}(\rho) = \int_0^\rho \prod_{v=1}^{n}\left(\mathbb{E}'_{\xi_v,\varrho}(t)\right)^{\eta_v}\left(e^{\mathbb{E}_{\xi_v,\varrho}(t)}\right)^{\zeta_v} dt, \tag{32}$$

so that, obviously,

$$\phi'(\rho) = \prod_{v=1}^{n}\left(\mathbb{E}'_{\xi_v,\varrho}(\rho)\right)^{\eta_v}\left(e^{\mathbb{E}_{\xi_v,\varrho}(\rho)}\right)^{\zeta_v} \tag{33}$$

and $\phi(\rho) = \phi'(\rho) - 1 = 0$.

Now we differentiate (33) logarithmically and multiply by ρ, we obtain

$$\frac{\rho\phi''(\rho)}{\phi'(\rho)} = \sum_{v=1}^{n}\eta_v\frac{\rho\mathbb{E}''_{\xi_v,\varrho}(\rho)}{\mathbb{E}'_{\xi_v,\varrho}(\rho)} + \sum_{v=1}^{n}\zeta_v\rho\mathbb{E}'_{\xi_v,\varrho}(\rho).$$

Furthermore, by (11), (13), (23) and (27) we obtain

$$\left|\frac{\rho\phi''(\rho)}{\phi'(\rho)}\right| \leqq \sum_{v=1}^{n}\left(|\eta_v|\left|\frac{\rho\mathbb{E}''_{\xi_v,\varrho}(\rho)}{\mathbb{E}'_{\xi_v,\varrho}(\rho)}\right| + |\zeta_v|\left|\rho\mathbb{E}'_{\xi_v,\varrho}(\rho)\right|\right)$$
$$\leqq \sum_{v=1}^{n}\left[|\eta_v|\frac{(\xi_v-\varrho+1)^3+2\varrho(\xi_v+1)^2}{(\xi_v-\varrho+1)^2+(\varrho-1)^2-(2\xi_v\varrho+1)} + |\zeta_v|\left(\frac{\xi_v+1}{\xi_v-\varrho+1}\right)^2\right] \tag{34}$$
$$\leqq \sum_{v=1}^{n}\left[|\eta_v|\frac{(\xi-\varrho+1)^3+2\varrho(\xi+1)^2}{(\xi-\varrho+1)^2+(\varrho-1)^2-(2\xi\varrho+1)} + |\zeta_v|\left(\frac{\xi+1}{\xi-\varrho+1}\right)^2\right].$$

Hence, from (34) we have

$$\left|\beta|\rho|^{2\gamma} + \left(1-|\rho|^{2\gamma}\right)\frac{\rho\phi''(\rho)}{\gamma\phi'(\rho)}\right|$$
$$\leqq |\beta| + \left|\frac{\rho\phi''(\rho)}{\phi'(\rho)}\right|$$
$$\leqq |\beta| + \frac{1}{|\gamma|}\left\{\sum_{v=1}^{n}|\eta_v|\frac{(\xi-\varrho+1)^3+2\varrho(\xi+1)^2}{(\xi-\varrho+1)^2+(\varrho-1)^2-(2\xi\varrho+1)} + \sum_{v=1}^{n}|\zeta_v|\left(\frac{\xi+1}{\xi-\varrho+1}\right)^2\right\}$$
$$\leqq 1,$$

which, in view of Lemma 1, implies that $\mathcal{L}^{\xi_1,\xi_2,\ldots,\xi_n,\varrho}_{\eta_1,\eta_2,\ldots,\eta_n;\zeta_1,\zeta_2,\ldots,\zeta_n;n;\gamma} \in \mathcal{S}$. □

Theorem 8. *Let the parameters $\varrho, \gamma, \eta_v, \xi_v$ and ζ_v $(v = 1, 2, \ldots, n)$ be as in Theorem 7. Suppose that $\xi = \min\{\xi_1, \xi_2, \ldots, \xi_n\}$ and that the following inequality holds true:*

$$\Re(\gamma) \geqq \left\{\sum_{v=1}^{n}|\eta_v|\frac{(\xi-\varrho+1)^3+2\varrho(\xi+1)^2}{(\xi-\varrho+1)^2+(\varrho-1)^2-(2\xi\varrho+1)} + \sum_{v=1}^{n}|\zeta_v|\left(\frac{\xi+1}{\xi-\varrho+1}\right)^2\right\}.$$

Then the function $\mathcal{L}^{\xi_1,\xi_2,\ldots,\xi_n;\varrho}_{\eta_1,\eta_2,\ldots,\eta_n;\zeta_1,\zeta_2,\ldots,\zeta_n;n;\gamma}$ defined by (7) is in the class $\mathcal{S}$.

Proof. By using (34) we obtain

$$\frac{1-|\rho|^{2\Re(\gamma)}}{\Re(\gamma)}\left|\frac{\rho\phi''(\rho)}{\phi'(\rho)}\right|$$
$$\leqq \frac{1-|\rho|^{2\Re(\gamma)}}{\Re(\gamma)}\left\{\sum_{v=1}^{n}|\eta_v|\frac{(\xi-\varrho+1)^3+2\varrho(\xi+1)^2}{(\xi-\varrho+1)^2+(\varrho-1)^2-(2\xi\varrho+1)} + \sum_{v=1}^{n}|\zeta_v|\left(\frac{\xi+1}{\xi-\varrho+1}\right)^2\right\}$$
$$\leqq \frac{1}{\Re(\gamma)}\left\{\sum_{v=1}^{n}|\eta_v|\frac{(\xi-\varrho+1)^3+2\varrho(\xi+1)^2}{(\xi-\varrho+1)^2+(\varrho-1)^2-(2\xi\varrho+1)} + \sum_{v=1}^{n}|\zeta_v|\left(\frac{\xi+1}{\xi-\varrho+1}\right)^2\right\}$$
$$\leqq 1,$$

which, in view of Lemma 2, implies that $\mathcal{L}^{\xi_1,\xi_2,\ldots,\xi_n;\varrho}_{\eta_1,\eta_2,\ldots,\eta_n;\zeta_1,\zeta_2,\ldots,\zeta_n;n;\gamma} \in \mathcal{S}$. □

Theorem 9. *Let $v = 1, 2, \ldots, n$, $\xi_v > -1$, $\varrho > 0$ and $\left(2+\sqrt{2}\right)\varrho - 1 < \xi_v$. Also, let γ, η_v and ζ_v be in $\mathbb{C}$ such that $\Re(\gamma) > 0$. Assume that these numbers satisfy the following inequality:*

$$0 < \sum_{v=1}^{n}|\eta_v|\frac{(\xi-\varrho+1)^3+2\varrho(\xi+1)^2}{(\xi-\varrho+1)^2+(\varrho-1)^2-(2\xi\varrho+1)} + \sum_{v=1}^{n}|\zeta_v|\left(\frac{\xi+1}{\xi-\varrho+1}\right)^2 \leqq 1,$$

where $\xi = \min\{\xi_1, \xi_2, \ldots, \xi_n\}$. *Then the function* $\mathcal{L}^{\xi_1,\xi_2,\ldots,\xi_n;\varrho}_{\eta_1,\eta_2,\ldots,\eta_n;\zeta_1,\zeta_2,\ldots,\zeta_n;n;1}$, *defined by (7) with* $\gamma = 1$, *is convex of order* δ *given by*

$$\delta = 1 - \sum_{v=1}^{n} |\eta_v| \frac{(\xi - \varrho + 1)^3 + 2\varrho(\xi + 1)^2}{(\xi - \varrho + 1)^2 + (\varrho - 1)^2 - (2\xi\varrho + 1)} - \sum_{v=1}^{n} |\zeta_v| \left(\frac{\xi + 1}{\xi - \varrho + 1}\right)^2.$$

Proof. From (34) and hypothesis of theorem, we obtain

$$\begin{aligned} \left|\frac{\rho\phi''(\rho)}{\phi'(\rho)}\right| &\leqq \sum_{v=1}^{n} |\eta_v| \frac{(\xi - \varrho + 1)^3 + 2\varrho(\xi + 1)^2}{(\xi - \varrho + 1)^2 + (\varrho - 1)^2 - (2\xi\varrho + 1)} + \sum_{v=1}^{n} |\zeta_v| \left(\frac{\xi + 1}{\xi - \varrho + 1}\right)^2 \\ &= 1 - \delta. \end{aligned}$$

Therefore, the function ϕ is convex of order δ. □

From Theorem 7 with $n = 1, \xi_1 = 1$ and $\varrho = 1/2$, we can get following result.

Corollary 9. *Let* γ, β, η *and* ζ *be in* $\mathbb{C}$ *such that* $\Re(\gamma) > 0, |\beta| \leq 1 (\beta \neq -1)$. *If these numbers satisfy the inequality:*

$$|\beta| + \frac{1}{|\gamma|}\left(\frac{59}{4}|\eta| + \frac{16}{9}|\zeta|\right) \leqq 1$$

then the function

$$\left[\gamma \int_0^{\rho} t^{\gamma-1} \left(e^{t/2}\right)^{\eta} \left(e^{2e^{t/2}-2}\right)^{\zeta} dt\right]^{1/\gamma}$$

is in the normalized univalent function class $\mathcal{S}$.

Example 3. *From Corollary 9 with* $\beta = 0, \gamma = 1, \eta = 0.01$ *and* $\zeta = 0.1$, *we obtain*

$$\hbar_3(\rho) = \int_0^{\rho} \left(e^{t/200}\right) \left(e^{\frac{e^{t/2}-1}{5}}\right) dt \in \mathcal{S}.$$

From Theorem 7 with $n = 1, \xi_1 = 3$ and $\varrho = 1$, we can get result below.

Corollary 10. *Let* γ, β, η *and* ζ *be in* $\mathbb{C}$ *such that* $\Re(\gamma) > 0$ *and* $\beta \neq -1$. *If these numbers satisfy the inequality*

$$|\beta| + \frac{1}{|\gamma|}\left(\frac{59}{2}|\eta| + \frac{16}{9}|\zeta|\right) \leqq 1$$

then the function

$$\left[6^{\eta}\gamma \int_0^{\rho} t^{-3\eta+\gamma-1} (te^t - 2e^t + t + 2)^{\eta} e^{3\zeta\left(\frac{2e^t - t^2 - 2t - 2}{t^2}\right)} dt\right]^{1/\gamma}$$

is in the normalized univalent function class $\mathcal{S}$.

From Theorem 9 with $n = 1, \xi_1 = 1$ and $\varrho = 1/2$, we have following result.

Corollary 11. *Let* η *and* ζ *be complex numbers such that*

$$\frac{59}{4}|\eta| + \frac{16}{9}|\zeta| \leqq 1.$$

Then the function

$$\int_0^{\rho} \left(e^{t/2}\right)^{\eta} \left(e^{2e^{t/2}-2}\right)^{\zeta} dt$$

is convex of order δ given by

$$\delta = 1 - \frac{59}{4}|\eta| - \frac{16}{9}|\zeta|.$$

From Theorem 9 with $n = 1, \xi_1 = 3$ and $\varrho = 1$, we have following result.

Corollary 12. *Let η and ζ be complex numbers such that*

$$\frac{59}{2}|\eta| + \frac{16}{9}|\zeta| \leqq 1.$$

Then the function

$$6^{\eta} \int_0^{\rho} t^{-3\eta} \left(te^t - 2e^t + t + 2\right)^{\eta} e^{3\zeta\left(\frac{2e^t - t^2 - 2t - 2}{t^2}\right)} dt$$

is convex of order δ given by

$$\delta = 1 - \frac{59}{2}|\eta| - \frac{16}{9}|\zeta|.$$

Example 4. *From Corollary 12 with $\eta = 0.01$ and $\zeta = 0.1$, we get*

$$\hbar_1(\rho) = 6^{1/100} \int_0^{\rho} t^{-3/100} \left(te^t - 2e^t + t + 2\right)^{1/100} e^{3\left(\frac{2e^t - t^2 - 2t - 2}{10t^2}\right)} dt$$

is convex of order $\delta = 949/1800$.

6. Conclusions

In the present investigation, we first introduced certain families of integral operators by using the Miller–Ross function which, in particular, plays a very important role in the study of pure and applied mathematical sciences. Therefore, it is important to know the geometric properties of special functions and their integral operators. For this reason, we aim to study the criteria for the univalence and convexity of these integral operators that are defined by using Miller–Ross functions. The various results, which we established in this paper, are believed to be new, and their importance is illustrated by several interesting consequences and examples together with the associated graphical illustrations.

Hopefully, the original results contained here would stimulate researchers' imagination and inspire them, just as all the operators introduced before in studies related to functions of a complex variable have done. Other geometric properties related to them could be investigated, and also they could prove useful in introducing special classes of functions based on those properties.

Author Contributions: Conceptualization, S.K., E.D. and L.-I.C.; methodology, S.K., E.D. and L.-I.C.; software, S.K., E.D. and L.-I.C.; validation, E.D. and L.-I.C.; formal analysis, S.K., E.D. and L.-I.C.; investigation, S.K., E.D. and L.-I.C.; resources, S.K., E.D. and L.-I.C.; data curation, S.K., E.D. and L.-I.C.; writing-original draft preparation, S.K., E.D. and L.-I.C.; writing-review and editing, S.K., E.D. and L.-I.C.; visualization, S.K., E.D. and L.-I.C.; supervision, E.D. and L.-I.C.; project administration, E.D. and L.-I.C.; funding acquisition, L.-I.C. All authors have read and agreed to the published version of the manuscript.

Funding: This research received no external funding.

Data Availability Statement: Not applicable.

Conflicts of Interest: The authors declare no conflict of interest.

References

1. Seenivasagan, N.; Breaz, D. Certain sufficient conditions for univalence. *General Math.* **2002**, *15*, 7–15.
2. Baricz, A.; Frasin, B.A. Univalence of integral operators involving Bessel functions. *Appl. Math. Lett.* **2002**, *23*, 371–376. [CrossRef]

3. Srivastava, H.M.; Deniz, E.; Orhan, H. Some general univalence criteria for a family of integral operators. *Appl. Math. Comput.* **2002**, *215*, 3696–3701. [CrossRef]
4. Breaz, D.; Breaz, N. Univalence conditions for certain integral operators. *Stud. Univ. Babeş-Bolyai Math.* **2002**, *47*, 9–15.
5. Breaz, D.; Owa, S.; Breaz, N. A new integral univalent operator. *Acta Univ. Apulensis Math. Inform.* **2002**, *16*, 11–16.
6. Kim, Y.J.; Merkes, E.P. On an integral of powers of a spirallike function. *Kyungpook Math. J.* **2002**, *12*, 249–252.
7. Pfaltzgraff, J.A. Univalence of the integral of $(f'(z))^{\lambda}$. *Bull. Lond. Math. Soc.* **2002**, *7*, 254–256. [CrossRef]
8. Pescar, V. Univalence of certain integral operators. *Acta Univ. Apulensis Math. Inform.* **2002**, *12*, 43–48.
9. Breaz, D.; Breaz, N. Univalence of an integral operator. *Mathematica* **2002**, *47*, 35–38.
10. Breaz, D.; Breaz, N.; Srivastava, H.M. An extension of the univalent condition for a family of integral operators. *Appl. Math. Lett.* **2002**, *22*, 41–44. [CrossRef]
11. Moldoveanu, S.; Pascu, N.N. Integral operators which preserve the univalence. *Mathematica* **2002**, *32*, 159–166.
12. Deniz, E.; Orhan, H.; Srivastava, H.M. Some sufficient conditions for univalence of certain families of integral operators involving generalized Bessel functions. *Taiwanese J. Math.* **2002**, *15*, 883–917.
13. Raza, M.; Noreen, S.; Malik, S.N. Geometric properties of integral operators defined by Bessel functions. *J. Inequal. Spec. Funct.* **2002**, *7*, 34–48.
14. Deniz, E. Convexity of integral operators involving generalized Bessel functions. *Integral Transform. Spec. Funct.* **2002**, *24*, 201–216. [CrossRef]
15. Al-Kharsani, H.A.; Al-Zahrani, A.M.; Al-Hajri, S.S.; Pogany, T.K. Univalence criteria for linear fractional differential operators associated with a generalized Bessel function. *Math. Commun.* **2002**, *21*, 171–188.
16. Srivastava, H.M.; Jan, R.; Jan, A.; Deebai, W.; Shutaywi, M. Fractional-calculus analysis of the transmission dynamics of the dengue infection. *Chaos* **2021**, *31*, 53130. [CrossRef]
17. Srivastava, H.M.; Owa, S. *Univalent Functions, Fractional Calculus, and Their Applications*; Halsted Press: Ultimo, Australia, 1989.
18. Miller, K.S.; Ross, B. *An Introduction to the Fractional Calculus and Fractional Differential Equations*; John Wiley and Sons: Hoboken, NJ, USA, 1993.
19. Sumer Eker, S.; Ece, S. Geometric Properties of the Miller–Ross Functions. *Iran. J. Sci. Technol. Trans. A Sci.* **2002**, *46*, 631–636. [CrossRef]
20. Şeker, B.; Sumer Eker, S.; Çekiç, B. On Subclasses of Analytic Functions Associated with Miller–Ross-Type Poisson Distribution Series. *Sahand Commun. Math. Anal.* **2002**, *19*, 69–79.
21. Kazımoğlu, S. Partial Sums of The Miller-Ross Function. *Turk. J. Sci.* **2021**, *6*, 167–173.
22. Kazımoğlu, S. Neighborhoods of Certain Classes of Analytic Functions Defined By Miller-Ross Function. *Caucasian J. Sci.* **2021**, *8*, 165–172. [CrossRef]
23. Arif, M.; Raza, M. Some properties of an integral operator defined by Bessel functions. *Acta Univ. Apulensis* **2002**, *26*, 69–74.
24. Frasin, B.A. Sufficient conditions for integral operator defined by Bessel functions. *J. Math. Inequal.* **2002**, *4*, 301–306. [CrossRef]
25. Mahmood, S.; Mahroz, S.; Rafiq, A.; Malik, S.N.; Raza, M. Convexity of Certain Integral Operators Defined by Struve Functions. *J. Funct. Spaces* **2018**, *2018*, 6327132. [CrossRef]
26. Mahmood, S.; Srivastava, H.M.; Malik, S.N.; Raza, M.; Shahzadi, N.; Zainab, S. A certain family of integral operators associated with the Struve functions. *Symmetry* **2002**, *11*, 463. [CrossRef]
27. Din, M.U.; Srivastava, H.M.; Raza, M. Univalence of certain integral operators involving generalized Struve functions. *Hacet. J. Math. Stat.* **2002**, *47*, 821–833.
28. Din, M.U.; Yalçın, S. Certain Geometric Properties Of Modified Lommel Functions. *Honam Math. J.* **2002**, *42*, 719–731.
29. Park, J.H.; Srivastava, H.M.; Cho, N.E. Univalence and convexity conditions for certain integral operators associated with the Lommel function of the first kind. *AIMS Math.* **2002**, *6*, 11380–11402. [CrossRef]
30. Srivastava, H.M.; Frasin, B.A.; Pescar, V. Univalence of integral operators involving Mittag–Leffler functions. *Appl. Math. Inform. Sci.* **2002**, *11*, 635–641. [CrossRef]
31. Oros, G.I. Study on new integral operators defined using confluent hypergeometric function. *Adv. Difference Equ.* **2002**, *2021*, 342. [CrossRef]
32. Raza, M.; Malik, S.N.; Xin, Q.; Din, M.U.; Cotirla, L.I. On Kudriasov Conditions for Univalence of Integral Operators Defined by Generalized Bessel Functions. *Mathematics* **2022**, *10*, 1361. [CrossRef]
33. Pescar, V. A new generalization of Ahlfor's and Becker's criterion of univalence. *Bull. Malaysian Math. Soc.* **2002**, *19*, 53–54.
34. Pascu, N.N. An Improvement of Becker's Univalence Criterion. In Proceedings of the Commemorative Session Simion Stoilow, Brasov, Romania, 1987; pp. 43–48.
35. Goodman, A.W. *Univalent Functions*; Mariner Publishing Company Incorporated: Tampa, FL, USA, 1983.

axioms

MDPI

Article

Faber Polynomial Coefficient Estimates for Bi-Close-to-Convex Functions Defined by the q-Fractional Derivative

Hari Mohan Srivastava [1,2,3,4,5], Isra Al-Shbeil [6,*], Qin Xin [7], Fairouz Tchier [8], Shahid Khan [9] and Sarfraz Nawaz Malik [10]

[1] Department of Mathematics and Statistics, University of Victoria, Victoria, BC V8W 3R4, Canada; harimsri@math.uvic.ca
[2] Department of Medical Research, China Medical University Hospital, China Medical University, Taichung 40402, Taiwan
[3] Center for Converging Humanities, Kyung Hee University, 26 Kyungheedae-ro, Dongdaemun-gu, Seoul 02447, Republic of Korea
[4] Department of Mathematics and Informatics, Azerbaijan University, 71 Jeyhun Hajibeyli Street, AZ1007 Baku, Azerbaijan
[5] Section of Mathematics, International Telematic University Uninettuno, I-00186 Rome, Italy
[6] Department of Mathematics, Faculty of Science, The University of Jordan, Amman 11942, Jordan
[7] Faculty of Science and Technology, University of the Faroe Islands, Vestarabryggja 15, FO 100 Torshavn, Faroe Islands, Denmark; qinx@setur.fo
[8] Mathematics Department, College of Science, King Saud University, P.O. Box 22452, Riyadh 11495, Saudi Arabia; ftchier@ksu.edu.sa
[9] Department of Mathematics, Abbottabad University of Science and Technology, Abbottabad 22500, Pakistan; shahidmath761@gmail.com
[10] Department of Mathematics, COMSATS University Islamabad, Wah Campus, Wah Cantt 47040, Pakistan; snmalik110@ciitwah.edu.pk or snmalik110@yahoo.com
* Correspondence: i.shbeil@ju.edu.jo

Abstract: By utilizing the concept of the q-fractional derivative operator and bi-close-to-convex functions, we define a new subclass of $\mathcal{A}$, where the class $\mathcal{A}$ contains normalized analytic functions in the open unit disk $\mathbb{E}$ and is invariant or symmetric under rotation. First, using the Faber polynomial expansion (FPE) technique, we determine the lth coefficient bound for the functions contained within this class. We provide a further explanation for the first few coefficients of bi-close-to-convex functions defined by the q-fractional derivative. We also emphasize upon a few well-known outcomes of the major findings in this article.

Keywords: quantum (or q-) calculus; analytic functions; q-derivative operator; bi-univalent functions; Faber polynomial expansions

Citation: Srivastava, H.M.; Al-Shbeil, I.; Xin, Q.; Tchier, F.; Khan, S.; Malik, S.N. Faber Polynomial Coefficient Estimates for Bi-Close-to-Convex Functions Defined by the q-Fractional Derivative. *Axioms* **2023**, *12*, 585. https://doi.org/10.3390/axioms12060585

Academic Editor: Georgia Irina Oros

Received: 3 April 2023
Revised: 28 April 2023
Accepted: 30 May 2023
Published: 13 June 2023

1. Introduction, Definitions and Motivation

Alexander [1] established the first integral operator in 1915, which he successfully applied in the investigation of analytical functions. This area of study of analytic functions, encompassing derivative and fractional derivative operators, has been a focus of ongoing research in geometric function theory of complex analysis. Several combinations of such operators are continually being developed [2,3]. Recent publications such as [4] provide an example of how important differential and integral fractional operators are in research. Recent research on differential and integral operators from a variety of angles, including quantum (or q-) calculus, has produced intriguing findings that have applications in other branches of physics and mathematics. Further investigation may reveal that such operators play a role in providing solutions to partial differential equations, since they have a role in the investigation of differential equations using functional analysis and operator theory. In his survey-cum-expository review study, Srivastava [5] highlights the intriguing operator applications that are emerging from such a methodology.

Many applications of the q-calculus can be found in both the field of mathematics and in other scientific disciplines such as numerical analysis, fractional calculus, special polynomials, analytic number theory and quantum group theory. Mathematicians and physicists are becoming interested in the large field of fractional calculus. The theory of analytical functions has been integrated with the theory of fractional calculus. The fractional differential equations are used in numerous mathematical models. In fact, nonlinear differential equations are considered to be a rival to fractional differential equations as a model (see, for example, Refs. [6–9]).

Researchers, who have created and examined a significant number of new analytic function subclasses in the field of geometric function theory (GFT), have extensively used the q-calculus. In the year 1909, Jackson [10,11] is to be acknowledged for the formal beginning of q-calculus because he provided the first definitions of the q-integrals and the q-derivatives. He proposed the q-calculus operator and the q-difference operator (D_q), which are extensions of the derivative and integral operators. Several mathematical and scientific disciplines, including mechanics, the theory of relativity, control theory, basic hypergeometric functions, combinatorics, number theory, and statistics, use the q-calculus. Ismail et al. [12] established the generalized version of the starlike functions, which was one of the very first contributions of the use of q-calculus in GFT. They gave this newly created class the name "class of q-starlike functions" because they defined it by using q-derivatives. It took a while for this area of research to advance, but the recent works of Anastassiu and Gal [13,14] based upon their complex operators research with their separate q-generalizations happen to provide a fine addition. Those were termed as q-Gauss–Weierstrass and q-Picard singular integral operators, respectively (see also the work of Mason [15] on the solution of linear q-difference equations with entire-function coefficients). By utilizing fundamental q-hypergeometric functions, Srivastava [5] built a solid foundation for the use of the q-calculus in GFT. Aral and Gupta [16–18] provided a further set of contributions by using q-beta functions. Aldweby et al. [19,20] established the q-analogue of certain operators by utilizing the convolution techniques for analytic functions. Additionally, they explored the composition of q-operators in the context of analytic functions that involve the q-version of hypergeometric functions. The subject of q-calculus has drawn the interest of several researchers in recent years, and the papers [21–23] contain a variety of new observations. Further current details on convex and starlike functions with regard to their symmetric points can be found in [24,25] and the references therein. As a consequence of ongoing research on differential and integral operators, we in this study present a novel fractional differential operator. With the aid of this operator, we intend to introduce a new family of analytic functions which are geometrically close-to-convex.

The class $\mathcal{A}$ contains all functions h which are analytic in $\mathbb{E}$ and which also satisfy the normalization condition given by

$$h(0) = 0 \quad \text{and} \quad h'(0) = 1,$$

where

$$\mathbb{E} = \{z : z \in \mathbb{C} \quad \text{and} \quad |z| < 1\},$$

$\mathbb{C}$ being the set of complex numbers. Thus, clearly, each function $h \in \mathcal{A}$ can be expressed as follows:

$$h(z) = \sum_{l=1}^{\infty} a_l z^l \qquad (z \in \mathbb{E};\ a_1 := 1). \tag{1}$$

Let the class $\mathcal{S} \subset \mathcal{A}$ consist of univalent functions in $\mathbb{E}$. The commonly known subclasses of $\mathcal{S}$ are the classes of convex, starlike and close-to-convex functions, which are denoted by and defined, respectively, as follows:

$$\mathcal{C} := \left\{ h : h \in \mathcal{S} \quad \text{and} \quad \Re\left(\frac{\left(zh'(z)\right)'}{h'(z)} \right) > 0 \right\} \qquad (z \in \mathbb{E}),$$

$$\mathcal{S}^* := \left\{ h : h \in \mathcal{S} \quad \text{and} \quad \Re\left(\frac{zh'(z)}{h(z)}\right) > 0 \right\} \qquad (z \in \mathbb{E})$$

and

$$\mathcal{K} := \left\{ h : h \in \mathcal{S},\, g \in \mathcal{S}^* \quad \text{and} \quad \Re\left(\frac{zh'(z)}{g(z)}\right) > 0 \right\} \qquad (z \in \mathbb{E})$$

or, equivalently,

$$\mathcal{K} := \left\{ h : h \in \mathcal{A},\, g \in \mathcal{C} \quad \text{and} \quad \Re\left(\frac{h'(z)}{g'(z)}\right) > 0 \right\} \qquad (z \in \mathbb{E})$$

For $h_1, h_2 \in \mathcal{A}$, h_1 is said to be subordinate to h_2 in $\mathbb{E}$, denoted by

$$h_1(z) \prec h_2(z) \qquad (z \in \mathbb{E}),$$

if we have a Schwarz function ℓ in $\mathbb{E}$ such that $\ell \in \mathcal{A}$, $|\ell(z)| < 1$ and $\ell(0) = 0$, and

$$h_1(z) = h_2(\ell(z)) \qquad (z \in \mathbb{E}).$$

The image of $\mathbb{E}$ under every $h \in \mathcal{A}$ contains a disk of radius $\frac{1}{4}$ and each function $h \in \mathcal{S}$ has an inverse $h^{-1} = \gamma$ given by

$$\gamma(h(z)) = z \qquad (z \in \mathbb{E})$$

and

$$h(\gamma(\vartheta)) = \vartheta \qquad (|\vartheta| < r_0(h)),$$

where $r_0(h)$ is the radius of the disk with $r_0(h) \geqq \frac{1}{4}$. The inverse function $\gamma(\vartheta)$ has the following series expansion:

$$\gamma(\vartheta) = \vartheta - a_2\vartheta^2 + (2a_2^2 - a_3)\vartheta^3 - (5a_2^3 - 5a_2a_3 + a_4)\vartheta^4 + \cdots. \tag{2}$$

If both h and h^{-1} are in the univalent function class $\mathcal{S}$, then the function h is called bi-univalent in $\mathbb{E}$. The set of bi-univalent functions in $\mathbb{E}$ is denoted by Σ. In GFT, the issue of finding bounds on the coefficients has always been important. Many characteristics of analytic functions, such as univalency, rate of growth and distortion, can be affected by the size of their coefficients. The pioneering work, which actually revived the study of analytic and bi-univalent functions, was presented in the year 2010 by Srivastava et al. [26]. In 1914, for $0 \leqq \alpha < 1$, Hamidi and Jahangiri [27] defined the class of bi-close-to-convex functions and investigated some useful results by using the Faber polynomial expansion technique. To overcome some the aforementioned problems, several researchers employed various other techniques. Finding coefficient estimates of functions belonging to Σ had already attracted a lot of interest, just like for univalent functions. For $h \in \Sigma$, Levin [28] demonstrated that $|a_2| < 1.51$ and after that, Branan and Clunie [29] contributed the improvement of $|a_2|$ and demonstrated that $|a_2| \leqq \sqrt{2}$. Furthermore, for $h \in \Sigma$, Netanyahu [30] proved that (see, for details, Refs. [31,32])

$$\max|a_2| = \frac{4}{3}.$$

In many of these efforts, only non-sharp estimates of the initial coefficients were derived. In [33], Alharbi et al. investigated two new subclasses of Σ by using the Sălăgean-Erdélyi-Kober operator and problems related to coefficients, such as the Fekete-Szegä problem, were also investigated. Recently, Oros et al. [34] defined some new subfamilies of bi-univalent functions and found the coefficient estimates for these subfamilies.

Our current work is primarily driven by the discovery of numerous intriguing and productive applications of special polynomials in GFT. One of these is the well-known Faber polynomial that has recently gained immense importance in the study of mathematics and other scientific disciplines. Faber [35] introduced Faber polynomials and these polynomials have important uses in many areas of mathematics, especially in GFT of Complex Analysis. Schiffer [36] discussed the applications of the Faber polynomials in 1948 (see also [37]). Following that, Pommerenke [38–40] significantly added to the facts that were already known about the structure of the Faber polynomial expansion (FPE). By using the FPE technique and defining subclasses of the bi-univalent function class Σ, Hamidi and Jahangiri [27,41] found some new coefficient bounds. Furthermore, many authors (see, for example, Refs. [42–51]) applied the technique of Faber polynomials and determined some interesting results for bi-univalent functions (see, for details, Ref. [44]).

For understanding the concepts of this article, it is now necessary to review certain fundamental definitions and notions relevant to the q-calculus.

Definition 1. *The q-shifted factorial $(\varkappa;q)_l$ is presented as*

$$(\varkappa;q)_l = \prod_{j=0}^{l-1}\left(1-\varkappa q^j\right) \qquad (l \in \mathbb{N};\ \varkappa, q \in \mathbb{C}), \tag{3}$$

where, as usual, $\mathbb{C}$ is the set of complex numbers. If $\varkappa \neq q^{-m}$ $(m \in \mathbb{N}_0 := \{0,1,2,3,\cdots\})$, then

$$(\varkappa;q)_\infty = \prod_{j=0}^{\infty}\left(1-\varkappa q^j\right) \qquad (\varkappa \in \mathbb{C};\ |q|<1). \tag{4}$$

In the case when $\varkappa \neq 0$ and $q \geqq 1$, $(\varkappa;q)_\infty$ diverges. Therefore, when we take $(\varkappa;q)_\infty$, then we will assume that $|q|<1$.

Remark 1. *For $q \to 1-$ in $(\varkappa;q)_l$, we have*

$$(\varkappa;q)_l = (\varkappa)_l = \prod_{j=0}^{l-1}(\varkappa+j) \qquad (l \in \mathbb{N}).$$

The q-factorial $[l]_q!$ is defined by

$$[n]_q! = \prod_{l=1}^{n}[l]_q \qquad (l \in \mathbb{N}), \tag{5}$$

where the q-number $[l]_q$ is given below:

$$[l]_q = \frac{1-q^l}{1-q} \qquad (l \in \mathbb{N}).$$

If $l=0$, then $[l]_q! = 1$.

Definition 2. *The $(\varkappa;q)_l$ in* (3) *can be given more precisely in the form of the q-gamma function as follows:*

$$\Gamma_q(\varkappa) = \frac{(1-q)^{1-\alpha}(q;q)_\infty}{(q^a;q)_\infty} \qquad (0<q<1),$$

or

$$(q^\varkappa;q)_l = \frac{\left(1-q^l\right)\Gamma_q(\varkappa+l)}{\Gamma_q(\varkappa)} \qquad (l \in \mathbb{N}).$$

Definition 3 (Jackson [10])**.** *For $h \in \mathcal{A}$, the q-difference operator is defined by*

$$D_q h(z) = \frac{h(z)-h(qz)}{z(1-q)} \qquad (z \in \mathbb{E}).$$

We recall that for $l \in \mathbb{N}$ and $z \in \mathbb{E}$, we have

$$D_q(z^l) = [l]_q z^{l-1} \qquad \text{and} \qquad D_q\left(\sum_{l=1}^{\infty} a_l z^l\right) = \sum_{l=1}^{\infty} [l]_q a_l z^{l-1},$$

where the q-number $[l]_q$ is already given along with (5).

The q-generalized Pochhammer symbol is expressed as follows:

$$[\varkappa]_{q,l} = \frac{\Gamma_q(\varkappa + l)}{\Gamma_q(\varkappa)} \qquad (l \in \mathbb{N};\ \varkappa \in \mathbb{C}).$$

Remark 2. *If $q \to 1-$, then*

$$[\varkappa]_{q,l} = (\varkappa)_l = \frac{\Gamma(\varkappa + l)}{\Gamma(\varkappa)}.$$

Definition 4 (see [52]). *For $\varrho > 0$, the fractional q-integral operator is defined by*

$$I^{\varrho}_{q,z} h(z) = \frac{1}{\Gamma_q(\varrho)} \int_0^z (z - tq)_{\varrho - 1}\, h(t)\, d_q(t), \tag{6}$$

where $(z - tq)_{\varrho-1}$ is given by

$$(z - tq)_{\varrho - 1} = z^{\varrho - 1}\,{}_1\Phi_0\left(q^{-\varrho+1}; —; q, \frac{tq^{\varrho}}{z}\right).$$

The representation of the q-binomial series ${}_1\Phi_0$ is given by

$${}_1\Phi_0(a; —; q, z) = 1 + \sum_{l=1}^{\infty} \frac{(a,q)_l}{(q,q)_l} z^l \qquad (|q| < 1;\ |z| < 1).$$

Definition 5 (see, for example, [53,54]). *For an analytic function h, the fractional q-derivative operator $\mathfrak{D}_q$ of order ϱ is described by*

$$\begin{aligned}\mathfrak{D}_q h(z) &= D_q I^{1-\varrho}_{q,z} h(z) \\ &= \frac{1}{\Gamma_q(1-\varrho)} D_q \int_0^z (z - tq)_{-\varrho} h(t) d_q(t) \qquad (0 \leqq \varrho < 1).\end{aligned}$$

In Geometric Function Theory, linear operators (both derivative and integral operators) are extensively utilized. The most important aspect of this study is that we are simultaneously examining the characteristics of many classes of analytic functions under a certain linear operator. Taking the aforementioned importance of linear operators into consideration, we now define the operator below.

Definition 6. *The extended fractional q-derivative $\mathfrak{D}^{\varrho}_q$ of order ϱ is specified as follows:*

$$\mathfrak{D}^{\varrho}_q h(z) = D^m_q I^{m-\varrho}_{q,z} h(z), \tag{7}$$

where m is assumed to be the smallest integer. We find from (7) that

$$\mathfrak{D}^{\varrho}_q z^l = \frac{\Gamma_q(l+1)}{\Gamma_q(l+1-\varrho)} z^{l-\varrho} \qquad (0 \leqq \varrho;\ l > -1).$$

Remark 3. *For $-\infty < \varrho < 0$, $\mathfrak{D}^{\varrho}_q$ denotes a fractional q-integral of h of order ϱ. Additionally, for $0 \leqq \varrho < 2$, $\mathfrak{D}^{\varrho}_q$ denotes a q-derivative of h of order ϱ.*

Definition 7. *Following the work of Selvakumaran et al. [55], we introduce the* (ϱ, q)*-differintegral operator* $\mathbf{\Omega}_q^{\varrho} : \mathcal{A} \to \mathcal{A}$*, which they defined as follows:*

$$\begin{aligned} \mathbf{\Omega}_q^{\varrho} h(z) &= \frac{\Gamma_q(2-\varrho)}{\Gamma_q(2)} z^{\varrho} \mathfrak{D}_q^{\varrho} h(z) \\ &= z + \sum_{l=2}^{\infty} \frac{\Gamma_q(2-\varrho)\Gamma_q(l+1)}{\Gamma_q(2)\Gamma_q(l+1-\varrho)} a_l z^l \qquad (z \in \mathbb{E}), \end{aligned} \tag{8}$$

where $0 \leqq \varrho < 2$ *and* $0 < q < 1$.

Each of the following properties of the (ϱ, q)-differintegral operator $\mathbf{\Omega}_q^{\varrho} h$ are worthy of note.

Property 1.

$$\lim_{\varrho \to 1} \mathbf{\Omega}_q^{\varrho} h(z) = \mathbf{\Omega}_q^{\varrho} h(z) = z D_q h(z).$$

Property 2.

$$\mathbf{\Omega}_q^{\varrho}\left(\Omega_q^{\delta} h(z)\right) = \Omega_q^{\delta}\left(\mathbf{\Omega}_q^{\varrho} h(z)\right) = z + \sum_{l=2}^{\infty} \frac{\Gamma_q(2-\varrho)\Gamma_q(2-\delta)\left(\Gamma_q(l+1)\right)^2}{\Gamma_q(2)\Gamma_q(l+1-\varrho)\Gamma_q(l+1-\delta)} a_l z^l.$$

Property 3.

$$\frac{D_q\left(\mathbf{\Omega}_q^{\varrho} h(z)\right)}{\mathbf{\Omega}_q^{\varrho} h(z)} = \begin{cases} \dfrac{z D_q h(z)}{h(z)} & (\varrho = 0) \\[2ex] 1 + z \frac{D_q\left(D_q h(z)\right)}{D_q h(z)} & (\varrho = 1). \end{cases}$$

Considering the operator $\mathbf{\Omega}_q^{\varrho}$ defined in Definition 7 and inspired by the work given in [27], a new subclass of the class Σ is introduced by means of this operator. The next section will provide proofs of the original findings by using the Faber polynomial method and one lemma.

Definition 8. *Let the function h be of the form* (1)*. Then, h is referred to as* ϱ*-fractional bi-close-to-convex function in* $\mathbb{E}$ *if a suitable function* $g \in \mathcal{S}^*$ *exists such that*

$$\Re\left(\frac{D_q\left(\mathbf{\Omega}_q^{\varrho} h(z)\right)}{g(z)}\right) > \alpha$$

and

$$\Re\left(\frac{D_q\left(\mathbf{\Omega}_q^{\varrho} \alpha(\vartheta)\right)}{\delta(\vartheta)}\right) > \alpha,$$

where $0 \leqq \alpha < 1,\ 0 \leqq \varrho < 2$ *and* $z, \vartheta \in \mathbb{E}$*. All such functions are symbolized by* $\mathcal{K}_{\Sigma}(q, \alpha, \varrho)$.

Remark 4. *If we let* $q \to 1-$ *and* $\varrho = 0$*, then* $\mathcal{K}_{\Sigma}(q, \alpha, \varrho)$ *reduces to the class introduced by Hamidi and Jahangiri in [27].*

Remark 5. *If* $q \to 1-$ *and* $\alpha = 0$*, then* $\mathcal{K}_{\Sigma}(q, \alpha, \varrho)$ *reduces to the class introduced by Sakar and Güney in [56].*

2. The Faber Polynomial Expansion Method and Its Applications

The coefficients of the inverse mapping $\gamma = h^{-1}$ can be expressed by using the Faber polynomial method for analytic functions h and as follows (see [43,57]):

$$\gamma(\vartheta) = h^{-1}(\vartheta) = \vartheta + \sum_{l=2}^{\infty} \frac{1}{l} \mathfrak{q}_{l-1}^{l}(a_2, a_3, \cdots, a_l)\vartheta^l,$$

where

$$\mathfrak{q}_{l-1}^{-l} = \frac{(-l)!}{(-2l+1)!(l-1)!} a_2^{l-1} + \frac{(-l)!}{[2(-l+1)]!(l-3)!} a_2^{l-3} a_3$$

$$+ \frac{(-l)!}{(-2l+3)!(l-4)!} a_2^{l-4} a_4$$

$$+ \frac{(-l)!}{[2(-l+2)]!(l-5)!} a_2^{l-5} \left[a_5 + (-l+2)a_3^2\right]$$

$$+ \frac{(-l)!}{(-2l+5)!(l-6)!} a_2^{l-6} [a_6 + (-2l+5)a_3 a_4]$$

$$+ \sum_{\mathrm{i} \geqq 7} a_2^{l-\mathrm{i}} S_{\mathrm{i}}$$

and a homogeneous polynomial in $a_2, a_3, \cdots, a_l$ is denoted by S_{i} for $7 \leqq \mathrm{i} \leqq l$. Especially, the first three terms of $\mathfrak{q}_{l-1}^{-l}$ are given below:

$$\frac{1}{2}\mathfrak{q}_1^{-2} = -a_2,$$

$$\frac{1}{3}\mathfrak{q}_2^{-3} = 2a_2^2 - a_3$$

and

$$\frac{1}{4}\mathfrak{q}_3^{-4} + -(5a_2^3 - 5a_2 a_3 + a_4).$$

Generally, an extension of $\mathfrak{q}_l^r$ of the following type is used for $r \in \mathbb{Z}$ $(\mathbb{Z} := 0, \pm 1, \pm 2, \cdots)$ and $l \geqq 2$:

$$\mathfrak{q}_l^r = r a_l + \frac{r(r-1)}{2} \mathcal{V}_l^2 + \frac{r!}{(r-3)!3!} \mathcal{V}_l^3 + \cdots + \frac{r!}{(r-l)!(l)!} \mathcal{V}_l^l,$$

where

$$\mathcal{V}_l^r = \mathcal{V}_l^r(a_2, a_3, \cdots)$$

and, by using [57], we have

$$\mathcal{V}_l^v(a_2, \cdots, a_l) = \sum_{l=1}^{\infty} \frac{v!(a_2)^{\mu_1} \cdots (a_l)^{\mu_l}}{\mu_1!, \cdots, \mu_l!} \qquad (a_1 = 1;\ v \leqq l).$$

Clearly, upon adding all non-negative integers $\mu_1, \cdots, \mu_l$, which satisfy

$$\mu_1 + \mu_2 + \cdots + \mu_l = v \quad \text{and} \quad \mu_1 + 2\mu_2 + \cdots + l\mu_l = l,$$

we find that

$$\mathcal{V}_l^l(a_1, \cdots, a_l) = \mathcal{V}_1^l$$

and that the first and last polynomials are given by

$$\mathcal{V}_l^l = a_1^l \quad \text{and} \quad \mathcal{V}_l^1 = a_l.$$

Lemma 1 (see [58]). *If p is a function with a positive real part and*

$$p(z) = 1 + \sum_{l=1}^{\infty} c_l z^l,$$

then

$$|c_l| \leqq 2.$$

The problem of finding bounds for the coefficients has always been a key concern in geometric function theory. The size of their coefficients can determine a number of properties of analytic functions, including univalency, rate of growth and distortion. Many scholars have used a variety of methods to overcome the aforementioned issues. Similar to univalent functions, bi-univalent function coefficient estimation has received a lot of interest lately. As a result of the significance of studying the coefficient problems described above, in this section, we utilize the $(varrho, q)$-fractional derivative operator and the Fabor polynomial technique to obtain coefficient estimates for $|a_l|$ and discuss the unpredictable behavior of the initial coefficient bounds for $|a_2|$ and $|a_3|$. We also investigate the Fekete–Szegö problem and give some examples. We also demonstrate how some of the previously published results would be improved and generalized as a result of our primary findings as well as their corollaries and consequences.

3. Main Results

Our first main result is asserted by Theorem 1 below.

Theorem 1. *If h has the series representation stated in* (1) *and belongs to the class $\mathcal{K}_\Sigma(q, \alpha, \varrho)$, and if $a_i = 0$ and $2 \leqq i \leqq l-1$, then*

$$|a_l| \leqq \frac{\Gamma_q(2)\Gamma_q(l+1-\varrho)(2(1-\alpha)+l)}{[l]_q\Gamma_q(2-\varrho)\Gamma_q(l+1)} \qquad (l \geqq 3).$$

Proof. For $h \in \mathcal{K}_\Sigma(q, \alpha, \varrho)$, there exists a function g. The FPE for $\frac{D_q\left(\Omega_q^\varrho h(z)\right)}{g(z)}$ is given by

$$\frac{D_q\left(\Omega_q^\varrho h(z)\right)}{g(z)} = 1 + \sum_{l=2}^{\infty} \left[\begin{array}{c} \left([l]_q \frac{\Gamma_q(2-\varrho)\Gamma_q(l+1)}{\Gamma_q(2)\Gamma_q(l+1-\varrho)} a_l - b_l\right) \sum_{l=1}^{l-2} \mathfrak{q}_l^{-1}(b_2, b_3, \cdots, b_{l+1}) \\ \cdot\left(\left([l]_q - l\right) \frac{\Gamma_q(2-\varrho)\Gamma_q(l+1)}{\Gamma_q(2)\Gamma_q(l+1-\varrho)} a_{l-l} - b_{l-l}\right) \end{array} \right] z^{l-1}. \quad (9)$$

Additionally, regarding the inverse maps $\gamma = h^{-1}$ and $\delta = g^{-1}$, we obtain

$$\frac{D_q\left(\Omega_q^\varrho \alpha(\vartheta)\right)}{\delta(\vartheta)} = 1 + \sum_{l=2}^{\infty} \left[\begin{array}{c} \left([l]_q \frac{\Gamma_q(2-\varrho)\Gamma_q(l+1)}{\Gamma_q(2)\Gamma_q(l+1-\varrho)} A_l - B_l\right) \sum_{l=1}^{l-2} \mathfrak{q}_l^{-1}(B_2, B_3, \cdots, B_{l+1}) \\ \cdot\left(\left([l]_q - l\right) \frac{\Gamma_q(2-\varrho)\Gamma_q(l+1)}{\Gamma_q(2)\Gamma_q(l+1-\varrho)} A_{l-l} - B_{l-l}\right) \end{array} \right] \vartheta^{l-1}. \quad (10)$$

As opposed to that, since

$$\Re\left(\frac{D_q\left(\Omega_q^\varrho h(z)\right)}{g(z)}\right) > \alpha \qquad (z \in \mathbb{E}),$$

there must exist a function $p(z)$ given by

$$p(z) = 1 + \sum_{l=1}^{\infty} c_l z^l$$

such that

$$\begin{aligned}\frac{D_q\left(\Omega_q^{\varrho} h(z)\right)}{g(z)} &= 1 + (1-\alpha)p(z) \\ &= 1 + (1-\alpha)\sum_{l=1}^{\infty} c_l z^l. \end{aligned} \tag{11}$$

Similarly, since

$$\Re\left(\frac{D_q\left(\Omega_q^{\varrho}\gamma(\vartheta)\right)}{\delta(\vartheta)}\right) > \alpha \qquad (0 \leqq \alpha < 1;\ z \in \mathbb{E}),$$

there must exist a function $\mathfrak{r}$ given by

$$\mathfrak{r}(\vartheta) = 1 + \sum_{l=1}^{\infty} d_l \vartheta^l$$

such that

$$\begin{aligned}\frac{D_q\left(\Omega_q^{\varrho}\gamma(\vartheta)\right)}{\delta(\vartheta)} &= 1 + (1-\alpha)q(\vartheta) \\ &= 1 + (1-\alpha)\sum_{l=1}^{\infty} d_l \vartheta^l. \end{aligned} \tag{12}$$

For each $l \geqq 2$, evaluating the coefficients of the Equations (9) and (11), we obtain

$$\left\{\begin{array}{c}\left([l]_q \frac{\Gamma_q(2-\varrho)\Gamma_q(l+1)}{\Gamma_q(2)\Gamma_q(l+1-\varrho)} a_l - b_l\right) \sum_{l=1}^{l-2} \mathfrak{q}_l^{-1}(b_2, b_3, \cdots, b_{l+1}) \\ \cdot\left(([l]_q - l)\frac{\Gamma_q(2-\varrho)\Gamma_q(l+1)}{\Gamma_q(2)\Gamma_q(l+1-\varrho)} a_{l-l} - b_{l-l}\right)\end{array}\right\} = (1-\alpha)c_{l-1}. \tag{13}$$

Additionally, by evaluating the coefficients of the Equations (10) and (12), for any $l \geqq 2$, we have

$$\left\{\begin{array}{c}\left([l]_q \frac{\Gamma_q(2-\varrho)\Gamma_q(l+1)}{\Gamma_q(2)\Gamma_q(l+1-\varrho)} A_l - B_l\right) \sum_{l=1}^{l-2} \mathfrak{q}_l^{-1}(B_2, B_3, \cdots, B_{l+1}) \\ \cdot\left(([l]_q - l)\frac{\Gamma_q(2-\varrho)\Gamma_q(l+1)}{\Gamma_q(2)\Gamma_q(l+1-\varrho)} A_{l-l} - B_{l-l}\right)\end{array}\right\} = (1-\alpha)d_{l-1}. \tag{14}$$

Using the Equations (13) and (14), we derive the following for the particular case when $l = 2$:

$$\frac{[2]_q\Gamma_q(2-\varrho)\Gamma_q(3)}{\Gamma_q(2)\Gamma_q(3-\varrho)} a_2 - b_2 = (1-\alpha)c_1$$

$$\frac{[2]_q\Gamma_q(2-\varrho)\Gamma_q(3)}{\Gamma_q(2)\Gamma_q(3-\varrho)} A_2 - B_2 = (1-\alpha)d_1$$

and

$$a_2 = \frac{\Gamma_q(2)\Gamma_q(3-\varrho)}{[2]_q\Gamma_q(2-\varrho)\Gamma_q(3)}((1-\alpha)c_1 + b_2)$$
$$A_2 = \frac{\Gamma_q(2)\Gamma_q(3-\varrho)}{[2]_q\Gamma_q(2-\varrho)\Gamma_q(3)}((1-\alpha)d_1 + B_2).$$

We now solve for a_l and apply Lemma 1 and the moduli, so that

$$|a_2| \leqq \frac{2[\Gamma_q(2)\Gamma_q(3-\varrho)}{[2]_q\Gamma_q(2-\varrho)\Gamma_q(3)}(2-\alpha).$$

However, assuming that $2 \leqq k \leqq l-1$ and $a_k = 0$ are true, the following results are obtained.

$$A_l = -a_l$$

and

$$\frac{[l]_q\Gamma_q(2-\varrho)\Gamma_q(l+1)}{\Gamma_q(2)\Gamma_q(l+1-\varrho)}a_l - b_l = (1-\alpha)c_{l-1},$$
$$-\frac{[l]_q\Gamma_q(2-\varrho)\Gamma_q(l+1)}{\Gamma_q(2)\Gamma_q(l+1-\varrho)}a_l - B_l = (1-\alpha)d_{l-1}$$

and

$$a_l = \frac{\Gamma_q(2)\Gamma_q(l+1-\varrho)}{[l]_q\Gamma_q(2-\varrho)\Gamma_q(l+1)}((1-\alpha)c_{l-1} + b_l)$$
$$-a_l = \frac{\Gamma_q(2)\Gamma_q(l+1-\varrho)}{[l]_q\Gamma_q(2-\varrho)\Gamma_q(l+1)}((1-\alpha)d_{l-1} + B_l)$$

By solving for a_l and using Lemma 1 and the moduli, we can derive

$$|a_l| \leqq \frac{\Gamma_q(2)\Gamma_q(l+1-\varrho)(2(1-\alpha)+l)}{[l]_q\Gamma_q(2-\varrho)\Gamma_q(l+1)},$$

upon noticing that

$$|b_l| \leqq l \text{ and } |B_l| \leqq l.$$

This completes the proof of Theorem 1. □

The following corollaries can be obtained by putting different values of the parameters involved.

Corollary 1. *If the function h has the series representation stated in* (1) *and belongs to the class* $\mathcal{K}_\Sigma(q,0,1)$, *and if*

$$a_i = 0 \ \ (2 \leqq i \leqq l-1),$$

then

$$|a_l| \leqq \frac{\Gamma_q(2)\Gamma_q(l)(2+l)}{[l]_q\Gamma_q(l+1)} \qquad (l \geqq 3).$$

Corollary 2. *If the function h has the series representation stated in* (1) *and belongs to* $\mathcal{K}_\Sigma(q,\alpha,1)$, *and if* $a_i = 0 \ \ (2 \leqq i \leqq l-1)$, *then*

$$|a_l| \leqq \frac{\Gamma_q(2)\Gamma_q(l)(2(1-\alpha)+l)}{[l]_q\Gamma_q(l+1)} \qquad (l \geqq 3).$$

Corollary 3. *If the function h has the series representation stated in* (1) *and belongs to the class* $\mathcal{K}_\Sigma(q \to 1-, \alpha, \varrho)$*, and if* $a_i = 0 \ (2 \leqq i \leqq l-1)$*, then*

$$|a_l| \leqq \frac{\Gamma(2)\Gamma(l+1-\varrho)(2(1-\alpha)+l)}{l\Gamma(2-\varrho)\Gamma(l+1)} \qquad (l \geqq 3).$$

Corollary 4. *If the h has the series representation stated in* (1) *and belongs to the class* $\mathcal{K}_\Sigma(q \to 1-, \alpha, 1)$*, and if* $a_i = 0 \ (2 \leqq i \leqq l-1)$*, then*

$$|a_l| \leqq \frac{\Gamma(2)\Gamma(l)(2(1-\alpha)+l)}{l\Gamma(l+1)} \qquad (l \geqq 3).$$

The following known consequence of Theorem 1 for $\varrho = 0$ and $q \to 1-$ was demonstrated in [27].

Corollary 5 (see [27])**.** *Let* $h \in \mathcal{K}_\Sigma(\alpha)$*. If* $a_{i+1} = 0 \ (1 \leqq i \leqq l)$*, then*

$$|a_l| \leqq 1 + \frac{2(1-\alpha)}{l} \qquad (l \geqq 3).$$

Corollary 6 (see [56])**.** *If the function h has the series representation stated in* (1) *and belongs to the class* $\mathcal{K}_\Sigma(q \to 1-, 0, \varrho)$*, and if* $a_i = 0 \ (2 \leqq i \leqq l-1)$*, then*

$$|a_l| \leqq \frac{(2+l)\Gamma(l+1-\varrho)}{l\Gamma(2-\varrho)\Gamma(l+1)} \qquad (l \geqq 3).$$

As a special form of Theorem 1, our next result (Theorem 2 below) provides estimates for the initial coefficients $|a_2|$ and $|a_3|$, and also for the Fekete–Szegö-type functional involved in $|a_3 - a_2^2|$ for functions in the class $\mathcal{K}_\Sigma(m, \alpha, q)$.

Theorem 2. *Let the function* $h \in \mathcal{K}_\Sigma(q, \alpha, \varrho)$ *be given by* (1)*. Then,*

$$|a_2| \leqq \begin{cases} \sqrt{\dfrac{2\Gamma_q(2)\Gamma_q(3-\varrho)\Gamma_q(4-\varrho)(1-\alpha)}{\Gamma_q(2-\varrho)\Big([3]_q\Gamma_q(4)\Gamma_q(3-\varrho) - [2]_q\Gamma_q(3)\Gamma_q(4-\varrho)\Big)}} \\ (0 \leqq \alpha < 1 - \phi(q,\varrho)) \\ \\ \dfrac{2\Gamma_q(2)\Gamma_q(3-\varrho)(1-\alpha)}{[2]_q\Gamma_q(2-\varrho)\Gamma_q(3) - \Gamma_q(2)\Gamma_q(3-\varrho)} \\ (1 - \phi(q,\varrho) \leqq \alpha < 1) \end{cases}$$

and

$$|a_3| \leqq \frac{2\Gamma_q(2)\Gamma_q(4-\varrho)(1-\alpha)}{[3]_q\Gamma_q(4)\Gamma_q(2-\varrho) - \Gamma_q(2)\Gamma_q(4-\varrho)} \cdot \frac{[2]_q\Gamma_q(2-\varrho)\Gamma_q(3) - \Gamma_q(2)\Gamma_q(3-\varrho) + 2(1-\alpha)\Gamma_q(2)\Gamma_q(3-\varrho)}{[2]_q\Gamma_q(2-\varrho)\Gamma_q(3) - \Gamma_q(2)\Gamma_q(3-\varrho)},$$

where

$$\phi(q,\varrho) := \frac{\Gamma_q(2)\Gamma_q(4-\varrho)\{[2]_q\Gamma_q(2-\varrho)\Gamma_q(3) - \Gamma_q(2)\Gamma_q(3-\varrho)\}^2}{2\Gamma_q(3-\varrho)\Gamma_q(2)([3]_q\Gamma_q(4)\Gamma_q(2-\varrho)\Gamma_q(3-\varrho) - [2]_q\Gamma_q(3)\Gamma_q(2-\varrho)\Gamma_q(4-\varrho))}.$$

Furthermore, it is asserted that

$$\left|a_3 - a_2^2\right| \leqq \frac{2\Gamma_q(2)\Gamma_q(4-\varrho)(1-\alpha)}{[3]_q\Gamma_q(2-\varrho)\Gamma_q(4) - \Gamma_q(2)\Gamma_q(4-\varrho)}.$$

Proof. Taking a function $g(z) = \Omega_q^{\varrho} h(z)$ in the proof of Theorem 1, we obtain $a_l = -b_l$. For $l = 2$, the Equations (13) and (14), respectively, yield

$$a_2\left(\frac{[2]_q\Gamma_q(2-\varrho)\Gamma_q(3)}{\Gamma_q(2)\Gamma_q(3-\varrho)} - 1\right) = (1-\alpha)c_1,$$

$$a_2\left(\frac{-[2]_q\Gamma_q(2-\varrho)\Gamma_q(3)}{\Gamma_q(2)\Gamma_q(3-\varrho)} + 1\right) = (1-\alpha)d_1;$$

and

$$a_2 = \frac{\Gamma_q(2)\Gamma_q(3-\varrho)}{[2]_q\Gamma_q(2-\varrho)\Gamma_q(3) - \Gamma_q(2)\Gamma_q(3-\varrho)}(1-\alpha)c_1,$$

$$-a_2 = \frac{\Gamma_q(2)\Gamma_q(3-\varrho)}{[2]_q\Gamma_q(2-\varrho)\Gamma_q(3) - \Gamma_q(2)\Gamma_q(3-\varrho)}(1-\alpha)d_1.$$

If we use moduli of either of these two equations, we obtain

$$|a_2| \leqq \frac{2\Gamma_q(2)\Gamma_q(3-\varrho)(1-\alpha)}{[2]_q\Gamma_q(2-\varrho)\Gamma_q(3) - \Gamma_q(2)\Gamma_q(3-\varrho)}.$$

For $l = 3$, the Equations (13) and (14), respectively, yield

$$\left(\frac{[3]_q\Gamma_q(2-\varrho)\Gamma_q(4)}{\Gamma_q(2)\Gamma_q(4-\varrho)} - 1\right)a_3 - \left(\frac{[2]_q\Gamma_q(2-\varrho)\Gamma_q(3)}{\Gamma_q(2)\Gamma_q(3-\varrho)} - 1\right)a_2^2 = (1-\alpha)c_2 \tag{15}$$

and

$$\left(2a_2^2 - a_3\right)\left(\frac{[3]_q\Gamma_q(2-\varrho)\Gamma_q(4)}{\Gamma_q(2)\Gamma_q(4-\varrho)} - 1\right) - \left(\frac{[2]_q\Gamma_q(2-\varrho)\Gamma_q(3)}{\Gamma_q(2)\Gamma_q(3-\varrho)} - 1\right)a_2^2 = (1-\alpha)d_2. \tag{16}$$

By combining the two equations mentioned above, we obtain

$$2a_2^2\left(\frac{[3]_q\Gamma_q(2-\varrho)\Gamma_q(4)}{\Gamma_q(2)\Gamma_q(4-\varrho)} - 1\right) - 2\left(\frac{[2]_q\Gamma_q(2-\varrho)\Gamma_q(3)}{\Gamma_q(2)\Gamma_q(3-\varrho)} - 1\right)a_2^2 = (1-\alpha)(c_2 + d_2),$$

$$2a_2^2\left(\frac{[3]_q\Gamma_q(2-\varrho)\Gamma_q(4)}{\Gamma_q(2)\Gamma_q(4-\varrho)} - \frac{[2]_q\Gamma_q(2-\varrho)\Gamma_q(3)}{\Gamma_q(2)\Gamma_q(3-\varrho)}\right) = (1-\alpha)(c_2 + d_2)$$

or

$$2a_2^2 = \frac{[3]_q\Gamma_q(3-\varrho)\Gamma_q(2-\varrho)\Gamma_q(4) - [2]_q\Gamma_q(4-\varrho)\Gamma_q(2-\varrho)\Gamma_q(3)}{\Gamma_q(2)\Gamma_q(3-\varrho)\Gamma_q(4-\varrho)} = (1-\alpha)(c_2 + d_2)$$

Now, by finding $|a_2|$, we arrive at

$$\left|a_2^2\right| = \frac{\Gamma_q(2)\Gamma_q(3-\varrho)\Gamma_q(4-\varrho)(1-\alpha)|d_2 + c_2|}{2\Gamma_q(2-\varrho)\left\{[3]_q\Gamma_q(4)\Gamma_q(3-\varrho) - [2]_q\Gamma_q(3)\Gamma_q(4-\varrho)\right\}}.$$

Additionally, by applying Lemma 1, we obtain

$$|a_2| \leqq \sqrt{\frac{2\Gamma_q(2)\Gamma_q(3-\varrho)\Gamma_q(4-\varrho)(1-\alpha)}{\Gamma_q(2-\varrho)\left([3]_q\Gamma_q(4)\Gamma_q(3-\varrho) - [2]_q\Gamma_q(3)\Gamma_q(4-\varrho)\right)}}.$$

As a result, we obtain the following estimate:

$$\sqrt{\frac{2\Gamma_q(2)\Gamma_q(3-\varrho)\Gamma_q(4-\varrho)(1-\alpha)}{\Gamma_q(2-\varrho)\Big([3]_q\Gamma_q(4)\Gamma_q(3-\varrho)-[2]_q\Gamma_q(3)\Gamma_q(4-\varrho)\Big)}}$$
$$<\frac{2\Gamma_q(2)\Gamma_q(3-\varrho)\Gamma_q(4-\varrho)(1-\alpha)}{\Gamma_q(2-\varrho)\Big([3]_q\Gamma_q(4)\Gamma_q(3-\varrho)-[2]_q\Gamma_q(3)\Gamma_q(4-\varrho)\Big)}.$$

Upon substituting

$$a_2=\frac{c_1(1-\alpha)\Gamma_q(2)\Gamma_q(3-\varrho)}{[2]_q\Gamma_q(2-\varrho)\Gamma_q(3)-\Gamma_q(2)\Gamma_q(3-\varrho)}$$

into (15), we have

$$a_3=\frac{\Gamma_q(2)\Gamma_q(4-\varrho)(1-\alpha)}{[3]_q\Gamma_q(4)\Gamma_q(2-\varrho)-\Gamma_q(2)\Gamma_q(4-\varrho)}$$
$$\cdot\left(c_2+\frac{(1-\alpha)\Gamma_q(2)\Gamma_q(3-\varrho)}{[2]_q\Gamma_q(2-\varrho)\Gamma_q(3)-\Gamma_q(2)\Gamma_q(3-\varrho)}c_1^2\right).$$

Taking the moduli on both sides, we find that

$$|a_3|\leqq\frac{\Gamma_q(2)\Gamma_q(4-\varrho)(1-\alpha)}{[3]_q\Gamma_q(4)\Gamma_q(2-\varrho)-\Gamma_q(2)\Gamma_q(4-\varrho)}$$
$$\cdot\left(|c_2|+\frac{(1-\alpha)\Gamma_q(2)\Gamma_q(3-\varrho)}{[2]_q\Gamma_q(2-\varrho)\Gamma_q(3)-\Gamma_q(2)\Gamma_q(3-\varrho)}\left|c_1^2\right|\right).$$

Applying Lemma 1, we obtain

$$|a_3|\leqq\frac{\Gamma_q(2)\Gamma_q(4-\varrho)(1-\alpha)}{[3]_q\Gamma_q(4)\Gamma_q(2-\varrho)-\Gamma_q(2)\Gamma_q(4-\varrho)}$$
$$\cdot\left(2+\frac{4(1-\alpha)\Gamma_q(2)\Gamma_q(3-\varrho)}{[2]_q\Gamma_q(2-\varrho)\Gamma_q(3)-\Gamma_q(2)\Gamma_q(3-\varrho)}\right),$$

that is,

$$|a_3|\leqq\frac{2\Gamma_q(2)\Gamma_q(4-\varrho)(1-\alpha)}{[3]_q\Gamma_q(4)\Gamma_q(2-\varrho)-\Gamma_q(2)\Gamma_q(4-\varrho)}$$
$$\cdot\left(\frac{[2]_q\Gamma_q(2-\varrho)\Gamma_q(3)-\Gamma_q(2)\Gamma_q(3-\varrho)+2(1-\alpha)\Gamma_q(2)\Gamma_q(3-\varrho)}{[2]_q\Gamma_q(2-\varrho)\Gamma_q(3)-\Gamma_q(2)\Gamma_q(3-\varrho)}\right).$$

Lastly, upon subtracting Equation (15) from Equation (16), we have

$$\left|a_3-a_2^2\right|\leqq\frac{2\Gamma_q(2)\Gamma_q(4-\varrho)(1-\alpha)}{[3]_q\Gamma_q(2-\varrho)\Gamma_q(4)-\Gamma_q(2)\Gamma_q(4-\varrho)}.$$

Our proof of Theorem 2 is thus completed. □

Several corollaries and consequences of Theorem 2 are presented below.

Corollary 7. *Let the function $h \in \mathcal{K}_\Sigma(q,\alpha,1)$ be given by* (1). *Then,*

$$|a_2| \leqq \begin{cases} \sqrt{\dfrac{2\Gamma_q(2)\Gamma_q(2)\Gamma_q(3)(1-\alpha)}{([3]_q\Gamma_q(4)\Gamma_q(2) - [2]_q\Gamma_q(3)\Gamma_q(3))}} \\ (0 \leqq \alpha < 1 - \varphi_1(q)) \\ \\ \dfrac{2\Gamma_q(2)\Gamma_q(2)(1-\alpha)}{[2]_q\Gamma_q(3) - \Gamma_q(2)\Gamma_q(2)} \\ (1 - \varphi_1(q) \leqq \alpha < 1), \end{cases}$$

$$|a_3| \leqq \frac{2\Gamma_q(2)\Gamma_q(3)(1-\alpha)}{[3]_q\Gamma_q(4) - \Gamma_q(2)\Gamma_q(3)} \cdot \left(\frac{[2]_q\Gamma_q(3) - \Gamma_q(2)\Gamma_q(2) + 2(1-\alpha)\Gamma_q(2)\Gamma_q(2)}{[2]_q\Gamma_q(3) - \Gamma_q(2)\Gamma_q(2)} \right)$$

and

$$\left|a_3 - a_2^2\right| \leqq \frac{2\Gamma_q(2)\Gamma_q(3)(1-\alpha)}{[3]_q\Gamma_q(4) - \Gamma_q(2)\Gamma_q(3)},$$

where

$$\varphi_1(q) = \frac{\Gamma_q(2)\Gamma_q(3)\left([2]_q\Gamma_q(3) - \Gamma_q(2)\Gamma_q(2)\right)^2}{2\Gamma_q(2)\Gamma_q(2)\left([3]_q\Gamma_q(4)\Gamma_q(2) - [2]_q\Gamma_q(3)\Gamma_q(3)\right)}.$$

Corollary 8. *Let $h \in \mathcal{K}_\Sigma(q,0,1)$ be given by* (1). *Then,*

$$|a_2| \leqq \begin{cases} \sqrt{\dfrac{2\Gamma_q(2)\Gamma_q(2)\Gamma_q(3)}{[3]_q\Gamma_q(4)\Gamma_q(2) - [2]_q\Gamma_q(3)\Gamma_q(3)}} \\ (0 \leqq \alpha < 1 - \varphi_2(q)) \\ \\ \dfrac{2\Gamma_q(2)\Gamma_q(2)}{[2]_q\Gamma_q(3) - \Gamma_q(2)\Gamma_q(2)} (1 - \varphi_2(q) \leqq \alpha < 1), \end{cases}$$

$$|a_3| \leqq \frac{2\Gamma_q(2)\Gamma_q(3)}{[3]_q\Gamma_q(4) - \Gamma_q(2)\Gamma_q(3)} \cdot \frac{[2]_q\Gamma_q(3) - \Gamma_q(2)\Gamma_q(2) + \Gamma_q(2)\Gamma_q(2)}{[2]_q\Gamma_q(3) - \Gamma_q(2)\Gamma_q(2)}$$

and

$$\left|a_3 - a_2^2\right| \leqq \frac{2\Gamma_q(2)\Gamma_q(3)}{[3]_q\Gamma_q(4) - \Gamma_q(2)\Gamma_q(3)},$$

where

$$\varphi_2(q) = \frac{\Gamma_q(2)\Gamma_q(3)\left\{[2]_q\Gamma_q(3) - \Gamma_q(2)\Gamma_q(2)\right\}^2}{2\Gamma_q(2)\Gamma_q(2)\left\{[3]_q\Gamma_q(4)\Gamma_q(2) - [2]_q\Gamma_q(3)\Gamma_q(3)\right\}}.$$

Corollary 9. *Let $h \in \mathcal{K}_\Sigma(q \to 1-, \alpha, \varrho)$ be given by* (1). *Then,*

$$|a_2| \leqq \begin{cases} \sqrt{\dfrac{2\Gamma(2)\Gamma(3-\varrho)\Gamma(4-\varrho)(1-\alpha)}{\Gamma(2-\varrho)\{3\Gamma(4)\Gamma(3-\varrho)-2\Gamma(3)\Gamma(4-\varrho)\}}} \\ (0 \leqq \alpha < 1-\varphi_3(\varrho)) \\ \\ \dfrac{2\Gamma(2)\Gamma(3-\varrho)(1-\alpha)}{2\Gamma(2-\varrho)\Gamma(3)-\Gamma(2)\Gamma(3-\varrho)} \\ (1-\varphi_3(\varrho) \leqq \alpha < 1), \end{cases}$$

$$|a_3| \leqq \frac{2\Gamma(2)\Gamma(4-\varrho)(1-\alpha)}{3\Gamma(4)\Gamma(2-\varrho)-\Gamma(2)\Gamma(4-\varrho)} \cdot \frac{2\Gamma(2-\varrho)\Gamma(3)-\Gamma(2)\Gamma(3-\varrho)+2(1-\alpha)\Gamma(2)\Upsilon(3-\varrho)}{2\Gamma(2-\varrho)\Gamma(3)-\Gamma(2)\Gamma(3-\varrho)}$$

and

$$\left|a_3-a_2^2\right| \leqq \frac{2\Gamma(2)\Gamma(4-\varrho)(1-\alpha)}{3\Gamma(2-\varrho)\Gamma(4)-\Gamma(2)\Gamma(4-\varrho)},$$

where

$$\varphi_3(\varrho) = \frac{\Gamma(2)\Gamma(4-\varrho)\{2\Upsilon(2-\varrho)\Gamma(3)-\Gamma(2)\Gamma(3-\varrho)\}^2}{2\Gamma(3-\varrho)\Gamma(2)\{3\Gamma(4)\Gamma(2-\varrho)\Gamma(3-\varrho)-2\Gamma(3)\Gamma(2-\varrho)\Gamma(4-\varrho)\}}.$$

As another application of Theorem 2 for $\varrho = 4$ and $q \to 1-$, we obtain the result given in [27].

Corollary 10 (see [27]). *Let $h \in \mathcal{K}_\Sigma(q \to 1-, \alpha, 0)$. Then,*

$$|a_2| \leqq \begin{cases} \sqrt{2(1-\alpha)} & \left(0 \leqq \alpha < \frac{1}{2}\right) \\ \\ 2(1-\alpha) & \left(\frac{1}{2} \leqq \alpha < 1\right) \end{cases}$$

and

$$|a_3| \leqq \begin{cases} 2(1-\alpha) & \left(0 \leqq \alpha < \frac{1}{2}\right) \\ \\ (1-\alpha)(3-2\alpha) & \left(\frac{1}{2} \leqq \alpha < 1\right). \end{cases}$$

Corollary 11 (see [56]). *Let $h \in \mathcal{K}_\Sigma(q \to 1-, 0, \varrho)$ be given by* (1). *Then,*

$$|a_2| \leqq \min\left(\begin{array}{c} \sqrt{\dfrac{2\Gamma(3-\varrho)\Gamma(4-\varrho)}{\Gamma(2-\varrho)\{3\Gamma(4)\Gamma(3-\varrho)-2\Gamma(3)\Gamma(4-\varrho)\}}}, \\ \\ \dfrac{2\Gamma(2)\Gamma(3-\varrho)}{2\Gamma(2-\varrho)\Gamma(3)-\Gamma(2)\Gamma(3-\varrho)} \end{array} \right),$$

$$|a_3| \leqq \frac{2\Gamma_q(4-\varrho)}{3\Gamma(4)\Gamma(2-\varrho)-\Gamma(4-\varrho)} \cdot \left(\frac{2\Gamma(2-\varrho)\Gamma(3)-\Gamma(3-\varrho)+2\Gamma(3-\varrho)}{2\Gamma(2-\varrho)\Gamma(3)-\Gamma(3-\varrho)}\right)$$

and
$$\left|a_3 - a_2^2\right| \leqq \frac{2\Gamma(2)\Gamma(4-\varrho)}{3\Gamma(2-\varrho)\Gamma(4) - \Gamma(4-\varrho)}.$$

Example 1. *For $l \geqq 3$, we will demonstrate that $h(z)$ given by*
$$h(z) = z + \frac{1-\alpha}{l-1} z^l$$
is a bi-close-to-convex function of order α, where $\alpha \in [0,1)$ in $\mathbb{E}$. Indeed, since the function
$$g(z) = z - \frac{1-\alpha}{l-\alpha} z^l$$
is starlike in $\mathbb{E}$, we have
$$\begin{aligned}\frac{D_q \boldsymbol{\Omega}_q^{\varrho} h(z)}{g(z)} &= \frac{1 + \left(\frac{\Psi_l(q,\varrho)[l]_q(1-\alpha)}{l-1}\right) z^{l-1}}{1 - \left(\frac{1-\alpha}{l-\alpha}\right) z^{l-1}} \\ &= 1 + \sum_{j=1}^{\infty} \left(\frac{(1-\alpha)^j}{(l-\alpha)^j} + \frac{\Psi_l(q,\varrho)[l]_q(1-\alpha)j}{(l-1)(l-\alpha)^{j-1}} \right) z^{(l-1)k},\end{aligned}$$
where
$$\Psi_l(q,\varrho) = \frac{\Gamma_q(2-\varrho)\Gamma_q(l+1)}{\Gamma_q(2)\Gamma_q(l+1-\varrho)}.$$

Therefore, we obtain
$$\begin{aligned}\frac{\frac{D_q \boldsymbol{\Omega}_q^{\varrho} h(z)}{g(z)} - \alpha}{1-\alpha} &= 1 + \sum_{j=1}^{\infty} \left(\frac{l(\Psi_l(q,\varrho)[l]_q + 1) - \Psi_l(q,\varrho)[l]_q \alpha - 1}{(l-1)(l-\alpha)} \right) \\ &\quad \cdot \left(\frac{1-\alpha}{l-\alpha} \right)^{j-1} z^{(l-1)j}.\end{aligned}$$

Obviously, we also have
$$\Re\left(\frac{D_q \boldsymbol{\Omega}_q^{\varrho} h(z)}{g(z)} \right) - \alpha > 0 \qquad (z \in \mathbb{E}).$$

For $\gamma = h^{-1}$ and $\delta = g^{-1}$, it is easily seen that
$$\gamma(\vartheta) = \vartheta - \frac{1-\alpha}{l-1}\, \vartheta^l,$$
and if we set
$$\delta(\vartheta) = \vartheta + \frac{1-\alpha}{l-\alpha}\, \vartheta^l$$
which is starlike in $\mathbb{E}$. As a result, we have
$$\begin{aligned}\frac{\frac{D_q \boldsymbol{\Omega}_q^{\varrho} \gamma(\vartheta)}{\delta(z)} - \alpha}{1-\alpha} &= 1 + \sum_{j=1}^{\infty} (-1)^j \left(\frac{l(\Psi_l(q,\varrho)[l]_q + 1) - \Psi_l(q,\varrho)[l]_q \alpha - 1}{(l-1)(l-\alpha)} \right) \\ &\quad \cdot \left(\frac{1-\alpha}{l-\alpha} \right)^{j-1} \vartheta^{(l-1)j}.\end{aligned}$$

Thus, clearly, we find that

$$\Re\left(\frac{D_q\mathbf{\Omega}_q^{\varrho}\gamma(\vartheta)}{\delta(\vartheta)}-\alpha\right)>0 \qquad (z\in\mathbb{E}).$$

4. Conclusions

In this article, we have used the notions of the q-fractional derivative, bi-univalent functions and FPE to define some new subfamilies of Σ. We investigated lth coefficient bounds and the Fekete–Szegö functional for these newly defined classes. Our study has also demonstrated how the results are enhanced and expanded by appropriate specialization of the parameters, including some recently released findings.

This article is composed of three sections. We briefly reviewed some fundamental geometric function theory ideas in Section 1 because they were important to deriving our main findings. All of these components are well-known, and we have correctly cited them. In Section 2, we provide the Faber polynomial approach and its applications and some initial lemmas. In Section 3, we present our key findings.

For future studies, researchers can use other extended q-operators instead of the $(\varrho;q)$-differintegral operator and define a number of new subclasses of the bi-univalent function class Σ. Furthermore, by using the Faber polynomial technique, the interested researchers can discuss the behavior of coefficient estimates for different types of newly defined subclasses of bi-univalent functions. Researchers may also investigate a variety of methods, depending on how inspired they are by the knowledge gained in this subject. Fractional derivative operators have made it possible to study differential equations from the perspectives of functional analysis and operator theory. Using the operator method for resolving differential equations, various properties fractional derivative operator are used extensively.

It is a clearly presented fact that the transition from our q-results to the corresponding $(\mathfrak{p},q)$-results is a rather trivial exercise because the additional forced-in parameter $\mathfrak{p}$ is obviously redundant (see, for details, ([5], p. 340) and ([54], Section 5, pp. 1511–1512); see also [59–62]).

Author Contributions: Conceptualization, H.M.S., S.K. and Q.X.; methodology, H.M.S., S.K. and Q.X.; software, I.A.-S.; validation, S.N.M. and F.T.; formal analysis, H.M.S. and S.N.M.; investigation, H.M.S., S.K. and Q.X.; resources, I.A.-S.; data curation, I.A.-S.; writing—original draft preparation, H.M.S. and S.K.; writing—review and editing, H.M.S. and S.K.; visualization, S.N.M.; supervision, S.N.M.; project administration, I.A.-S. and F.T.; funding acquisition, F.T. All authors have read and agreed to the published version of the manuscript.

Funding: This research received no external funding.

Data Availability Statement: No data is used in this work.

Acknowledgments: This research was supported by the Researchers Supporting Project Number (RSP2023R401), King Saud University, Riyadh, Saudi Arabia.

Conflicts of Interest: The authors declare that they have no conflict of interest.

References

1. Alexander, J.W. Functions which map the interior of the unit circle upon simple regions. *Ann. Math.* **1915**, *17*, 12–22. [CrossRef]
2. Alb Lupaş, A.; Oros, G.I. Differential subordination and superordination results using fractional integral of confluent hypergeometric function. *Symmetry* **2021**, *13*, 327. [CrossRef]
3. Oros, G.I. Study on new integral operators defined using confluent hypergeometric function. *Adv. Differ. Equ.* **2021**, *2021*, 342. [CrossRef]
4. Khan, Ş.S.; Altinkaya; Xin, Q.; Tchier, F.; Malik, S.N.; Khan, N. Faber Polynomial coefficient estimates for Janowski type bi-close-to-convex and bi-quasi-convex functions. *Symmetry* **2023**, *15*, 604. [CrossRef]
5. Srivastava, H.M. Operators of basic (or q-) calculus and fractional q-Calculus and their applications. *Iran. J. Sci. Technol. Trans. A Sci.* **2020**, *44*, 327–344. [CrossRef]

6. Ahmad, B.; Ntouyas, S.K.; Alsaedi, A. New existence results for nonlinear fractional differential equations with three-point integral boundary conditions. *Adv. Differ. Equ.* **2011**, *2011*, 107384. [CrossRef]
7. Hilfer, R. *Applications of Fractional Calculus in Physics*; World Scientific Publishing Company: Singapore, 2000.
8. Ibrahim, R.W. On holomorphic solutions for nonlinear singular fractional differential equations. *Comput. Math. Appl.* **2011**, *62*, 1084–1090. [CrossRef]
9. Ibrahim, R.W. On solutions for fractional diffusion problems. *Electron. J. Differ. Equ.* **2010**, *147*, 1–11.
10. Jackson, F.H. On q-functions and a certain difference operator. *Earth Environ. Sci. Trans. R. Soc. Edinb.* **1909**, *46*, 253–281. [CrossRef]
11. Jackson, F.H. On q-definite integrals. *Q. J. Pure Appl. Math.* **1910**, *41*, 193–203.
12. Ismail, M.E.H.; Merkes, E.; Styer, D. A generalization of starlike functions. *Complex Var. Theory Appl.* **1990**, *14*, 77–84. [CrossRef]
13. Anastassiou, G.A.; Gal, S.G. Geometric and approximation properties of some singular integrals in the unit disk. *J. Inequal. Appl.* **2006**, *2006*, 17231. [CrossRef]
14. Anastassiou, G.A.; Gal, S.G. Geometric and approximation properties of generalized singular integrals in the unit disk. *J. Korean Math. Soc.* **2006**, *43*, 425–443. [CrossRef]
15. Mason, T.E. On properties of the solution of linear q-difference equations with entire function coefficients. *Am. J. Math.* **1915**, *37*, 439–444. [CrossRef]
16. Aral, A.; Gupta, V. On q-Baskakov type operators. *Demonstr. Math.* **2009**, *42*, 109–122.
17. Aral, A.; Gupta, V. On the Durrmeyer type modification of the q-Baskakov type operators. *Nonlinear Anal. Theory Methods Appl.* **2010**, *72*, 1171–1180. [CrossRef]
18. Aral, A.; Gupta, V. Generalized q-Baskakov operators. *Math. Slovaca* **2011**, *61*, 619–634. [CrossRef]
19. Aldweby, H.; Darus, M. On harmonic meromorphic functions associated with basic hypergeometric functions. *Sci. World J.* **2013**, *2013*, 164287.
20. Aldweby, H.; Darus, M. A subclass of harmonic univalent functions associated with q-analogue of Dziok-Serivastva operator. *ISRN Math. Anal.* **2013**, *2013*, 382312.
21. Kanas, S.; Răducanu, D. Some class of analytic functions related to conic domains. *Math. Slovaca* **2014**, *64*, 1183–1196. [CrossRef]
22. Srivastava, H.M. Univalent functions, fractional calculus, and associated generalized hypergeometric functions. In *Univalent Functions, Fractional Calculus, and Their Applications*; Srivastava, H.M., Owa, S., Eds.; Ellis Horwood: Chichester, UK, 1989; pp. 329–354.
23. Wanas, A.K.; Cotîrlă, L.-I. Initial coefficient estimates and Fekete-Szegö inequalities for new families of bi-univalent functions governed by (p,s)-Wanas operator. *Symmetry* **2021**, *13*, 2118. [CrossRef]
24. Saliu, A.; Al-Shbeil, I.; Gong, J.; Malik, S.N.; Aloraini, N. Properties of q-symmetric starlike functions of Janowski type. *Symmetry* **2022**, *14*, 1907. [CrossRef]
25. Çentikaya, A.; Cotîrlă, L.-I. Quasi-Hadamard product and partial sums for Sakaguchi-type function classes involving q-difference operator. *Symmetry* **2022**, *14*, 709.
26. Srivastava, H.M.; Mishra, A.K.; Gochhayat, P. Certain subclasses of analytic and bi-univalent functions. *Appl. Math. Lett.* **2010**, *23*, 1188–1192. [CrossRef]
27. Hamidi, S.G.; Jahangiri, J.M. Faber polynomials coefficient estimates for analytic bi-close-to-convex functions. *C. R. Math.* **2014**, *352*, 17–20. [CrossRef]
28. Lewin, M. On a coefficient problem for bi-univalent functions. *Proc. Am. Math. Soc.* **1967**, *18*, 63–68. [CrossRef]
29. Brannan, D.A.; Clunie, J.G. Aspects of contemporary complex analysis. In Proceedings of the NATO Advanced Study Institute Held at University of Durham, Durham, UK, 29 August–10 September 1979; Academic Press: New York, NY, USA, 1979.
30. Netanyahu, E. The minimal distance of the image boundary from the origin and the second coefficient of a univalent function in $|\tau| < 1$. *Arch. Ration. Mech. Anal.* **1967**, *32*, 100–112.
31. Brannan, D.A.; Taha, T.S. On some classes of bi-univalent function. *Stud. Univ.-Babes-Bolyai Math.* **1986**, *31*, 70–77.
32. Hayami, T.; Owa, S. Coefficient bounds for bi-univalent functions. *Panam. Math. J.* **2012**, *22*, 15–26.
33. Alharbi, A.; Murugusundaramoorthy, G.; El-Deeb, S.M. Yamaguchi-Noshiro type bi-univalent functions associated with Salagean-Erdélyi-Kober operator. *Mathematics* **2022**, *10*, 2241. [CrossRef]
34. Oros, G.I.; Cotîrlă, L.-I. Coefficient estimates and the Fekete-Szegö problem for new classes of m-fold symmetric bi-univalent functions. *Mathematics* **2022**, *10*, 129. [CrossRef]
35. Faber, G. Über polynomische Entwickelungen. *Math. Ann.* **1903**, *57*, 1569–1573. [CrossRef]
36. Schiffer, M. Faber polynomials in the theory of univalent functions. *Bull. Am. Soc.* **1948**, *54*, 503–517. [CrossRef]
37. Gong, S. *The Bieberbach Conjecture: AMS/IP Studies in Advanced Mathematics*; American Mathematical Society: Providence, RI, USA, 1999; Volume 12.
38. Pommerenke, C. Über die Faberschen Polynome schlichter Funktionen. *Math. Z.* **1964**, *85*, 197–208. [CrossRef]
39. Pommerenke, C. Konform Abbildung und Fekete-Punkte. *Math. Z.* **1965**, *89*, 422–438. [CrossRef]
40. Pommerenke, C. Über die Verteilung der Fekete-Punkte. *Math. Ann.* **1967**, *168*, 111–127. [CrossRef]
41. Hamidi, S.G.; Jahangiri, J.M. Faber polynomial coefficient estimates for bi-univalent functions defined by subordinations. *Bull. Iran. Math. Soc.* **2015**, *41*, 1103–1119.
42. Airault, H. Remarks on Faber polynomials. *Int. Math. Forum* **2008**, *3*, 449–456.

43. Attiya, A.A.; Lashin, A.M.; Ali, E.E.; Agarwal, P. Coefficient bounds for certain classes of analytic functions associated with Faber polynomial. *Symmetry* **2021**, *13*, 302. [CrossRef]
44. Altinkaya, Ş.; Yalçin, S. Faber polynomial coefficient bounds for a subclass of bi-univalent functions. *C. R. Math.* **2015**, *353*, 1075–1080; reprinted in *Stud. Univ.-Babes-Bolyai Math.* **2016**, *61*, 37–44. [CrossRef]
45. Bulut, S. Faber polynomial coefficients estimates for a comprehensive subclass of analytic bi-univalent functions. *C. R. Math.* **2014**, *352*, 479–484. [CrossRef]
46. Bulut, S. Faber polynomial coefficient estimates for certain subclasses of meromorphic bi-univalent functions. *C. R. Math.* **2015**, *353*, 113–116. [CrossRef]
47. Hamidi, S.G.; Jahangiri, J.M. Faber polynomial coefficients of bi-subordinate functions. *C. R. Math.* **2016**, *354*, 365–370. [CrossRef]
48. Cotırlă, L.-I.; Wanas, A.K. Coefficient-related studies and Fekete-Szegö type inequalities for new classes of bi-starlike and bi-convex functions. *Symmetry* **2022**, *14*, 2263. [CrossRef]
49. Páll-Szabö, Á.O.; Oros, G.I. Coefficient related studies for new classes of bi-univalent functions. *Mathematics* **2020**, *8*, 1110. [CrossRef]
50. Srivastava, H.M.; Eker, S.S.; Hamidi, S.G.; Jahangiri, J.M. Faber polynomial coefficient estimates for bi-univalent functions defined by the Tremblay fractional derivative operator. *Bull. Iran. Math. Soc.* **2018**, *44*, 149–157. [CrossRef]
51. Al-Shbeil, I.; Khan, N.; Tchier, F.; Xin, Q.; Malik, S.N.; Khan, S. Coefficient bounds for a family of s-fold symmetric bi-univalent functions. *Axioms* **2023**, *12*, 317. [CrossRef]
52. Purohit, S.D.; Raina, R.K. Certain subclasses of analytic functions associated with fractional q-calculus operators. *Math. Scand.* **2011**, *109*, 55–70. [CrossRef]
53. Srivastava, H.M.; Choi, J. *Zeta and q-Zeta Functions and Associated Series and Integrals*; Elsevier Science Publishers: Amsterdam, The Netherlands, 2012.
54. Srivastava, H.M. Some parametric and argument variations of the operators of fractional calculus and related special functions and integral transformations. *J. Nonlinear Convex Anal.* **2021**, *22*, 1501–1520.
55. Selvakumaran, K.A.; Choi, J.; Purohit, S.D. Certain subclasses of analytic functions defined by fractional q-calculus operators. *Appl. Math. E-Notes* **2021**, *21*, 72–80.
56. Sakar, F.M.; Güney, H.O. Faber polynomial coefficient bounds for analytic bi-close to convex functions defined by fractional calculus. *J. Fract. Calc. Appl.* **2018**, *9*, 64–71.
57. Airault, H. Symmetric sums associated to the factorizations of Grunsky coefficients. In *Groups and Symmetries: From Neolithic Scots to John McKay*; American Mathematical Society: Montreal, QC, Canada, 2007.
58. Duren, P.L. Univalent Functions. In *Grundlehren der Mathematischen Wissenschaften, Band 259*; Springer: Berlin/Heidelberg, Germany, 1983.
59. Srivastava, H.M. An introductory overview of Bessel polynomials, the generalized Bessel polynomials and the q-Bessel polynomials. *Symmetry* **2023**, *15*, 822. [CrossRef]
60. Al-Shbeil, I.; Shaba, T.G.; Cătaş, A. Second Hankel determinant for the subclass of bi-univalent functions using q-Chebyshev polynomial and Hohlov operator. *Fractal Fract.* **2022**, *6*, 186. [CrossRef]
61. Al-Shbeil, I.; Srivastava, H.M.; Arif, M.; Haq, M.; Khan, N.K. Majorization results based upon the Bernardi integral operator. *Symmetry* **2022**, *14*, 1404. [CrossRef]
62. Al-Shbeil, I.; Cătaş, A.; Srivastava, H.M.; Aloraini, N. Coefficient estimates of new families of analytic functions associated with q-Hermite polynomials. *Axioms* **2023**, *12*, 52. [CrossRef]

axioms

MDPI

Article

Classes of Harmonic Functions Related to Mittag-Leffler Function

Abeer A. Al-Dohiman [1], Basem Aref Frasin [2,*], Naci Taşar [3] and Fethiye Müge Sakar [3]

1 Department of Mathematics, Faculty of Science, Jouf University, Sakaka P.O. Box 2014, Saudi Arabia; a.aldohiman@ju.edu.sa
2 Faculty of Science, Department of Mathematics, Al al-Bayt University, Mafraq 25113, Jordan
3 Department of Management, Faculty of Economics and Administrative Sciences, Dicle University, Diyarbakir 21280, Turkey; nacitasar_72@hotmail.com (N.T.); mugesakar@hotmail.com (F.M.S.)
* Correspondence: bafrasin@yahoo.com

Abstract: The purpose of this paper is to find new inclusion relations of the harmonic class $\mathcal{HF}(\varrho,\gamma)$ with the subclasses $\mathcal{S}^*_{\mathcal{HF}}$, $\mathcal{K}_{\mathcal{HF}}$ and $\mathcal{T}\mathfrak{N}_{\mathcal{HF}}(\tau)$ of harmonic functions by applying the convolution operator $\Theta(\Im)$ associated with the Mittag-Leffler function. Further for $\varrho = 0$, several special cases of the main results are also obtained.

Keywords: harmonic; univalent functions; harmonic starlike; harmonic convex; Mittag-Leffler function

MSC: 30C45

1. Introduction

Harmonic functions play important roles in many problem in applied mathematics and they are also famous for their use in the study of minimal surfaces. Several differential geometers such as Choquest [1], Kneser [2], Lewy [3] and Rado [4] studied the harmonic functions. In 1984, Clunie and Sheil-Small [5] developed the basic theory of complex harmonic univalent functions $\Im$ defined in the open unit disk $\Xi = \{\xi : |\xi| < 1\}$ for which $\Im(0) = \Im_{\xi}(0) - 1 = 0$.

Let $\mathcal{HF}$ be the family of all harmonic functions of the form $\Im = \phi + \overline{\psi}$, where

$$\phi(\xi) = \xi + \sum_{\nu=2}^{\infty} a_\nu \xi^\nu, \qquad \psi(\xi) = \sum_{\nu=1}^{\infty} b_\nu \xi^\nu, \quad |b_1| < 1. \tag{1}$$

are analytic in the open unit disk Ξ. Furthermore, let $\mathcal{S}_{\mathcal{HF}}$ denote the family of functions $\Im = \phi + \overline{\psi}$ that are harmonic univalent and sense preserving in Ξ. Note that the family $\mathcal{S}_{\mathcal{HF}} = \mathcal{S}$ if ψ is zero.

We also let the subclass $\mathcal{S}^0_{\mathcal{HF}}$ of $\mathcal{S}_{\mathcal{HF}}$ as

$$\mathcal{S}^0_{\mathcal{HF}} = \left\{\Im = \phi + \overline{\psi} \in \mathcal{S}_{\mathcal{HF}} : \psi'(0) = b_1 = 0\right\}.$$

The classes $\mathcal{S}^0_{\mathcal{HF}}$ and $\mathcal{S}_{\mathcal{HF}}$ were first studied in [5].

A sense-preserving harmonic mapping $\Im \in \mathcal{S}^0_{\mathcal{HF}}$ is in the class $\mathcal{S}_{\mathcal{HF}}$ if the range $\Im(\Xi)$ is starlike with respect to the origin. The function $\Im \in \mathcal{S}^*_{\mathcal{HF}}$ is called a harmonic starlike mapping in Ξ. Also, the function $\Im$ defined in Ξ belongs to the class $\mathcal{K}_{\mathcal{HF}}$ if $\Im \in \mathcal{S}^0_{\mathcal{HF}}$ and if $\Im(\Xi)$ is a convex domain. The function $\Im \in \mathcal{K}_{\mathcal{HF}}$ is called harmonic convex in Ξ. Analytically, we have

$$\Im \in \mathcal{S}^*_{\mathcal{HF}} \text{ iff } arg\left(\frac{\partial}{\partial\theta}\Im\left(re^{i\theta}\right)\right) \geq 0,$$

Citation: Al-Dohiman, A.A.; Frasin, B.A.; Taşar, N.; Sakar, F.M. Classes of Harmonic Functions Related to Mittag-Leffler Function. *Axioms* **2023**, *12*, 714. https://doi.org/10.3390/axioms12070714

Academic Editor: Georgia Irina Oros

Received: 25 June 2023
Revised: 20 July 2023
Accepted: 21 July 2023
Published: 23 July 2023

and

$$\Im \in \mathcal{K}_{\mathcal{HF}} \text{ iff } \frac{\partial}{\partial\theta}\left\{arg\left(arg\left(\frac{\partial}{\partial\theta}\Im\left(re^{i\theta}\right)\right)\right)\right\} \geq 0,$$
$$\xi = re^{i\theta} \in \Xi,\ 0 \leq \theta \leq 2\pi,\ 0 \leq r \leq 1.$$

For definitions and properties of these classes, one may refer to [6] and for other subclasses of harmonic functions one can see [7–17].

Let $\mathcal{T}_{\mathcal{HF}}$ be the class of functions in $\mathcal{S}_{\mathcal{HF}}$ that may be expressed as $\Im = \phi + \overline{\psi}$, where

$$\begin{aligned} \phi(\xi) &= \xi - \sum_{\nu=2}^{\infty}|a_\nu|\xi^\nu, \\ \psi(\xi) &= \sum_{\nu=1}^{\infty}|b_\nu|\xi^\nu \quad |b_1| < 1. \end{aligned} \tag{2}$$

For $0 \leq \tau < 1$, let

$$\mathfrak{N}_{\mathcal{HF}}(\tau) = \left\{\Im \in \mathcal{HF} : \mathrm{Re}\left(\frac{\Im'(\xi)}{\xi'}\right) \geq \tau,\ \xi = re^{i\theta} \in \Xi\right\},$$

and

$$\mathfrak{R}_{\mathcal{HF}}(\tau) = \left\{\Im \in \mathcal{HF} : \mathrm{Re}\left(\frac{\Im''(\xi)}{\xi''}\right) \geq \tau,\ \xi = re^{i\theta} \in \Xi\right\}$$

where

$$\xi' = \frac{\partial}{\partial\theta}\left(\xi = re^{i\theta}\right), \xi'' = \frac{\partial}{\partial\theta}(\xi'), \Im'(\xi) = \frac{\partial}{\partial\theta}\Im\left(re^{i\theta}\right), \Im'' = \frac{\partial}{\partial\theta}(\Im'(\xi)).$$

Define

$$\mathcal{T}\mathfrak{N}_{\mathcal{HF}}(\tau) = \mathfrak{N}_{\mathcal{HF}}(\tau) \cap \mathcal{T}_{\mathcal{HF}} \quad \text{and} \quad \mathcal{T}\mathfrak{R}_{\mathcal{HF}}(\tau) = \mathfrak{R}_{\mathcal{HF}}(\tau) \cap \mathcal{T}_{\mathcal{HF}}.$$

For more details about the classes $\mathcal{T}_{\mathcal{HF}}$, $\mathfrak{N}_{\mathcal{HF}}(\tau)$, $\mathcal{T}\mathfrak{N}_{\mathcal{HF}}(\tau)$, $\mathfrak{R}_{\mathcal{HF}}(\tau)$ and $\mathcal{T}\mathfrak{R}_{\mathcal{HF}}(\tau)$ see [13,18].

In [19] Sokòl et al., introduced the class $\mathcal{HF}(\varrho, \gamma)$ of functions $\Im \in \mathcal{HF}$ that satisfy

$$\mathrm{Re}\left\{\phi'(\xi) + \psi'(\xi) + 3\varrho\xi(\phi''(\xi) + \psi''(\xi)) + \varrho\xi^3(\phi'''(\xi) + \psi'''(\xi))\right\} > \gamma,$$

for some $\varrho \geq 0$ and $0 \leq \gamma < 1$. For $\varrho = 0$, we obtain the class $\mathcal{HF}(\gamma)$ which satisfy

$$\mathrm{Re}\{\phi'(\xi) + \psi'(\xi)\} > \gamma.$$

2. Mittag-Leffler Function

The two-parameter Mittag-Leffler $\mathbb{E}_{\rho,\epsilon}(\xi)$ (also known as the Wiman function [20]) was given by

$$\mathbb{E}_{\rho,\epsilon}(\xi) = \sum_{\nu=0}^{\infty}\frac{\xi^\nu}{\Gamma(\rho\nu + \epsilon)}, \quad (\xi, \rho, \epsilon \in \mathbb{C}, \text{ with } \mathrm{Re}\rho > 0, \mathrm{Re}\epsilon > 0), \tag{3}$$

while in 1903, the one-parameter Mittag-Leffler $\mathbb{E}_\rho(\xi)$ was introduced for $\epsilon = 1$, and given by

$$\mathbb{E}_\rho(\xi) = \sum_{\nu=0}^{\infty}\frac{\xi^\nu}{\Gamma(\rho\nu + 1)}, \quad (\xi, \rho \in \mathbb{C}, \text{ with } \mathrm{Re}\rho > 0).$$

As its special case, the function $\mathbb{E}_{\rho,\epsilon}(\xi)$ has many well known functions for example, $\mathbb{E}_{\mathbf{0,0}}(\xi) = \sum_{\nu=0}^{\infty}\xi^\nu$, $\mathbb{E}_{\mathbf{1,1}}(\xi) = e^\xi$, $\mathbb{E}_{\mathbf{1,2}}(\xi) = \frac{e^\xi - 1}{\xi}$, $\mathbb{E}_{\mathbf{2,1}}(\xi^2) = cosh\xi$, $\mathbb{E}_{\mathbf{2,1}}(-\xi^2) = cos\xi$,

$\mathbb{E}_{2,2}(\xi^2) = \frac{sinh\xi}{\xi}$, $\mathbb{E}_{2,2}(-\xi^2) = \frac{sin\xi}{\xi}$, $\mathbb{E}_4(\xi) = \frac{1}{2}[cos\xi^{\frac{1}{4}} + cosh\xi^{\frac{1}{4}}]$ and $\mathbb{E}_3(\xi) = \frac{1}{2}[e^{\xi^{\frac{1}{3}}} + 2e^{-\frac{1}{2}\xi^{\frac{1}{3}}}cos(\frac{\sqrt{3}}{2}\xi^{\frac{1}{3}})]$.

Putting $\rho = \frac{1}{2}$ and $\epsilon = 1$, we get

$$\mathbb{E}_{\frac{1}{2},1}(\xi) = e^{\xi^2}.erfc(-\xi) = e^{\xi^2}\left(1 + \frac{2}{\sqrt{\pi}}\sum_{\nu=0}^{\infty}\frac{(-1)^{\nu}}{\nu!(2\nu+1)}\xi^{2\nu+1}\right).$$

Numerous properties of the one-parameter Mittag-Leffler $\mathbb{E}_{\rho}(\xi)$ and the two-parameter Mittag-Leffler $\mathbb{E}_{\rho,\epsilon}(\xi)$ can be found e.g., in [21–24].

It is clear that the two-parameter Mittag-Leffler function $\mathbb{E}_{\rho,\epsilon}(\xi) \notin \mathcal{A}$. Thus, we have the following normalization due to Bansal and Prajapat [22]:

$$\chi_{\rho,\epsilon}(\xi) = \xi\Gamma(\epsilon)\mathbb{E}_{\rho,\epsilon}(\xi) = \xi + \sum_{\nu=2}^{\infty}\frac{\Gamma(\epsilon)}{\Gamma(\rho(\nu-1)+\epsilon)}\xi^{\nu},$$

where $\rho,\epsilon,\xi \in \mathbb{C}$, with $\mathrm{Re}\rho > 0$ and $\mathrm{Re}\epsilon > 0$. In this study, we let ρ, ϵ to be real numbers and $\xi \in \Xi$.

The study of operators plays an important role in the geometric function theory. Many differential and integral operators can be written in terms of convolution of certain analytic functions, (see [25–29]).

Very recently, and for the functions

$$\chi_{\rho,\epsilon}(\xi) = \xi + \sum_{\nu=2}^{\infty}\frac{\Gamma(\epsilon)}{\Gamma(\rho(\nu-1)+\epsilon)}\xi^{\nu}, \text{ and } \chi_{\eta,\delta}(\xi) = \sum_{\nu=1}^{\infty}\frac{\Gamma(\delta)}{\Gamma(\eta(\nu-1)+\delta)}\xi^{\nu}. \quad (4)$$

Murugusundaramoorthy et al. [30] defined the following convolution operator $\Theta(\Im)$ given by

$$\begin{aligned}\mathfrak{F}(\xi) = \Theta\Im(\xi) &= \phi(\xi) * \chi_{\rho,\epsilon}(\xi) + \overline{\psi(\xi) * \chi_{\eta,\delta}(\xi)} \\ &= \xi + \sum_{\nu=2}^{\infty}\frac{\Gamma(\epsilon)}{\Gamma(\rho(\nu-1)+\epsilon)}a_{\nu}\xi^{\nu} + \overline{\sum_{\nu=1}^{\infty}\frac{\Gamma(\delta)}{\Gamma(\eta(\nu-1)+\delta)}b_{\nu}\xi^{\nu}},\end{aligned} \quad (5)$$

where $\rho, \eta, \epsilon, \delta$ are real with $\rho, \eta, \epsilon, \delta \notin \mathbb{Z}_0^- = \{0, -1, -2, \ldots\} \cup \{0\}$.

Inclusion relations between different subclasses of analytic and univalent functions by using hypergeometric functions [10,31], generalized Bessel function [32–34] and by the recent investigations related with distribution series [35–41], were studied in the literature. Very recently, several authors have investigated mapping properties and inclusion results for the families of harmonic univalent functions, including various linear and nonlinear operators (see [42–48]).

The paper is organized as follows. In Section 3, we recall some lemmas, which will be useful to prove the main results. Section 4 is devoted to establishing some inclusion relations of the harmonic class $\mathcal{HF}(\varrho,\gamma)$ the classes $\mathcal{S}^*_{\mathcal{HF}}$, $\mathcal{K}_{\mathcal{HF}}$, $\mathfrak{N}_{\mathcal{HF}}(\tau)$, and $\mathfrak{R}_{\mathcal{HF}}(\tau)$ by applying the convolution operator Θ related with Mittag-Leffler function following the work performed in [30]. Finally, in Section 5, several special cases of the main results are also obtained when $\varrho = 0$.

3. Preliminary Lemmas

We shall use the following lemmas in our proofs.

Lemma 1 ([19]). *Let $\Im = \phi + \overline{\psi}$ where ϕ and ψ are given by (1) and suppose that $\varrho \geq 0$, $0 \leq \gamma < 1$ and*

$$\sum_{\nu=2}^{\infty} \nu[1+\varrho\left(\nu^2-1\right)]|a_\nu| + \sum_{\nu=1}^{\infty} \nu[1+\varrho\left(\nu^2-1\right)]|b_\nu| \leq 1-\gamma. \tag{6}$$

then $\Im$ is harmonic, sense-preserving univalent functions in Ξ and $\Im \in \mathcal{HF}(\varrho,\gamma)$.

Moreover, if $\Im \in \mathcal{HF}(\varrho,\gamma)$, then

$$|a_\nu| \leq \frac{1-\gamma}{\nu[1+\varrho(\nu^2-1)]},\ \nu \geq 2, \tag{7}$$

and

$$|b_\nu| \leq \frac{1-\gamma}{\nu[1+\varrho(\nu^2-1)]},\ \nu \geq 1. \tag{8}$$

Lemma 2 ([6]). *Let $\Im = \phi + \overline{\psi}$ where ϕ and ψ are given by (2) and suppose that $0 \leq \tau < 1$. Then $\Im \in \mathcal{T}\mathfrak{N}_{\mathcal{HF}}(\tau)$ if and only if*

$$\sum_{\nu=2}^{\infty} \nu|a_\nu| + \sum_{\nu=1}^{\infty} \nu|b_\nu| \leq 1-\tau. \tag{9}$$

Moreover, if $\Im \in \mathcal{T}\mathfrak{N}_{\mathcal{HF}}(\tau)$, then

$$|a_\nu| \leq \frac{1-\tau}{\nu}, \nu \geq 2, \tag{10}$$

and

$$|b_\nu| \leq \frac{1-\tau}{\nu}, \nu \geq 1. \tag{11}$$

Lemma 3 ([18]). *Let $\Im = \phi + \overline{\psi}$ where ϕ and ψ are given by (2), and suppose that $0 \leq \tau < 1$. Then $\Im \in \mathcal{T}\mathfrak{R}_{\mathcal{HF}}(\tau)$ if and only if*

$$\sum_{\nu=2}^{\infty} \nu^2|a_\nu| + \sum_{\nu=1}^{\infty} \nu^2|b_\nu| \leq 1-\tau. \tag{12}$$

Moreover, if $\Im \in \mathcal{T}\mathfrak{R}_{\mathcal{HF}}(\tau)$, then

$$|a_\nu| \leq \frac{1-\tau}{\nu^2},\ \nu \geq 2 \tag{13}$$

and

$$|b_\nu| \leq \frac{1-\tau}{\nu^2},\ \nu \geq 1. \tag{14}$$

Lemma 4 ([5]). *If $\Im = \phi + \overline{\psi} \in \mathcal{S}^*_{\mathcal{HF}}$ where ϕ and ψ are given by (1) with $b_1 = 0$, then*

$$|a_\nu| \leq \frac{(2\nu+1)(\nu+1)}{6} \text{ and } |b_\nu| \leq \frac{(2\nu-1)(\nu-1)}{6}. \tag{15}$$

Lemma 5 ([5]). *If $\Im = \phi + \overline{\psi} \in \mathcal{K}_{\mathcal{HF}}$ where ϕ and ψ are given by (1) with $b_1 = 0$, then*

$$|a_\nu| \leq \frac{\nu+1}{2} \text{ and } |b_\nu| \leq \frac{\nu-1}{2}. \tag{16}$$

Throughout the sequence, we use the following:

$$\chi_{\rho,\epsilon}(\xi) = \xi + \sum_{\nu=2}^{\infty} \frac{\Gamma(\epsilon)}{\Gamma(\rho(\nu-1)+\epsilon)}\xi^{\nu}; \quad \chi_{\rho,\epsilon}(1) = 1 + \sum_{\nu=2}^{\infty} \frac{\Gamma(\epsilon)}{\Gamma(\rho(\nu-1)+\epsilon)}, \tag{17}$$

$$\chi'_{\rho,\epsilon}(\xi) = 1 + \sum_{\nu=2}^{\infty} \frac{\nu\Gamma(\epsilon)}{\Gamma(\rho(\nu-1)+\epsilon)}\xi^{\nu-1}; \quad \chi'_{\rho,\epsilon}(1) - 1 = \sum_{\nu=2}^{\infty} \frac{\nu\Gamma(\epsilon)}{\Gamma(\rho(\nu-1)+\epsilon)}, \tag{18}$$

$$\chi''_{\rho,\epsilon}(1) = \sum_{\nu=2}^{\infty} \frac{\nu(\nu-1)\Gamma(\epsilon)}{\Gamma(\rho(\nu-1)+\epsilon)}, \tag{19}$$

$$\chi'''_{\rho,\epsilon}(1) = \sum_{\nu=2}^{\infty} \frac{\nu(\nu-1)(\nu-2)\Gamma(\epsilon)}{\Gamma(\rho(\nu-1)+\epsilon)}, \tag{20}$$

and in general, we have

$$\chi^{(j)}_{\rho,\epsilon}(1) = \sum_{\nu=2}^{\infty} \frac{\nu(\nu-1)(\nu-2)\cdots(\nu-(j-1))\Gamma(\epsilon)}{\Gamma(\rho(\nu-1)+\epsilon)}, j = 1, 2, \ldots \tag{21}$$

4. Inclusion Relations of the Class $\mathcal{HF}(\varrho, \gamma)$

In this section we shall prove that $\Theta(\mathcal{S}^*_{\mathcal{HF}}) \subset \mathcal{HF}(\varrho, \gamma)$ and $\Theta(\mathcal{K}_{\mathcal{HF}}) \subset \mathcal{HF}(\varrho, \gamma)$.

Theorem 1. *Let $\varrho \geq 0$, $\gamma \in [0, 1)$ and $\rho, \epsilon, \eta, \delta \notin \mathbb{Z}_0^-$. If*

$$\begin{aligned}
&\Big[2\varrho\Big(\chi^{(5)}_{\rho,\epsilon}(1) + \chi^{(5)}_{\eta,\epsilon}(1)\Big) + 23\varrho\chi^{(4)}_{\rho,\epsilon}(1) + (67\varrho + 2)\chi^{(3)}_{\rho,\epsilon}(1) \\
&+ (45\varrho + 9)\chi^{(2)}_{\rho,\epsilon}(1) + 6\chi'_{\rho,\epsilon}(1) \\
&+ 17\varrho\chi^{(4)}_{\eta,\epsilon}(1) + (31\varrho + 2)\chi^{(3)}_{\eta,\epsilon}(1) + (9\varrho + 3)\chi^{(2)}_{\eta,\epsilon}(1)\Big] \\
&\leq 6(1-\gamma),
\end{aligned} \tag{22}$$

then

$$\Theta(\mathcal{S}^*_{\mathcal{HF}}) \subset \mathcal{HF}(\varrho, \gamma).$$

Proof. Let $\Im = \phi + \overline{\psi} \in \mathcal{S}^*_{\mathcal{HF}}$ where ϕ and ψ are of the form (1) with $b_1 = 0$. We need to show that $\Theta(\Im) = \mathfrak{F}(\xi) \in \mathcal{HF}(\varrho, \gamma)$, which given by (5) with $b_1 = 0$. In view of Lemma 1, we need to prove that

$$\mathcal{Q}(\varrho, \epsilon, \delta, \eta) \leq 1 - \gamma,$$

where

$$\begin{aligned}
\mathcal{Q}(\varrho, \epsilon, \delta, \eta) = &\sum_{\nu=2}^{\infty} \nu\Big(1 + \varrho\Big(\nu^2 - 1\Big)\Big)\left|\frac{\Gamma(\epsilon)}{\Gamma(\rho(\nu-1)+\epsilon)}a_\nu\right| \\
&+ \sum_{\nu=2}^{\infty} \nu\Big(1 + \varrho\Big(\nu^2 - 1\Big)\Big)\left|\frac{\Gamma(\delta)}{\Gamma(\eta(\nu-1)+\delta)}b_\nu\right|.
\end{aligned} \tag{23}$$

Using the inequalities (15) of Lemma 4, we get

$$
\begin{aligned}
&Q(\varrho,\epsilon,\delta,\eta) \\
&\leq \frac{1}{6}\left[\sum_{\nu=2}^{\infty}(2\nu+1)(\nu+1)\left(\nu+\varrho\nu\left(\nu^2-1\right)\right)\frac{\Gamma(\epsilon)}{\Gamma(\rho(\nu-1)+\epsilon)}\right. \\
&\left.+\sum_{\nu=2}^{\infty}(2\nu-1)(\nu-1)\left(\nu+\varrho\nu\left(\nu^2-1\right)\right)\frac{\Gamma(\delta)}{\Gamma(\eta(\nu-1)+\delta)}\right] \\
&=\frac{1}{6}\left[\sum_{\nu=2}^{\infty}\left[2\varrho\nu^5+3\varrho\nu^4+(2-\varrho)\nu^3+(3-3\varrho)\nu^2+(1-\varrho)\nu\right]\frac{\Gamma(\epsilon)}{\Gamma(\rho(\nu-1)+\epsilon)}\right. \\
&\left.+\sum_{\nu=2}^{\infty}\left[2\varrho\nu^5-3\varrho\nu^4+(2-\varrho)\nu^3+(3\varrho-3)\nu^2+(1-\varrho)\nu\right]\frac{\Gamma(\delta)}{\Gamma(\eta(\nu-1)+\delta)}\right]
\end{aligned}
\tag{24}
$$

Writing

$$\nu^2=\nu(\nu-1)+\nu, \tag{25}$$

$$\nu^3=\nu(\nu-1)(\nu-2)+3\nu(\nu-1)+\nu, \tag{26}$$

$$\nu^4=\nu(\nu-1)(\nu-2)(\nu-3)+6\nu(\nu-1)(\nu-2)+7\nu(\nu-1)+\nu, \tag{27}$$

and

$$
\begin{aligned}
\nu^5=&\ \nu(\nu-1)(\nu-2)(\nu-3)(\nu-4)+10\nu(\nu-1)(\nu-2)(\nu-3)+25\nu(\nu-1)(\nu-2) \\
&+15\nu(\nu-1)+\nu,
\end{aligned}
\tag{28}
$$

in (24), we have

$$
\begin{aligned}
&Q(\varrho,\epsilon,\delta,\eta) \\
&\leq \frac{1}{6}\left[\sum_{\nu=2}^{\infty}[2\varrho\nu(\nu-1)(\nu-2)(\nu-3)(\nu-4)+23\varrho\nu(\nu-1)(\nu-2)(\nu-3)\right. \\
&+(67\varrho+2)\nu(\nu-1)(\nu-2)+(45\varrho+9)\nu(\nu-1) \\
&+6\nu]\frac{\Gamma(\epsilon)}{\Gamma(\rho(\nu-1)+\epsilon)} \\
&+\sum_{\nu=2}^{\infty}[2\varrho\nu(\nu-1)(\nu-2)(\nu-3)(\nu-4)+17\varrho\nu(\nu-1)(\nu-2)(\nu-3) \\
&\left.+(31\varrho+2)\nu(\nu-1)(\nu-2)+(9\varrho+3)\nu(\nu-1)]\frac{\Gamma(\delta)}{\Gamma(\eta(\nu-1)+\delta)}\right] \\
&=\frac{1}{6}\left[2\varrho\chi_{\rho,\epsilon}^{(5)}(1)+23\varrho\chi_{\rho,\epsilon}^{(4)}(1)+(67\varrho+2)\chi_{\rho,\epsilon}^{(3)}(1)\right. \\
&+(45\varrho+9)\chi_{\rho,\epsilon}^{(2)}(1)+6\chi_{\rho,\epsilon}'(1) \\
&\left.+2\varrho\chi_{\eta,\epsilon}^{(5)}(1)+17\varrho\chi_{\eta,\epsilon}^{(4)}(1)+(31\varrho+2)\chi_{\eta,\epsilon}^{(3)}(1)+(9\varrho+3)\chi_{\eta,\epsilon}^{(2)}(1)\right].
\end{aligned}
$$

Now $Q(\varrho,\epsilon,\delta,\eta)\leq 1-\gamma$ if (22) holds. $\square$

Theorem 2. *Let $\varrho \geq 0$, $\gamma \in [0,1)$ and $\rho, \epsilon, \eta, \delta \notin \mathbb{Z}_0^-$. If*

$$\begin{aligned}&[\varrho\chi^{(4)}_{\rho,\epsilon}(1) + 7\varrho\chi^{(3)}_{\rho,\epsilon}(1) + (9\varrho + 1)\chi^{(2)}_{\rho,\epsilon}(1) + 2\chi'_{\rho,\epsilon}(1) + \varrho\chi^{(4)}_{\eta,\epsilon} + 5\varrho\chi^{(3)}_{\eta,\epsilon}(1)\\ &+ (5\varrho - 1)\chi^{(2)}_{\eta,\epsilon} + 2(\varrho - 1)\chi'_{\eta,\epsilon}(1)].\\ &\leq 2(1-\gamma),\end{aligned} \tag{29}$$

then

$$\Theta(\mathcal{K}_{\mathcal{HF}}) \subset \mathcal{HF}(\varrho, \gamma).$$

Proof. Let $\Im = \phi + \overline{\psi} \in \mathcal{K}_{\mathcal{HF}}$ where ϕ and ψ are of the form (2) with $b_1 = 0$. We need to show that $\Theta(\Im) = \mathfrak{F}(\xi) \in \mathcal{HF}(\varrho, \gamma)$ which given by (5) with $b_1 = 0$. In view of Lemma 1, we need to prove that$Q(\varrho, \epsilon, \delta, \eta)$

$$Q(\varrho, \epsilon, \delta, \eta) \leq 1 - \gamma,$$

where $Q(\varrho, \epsilon, \delta, \eta)$ as given in (23). Using the inequalities (16) of Lemma 5, we get

$$\begin{aligned}Q(\varrho, \epsilon, \delta, \eta) \leq &\frac{1}{2}\Bigg[\sum_{\nu=2}^{\infty}(\nu+1)\left(\nu + \varrho\nu\left(\nu^2-1\right)\right)\frac{\Gamma\epsilon)}{\Gamma(\rho(\nu-1)+\epsilon)}\\ &+\sum_{\nu=2}^{\infty}(\nu-1)\left(\nu + \varrho\nu\left(\nu^2-1\right)\right)\frac{\Gamma(\delta)}{\Gamma(\eta(\nu-1)+\delta)}\Bigg]\\ =&\frac{1}{2}\Bigg[\sum_{\nu=2}^{\infty}\left[\varrho\nu^4 + \varrho\nu^3 + (1-\varrho)\nu^2 + (1-\varrho)\nu\right]\frac{\Gamma(\epsilon)}{\Gamma(\rho(\nu-1)+\epsilon)}\\ &+\sum_{\nu=2}^{\infty}\left[\varrho\nu^4 - \varrho\nu^3 + (1-\varrho)\nu^2 + (\varrho-1)\nu\right]\frac{\Gamma(\delta)}{\Gamma(\eta(\nu-1)+\delta)}\Bigg].\end{aligned}$$

Using the Equations (25)–(27), we have

$$\begin{aligned}&Q(\varrho, \epsilon, \delta, \eta) \leq \frac{1}{2}\Bigg[\sum_{\nu=2}^{\infty}[\varrho\nu(\nu-1)(\nu-2)(\nu-3) + 7\varrho\nu(\nu-1)(\nu-2)\\ &+(9\varrho+1)\nu(\nu-1) + 2\nu]\frac{\Gamma(\epsilon)}{\Gamma(\rho(\nu-1)+\epsilon)}\Bigg]\\ &+\frac{1}{2}\sum_{\nu=2}^{\infty}[\varrho\nu(\nu-1)(\nu-2)(\nu-3) + 5\varrho\nu(\nu-1)(\nu-2) + (5\varrho-1)\nu(\nu-1)\\ &2(\varrho-1)\nu]\frac{\Gamma(\delta)}{\Gamma(\eta(\nu-1)+\delta)}\\ &=\frac{1}{2}[\varrho\chi^{(4)}_{\rho,\epsilon}(1) + 7\varrho\chi^{(3)}_{\rho,\epsilon}(1) + (9\varrho+1)\chi^{(2)}_{\rho,\epsilon}(1) + 2\chi'_{\rho,\epsilon}(1) + \varrho\chi^{(4)}_{\eta,\epsilon} + 5\varrho\chi^{(3)}_{\eta,\epsilon}(1) + (5\varrho-1)\chi^{(2)}_{\eta,\epsilon}\\ &+2(\varrho-1)\chi'_{\eta,\epsilon}(1)].\end{aligned}$$

Now $Q(\varrho, \epsilon, \delta, \eta) \leq 1 - \gamma$ if (29) holds. □

The connection between $\mathcal{TN}_{\mathcal{HF}}(\tau)$ and $\mathcal{HF}(\varrho, \gamma)$ is given below in the next theorem.

Theorem 3. *Let $\varrho \geq 0$, $\gamma, \tau \in [0,1)$ and $\rho, \epsilon, \eta, \delta \notin \mathbb{Z}_0^-$. If*

$$\begin{aligned}&(1-\tau)\left[\varrho\left(\chi^{(2)}_{\rho,\epsilon}(1) + \chi^{(2)}_{\eta,\epsilon}(1)\right) + \varrho\left(\chi'_{\rho,c}(1) + \chi'_{\eta,c}(1)\right) + (1-\varrho)\left(\chi_{\rho,c}(1) + \chi_{\eta,c}(1) - 2\right)\right]\\ &\leq 1 - \gamma - |b_1|,\end{aligned}$$

then

$$\Theta(\mathcal{T}\mathfrak{N}_{\mathcal{HF}}(\tau)) \subset \mathcal{HF}(\varrho, \gamma).$$

Proof. Let $\Im = \phi + \overline{\psi} \in \mathcal{T}\mathfrak{N}_{\mathcal{HF}}(\tau)$ where ϕ and ψ are given by (2). In view of Lemma 1, it is enough to show that $P(\varrho, \epsilon, \delta, \eta) \leq 1 - \gamma$, where

$$\begin{aligned} P(\varrho, \epsilon, \delta, \eta) = & \sum_{\nu=2}^{\infty} \left(\nu + \varrho\nu\left(\nu^2 - 1\right)\right) \left| \frac{\Gamma(\epsilon)}{\Gamma(\rho(\nu-1)+\epsilon)} a_\nu \right| \\ & + |b_1| + \sum_{\nu=2}^{\infty} \left(\nu + \varrho\nu\left(\nu^2 - 1\right)\right) \left| \frac{\Gamma(\delta)}{\Gamma(\eta(\nu-1)+\delta)} b_\nu \right|. \end{aligned} \tag{30}$$

Using the inequalities (10) and (11) of Lemma 2, it follows that

$$\begin{aligned} P(\varrho, \epsilon, \delta, \eta) \leq & (1-\tau) \left[\sum_{\nu=2}^{\infty} \left(\varrho\nu^2 + 1 - \varrho\right) \frac{\Gamma(\epsilon)}{\Gamma(\rho(\nu-1)+\epsilon)} \right. \\ & \left. + \sum_{\nu=2}^{\infty} \left(\varrho\nu^2 + 1 - \varrho\right) \frac{\Gamma(\delta)}{\Gamma(\eta(\nu-1)+\delta)} \right] + |b_1| \\ = & (1-\tau) \left[\sum_{\nu=2}^{\infty} [\varrho\nu(\nu-1) + \varrho\nu + 1 - \varrho] \frac{\Gamma(\epsilon)}{\Gamma(\rho(\nu-1)+\epsilon)} \right. \\ & \left. + \sum_{\nu=2}^{\infty} [\varrho\nu(\nu-1) + \varrho\nu + 1 - \varrho] \frac{\Gamma(\delta)}{\Gamma(\eta(\nu-1)+\delta)} \right] + |b_1| \\ = & (1-\tau) \Big[\varrho\chi_{\rho,\epsilon}^{(2)}(1) + \varrho\chi'_{\rho,\epsilon}(1) + (1-\varrho)\left(\chi_{\rho,\epsilon}(1) - 1\right) \\ & + \varrho\chi_{\eta,\epsilon}^{(2)}(1) + \varrho\chi'_{\eta,\epsilon}(1) + (1-\varrho)\left(\chi_{\eta,\epsilon}(1) - 1\right) \Big] + |b_1| \\ \leq & 1 - \gamma, \end{aligned}$$

by the given hypothesis. □

Below we prove that $\Theta(\mathcal{T}\mathfrak{R}_{\mathcal{HF}}(\tau)) \subset \mathcal{HF}(\varrho, \gamma)$.

Theorem 4. *Let* $\varrho \geq 0$, $\gamma, \tau \in [0,1)$ *and* $\rho, \epsilon, \eta, \delta \notin \mathbb{Z}_0^-$. *If*

$$\begin{aligned} & (1-\tau) \left[\varrho\left(\chi'_{\rho,\epsilon}(1) + \chi'_{\eta,\epsilon}(1)\right) + \int_0^1 \frac{\chi_{\rho,\epsilon}(s)}{s} ds + \int_0^1 \frac{\chi_{\eta,\epsilon}(s)}{s} ds \right] \\ & \leq 1 - \delta - |b_1|, \end{aligned}$$

then

$$\Theta(\mathcal{T}\mathfrak{R}_{\mathcal{HF}}(\tau)) \subset \mathcal{HF}(\varrho, \gamma).$$

Proof. Making use of Lemma 1, we need only to prove that $P(\varrho,\epsilon,\delta,\eta) \leq 1-\gamma$, where $P(\varrho,\epsilon,\delta,\eta)$ as given in (30). Using the inequalities (13) and (14) of Lemma 3, it follows that

$$\begin{aligned} P(\varrho,\epsilon,\delta,\eta) &= \sum_{\nu=2}^{\infty}\left(\nu+\varrho\nu\left(\nu^2-1\right)\right)\left|\frac{\Gamma(\epsilon)}{\Gamma(\rho(\nu-1)+\epsilon)}a_\nu\right| \\ &+|b_1|+\sum_{\nu=2}^{\infty}\left(\nu+\varrho\nu\left(\nu^2-1\right)\right)\left|\frac{\Gamma(\delta)}{\Gamma(\eta(\nu-1)+\delta)}b_\nu\right| \\ &\leq (1-\tau)\left[\sum_{\nu=2}^{\infty}\left(\varrho\nu+\frac{1-\varrho}{\nu}\right)\frac{\Gamma(\epsilon)}{\Gamma(\rho(\nu-1)+\epsilon)}\right. \\ &\left.+\sum_{\nu=2}^{\infty}\left(\varrho\nu+\frac{1-\varrho}{\nu}\right)\frac{\Gamma(\delta)}{\Gamma(\eta(\nu-1)+\delta)}\right] \\ &= (1-\tau)\left[\varrho\chi'_{\rho,\epsilon}(1)+\int_0^1\frac{\chi_{\rho,\epsilon}(s)}{s}dt+\varrho\chi'_{\eta,\epsilon}(1)+\int_0^1\frac{\chi_{\eta,\epsilon}(s)}{s}ds\right]+|b_1| \\ &\leq 1-\gamma, \end{aligned}$$

by given hypothesis. □

Theorem 5. *Let $\varrho \geq 0$, $\gamma,\tau \in [0,1)$ and $\rho,\epsilon,\eta,\delta \notin \mathbb{Z}_0^-$. If*

$$\chi_{\rho,\epsilon}(1)+\chi_{\eta,\epsilon}(1) \leq 3-\frac{|b_1|}{1-\gamma}$$

then

$$\Theta(\mathcal{HF}(\varrho,\gamma)) \subset \mathcal{HF}(\varrho,\gamma).$$

Proof. Using Lemma 1 and the inequalities (7) and (8) of Lemma 1, we obtain

$$\begin{aligned} P(\varrho,\epsilon,\delta,\eta) &\leq (1-\gamma)\left[\sum_{\nu=2}^{\infty}\frac{\Gamma(\epsilon)}{\Gamma(\rho(\nu-1)+\epsilon)}+\sum_{\nu=2}^{\infty}\frac{\Gamma(\delta)}{\Gamma(\eta(\nu-1)+\delta)}\right]+|b_1| \\ &= (1-\gamma)\left[(\chi_{\rho,\epsilon}(1)-1)+(\chi_{\eta,\epsilon}(1)-1)\right]+|b_1| \\ &= (1-\gamma)[\chi_{\rho,\epsilon}(1)+\chi_{\eta,\epsilon}(1)-2]+|b_1| \\ &\leq 1-\gamma, \end{aligned}$$

by the given condition and this completes the proof of the theorem. □

5. Special Cases

Putting $\varrho = 0$ in Theorems 1–4, we obtain the following results.

Corollary 1. *Let $\gamma \in [0,1)$ and $\rho,\epsilon,\eta,\delta \notin \mathbb{Z}_0^-$. If*

$$2\left(\chi^{(3)}_{\rho,\epsilon}(1)+\chi^{(3)}_{\eta,\epsilon}(1)\right)+9\chi^{(2)}_{\rho,\epsilon}(1)+6\chi'_{\rho,\epsilon}(1)+3\chi^{(2)}_{\eta,\epsilon}(1) \leq 6(1-\gamma),$$

then

$$\Theta(\mathcal{S}^*_{\mathcal{HF}}) \subset \mathcal{HF}(\gamma).$$

Corollary 2. *Let $\gamma \in [0,1)$ and $\rho,\epsilon,\eta,\delta \notin \mathbb{Z}_0^-$. If*

$$\begin{aligned} &[\chi^{(2)}_{\rho,\epsilon}(1)-\chi^{(2)}_{\eta,\epsilon}(1)+2\left(\chi'_{\rho,\epsilon}(1)-\chi'_{\eta,\epsilon}(1)\right)] \\ &\leq 2(1-\gamma), \end{aligned} \tag{31}$$

then

$$\Theta(\mathcal{K}_{\mathcal{HF}}) \subset \mathcal{HF}(\gamma).$$

Corollary 3. *Let $\gamma \in [0,1)$ and $\rho, \epsilon, \eta, \delta \notin \mathbb{Z}_0^-$. If*

$$(1-\tau)\left[\left(\chi_{\rho,\epsilon}(1) + \chi_{\eta,\epsilon}(1)\right) - 2\right] \leq 1 - \gamma - |b_1|,$$

then

$$\Theta(\mathcal{T}\mathfrak{N}_{\mathcal{HF}}(\tau)) \subset \mathcal{HF}(\gamma).$$

Corollary 4. *Let $\gamma \in [0,1)$ and $\rho, \epsilon, \eta, \delta \notin \mathbb{Z}_0^-$. If*

$$(1-\tau)\left[\int_0^1 \frac{\chi_{\rho,\epsilon}(s)}{s} dt + \int_0^1 \frac{\chi_{\eta,\epsilon}(s)}{s} dt\right] \leq 1 - \gamma - |b_1|,$$

then

$$\Theta(\mathcal{T}\mathfrak{R}_{\mathcal{HF}}(\tau)) \subset \mathcal{HF}(\gamma).$$

6. Conclusions

Making use of the of the operator Θ given in (5) related with Mittag-Leffler function, we found some inclusion relations of the harmonic class $\mathcal{HF}(\varrho, \delta)$ with other classes of harmonic analytic function defined in the open disk. Further, and for $\varrho = 0$, several results of the main results are given. Following this study, one can find new inclusion relations for new harmonic classes of analytic functions using the operator Θ.

Author Contributions: Conceptualization, B.A.F. and F.M.S.; methodology, B.A.F.; validation, A.A.A.-D.; B.A.F.; N.T. and F.M.S.; formal analysis, A.A.A.-D. and B.A.F.; investigation, A.A.A.-D., B.A.F. and F.M.S.; writing original draft preparation, B.A.F. and A.A.A.-D.; writing—review and editing, A.A.A.-D.; B.A.F.; N.T. and F.M.S.; supervision, B.A.F. All authors have read and agreed to the published version of the manuscript.

Funding: This research was supported by the Deanship of Scientific Research at Jouf University through research grant no. (DSR-2021-03-0221).

Institutional Review Board Statement: Not applicable.

Informed Consent Statement: Not applicable.

Data Availability Statement: No data were used to support this study.

Acknowledgments: The authors would like to extend their appreciation to the Deanship of Scientific 224 Research at Jouf University for funding this work through research grant no. (DSR-2021-225 03-0221).

Conflicts of Interest: The authors declare no conflict of interest.

References

1. Choquet, G. Sur un type de transformation analytique généralisant la représentation conforme et définie au moyen de fonctions harmoniques. *Bull. Sci. Math.* **1945**, *89*, 156–165.
2. Kneser, H. Losung der Aufgabe 41. *Jahresber. Dtsch. Math.-Ver.* **1926**, *36*, 123–124.
3. Lewy, H. On the non-vanishing of the Jacobian in certain one-to-one mappings. *Bull. Amer. Math. Soc.* **1936**, *42*, 689–692. [CrossRef]
4. Rado, T. Aufgabe 41. *Jahresber. Dtsch. Math. Ver.* **1926**, *35*, 49.
5. Clunie, J.; Sheil-Small, T. Harmonic univalent functions. *Ann. Acad. Sci. Fen. Series A I Math.* **1984**, *9*, 3–25. [CrossRef]
6. Ahuja, O.P.; Jahangiri, J.M. Noshiro-type harmonic univalent functions. *Sci. Math. Jap.* **2002**, *6*, 253–259.
7. Duren, P. *Harmonic Mappings in the Plane. Cambridge Tracts in Mathematics*; Cambridge University Press: Cambridge, UK, 2004; Volume 156. [CrossRef]
8. Frasin, B.A. Comprehensive family of harmonic univalent functions. *SUT J. Math.* **2006**, *42*, 145–155. [CrossRef]

9. Frasin, B.A.; Magesh, N. Certain subclasses of uniformly harmonic β-starlike functions of complex order. *Stud. Univ. Babes-Bolyai Math.* **2013**, *58*, 147–158.
10. Jahangiri, J.M. Harmonic functions starlike in the unit disk. *J. Math. Anal. Appl.* **1999**, *235*, 470–477. [CrossRef]
11. Murugusundaramoorthy, G.; Vijaya, K.; Frasin, B.A. A subclass of harmonic functions with negative coefficients defined by Dziok-Srivastava operator. *Tamkang J. Math.* **2011**, *42*, 463–473. [CrossRef]
12. Ponnusamy, S.; Rasila, A. Planar harmonic mappings. *RMS Math. Newsl.* **2007**, *17*, 40–57.
13. Silverman, H. Harmonic univalent function with negative coefficients. *J. Math. Anal. Appl.* **1998**, *220*, 283–289. [CrossRef]
14. Alsoboh, A.; Darus, M.; Amourah, A.; Atshan, W.G. A Certain Subclass of Harmonic Meromorphic Functions with Respect to k-Symmetric Points. *Int. J. Open Probl. Complex Anal.* **2023**, *15*, 1–16.
15. Silverman, H.; Silvia, E.M. Subclasses of harmonic univalent functions. *N. Z. J. Math.* **1999**, *28*, 275–284.
16. Alsoboh, A.; Amourah, A.; Darus, M.; Rudder, C.A. Studying the Harmonic Functions Associated with Quantum Calculus. *Mathematics* **2023**, *11*, 2220. [CrossRef]
17. Alsoboh, A.; Darus, M. A q-Starlike Class of Harmonic Meromorphic Functions Defined by q-Derivative Operator. In *International Conference on Mathematics and Computations*; Springer Nature: Singapore, 2022; pp. 257–269.
18. Ahuja, O.P.; Jahangiri, J.M. A subclass of harmonic univalent functions. *J. Nat. Geom.* **2001**, *20*, 45–56.
19. Sokòl, J.; Ibrahim, R.W.; Ahmad, M.Z.; Al-Janaby, H.F. Inequalities of harmonic univalent functions with connections of hypergeometric functions. *Open Math.* **2015**, *13*, 691–705. [CrossRef]
20. Wiman, A. Uber die Nullstellun der Funcktionen $E(x)$. *Acta Math.* **1905**, *29*, 191–201. [CrossRef]
21. Attiya, A.A. Some applications of Mittag-Leffler function in the unit disk. *Filomat* **2016**, *30*, 2075–2081. Available online: http://www.jstor.org/stable/24898778 (accessed on 24 June 2023). [CrossRef]
22. Bansal, D.; Prajapat, J.K. Certain geometric properties of the Mittag-Leffler functions. *Complex Var. Elliptic Equations* **2016**, *61*, 338–350. [CrossRef]
23. Mittag-Leffler, G.M. Sur la nouvelle fonction $E(x)$. *Comptes Rendus Acad. Sci. Paris* **1903**, *137*, 554–558.
24. Sahoo, S.K.; Ahmad, H.; Tariq, M.; Kodamasingh, B.; Aydi, H.; De la Sen, M. Hermite-Hadamard type inequalities involving k-fractional operator for (h, m)-convex functions. *Symmetry* **2021**, *13*, 1686. [CrossRef]
25. Bernardi, S.D. Convex and starlike univalent functions. *Trans. Am. Math. Soc.* **1969**, *135*, 429–446. [CrossRef]
26. Carlson, B.C.; Shaffer, D.B. Starlike and prestarlike hypergeometric functions. *SIAM J. Math. Anal.* **1984**, *15*, 737–745. [CrossRef]
27. Frasin, B.A. Convexity of integral operators of p-valent functions. *Math. Comput. Model.* **2010**, *51*, 601–605. [CrossRef]
28. Hohlov, Y.E. Convolution operators preserving univalent functions. *Ukr. Math. J.* **1985**, *37*, 220–226. [CrossRef]
29. Ruscheweyh, S. New criteria for univalent functions. *Proc. Am. Math. Soc.* **1975**, *49*, 109–115. [CrossRef]
30. Murugusundaramoorthy, G.; Vijaya, K.; Hijaz, A.; Mahmoud, K.H.; Khalil, E.M. Mapping properties of Janowski-type harmonic functions involving Mittag-Leffler function. *AIMS Math.* **2021**, *6*, 13235–13246. [CrossRef]
31. Frasin, B.A.; Al-Hawary, T.; Yousef, F. Necessary and sufficient conditions for hypergeometric functions to be in a subclass of analytic functions. *Afr. Mat.* **2019**, *30*, 223–230. [CrossRef]
32. Frasin, B.A.; Aldawish, I. On subclasses of uniformly spiral-like functions associated with generalized Bessel functions. *J. Funct. Spaces.* **2019**, *2019*. [CrossRef]
33. Al-Hawary, T.; Amourah, A.; Aouf, M.K.; Frasin, B.A. Certain subclasses of analytic functions with complex order associated with generalized Bessel functions. In *Bulletin of the Transilvania University of Brasov*; Series III: Mathematics and Computer Science; Transilvania University Press: Brasov, Romania, 2023; pp. 27–40.
34. El-Ashwah, R.M.; Hassan, A.H. Some characterizations for a certain generalized Bessel function of the first kind to be in certain subclasses of analytic functions. *Int. J. Open Probl. Complex Anal.* **2017**, *9*, 14–37. [CrossRef]
35. Bulboaca, T.; Murugusundaramoorthy, G. Univalent functions with positive coefficients involving Pascal distribution series. *Commun. Korean Math. Soc.* **2020**, *35*, 867–877. [CrossRef]
36. Frasin, B.A. Subclasses of analytic functions associated with Pascal distribution series. *Adv. Theory Nonlinear Anal. Appl.* **2020**, *4*, 92–99. [CrossRef]
37. Frasin, B.A.; Alb Lupas, A. An Application of Poisson Distribution Series on Harmonic Classes of Analytic Functions. *Symmetry* **2023**, *15*, 590. [CrossRef]
38. Murugusundaramoorthy, G. Subclasses of starlike and convex functions involving Poisson distribution series. *Afr. Mat.* **2017**, *28*, 1357–1366. [CrossRef]
39. Amourah, A.; Frasin, B.A.; Ahmad, M.; Yousef, F. Exploiting the Pascal Distribution Series and Gegenbauer Polynomials to Construct and Study a New Subclass of Analytic Bi-Univalent Functions. *Symmetry* **2022**, *14*, 147. [CrossRef]
40. Alsoboh, A.; Amourah, A.; Darus, M.; Rudder, C.A. Investigating New Subclasses of Bi-Univalent Functions Associated with q-Pascal Distribution Series Using the Subordination Principle. *Symmetry* **2023**, *15*, 1109. [CrossRef]
41. Alsoboh, A.; Amourah, A.; Darus, M.; Sharefeen, R.I.A. Applications of Neutrosophic q-Poisson distribution Series for Subclass of Analytic Functions and Bi-Univalent Functions. *Mathematics* **2023**, *11*, 868. [CrossRef]
42. Porwal, S.; Dixit, K.K. An application of hypergeometric functions on harmonic univalent functions. *Bull. Math. Anal. Appl.* **2010**, *2*, 97–105.
43. Porwal, S.; Vijaya, K.; Kasthuri, M. Connections between various subclasses of planar harmonic mappings involving generalized Bessel functions. *Le Matematiche* **2016**, *71*, 99–114. [CrossRef]

44. Srivastava, H.M.; Khan, N.; Khan, S.; Ahmad, Q.Z.; Khan, B. A Class of k-Symmetric Harmonic Functions Involving a Certain q-Derivative Operator. *Mathematics* **2021**, *9*, 1812. [CrossRef]
45. Tariq, M.; Ahmad, H.; Sahoo, S.K. The Hermite-Hadamard type inequality and its estimations via generalized convex functions of Raina type. *Math. Mod. Num. Sim. Appl.* **2021**, *1*, 32–43. [CrossRef]
46. Yaşar, E. Harmonic k-Uniformly Convex, k-Starlike Mappings and Pascal Distribution Series. *Math. Sci. Appl. E-Notes* **2020**, *8*, 1–9. https://doi.org10.36753/mathenot.683486. [CrossRef]
47. Yalçın, S.; Murugusundaramoorthy, G.; Vijaya, K. Inclusion results on subclasses of harmonic univalent functions associated with Pascal distribution series. *Palestine J. Math.* **2022**, *11*, 267–275.
48. Yousef, A.T.; Salleh, Z. On a Harmonic Univalent Subclass of Functions Involving a Generalized Linear Operator. *Axioms* **2020**, *9*, 32. [CrossRef]

axioms

MDPI

Article

Starlike Functions Associated with Bernoulli's Numbers of Second Kind

Mohsan Raza [1], Mehak Tariq [1], Jong-Suk Ro [2,3,*], Fairouz Tchier [4] and Sarfraz Nawaz Malik [5,*]

1 Department of Mathematics, Government College University Faisalabad, Faisalabad 38000, Pakistan; mohsanraza@gcuf.edu.pk or mohsan976@yahoo.com (M.R.); mehaktariq988@gmail.com (M.T.)
2 School of Electrical and Electronics Engineering, Chung-Ang University, Dongjak-gu, Seoul 06974, Republic of Korea
3 Department of Intelligent Energy and Industry, Chung-Ang University, Dongjak-gu, Seoul 06974, Republic of Korea
4 Mathematics Department, College of Science, King Saud University, P.O. Box 22452, Riyadh 11495, Saudi Arabia; ftchier@ksu.edu.sa
5 Department of Mathematics, COMSATS University Islamabad, Wah Campus, Wah Cantt 47040, Pakistan
* Correspondence: jongsukro@gmail.com (J.-S.R.); snmalik110@ciitwah.edu.pk or snmalik110@yahoo.com (S.N.M.)

Abstract: The aim of this paper is to introduce a class of starlike functions that are related to Bernoulli's numbers of the second kind. Let $\varphi_{BS}(\xi) = \left(\frac{\xi}{e^{\xi}-1}\right)^2 = \sum_{n=0}^{\infty} \frac{\xi^n B_n^2}{n!}$, where the coefficients of B_n^2 are Bernoulli numbers of the second kind. Then, we introduce a subclass of starlike functions $\digamma$ such that $\frac{\xi \digamma'(\xi)}{\digamma(\xi)} \prec \varphi_{BS}(\xi)$. We found out the coefficient bounds, several radii problems, structural formulas, and inclusion relations. We also found sharp Hankel determinant problems of this class.

Keywords: starlike functions; subordination; Bernoulli's number of second kind; radii problems; inclusion results; coefficient bounds; Hankel determinants

MSC: 30C45; 30C50

Citation: Raza, M.; Tariq, M.; Ro, J.-S.; Tchier, F.; Malik, S.N. Starlike Functions Associated with Bernoulli's Numbers of Second Kind. *Axioms* **2023**, *12*, 764. https://doi.org/10.3390/axioms12080764

Academic Editor: Georgia Irina Oros

Received: 11 July 2023
Revised: 26 July 2023
Accepted: 1 August 2023
Published: 3 August 2023

1. Introduction and Preliminaries

The Bernoulli numbers first appeared in the posthumous publications of Jakob Bernoulli in (1713), and they were independently discovered by the Japanese mathematician Seki Takakazu in 1712 [1]. We define the Bernoulli numbers of the k kind as follows:

$$\varphi_{BS}(\xi) = \left(\frac{\xi}{e^{\xi}-1}\right)^k = \sum_{n=0}^{\infty} \frac{\xi^n B_n^k}{n!}. \tag{1}$$

Bernoulli numbers of the k kind are denoted by B_n^k. The function defined in (1) for $k = 1$ is known as the Bernoulli function. The convexity of the function φ_{BS} given in (1), as well as its reciprocal function $(e^{\xi} - 1)/\xi$ are studied in [2,3]; see also [4].

Let $\mathbf{H}$ denote a class of analytic functions in $\mathbf{E} = [\xi \in \mathbb{C} : |\xi| < 1]$. Let $\mathbf{A}_n \subset \mathbf{H}$ represent the functions $\digamma$ having the series expansion $\digamma(\xi) = \xi + d_{n+1}\xi^{n+1} + d_{n+2}\xi^{n+2} + \cdots$ in $\mathbf{E}$. The class $\mathbf{A}_1 = \mathbf{A}$ represents the function $\digamma$ with a power series representation:

$$\digamma(\xi) = \xi + \sum_{n=2}^{\infty} d_n \xi^n, \quad \xi \in \mathbf{E}. \tag{2}$$

The class $\mathbf{S} \subset \mathbf{A}$ contains the univalent function $\digamma$ (i.e., $\digamma(\xi_1) = \digamma(\xi_2)$, which implies that $\xi_1 = \xi_2$ in $\mathbf{E}$). Let $\digamma \in \mathbf{A}$. Then, $\digamma$ is in the $\mathbf{S}^*$ of univalent starlike functions if, and only if

$$Re\left\{\frac{\xi \digamma'(\xi)}{\digamma(\xi)}\right\} > 0, \quad \xi \in \mathbf{E}.$$

Let $\mathbf{B} \subset \mathbf{H}$ represent a class of self maps ϖ (Schwarz functions) in $\mathbf{E}$ with $\varpi(0) = 0$. Assume that F and g are analytic (holomorphic) in $\mathbf{E}$. Then, $F \prec g$ and reads as F, which is subordinated by g such that $F(\xi) = g(\varpi(\xi))$ for $\xi \in \mathbf{E}$ and $\varpi \in \mathbf{B}$ if the subordinating function g is univalent. Then,

$$F(0) = g(0) \Leftrightarrow F(\mathbf{E}) \subseteq g(\mathbf{E}).$$

In [5], the authors have introduced a subclass of $\mathbf{S}^*$ defined by

$$\mathbf{S}^*(\varphi) = \left\{ F \in \mathbf{A} : \frac{\xi F'(\xi)}{F(\xi)} \prec \varphi(\xi) \right\}.$$

The function φ is one-to-one in $\mathbf{E}$, and maps $\mathbf{E}$ onto a starlike domain with respect to $\varphi(0) = 1$, with $\varphi'(0) > 0$ being symmetric about the real axis . We obtain subclasses of $\mathbf{S}^*$ by taking particular φ. The functions in class $\mathbf{S}^*[a,b] := \mathbf{S}^*((1+a\xi)/(1+b\xi))$ are Janowski starlike functions [6]. Furthermore, $\mathbf{S}^*(\lambda) := \mathbf{S}^*[1-2\lambda, -1]$ represents starlike functions of order $\lambda \in [0,1)$, whereas $\mathbf{S}^*(0) = \mathbf{S}^*$. The class

$$\mathbf{SS}^*(\beta) := \mathbf{S}^*[(1+\xi)/(1-\xi)]^{\beta} = \{F \in \mathbf{A} : |\arg(\xi F'(\xi)/F(\xi))| < \beta\pi/2\},\ \beta \in (0,1]$$

represents strongly starlike functions in $\mathbf{E}$. The class $\mathbf{SL}^* := \mathbf{S}^*(\sqrt{1+\xi})$ contains starlike functions related with a lemniscate of the Bernoulli; see [7]. The classes

$$\mathbf{S}^*_{\mathbf{RL}} := \mathbf{S}^*\left(\sqrt{2} - \left(\sqrt{2}-1\right)\left((1-\xi)/\left(1+2\left(\sqrt{2}-1\right)\xi\right)\right)^{1/2}\right)$$

and $\mathbf{S}^*_e := \mathbf{S}^*(e^{\xi})$ were studied in [8,9]. The class $\mathbf{S}^*_C := \mathbf{S}^*(1+4\xi/3+2\xi^2/3)$ represents starlike functions related with a cardioid [10]. The classes $\mathbf{S}^*_s := \mathbf{S}^*(1+\sin\xi)$ and $\mathbf{S}^*_{\cos} := \mathbf{S}^*(\cos\xi)$ are related with sine and cosine functions, respecitvely; see [11] and [12] respectively. The class $\mathbf{S}^*_{\Delta} = \mathbf{S}^*\left(\xi + \sqrt{1+\xi^2}\right)$ is related with the lune, see [13], whereas the class $\mathbf{BS}^*(\lambda) := \mathbf{S}^*(1+\xi/(1-\lambda\xi^2))$, $\lambda \in [0,1]$ is related with the Booth lemniscate; see [14]. The class $\mathbf{S}^*_{\mathbf{B}} := \mathbf{S}^*(e^{e^{\xi}} - 1)$ is related to the Bell numbers; see [15]. The class $\mathbf{S}^*_{\mathbf{T}} = \mathbf{S}^*(e^{(\xi+\mu\frac{\xi^2}{2})})$ is related to telephone numbers; see [16]. The class $\mathbf{S}^*_{\mathbf{BF}} = \mathbf{S}^*(\xi/e^{\xi}-1)$ contains starlike functions related with Bernoulli functions' see [17].

For some recent work, we refer to [18–23] and the references therein.

We now define the class $\mathbf{S}^*_{BS}$ associated with the Bernoulli numbers of the second kind.

Definition 1. *Let $F \in \mathbf{A}$. Then, $F \in \mathbf{S}^*_{BS}$ if and only if*

$$\frac{\xi F'(\xi)}{F(\xi)} \prec \left(\frac{\xi}{e^{\xi}-1}\right)^2 = \varphi_{BS}(\xi), \quad \xi \in \mathbf{E}.$$

In other words, a function $F \in \mathbf{S}^*_{BS}$ can be written as

$$F(\xi) = \xi \exp\left(\int_0^{\xi} \frac{\varphi(s)-1}{s} ds\right), \tag{3}$$

where φ is analytic and satisfies $\varphi(\xi) \prec \varphi_{BS}(\xi) = (\frac{\xi}{e^{\xi}-1})^2$ $(\xi \in \mathbf{E})$.

To give some examples of functions in the class $\mathbf{S}^*_{BS}$, consider

$$\varphi_1(\xi) = 1 + \frac{\xi}{4}, \quad \varphi_2(\xi) = \frac{5+2\xi}{5+\xi}, \quad \varphi_3(\xi) = \frac{3+\xi e^{\xi}}{3}, \quad \varphi_4(\xi) = 1 + \frac{\xi\cos(\xi)}{4}.$$

The function $\varphi_0(\xi) = (\frac{\xi}{e^{\xi}-1})^2$ is univalent in **E**, $\varphi_i(0) = \varphi_0(0)$ $(i = 1,2,3,4)$ and $\varphi_i(\mathbf{E}) \subset \varphi_0(\mathbf{E})$; it is easy to conclude that $\varphi_i(\xi) \prec \varphi_0(\xi)$. The functions $\digamma_i \in \mathbf{S}^*_{BS}$ corresponding to every φ_i. respectively, are given as follows:

$$\begin{aligned}
\digamma_1(\xi) &= \xi e^{\xi/4}, \quad \digamma_2(\xi) = \xi\left(1+\frac{\xi}{5}\right), \\
\digamma_3(\xi) &= \xi \exp\left(\frac{e^{\xi}-1}{3}\right), \quad \digamma_4(\xi) = \xi \exp\left(\frac{\sin(\xi)}{4}\right).
\end{aligned}$$

In particular, if $\varphi_0(\xi) = \left(\frac{\xi}{e^{\xi}-1}\right)^2$, then (3) takes the form

$$\begin{aligned}
\digamma_0(\xi) &= \xi \exp\left(\int_0^{\xi} \frac{\varphi_0(s)-1}{s} ds\right) = \xi - \xi^2 + \frac{17\xi^3}{24} - \frac{29\xi^4}{72} \\
&+ \frac{377\xi^5}{1920} - \frac{11\xi^6}{120} + \cdots.
\end{aligned} \tag{4}$$

The above function acts as an extremal function for $\mathbf{S}^*_{BS}$.

The following theorem gives the sharp estimates for φ_{BS}:

Lemma 1. *The function* $\varphi_{BS}(\xi) = \left(\frac{\xi}{e^{\xi}-1}\right)^2$ *satisfies*

$$\begin{aligned}
\min_{|\xi|=\ell} Re\, \varphi_{BS}(\xi) &= \varphi_{BS}(\ell) = \min_{|\xi|=\ell} |\varphi_{BS}(\xi)| \\
\max_{|\xi|=\ell} Re\, \varphi_{BS}(\xi) &= \varphi_{BS}(-\ell) = \max_{|\xi|=\ell} |\varphi_{BS}(\xi)|,
\end{aligned}$$

whenever $\ell \in (0,1)$.

2. Inclusion and Radius Problems

Theorem 1. *The class* $\mathbf{S}^*_{BS}$ *satisfies the following inclusion relations:*

1. *If* $0 \leq \lambda \leq \frac{1}{(e-1)^2}$, *then* $\mathbf{S}^*_{BS} \subset \mathbf{S}^*(\lambda)$.
2. *If* $\beta \geq (\frac{e}{e-1})^2$, *then* $\mathbf{S}^*_{BS} \subset \mathbf{RS}^*(1/\beta) \subset \mathbf{M}(\beta)$.
3. $\mathbf{S}^*_{BS} \subset \mathbf{SS}^*(\beta)$, *where* $\beta_0 \leq \beta \leq 1$, *wherein* $\beta_0 = 2\mathrm{h}(y_2)/\pi \approx 0.6454469651m$ *and* h *is defined in* (5).

Proof. (1) If $\digamma \in \mathbf{S}^*_{BS}$, then $\frac{\xi \digamma'(\xi)}{\digamma(\xi)} \prec (\frac{\xi}{e^{\xi}-1})^2$. According to Lemma 1, we have

$$\min_{|\xi|=1} Re\left(\frac{\xi}{e^{\xi}-1}\right)^2 < Re\frac{\xi\digamma'(\xi)}{\digamma(\xi)} < \max_{|\xi|=1} Re\left(\frac{\xi}{e^{\xi}-1}\right)^2;$$

therefore,

$$Re\frac{\xi\digamma'(\xi)}{\digamma(\xi)} > \frac{1}{(e-1)^2}.$$

(2) Similarly,

$$Re\frac{\xi\digamma'(\xi)}{\digamma(\xi)} < \frac{e^2}{(e-1)^2}.$$

Thus, $\digamma \in \mathbf{S}^*\left(\frac{1}{(e-1)^2}\right) \cap \mathbf{M}\left(\frac{e^2}{(e-1)^2}\right)$. Now, we have the following:

$$Re\frac{\digamma(\xi)}{\xi\digamma'(\xi)} > \left(\frac{e-1}{e}\right)^2.$$

This implies that $F \in \mathbf{RS}^*(\beta)$ for $\beta \leq \left(\frac{e-1}{e}\right)^2$. Identically, $F \in \mathbf{RS}^*(1/\beta)$ for $\beta \geq \left(\frac{e}{e-1}\right)^2$. Also, $F \in \mathbf{RS}^*(1/\beta)$ if and only if

$$\left|\frac{\xi F'(\xi)}{F(\xi)} - \frac{\beta}{2}\right| < \frac{\beta}{2},$$

which leads to $Re(\xi F'(\xi)/F(\xi)) < \beta$. Therefore, $\mathbf{S}^*_{BS} \subset \mathbf{RS}^*(1/\beta) \subset \mathbf{M}(\beta)$ whenever $\beta \geq \left(\frac{e}{e-1}\right)^2$.

(3) If $F \in \mathbf{S}^*_{BS}$, then

$$\begin{aligned} \left|\arg\frac{\xi F'(\xi)}{F(\xi)}\right| &< \max_{|\xi|=1} \arg\left(\frac{\xi}{e^{\xi}-1}\right)^2 \\ &= \max_{0\leq y<2\pi} \arctan\left(\frac{V}{U}\right). \end{aligned}$$

Let

$$h(y) = \arctan\left(\frac{V}{U}\right), \tag{5}$$

where U and V are given as

$$\begin{aligned} U &= \cos(2y)\left(\begin{array}{c} \left(e^{\cos(y)}\right)^2(\cos(\sin(y)))^2 - 2\,e^{\cos(y)}\cos(\sin(y)) + 1 \\ -\left(e^{\cos(y)}\right)^2(\sin(\sin(y)))^2 \end{array}\right) \\ &\quad + \sin(2y)\left(2\left(e^{\cos(y)}\right)^2\cos(\sin(y))\sin(\sin(y)) - 2\,e^{\cos(y)}\sin(\sin(y))\right), \\ V &= \sin(2y)\left(\begin{array}{c} \left(e^{\cos(y)}\right)^2(\cos(\sin(y)))^2 - 2e^{\cos(y)}\cos(\sin(y)) + 1 \\ -\left(e^{\cos(y)}\right)^2(\sin(\sin(y)))^2 \end{array}\right) \\ &\quad - \cos(2y)\left(2\left(e^{\cos(y)}\right)^2\cos(\sin(y))\sin(\sin(y)) - 2e^{\cos(y)}\sin(\sin(y))\right). \end{aligned}$$

Here, $h'(y) = 0$ has $y_1 \approx 1.409746460$ and $y_2 \approx 4.873438847$ roots in $[0, 2\pi]$. In addition, $h''(y_2) \approx -1.0988577$. Hence, $\max_{0\leq y<2\pi} h(y) = h(y_2) \approx 1.013865722$, and $\left|\arg\frac{\xi F'(\xi)}{F(\xi)}\right| \leq \frac{\pi\beta}{2}$; that is, $\beta \geq 0.645186552$. This implies that $\mathbf{S}^*_{BS} \subset \mathbf{SS}^*_{\beta}$. □

Now, we discuss some radii problems for the class $\mathbf{S}^*_{BS}$. The following definitions and lemmas are needed to establish the results. The class $\mathbf{P}$ represents the functions p of the form

$$p(\xi) = 1 + \sum_{n=1}^{\infty} p_n \xi^n \tag{6}$$

that are analytic in $\mathbf{E}$ such that $Rep(\xi) > 0, \xi \in \mathbf{E}$. Let

$$\mathbf{P}_n[a,b] := \left\{p(\xi) = 1 + \sum_{k=n}^{\infty} c_n \xi^n : p(\xi) \prec \frac{1+a\xi}{1+b\xi},\ -1 \leq b < a \leq 1\right\}.$$

In particular, $\mathbf{P}_n(\lambda) := \mathbf{P}_n[1-2\lambda, -1]$, and $\mathbf{P}_n := \mathbf{P}_n(0)$. Let $\mathbf{S}^*_n[a,b] = \mathbf{A}_n \cap \mathbf{S}^*[a,b]$, and $\mathbf{S}^*_n(\lambda) := \mathbf{S}^*_n[1-2\lambda, -1]$. Also, let

$$\mathbf{S}^*_{BS,n} := \mathbf{A}_n \cap \mathbf{S}^*_{BS}, \quad \mathbf{S}^*_n(\lambda) := \mathbf{A}_n \cap \mathbf{S}^*(\lambda), \quad \mathbf{S}^*_{L,n} := \mathbf{A}_n \cap \mathbf{S}^*_L.$$

Additionally,

$$\mathbf{S}_n := \{F \in \mathbf{A}_n : F(\xi)/\xi \in \mathbf{P}_n\},$$

and

$$\mathbf{CS}_n(\lambda) := \left\{F \in \mathbf{A}_n : \frac{F(\xi)}{g(\xi)} \in \mathbf{P}_n,\ g \in \mathbf{S}_n^*(\lambda)\right\};$$

see [24].

Lemma 2 ([25]). *If $p \in \mathbf{P}_n(\lambda)$, then for $|\xi| = \ell$,*

$$\left|\frac{\xi p'(\xi)}{p(\xi)}\right| \leq \frac{2(1-\lambda)n\ell^n}{(1-\ell^n)(1+(1-2\lambda)\ell^n)}.$$

Lemma 3 ([26]). *Let $p \in \mathbf{P}$. Then,*

$$|jp_1^3 - kp_1p_2 + lp_3| \leq 2|j| + 2|k-2j| + 2|j-k+l|.$$

Lemma 4 ([27]). *If $p \in \mathbf{P}_n[a,b]$, then for $|\xi| = \ell$,*

$$\left|p(\xi) - \frac{1-ab\ell^{2n}}{1-b^2\ell^{2n}}\right| \leq \frac{(a-b)\ell^n}{1-b^2\ell^{2n}}.$$

If $p \in \mathbf{P}_n(\lambda)$, then for $|\xi| = \ell$,

$$\left|p(\xi) - \frac{(1+(1-2\lambda))\ell^{2n}}{1-\ell^{2n}}\right| \leq \frac{2(1-\lambda)\ell^n}{1-\ell^{2n}}.$$

In the following lemmas, we find disks centered at $(\nu,0)$ and $(1,0)$ of the largest and the smallest radii, respectively, such that $\mho_{BS} := \varphi_{BS}(\mathbf{E})$ lies in the disk with the smallest radius and contains the largest disk.

Lemma 5. *Let $\left(\frac{1}{e-1}\right)^2 \leq \nu \leq \left(\frac{e}{e-1}\right)^2$. Then,*

$$\{w \in \mathbb{C} : |w-\nu| < \ell_\nu\} \subset \mho_{BS} \subset \left\{w \in \mathbb{C} : |w-1| < \left(\frac{e}{e-1}\right)^2\right\},$$

where

$$\ell_\nu = \begin{cases} \nu - \left(\frac{1}{e-1}\right)^2, & \frac{1}{(e-1)^2} \leq \nu \leq \frac{e^2+1}{2(e-1)^2}, \\ \left(\frac{e}{e-1}\right)^2 - \nu, & \frac{e^2+1}{2(e-1)^2} \leq \nu \leq \left(\frac{e}{e-1}\right)^2. \end{cases}$$

Proof. Let $\cos(y) = \varrho$ and $\sin(y) = \varsigma$. Then, the square of the distance from the boundary $\mho_{BS}$ to the point $(\nu,0)$ is given by

$$\psi(y) = \left(\frac{\mathbf{A}}{(1-2e^{\varrho}cos(\varsigma)+(e^{\varrho})^2)^2} - \nu\right)^2 + \left(\frac{\mathbf{B}}{(1-2e^{\varrho}cos(\varsigma)+(e^{\varrho})^2)^2}\right)^2,$$

where

$$\begin{aligned} \mathbf{A} &= \cos(2y)\left\{1-2e^{\varrho}\cos(\varsigma)+(e^{\varrho})^2\cos(2\varsigma)\right\} + 2e^{\varrho}\{e^{\varrho}\cos(\varsigma)-1\}\sin(\varsigma)\sin(2y), \\ \mathbf{B} &= \sin(2y)\left\{1-2e^{\varrho}\cos(\varsigma)+(e^{\varrho})^2\cos(2\varsigma)\right\} - 2e^{\varrho}\{e^{\varrho}\cos(\varsigma)-1\}\sin(\varsigma)\cos(2y). \end{aligned}$$

To show that $|w-\nu| < \ell_\nu$ is largest disk contained in $\mho_{BS}$, it is enough to show that the $\min_{0\leq\leq 2\pi}\psi(y) = \ell_\nu$. Since $\psi(y) = \psi(-y)$, it is enough to take the range $0 \leq y \leq \pi$.

Case 1: When $\frac{1}{(e-1)^2} \leq \nu < \frac{e^2}{(2e^2-8e+9)(e-1)^2}$, then $\psi'(y) = 0$ has 0 and π roots. In addition, $\psi'(y) > 0$ for $y \in (0, \pi)$. Thus,

$$\min_{0 \leq \ell \leq \pi} \psi(y) = \min\{\psi(0),\ \psi(\pi)\} = \psi(0).$$

Hence,

$$\ell_\nu = \min_{0 \leq y \leq \pi} \sqrt{\psi(y)} = \sqrt{\psi(0)} = \frac{1}{(e-1)^2} - \nu.$$

Case 2: When $\frac{e^2}{(2e^2-8e+9)(e-1)^2} < \nu \leq \frac{e^2}{(e-1)^2}$, then $\psi'(y) = 0$ has 0, y_ν, and π roots, where y_ν depends on ν. In addition, $\psi'(y) > 0$ for $y \in (0, y_\nu)$, and $\psi'(y) < 0$ when $y \in (y_\nu, \pi)$. Therefore, $\psi(y)$ has minima at 0 or π. We also see that $\psi(0) < \psi(\pi)$ for $\frac{e^2}{(2e^2-8e+9)(e-1)^2} < \nu \leq \frac{e^2+1}{2(e-1)^2}$ and $\psi(0) > \psi(\pi)$ for $\frac{e^2+1}{2(e-1)^2} < \nu \leq \left(\frac{e}{e-1}\right)^2$.

Thus, the first part of the proof is completed.

Now, for the smallest disc that contains $\mho_{BS}$, the function $\psi(y)$ for $\nu = 1$ attains its maximum value at π. Thus, the disk with the smallest radius that contains $\mho_{BS}$ has a radius of $\left(\frac{e}{e-1}\right)^2$. □

Theorem 2. *The sharp $R_{\mathbf{S}^*_{BS,n}}$ for $\mathbf{S}_n$ is*

$$R_{\mathbf{S}^*_{BS,n}}(\mathbf{S}_n) = \left(\frac{e^2 - 2e}{\sqrt{n^2(e-1)^4 + (e^2-2e)} + n(e-1)^2} \right)^{1/n}.$$

Proof. Consider a function $\hbar(\xi) \in \mathbf{P}_n$ such that $\hbar(\xi) = \digamma(\xi)/\xi$. Now, we have the following:

$$\frac{\xi \digamma'(\xi)}{\digamma(\xi)} - 1 = \frac{\xi \hbar'(\xi)}{\hbar(\xi)}.$$

From Lemma 2, we have

$$\left| \frac{\xi \digamma'(\xi)}{\digamma(\xi)} - 1 \right| = \left| \frac{\xi \hbar'(\xi)}{\hbar(\xi)} \right| \leq \frac{2n\ell^n}{1-\ell^{2n}}.$$

From Lemma 4, the map of $|\xi| \leq \ell$ under $\xi\digamma'/\digamma$ lies in the $\mho_{BS}$ if the following is satisfied:

$$\frac{2n\ell^n}{1-\ell^{2n}} \leq 1 - \frac{1}{(e-1)^2}.$$

This is equivalently written as

$$((e-1)^2 - 1)\ell^{2n} + 2n(e-1)^2\ell^n + 1 - (e-1)^2 \leq 0.$$

Thus, the $\mathbf{S}^*_{BS,n}$ radius of the $\mathbf{S}_n$ is the root $\ell \subset (0,1)$ of

$$((e-1)^2 - 1)\ell^{2n} + 2n(e-1)^2\ell^n + 1 - (e-1)^2 = 0;$$

that is,

$$R_{\mathbf{S}^*_{BS,n}}(\mathbf{S}_n) = \left(\frac{e(e-2)}{n(e-1)^2 + \sqrt{1 + (n^2+1)(e-1)^4 - 2(e-1)^2}} \right)^{1/n}.$$

Consider $\digamma_0(\xi) = \xi(1+\xi^n)/1-\xi^n$. Then, $\hbar_0(\xi) = \digamma_0(\xi)/\xi = (1+\xi^n)/(1-\xi^n) > 0$. Thus, $\digamma_0 \in \mathbf{S}_n$, and $\xi\digamma_0'(\xi)/\digamma_0(\xi) = 1 + 2n\xi^n/(1-\xi^{2n})$. This is beacuse at $\xi = R_{\mathbf{S}^*_{BS,n}}$, we have

$$\frac{\xi \digamma_0'(\xi)}{\digamma_0(\xi)} - 1 = \frac{2n\xi^n}{1-\xi^{2n}} = 1 - \frac{1}{(e-1)^2}.$$

Therefore, F_0 gives a sharp result. Hence, the proof is completed. □

Theorem 3. *Let*

$$R_1 = \left(\frac{4e-e^2-1}{2(e-1)^2(1-2\lambda)+e^2+1}\right)^{\frac{1}{2n}},$$

$$R_2 = \left(\frac{(e-1)^2-1}{(1+n-\lambda)(e-1)^2+\sqrt{1+(2n(1-\lambda)+\lambda^2+n^2)(e-1)^4-2(e-1)^2\lambda}}\right)^{\frac{1}{n}},$$

$$R_3 = \left(\frac{e^2}{(1+n-\lambda)(e-1)^2+\sqrt{1+(1+n-\lambda)^2(e-1)^4-(1-2\lambda)e^4}}\right)^{\frac{1}{n}}.$$

Then, a sharp $\mathbf{S}^*_{BS,n}$-radius for the class $\mathbf{CS}_n(\lambda)$ is

$$R_{\mathbf{S}^*_{BS,n}}(\mathbf{CS}_n(\lambda)) = \begin{cases} R_2, & if\ R_2 \leq R_1, \\ R_3, & if\ R_2 > R_1. \end{cases}$$

Proof. Define a function $\hbar(\xi) = F(\xi)/g(\xi)$, where $g \in \mathbf{S}^*_n(\lambda)$. Then, $\hbar \in \mathbf{P}_n$, and $\xi g'(\xi)/g(\xi) \in P_n(\lambda)$. From the definition of $\hbar$, we have

$$\frac{\xi F'(\xi)}{F(\xi)} = \frac{\xi g'(\xi)}{g(\xi)} + \frac{\xi \hbar'(\xi)}{\hbar(\xi)}.$$

From Lemmas 2 and 3, we see that

$$\left|\frac{\xi F'(\xi)}{F(\xi)} - \frac{1+(1-2\lambda)\ell^{2n}}{1-\ell^{2n}}\right| \leq \frac{2(1+n-\lambda)\ell^n}{1-\ell^{2n}}. \tag{7}$$

Now, we find the values R_1, R_2 and R_3 for $0 < \ell < 1$ and $0 \leq \lambda < 1$. Firstly, we find R_1. For $\ell \leq R_1$, this can be found if and only if

$$\frac{1+(1-2\lambda)\ell^{2n}}{1-\ell^{2n}} \leq \frac{e^2+1}{2(e-1)^2}.$$

This implies that

$$\ell \leq \left(\frac{4e-e^2-1}{2(e-1)^2(1-2\lambda)+e^2+1}\right)^{\frac{1}{2n}}.$$

Now, we obtain R_2. For this, we must have

$$\frac{2(1+n-\lambda)\ell^n}{1-\ell^{2n}} \leq \frac{1+(1-2\lambda)\ell^{2n}}{1-\ell^{2n}} - \frac{1}{(e-1)^2}.$$

This implies that

$$\ell \leq \frac{(e-1)^2-1}{(1+n-\lambda)(e-1)^2+\sqrt{1+(-2n\lambda+\lambda^2+2n+n^2)(e-1)^4-2(e-1)^2\lambda}}.$$

For R_3, we have

$$\frac{2(1+n-\lambda)\ell^n}{1-\ell^{2n}} \leq \left(\frac{e}{e-1}\right)^2 - \frac{1+(1-2\lambda)\ell^{2n}}{1-\ell^{2n}}.$$

This implies that

$$\ell \leq \frac{e^2}{(1+n-\lambda)(e-1)^2+\sqrt{1+(1+n-\lambda)^2(e-1)^4-(1-2\lambda)e^4}}.$$

□

Theorem 4. *The* $\mathbf{S}^*_{BS,n}$*-radius for* $\mathbf{S}^*_n[a,b]$ *is*

$$R_{\mathbf{S}^*_{BS,n}}(\mathbf{S}^*_n[a,b]) = \begin{cases} \min\{1;\ell_1\}, & -1 \le b \le 0 < a \le 1, \\ \min\{1;\ell_2\}, & 0 < b < a \le 1, \end{cases}$$

where

$$\ell_1 = \left(\frac{2e-1}{(e-1)^2 a - be^2}\right)^{1/n},$$

and

$$\ell_2 = \left(\frac{e(e-2)}{a(e-1)^2 - b}\right)^{1/n}.$$

Proof. Let $F \in \mathbf{S}^*_n[a,b]$. Then, from Lemma 3, we can write

$$\left|\frac{\xi F'(\xi)}{F(\xi)} - C\right| \le \frac{(a-b)\ell^n}{1-b^2\ell^{2n}}, \tag{8}$$

where

$$C = \frac{1-ab\ell^{2n}}{1-b^2\ell^{2n}}, \ |\xi| = \ell$$

For $b < 0$, we see that $C \ge 1$. Also by using Lemma 4, $F \in \mathbf{S}^*_{BS,n}$ if

$$\frac{1+(a-b)\ell^n - ab\ell^{2n}}{1-b^2\ell^{2n}} \le \frac{e^2}{(e-1)^2},$$

which is equivalent to

$$\ell \le \left(\frac{2e-1}{(e-1)^2 a - be^2}\right)^{1/n} = \ell_1.$$

Furthermore, if $b = 0$, then $C = 1$. From (8), we have

$$\left|\frac{\xi F'(\xi)}{F(\xi)} - 1\right| \le a\ell^n, \quad (0 < a \le 1).$$

By using Lemma 4 with $a = 1$, this gives $\ell \le \left(\frac{e(e-2)}{a(e-1)^2}\right)^{1/n}$ for $F \in \mathbf{S}^*_{BS,n}$. We see that $C < 1$ for $0 < b < a \le 1$. Thus, from Lemma 4 and (8), we have $F \in \mathbf{S}^*_{BS,n}$ if

$$\frac{(a-b)\ell^n}{1-b^2\ell^{2n}} \le \frac{1-ab\ell^{2n}}{1-b^2\ell^{2n}} - \frac{1}{(e-1)^2},$$

or, equivalently, if

$$\ell \le \left(\frac{e(e-2)}{a(e-1)^2 - b}\right)^{1/n} = \ell_2.$$

This completes the result. □

Theorem 5. *Let* $-1 < b < a \le 1$*. If either*

(a) $(1-b) \le (e-1)^2(1-a)$ *and* $2(1-b^2) \le (1-ab)(e-1)^2 < (1-b^2)(1+e^2)$ *or if*

(b) $(a+1)(e-1)^2 \le e^2(1+b)$ *and* $(1-b^2)(1+e^2) \le 2(1-ab)(e-1)^2 \le 2e^2(1-b^2)$ *hold, then* $\mathbf{S}^*_n[a,b] \subset \mathbf{S}^*_{BS,n}$.

Proof. (a) Let $p(\xi) = \xi F'(\xi)/F(\xi)$. From Lemma 3, $F \in \mathbf{S}_n^*[a,b]$ if

$$\left| p(\xi) - \frac{1-ab}{1-b^2} \right| \leq \frac{a-b}{1-b^2}.$$

In connection with Lemma 4, $F \in \mathbf{S}_n^*[a,b]$ if

$$\frac{a-b}{1-b^2} \leq \frac{1-ab}{1-b^2} - \frac{1}{(e-1)^2},$$

and

$$\frac{1}{(e-1)^2} \leq \frac{1-ab}{1-b^2} \leq \frac{1}{2}\frac{1+e^2}{(e-1)^2},$$

which, upon simplification, reduce to (a).

(b) Let $p(\xi) = \xi F'(\xi)/F(\xi)$. Since $F \in \mathbf{S}_n^*[a,b]$, thus, in the view of Lemma 3,

$$\left| p(\xi) - \frac{1-ab}{1-b^2} \right| \leq \frac{a-b}{1-b^2}.$$

By using Lemma 4, we note that $F \in \mathbf{S}_n^*[a,b]$ if the following is satisfied:

$$\frac{a-b}{1-b^2} \leq \frac{e^2}{(e-1)^2} - \frac{1-ab}{1-b^2},$$

and

$$\frac{1}{2}\left(\frac{1+e^2}{(e-1)^2}\right) \leq \frac{1-ab}{1-b^2} \leq \frac{e^2}{(e-1)^2},$$

which reduced to the conditions (b). □

Theorem 6. *The sharp radii for* $\mathbf{S}_{\mathbf{L}}^*$, $\mathbf{S}_{\mathbf{RL}}^*$, $\mathbf{S}_{\mathbf{e}}^*$, *and* $\mathbf{S}_{\mathbf{lim}}^*$ *are*

$R_{\mathbf{S}_{BS}^*}(\mathbf{S}_{\mathbf{L}}^*) = \frac{(e-1)^4-1}{(e-1)^4} \approx 0.889,$

$R_{\mathbf{S}_{BS}^*}(\mathbf{S}_{\mathbf{RL}}^*) = \frac{(5+4\sqrt{2})(e-1)^4+(-6\sqrt{2}-8)(e-1)^2+3+2\sqrt{2}}{(5+4\sqrt{2})(e-1)^4+(8+4\sqrt{2})(e-1)^2+2+2\sqrt{2}} \approx 0.87193,$

$R_{\mathbf{S}_{BS}^*}(\mathbf{S}_{\mathbf{e}}^*) = 2 - 2\ln(e-1) \approx 0.917350,$

$R_{\mathbf{S}_{BS}^*}(\mathbf{S}_{\mathbf{lim}}^*) = \frac{\sqrt{2}(e-2)}{e-1} \approx 0.591174.$

Proof. (1) For $F \in \mathbf{S}_{\mathbf{L}}^*$, we have

$$\frac{\xi F'(\xi)}{F(\xi)} = \sqrt{1+\omega(\xi)}.$$

By the Schwarz Lemma $|\omega(\xi)| \leq |\xi|$, we thus have $\left|\sqrt{1+\omega(\xi)} - 1\right| \leq 1 - \sqrt{1-\ell}$. Thus, for $|\xi| = \ell$, we have

$$\left| \frac{\xi F'(\xi)}{F(\xi)} - 1 \right| \leq 1 - \sqrt{1-\ell}.$$

By Lemma 4, we have $1 - \sqrt{1-\ell} \leq 1 - \frac{1}{(e-1)^2}$. Consider $F_0(\xi) = \frac{4\xi \exp\{2(\sqrt{1+\xi}-1)\}}{(1+\sqrt{1+\xi})^2}$, which is in $\mathbf{S}_{\mathbf{L}}^*$ and $\frac{\xi F_0'(\xi)}{F_0(\xi)} = \sqrt{1+\xi} = \frac{1}{(e-1)^2}$ at $R_{\mathbf{S}_{BS}^*}(\mathbf{S}_{\mathbf{L}}^*)$. Hence, the sharpness is verified.

(2) Let $F \in \mathbf{S}^*_{\mathbf{RL}}$. Then, for $|\xi| = \ell$, we have

$$\left|\frac{\xi F'(\xi)}{F(\xi)} - 1\right| \le 1 - \sqrt{2} + (\sqrt{2}-1)\sqrt{\frac{1+\ell}{1-2(\sqrt{2}-1)\ell}}$$
$$\le 1 - \frac{1}{(e-1)^2}$$

provided that

$$\ell \le \frac{(5+4\sqrt{2})(e-1)^4 + (-6\sqrt{2}-8)(e-1)^2 + 3 + 2\sqrt{2}}{(5+4\sqrt{2})(e-1)^4 + (8+4\sqrt{2})(e-1)^2 + 2 + 2\sqrt{2}} = R_{\mathbf{S}^*_{BS}}(\mathbf{S}^*_{\mathbf{RL}}).$$

Consider the function F_1 defined by

$$F_1(\xi) = \xi \exp\left(\int_0^{\xi} \frac{\varphi_0(t)-1}{t} dt\right),$$

where

$$\varphi_0(\xi) = \sqrt{2} - (\sqrt{2}-1)\sqrt{\frac{1-\xi}{1+2(\sqrt{2}-1)\xi}}.$$

At $\xi = R_{\mathbf{S}^*_{BS}}(\mathbf{S}^*_{\mathbf{RL}})$, we have

$$\frac{\xi F_1'(\xi)}{F_1(\xi)} = \sqrt{2} - (\sqrt{2}-1)\sqrt{\frac{1-\xi}{1+2(\sqrt{2}-1)\xi}} = \frac{1}{(e-1)^2}.$$

Hence, the sharpness is verified.

(3) $F \in \mathbf{S}^*_e$, so we have

$$\left|\frac{\xi F'(\xi)}{F(\xi)} - 1\right| \le e^{\xi} - 1 \le \frac{e^2}{(e-1)^2} - 1.$$

The result is sharp for F_2 such that $\frac{\xi F_2'(\xi)}{F_2(\xi)} = e^{\xi}$.

(4) Suppose that $F \in (\mathbf{S}^*_{\mathbf{lim}})$; then $\frac{\xi F'(\xi)}{F(\xi)} \prec 1 + \sqrt{2}\xi + \frac{\xi^2}{2}$. Thus, for $|\xi| = \ell$, we can it write as

$$\left|\frac{\xi F'(\xi)}{F(\xi)} - 1\right| = \left|1 + \sqrt{2}\xi + \frac{\xi^2}{2} - 1\right| \le \sqrt{2}\ell - \frac{\ell^2}{2} \le 1 - \frac{1}{(e-1)^2},$$

which is satisfied for $\ell \le \frac{\sqrt{2}(e-2)}{e-1}$. Consider

$$F_3(\xi) = \xi \exp\frac{4\sqrt{2}\xi + \xi^2}{4}.$$

Since $\frac{\xi F_3'(\xi)}{F_3(\xi)} = 1 + \sqrt{2}\xi + \frac{\xi^2}{2}$, it follows that $F_3 \in (\mathbf{S}^*_{\mathbf{lim}})$ and at $\xi = R_{\mathbf{S}^*_{BS}}(\mathbf{S}^*_{\mathbf{lim}})$, so we have $\frac{\xi F_3'(\xi)}{F_3(\xi)} = \frac{1}{(e-1)^2}$. □

Consider the families:

$$\mathbf{F}_1 := \left\{F \in \mathbf{A}_n : Re\left(\frac{F(\xi)}{g(\xi)}\right) > 0 \text{ and } Re\left(\frac{g(\xi)}{\xi}\right) > 0,\ g \in \mathbf{A}_n\right\},$$

$$\mathbf{F}_2 := \left\{F \in \mathbf{A}_n : Re\left(\frac{F(\xi)}{g(\xi)}\right) > 0 \text{ and } Re\left(\frac{g(\xi)}{\xi}\right) > 1/2,\ g \in \mathbf{A}_n\right\},$$

and

$$\mathbf{F}_3 := \left\{ F \in \mathbf{A}_n : \left| \frac{F(\xi)}{g(\xi)} - 1 \right| < 1 \text{ and } Re\left(\frac{g(\xi)}{\xi} \right) > 0,\ g \in \mathbf{A}_n \right\}.$$

Theorem 7. *The sharp radii for functions in the families* $\mathbf{F}_1$, $\mathbf{F}_2$, *and* $\mathbf{F}_3$ *respectively, are:*

$$R_{\mathbf{S}^*_{BS,n}}(\mathbf{F}_1) = \left(\frac{e(e-2)}{2n(e-1)^2 + \sqrt{1+(4n^2+1)(e-1)^4 - 2(e-1)^2}} \right)^{1/n},$$
$$R_{\mathbf{S}^*_{BS,n}}(\mathbf{F}_2) = \left(\frac{2e(e-2)}{3n(e-1)^2 + \sqrt{(9n^2+4n+4)(e-1)^4 - 4(n+2)(e-1)^2 + 4}} \right)^{1/n},$$
$$R_{\mathbf{S}^*_{BS,n}}(\mathbf{F}_3) = \left(\frac{2e(e-2)}{3n(e-1)^2 + \sqrt{(9n^2+4n+4)(e-1)^4 - 4(n+2)(e-1)^2 + 4}} \right)^{1/n}.$$

Proof. (1) Let $F \in \mathbf{F}_1$ and define $p,\ \hbar : \mathbf{E} \to \mathbb{C}$ by $p(\xi) = \frac{g(\xi)}{\xi}$ and $\hbar(\xi) = \frac{F(\xi)}{g(\xi)}$. Then, clearly, $p,\ \hbar \in \mathbf{P}_n$, since $F(\xi) = \xi p(\xi)\hbar(\xi)$. By Lemma 2, and by combining the above inequalities, we have

$$\left| \frac{\xi F'(\xi)}{F(\xi)} - 1 \right| \leq \frac{4n\ell^n}{1-\ell^{2n}} \leq 1 - \frac{1}{(e-1)^2}.$$

After some simplification, we arrive at

$$\ell \leq \left(\frac{e(e-2)}{2n(e-1)^2 + \sqrt{1+(4n^2+1)(e-1)^4 - 2(e-1)^2}} \right)^{1/n} = R_{\mathbf{S}^*_{BS,n}}(\mathbf{F}_1).$$

To verify the sharpness of result, consider the functions defined by

$$F_4(\xi) = \xi \left(\frac{1+\xi^n}{1-\xi^n} \right)^2 \text{ and } g_0(\xi) = \xi \left(\frac{1+\xi^n}{1-\xi^n} \right).$$

Then, clearly $Re\left(\frac{F_4(\xi)}{g_0(\xi)} \right) > 0$, and $Re\left(\frac{g_0(\xi)}{\xi} \right) > 0$. Hence, $F_0 \in \mathbf{F}_1$. We see that at $\xi = R_{\mathbf{S}^*_{BS,n}}(\mathbf{F}_1) e^{i\pi/n}$ as follows:

$$\frac{\xi F_4'(\xi)}{F_4(\xi)} = 1 + \frac{4n\xi^n}{1-\xi^{2n}} = \frac{1}{(e-1)^2}.$$

Hence, the sharpness is satisfied.

(2) Let $F \in \mathbf{F}_2$. Define $p,\ \hbar : \mathbf{E} \to \mathbb{C}$ by $p(\xi) = \frac{g(\xi)}{\xi}$ and $\hbar(\xi) = \frac{F(\xi)}{g(\xi)}$. Then, $p \in \mathbf{P}_n$, and $\hbar \in \mathbf{P}_n(1/2)$. Since $F(\xi) = \xi p(\xi)\hbar(\xi)$, then according to Lemma 2, we have

$$\left| \frac{\xi F'(\xi)}{F(\xi)} - 1 \right| \leq \frac{3n\ell^n + n\ell^{2n}}{1-\ell^{2n}} \leq 1 - \frac{1}{(e-1)^2},$$

which implies that

$$\ell \leq \left(\frac{2e(e-2)}{3n(e-1)^2 + \sqrt{9n^2(e-1)^4 + 4[(n+1)(e-1)^2 - 1][e(e-2)]}} \right)^{1/n} = R_{\mathbf{S}^*_{BS,n}}(\mathbf{F}_2).$$

Thus, $F \in \mathbf{S}^*_{BS,n}$ for $\ell \leq R_{\mathbf{S}^*_{BS,n}}(\mathbf{F}_2)$.

For sharpness, consider the following:

$$F_5(\xi) = \frac{\xi(1+\xi^n)}{(1-\xi^n)^2} \text{ and } g_1(\xi) = \frac{\xi}{1-\xi^n}.$$

Then clearly $Re\left(\frac{F_5(\xi)}{g_1(\xi)}\right) > 0$, and $Re\left(\frac{g_1(\xi)}{\xi}\right) > \frac{1}{2}$. Hence, $F \in \mathbf{F}_2$. Now, at $\xi = R_{\mathbf{S}^*_{BS,n}}(\mathbf{F}_2)$

$$\frac{\xi F'_5(\xi)}{F_5(\xi)} = 1 + \frac{3n\xi^n + n\xi^{2n}}{1-\xi^{2n}} = \frac{1}{(e-1)^2}.$$

Hence, the sharpness is satisfied.

(3) Let $F \in \mathbf{F}_3$. Define $p, \hbar : \mathbf{E} \to \mathbb{C}$ by $p(\xi) = \frac{g(\xi)}{\xi}$ and $\hbar(\xi) = \frac{g(\xi)}{F(\xi)}$. Then, $p \in \mathbf{P}_n$ and

$$\left|\frac{1}{\hbar(\xi)} - 1\right| < 1 \iff Re(\hbar(\xi)) > 1/2;$$

therefore, $\hbar \in \mathbf{P}_n(1/2)$. Since $F(\xi)\hbar(\xi) = \xi p(\xi)$, then according to Lemma 2, we have

$$\left|\frac{\xi F'(\xi)}{F(\xi)} - 1\right| \leq \frac{3n\ell^n + n\ell^{2n}}{1-\ell^{2n}} \leq 1 - \frac{1}{(e-1)^2}.$$

This implies that

$$\ell \leq \left(\frac{2e(e-2)}{3n(e-1)^2 + \sqrt{(9n^2+4n+4)(e-1)^4 - 4(n+2)(e-1)^2+4}}\right)^{1/n} = R_{\mathbf{S}^*_{BS,n}}(\mathbf{F}_3).$$

Thus, $F \in \mathbf{S}^*_{BS,n}$ for $\ell \leq R_{\mathbf{S}^*_{BS,n}}(\mathbf{F}_3)$. For sharpness, consider the following:

$$F_6(\xi) = \frac{\xi(1+\xi^n)^2}{1-\xi^n} \text{ and } g_2(\xi) = \frac{\xi(1+\xi^n)}{1-\xi^n}.$$

We see that

$$Re\left(\frac{g_2(\xi)}{F_6(\xi)}\right) = Re\left(\frac{1}{1+\xi^n}\right) > \frac{1}{2},$$

and

$$Re\left(\frac{F_6(\xi)}{\xi}\right) = Re\left(\frac{1+\xi^n}{1-\xi^n}\right) > 0.$$

Therefore, $F_6 \in \mathbf{F}_3$. A computation shows that at $\xi = R_{\mathbf{S}^*_{BS,n}}(\mathbf{F}_3)e^{i\pi/n}$, which comes out to

$$\frac{\xi F'_6(\xi)}{F_6(\xi)} - 1 = \frac{3n\xi^n + n\xi^{2n}}{1-\xi^{2n}} = 1 - \frac{1}{(e-1)^2}.$$

Hence, the sharpness is satisfied. □

3. Coefficient and Hankel Determinant Problems for the Class $\mathbf{S}^*_{BS}$

Pommerenke [28] was the first to introduce the qth Hankel determinant for analytic functions, and it is stated as follows:

$$H_{q,n}(F) := \begin{vmatrix} d_n & d_{n+1} & \dots & d_{n+q-1} \\ d_{n+1} & d_{n+2} & \dots & d_{n+q} \\ \vdots & \vdots & \dots & \vdots \\ d_{n+q-1} & d_{n+q} & \dots & d_{n+2q-2} \end{vmatrix}, \tag{9}$$

where $n, q \in \mathbb{N}$. We note that

$$H_{2,1}(F) = d_3 - d_2^2, \quad H_{2,2}(F) = d_2 d_4 - d_3^2.$$

In this section, we focus on obtaining sharp coefficient bounds and bounds on $H_{2,1}(F)$ and $H_{2,2}(F)$.

We will use the following results related to the class $\mathbf{P}$.

Lemma 6 ([5]). *Let $p \in \mathbf{P}$ and be of the form (6). Then for v, a complex number*

$$|p_2 - vp_1^2| \le 2\max(1, |2v-1|).$$

Lemma 7 ([29,30]). *Let $p \in \mathbf{P}$ and be of the form (6) such that $|\rho| \le 1$, and $|\eta| \le 1$. Then,*

$$2p_2 = p_1^2 + \rho(4 - p_1^2), \tag{10}$$

$$4p_3 = p_1^3 + 2(4-p_1^2)p_1\rho - (4-p_1^2)p_1^2\rho + 2(4-p_1^2)(1-|\rho|^2)\eta, \tag{11}$$

Lemma 8 ([31]). *Let $\varpi \in \mathbf{B}$ be given by $\varpi(z) = \sum_{n=0}^{\infty} c_n \xi^n$, and thus*

$$\psi(u,v) = \left|c_3 + \mu_1 c_1 c_2 + \mu_2 c_1^3\right|.$$

Then, $\psi(u,v) \le |v|$ if $(u,v) \in D_6$, where

$$D_6 = \left\{(u,v) : 2 \le |\mu| \le 4, \quad v \ge \frac{1}{12}\left(\mu^2 + 8\right)\right\}.$$

Lemma 9 ([32]). *Let $\overline{\mathbf{E}} := \{\rho \in \mathbb{C} : |\rho| \le 1\}$, and, for j, k, and $l \in \mathbb{R}$, let*

$$Y(j,k,l) := \max\left\{|j + k\rho + l\rho^2| + 1 - |\rho|^2 : \rho \in \overline{\mathbf{E}}\right\}. \tag{12}$$

If $jl \ge 0$, then

$$Y(j,k,l) = \begin{cases} |j| + |k| + |l|, & |k| \ge 2(1-|l|), \\ 1 + |j| + \dfrac{k^2}{4(1-|l|)}, & |k| < 2(1-|l|). \end{cases}$$

If $jl < 0$, then

$$Y(j,k,l) = \begin{cases} 1 - |j| + \dfrac{k^2}{4(1-|l|)}, & -4jl(l^{-2}-1) \le k^2 \wedge |k| < 2(1-|l|), \\ 1 + |j| + \dfrac{k^2}{4(1+|l|)}, & k^2 < \min\{4(1+|l|)^2, -4jl(l^{-2}-1)\}. \\ R(j,k,l), & \text{otherwise.} \end{cases}$$

In such as case,

$$R(j,k,l) = \begin{cases} |j| + |k| - |l|, & |l|(|k| + 4|j|) \le |jk|, \\ 1 + |j| + \dfrac{k^2}{4(1+|l|)}, & |jk| < |l|(|k| - 4|j|) \le |jk|. \\ |l| + |j|\sqrt{1 - \dfrac{k^2}{4jl}}, & \text{otherwise.} \end{cases}$$

Theorem 8. *Let $F \in \mathbf{S}^*_{BS}$ and be of the form (2). Then,*

$$|d_2| \le 1, \quad |d_3| \le \frac{17}{24}, \quad |d_4| \le \frac{29}{72}.$$

These bounds are the best possible.

Proof. If $F \in \mathbf{S}^*_{BS}$, then

$$\frac{\xi F'(\xi)}{F(\xi)} = \left(\frac{\varpi(\xi)}{e^{\varpi(\xi)} - 1}\right)^2,$$

where $\varpi \in \mathbf{B}$. The class $\mathbf{B}$ consists of Schwarz functions ϖ that are analytic in $\mathbf{E}$, with $\varpi(0) = 0$, and $|\varpi(\xi)| \leq |\xi|$. Let p be of the form (6). Then,

$$\varpi(\xi) = \frac{p(\xi) - 1}{p(\xi) + 1}.$$

Now by using (2), we can write out the following:

$$\begin{aligned} \frac{\xi F'(\xi)}{F(\xi)} &= 1 + d_2\xi + (2d_3 - d_2^2)\xi^2 + (3d_4 - 3d_2d_3 + d_2^3)\xi^3 \\ &\quad + (4d_5 - 2d_3^2 - 4d_2d_4 + 4d_2^2d_3 - d_2^4)\xi^4 + \cdots. \end{aligned} \tag{13}$$

In addition,

$$\begin{aligned} \left(\frac{\mu(\xi)}{e^{\mu(\xi)} - 1}\right)^2 &= 1 - \frac{1}{2}p_1\xi + \left(\frac{29}{96}p_1^2 - \frac{1}{4}p_2\right)\xi^2 + \left(\frac{-109}{576}p_1^3 + \frac{13}{36}p_1p_2 - \frac{1}{6}p_3\right)\xi^3 \\ &\quad + \left(\frac{11011}{92160}p_1^4 - \frac{215}{576}p_2p_1^2 + \frac{25}{96}p_1p_3 + \frac{23}{192}p_2^2 - \frac{1}{8}p_4\right)\xi^4 + \cdots. \end{aligned} \tag{14}$$

From (13) and (14), we obtain

$$d_2 = \frac{1}{2}p_1, \tag{15}$$

$$d_3 = \frac{29}{96}p_1^2 - \frac{1}{4}p_2, \tag{16}$$

$$d_4 = \frac{-109}{576}p_1^3 + \frac{13}{36}p_1p_2 - \frac{1}{6}p_3. \tag{17}$$

From (15), we have $|d_2| = \frac{1}{2}|p_1| \leq 1$. From (16), we can write out the following:

$$|d_3| = \frac{1}{4}\left|p_2 - \frac{29}{24}p_1^2\right|.$$

An application of Lemma 6 for $v = \frac{29}{24}$ gives the required bound.

The function $\varpi \in \mathbf{B}$ can be written as a power series:

$$\varpi(z) = \sum_{n=1}^{\infty} c_n z^n, \quad z \in \mathbf{E}. \tag{18}$$

Since $p \in \mathbf{P}$, therefore,

$$p(z) = \frac{1 + \varpi(z)}{1 - \varpi(z)}.$$

By comparing the coefficients at powers of z in

$$[1 - \omega(z)]p(z) = 1 + \omega(z),$$

we obtain

$$p_1 = 2c_1, \quad p_2 = 2c_2 + 2c_1^2, \quad p_3 = 2c_3 + 4c_1c_2 + 2c_1^3.$$

By putting these values in (17), we obtain

$$d_4 = -\frac{1}{3}\left(c_3 + \mu_1c_1c_2 + \mu_2c_1^3\right),$$

where $\mu_1 = -\frac{7}{3}$, and $\mu_2 = \frac{29}{24}$. Now, by using Lemma 8, we have $2 \leq |\mu_1| \leq 4$, and $\mu_1 - \frac{1}{12}(\mu_2 + 8) = \frac{19}{216}$; therefore,

$$|d_4| \leq \frac{1}{3}|\mu_2| = \frac{29}{72}.$$

The equalities in each coefficient $|d_2|$, $|d_3|$, and $|d_4|$ are respectively obtained by taking the following:

$$F_1(\xi) = \xi \exp\left(\int_0^{\xi} \frac{(\frac{t}{e^t-1})^2 - 1}{t} dt\right) = \xi - \xi^2 + \frac{17}{24}\xi^3 - \frac{29}{72}\xi^4 + \cdots. \tag{19}$$

□

Theorem 9. *Let $F \in \mathbf{S}^*_{BS}$ and have the series representation given in (2). Then,*

$$|d_3 - d_2^2| \leq \frac{1}{2}. \tag{20}$$

Theorem 10. *Let $F \in \mathbf{S}^*_{BS}$ and have the series representation given in (2). Then,*

$$H_{2,2}(F) = |d_2 d_4 - d_3^2| \leq \frac{521}{576}. \tag{21}$$

The equality is obtained by the F_1 given in (19).

Proof. Using (15)–(17), we obtain

$$H_{2,2}(F) = d_2 d_4 - d_3^2 = -\frac{571}{3072}p_1^4 + \frac{191}{576}p_1^2 p_2 - \frac{1}{12}p_1 p_3 - \frac{1}{16}p_2^2. \tag{22}$$

As we can see that the functional $H_{2,2}(F)$ and the class $\mathbf{S}^*_{BS}$ are rotationally invariant, we may therefore take $p := p_1$ such that $p \in [0, 2]$. Then, by using Lemma 7, and after some computations, we may write out the following:

$$\begin{aligned} H_{2,2}(F) = &-\frac{571}{9216}p^4 + \frac{107}{1152}p^2(4-p^2)\rho - \frac{1}{192}(4-p^2)\left(12 - 7p^2\right)\rho^2 \\ &-\frac{1}{24}p(4-p^2)\left(1 - |\rho|^2\right)\eta, \end{aligned}$$

where ρ and η satisfy the relation $|\rho| \leq 1$ and $|\eta| \leq 1$.

Firstly, we consider the case when $p = 0$. Then, $|H_{2,2}(F)| = \left|-\frac{1}{4}\rho^2\right| \leq \frac{1}{4}$. Next, we assume that $p = 2$; then, $|H_{2,2}(F)| = \frac{521}{576}$. Now suppose that $p \in (0, 2)$; then,

$$|H_{2,2}(F)| \leq \frac{1}{24}p(4-p^2)\Phi(j,k,l),$$

where

$$\Phi(j,k,l) = \left|j + k\rho + l\rho^2\right| + 1 - |\rho|^2, \qquad \rho \in \overline{\mathbf{E}},$$

with $j = \dfrac{521p^3}{384(4-p^2)}$, $k = -\frac{107p}{48}$, and $l = \dfrac{(12-7p^2)}{8p}$; then clearly,

$$jl = \frac{521p^2(12-7p^2)}{3072(4-p^2)} \geq 0, \quad \text{for } p \in \left[\sqrt{\frac{12}{7}}, 2\right). \tag{23}$$

In addition,

$$|k| - 2(1 - |l|) = \frac{23p^2 - 96p + 144}{48p} > 0 \quad p \in \left[\sqrt{\frac{12}{7}}, 2\right)$$

so that $|k| > 2(1 - |l|)$, and by applying Lemma 9, we can obtain

$$|H_{2,2}(F)| \leq \frac{1}{24}p(4 - p^2)(|j| + |k| + |l|) = g(p),$$

where

$$g(p) = \frac{1}{9216}p^4 + \frac{24}{288}p^2 + \frac{1}{4}. \tag{24}$$

Clearly, $g'(p) > 0$, and so

$$\max g(p) = g(2) = \frac{521}{576}.$$

We also see from (23) that

$$jl = \frac{521p^2(12 - 7p^2)}{3072(4 - p^2)} < 0, \qquad \text{for } p \in \left(0, \sqrt{\frac{12}{7}}\right).$$

Thus,

$$k^2 - 4jl\left(l^{-2} - 1\right) = \frac{1}{576}\frac{p^2(889p^2 - 20280)}{7p^2 - 12} < 0, \quad p \in \left(0, \sqrt{\frac{12}{7}}\right).$$

This shows that $-4jl\left(l^{-2} - 1\right) \leq k^2 \wedge |k| < 2(1 - |l|)$. In addition,

$$\begin{aligned} \Phi(p) &= 4(1 + |l|)^2 + 4jl\left(l^{-2} - 1\right) \\ &= \frac{(7p - 6)(1295p^5 - 4266p^4 + 2688p^3 + 2073p^2 + 2304p - 13824)}{p^2(12 - 7p^2)}. \end{aligned}$$

We see that $\Phi(p) > 0$ for $p \in (0, 0.76032) \cup \left(\frac{6}{7}, \sqrt{\frac{12}{7}}\right)$, and $\Phi(p) < 0$ for $p \in (0.76032, \frac{6}{7})$. Hence, we conclude that

$$\min\left\{4(1 + |l|)^2, -4jl\left(l^{-2} - 1\right)\right\} = \begin{cases} -4jl\left(l^{-2} - 1\right), & p \in (0, 0.76032) \cup \left(\frac{6}{7}, \sqrt{\frac{12}{7}}\right), \\ 4(1 + |l|)^2 & (0.76032, \frac{6}{7}). \end{cases}$$

As a result,

$$k^2 - 4(1 + |l|)^2 - \frac{(23p^2 - 96p + 144)(191p^2 + 96p - 144)}{2304} > 0 \text{ for } \left(0.76032, \frac{6}{7}\right).$$

In addition,

$$k^2 + 4(1 + |l|)^2 = \frac{p^2(78365p^2 - 96828)}{1152(7p^2 - 12)} < 0 \text{ for } \left(\sqrt{\frac{96828}{78365}}, \sqrt{\frac{12}{7}}\right).$$

This shows that $k^2 < \min\{4(1 + |l|)^2, -4jl\left(l^{-2} - 1\right)\}$ hold for $p \in \left(\sqrt{\frac{96828}{78365}}, \sqrt{\frac{12}{7}}\right)$. By applying Lemma 9, we arrive at the following:

$$|H_{2,2}(F)| \leq \frac{1}{24}p(4 - p^2)\left(1 + |j| + \frac{k^2}{4(1 + |l|)}\right) = g_1(p),$$

where

$$g_1(p) = \frac{p(127p^4 - 1364p^3 - 1728p^2 - 8064p + 6912)}{6912(6 - 7p)}.$$

This attains its maxima at $p = \sqrt{\frac{12}{7}}$. Hence,

$$|H_{2,2}(F)| \leq \frac{\sqrt{21}\left(-4413 + 3034\sqrt{21}\right)}{-148176 + 49392\sqrt{21}} < \frac{521}{576}.$$

We are left with the case $p \in \left(0, \sqrt{\frac{96828}{78365}}\right)$. We also see that

$$|l|(|k| + 4|j|) - |jk| = \frac{4171p^4 - 55392p^2 + 246528}{18432(p^2 - 4)} < 0 \quad p \in \left(0, \sqrt{\frac{96828}{78365}}\right).$$

We conclude that $|l|(|k| + 4|j|) < |jk|$. By applying Lemma 9, we arrive at the following:

$$|H_{2,2}(F)| \leq \frac{1}{24}p(4 - p^2)(|j| + |k| - |l|) = g(p),$$

where g is given in (24), this giving us the required result. The function given in (19) belongs to the $\mathbf{S}^*_{BS}$, as $d_2 = -1$, $d_4 = -29/72$, and $d_3 = 17/24$, which yields the sharpness of (21). Hence, the proof is done. □

4. Conclusions

We have introduced a subclass of S^* associated with Bernoulli numbers of the second kind and studied some geometrical properties of the introduced class. These results include radii problems, inclusion problems, coefficient bounds, and Hankel determinants. The new defined class can further be studied for determining the bounds of Hankel and Toeplitz determinants, and the same can also be found for logarithmic coefficients and for the coefficients of inverse functions.

Author Contributions: Conceptualization, M.R. and M.T.; methodology, M.R. and M.T.; software, S.N.M.; validation, M.R. and S.N.M.; formal analysis, M.R.; investigation, M.R. and M.T.; resources, J.-S.R. and F.T.; data curation, J.-S.R. and F.T.; writing—original draft preparation, S.N.M.; writing—review and editing, S.N.M.; visualization, J.-S.R. and F.T.; supervision, M.R.; project administration, S.N.M.; funding acquisition, J.-S.R. and F.T. All authors have read and agreed to the published version of the manuscript.

Funding: This research received no external funding.

Institutional Review Board Statement: Not applicable.

Informed Consent Statement: Not applicable.

Data Availability Statement: Not applicable.

Acknowledgments: 1. This research was supported by the researchers Supporting Project Number (RSP2023R401), at King Saud University, Riyadh, Saudi Arabia. 2. This work was supported by the National Research Foundation of Korea (NRF) grant funded by the Korean government (MSIT) (No. NRF-2022R1A2C2004874). 3. This work was supported by the Korea Institute of Energy Technology Evaluation and Planning(KETEP), as well as the Ministry of Trade, Industry, and Energy (MOTIE) of the Republic of Korea (No. 20214000000280).

Conflicts of Interest: The authors declare no conflict of interest

References

1. Coen, L.E.S. Sums of Powers and the Bernoulli Numbers. Master's Thesis, Eastern Illinois University, Charleston, IL, USA , 1996.
2. Mocnu, P.T. Convexity of some particular functions. *Stud. Univ. Babes-Bolyai Math.* **1984**, *29*, 70–73.

3. Serb, I. The radius of convexity and starlikeness of a particular function. *Math Montisnigri.* **1996**, *7*, 65–69.
4. Miller, S.S.; Mocanu, P.T. *Differential Subordinations. Monographs and Textbooks in Pure and Applied Mathematics*; Dekker: New York, NY, USA, 2000; Volume 225.
5. Ma, W.; Minda, D. A unified treatment of some special classes of univalent functions. In *Proceeding of the Conference on Complex Analysis*; Li, Z., Ren, F., Yang, L., Zhang, S., Eds.; International Press: Boston, MA, USA, 1994; pp. 157–169.
6. Janowski, W. Extremal problems for a family of functions with positive real part and for some related families. *Ann. Polon. Math.* **1973**, *23*, 159–177. [CrossRef]
7. Sokół, J.; Stankiewicz, J. Radius of convexity of some subclasses of strongly starlike functions. *Zesz. Nauk. Politech. Rzesz. Mat.* **1996**, *19*, 101–105.
8. Mendiratta, R.; Nagpal, S.; Ravichandran, V. A subclass of starlike functions associated with left-half of the lemniscate of Bernoulli. *Int. J. Math.* **2014**, *25*, 1450090. [CrossRef]
9. Mendiratta, R.; Nagpal, S.; Ravichandran, V. On a subclass of strongly starlike functions associated with exponential function. *Bull. Malays. Math. Sci. Soc.* **2015**, *38*, 365–386. [CrossRef]
10. Sharma, K.; Jain, N.K.; Ravichandran, V. Starlike functions associated with a cardioid. *Afr. Math.* **2016**, *27*, 923–939. [CrossRef]
11. Cho, N.E.; Kumar, S.; Kumar, V.; Ravichandran, V. Radius problems for starlike functions associated with the sine function. *Bull. Iran. Math. Soc.* **2019**, *45*, 213–232. [CrossRef]
12. Bano, K.; Raza, M. Starlike functions associated with cosine functions. *Bull. Iran. Math. Soc.* **2021**, *47*, 1513–1532. [CrossRef]
13. Raina, R.K.; Sokół, J. On coefficient for certain class of starlike functions. *Hacet. J. Math. Stat.* **2015**, *44*, 1427–1433. [CrossRef]
14. Kargar, R.; Ebadian, A.; Sokół, J. On Booth lemniscate and starlike functions. *Anal. Math. Phys.* **2019**, *9*, 143–154. [CrossRef]
15. Cho, N.E.; Kumar, S.; Kumar, V.; Ravichandran, V.; Srivastava, H.M. Starlike functions related to the Bell numbers. *Symmetry* **2019**, *11*, 219. [CrossRef]
16. Deniz, E. Sharp coefficient bounds for starlike functions associated with generalized telephone numbers. *Bull. Malays. Math. Sci. Soc.* **2021**, *44*, 1525–1542. [CrossRef]
17. Raza, M.; Binyamin, M.A.; Riaz, A. A study of convex and related functions in the perspective of geometric function theory. In *Inequalities with Generalized Convex Functions and Applications*; Awan, M.U., Cristescu, G., Eds.; Springer: Berlin/Heidelberg, Germany, 2023; To be published.
18. Goel, P.; Kumar, S.S. Certain class of starlike functions associated with modified sigmoid function. *Bull. Malays. Math. Sci. Soc.* **2020**, *43*, 957–991. [CrossRef]
19. Kanas, S.; Masih, V.S. On the behaviour of analytic representation of the generalized Pascal snail. *Anal. Math. Phy.* **2021**, *11*, 77. [CrossRef]
20. Malik, S.N.; Raza, M.; Sokół, J.; Zainab, S. Analytic functions associated with cardioid domain. *Turk. J. Math.* **2020**, *44*, 1127–1136. [CrossRef]
21. Masih, V.S.; Kanas, S. Subclasses of starlike and convex functions associated with the limaçon domain. *Symmetry* **2020**, *12*, 942. [CrossRef]
22. Wani, L.A.; Swaminathan, A. Starlike and convex functions associated with nephroid domain. *Bull. Malays. Math. Sci. Soc.* **2021**, *44*, 79–104. [CrossRef]
23. Yunus, Y.;Halim, S.A.; Akbarally, A.B. Subclass of starlike functions associated with a limaçon. *AIP Conf. Proc.* **2018**, *1974*, 030023.
24. Ali, R.M.; Jain, N.K.; Ravichandran, V. Radii of starlikeness associated with the lemniscate of Bernoulli and the left-half plane. *Appl. Math. Comput.* **2012**, *128*, 6557–6565. [CrossRef]
25. Shah, G.M. On the univalence of some analytic functions. *Pac. J. Math.* **1972**, *43*, 239–250. [CrossRef]
26. Arif, M.; Raza, M.; Tang, H.; Hussain, S.; Khan, H. Hankel determinant of order three for familiar subsets of analytic functions related with sine function. *Open Math.* **2019**, *17*, 1615–1630. [CrossRef]
27. Ravichandran, V.; Rønning, F.; Shanmugam, T.N. Radius of convexity and radius of starlikeness for some classes of analytic functions. *Complex Var.* **1997**, *33*, 265–280. [CrossRef]
28. Pommerenke, C. On the coefficients and Hankel determinants of univalent functions. *J. Lond. Math. Soc.* **1966**, *41*, 111–122. [CrossRef]
29. Kwon, O.S.; Lecko, A.; Sim, Y.J. On the fourth coefficient of functions in the Carathéodory class. *Comput. Methods Funct. Theory* **2018**, *18*, 307–314. [CrossRef]
30. Libera, R.J.; Zlotkiewicz, E.J. Early coefficients of the inverse of a regular convex functions. *Proc. Am. Math. Soc.* **1982**, *85*, 225–230. [CrossRef]
31. Prokhorov, D.V.; Szynal, J. Inverse coeffiecients for (α, β)-convex functions. *Ann. Univ. Mariae Curie-Sklodowska Sect. A* **1981**, *35*, 125–143.
32. Choi, J.H.; Kim, Y.C.; Sugawa, T. A general approach to the Fekete–Szegö problem. *J. Math. Soc. Jpn.* **2007**, *59*, 707–727. [CrossRef]

axioms MDPI

Article

Bi-Univalent Functions Based on Binomial Series-Type Convolution Operator Related with Telephone Numbers

Hasan Bayram [1,*], Kaliappan Vijaya [2], Gangadharan Murugusundaramoorthy [2] and Sibel Yalçın [1,*]

[1] Department of Mathematics, Faculty of Arts and Science, Bursa Uludağ University, Görükle 16059, Bursa, Turkey
[2] School of Advanced Sciences, Vellore Institute of Technology, Vellore 632014, TN, India; kvijaya@vit.ac.in (K.V.); gmsmoorthy@yahoo.com (G.M.)
* Correspondence: hbayram@uludag.edu.tr (H.B.); syalcin@uludag.edu.tr (S.Y.)

Abstract: This paper introduces two novel subclasses of the function class Σ for bi-univalent functions, leveraging generalized telephone numbers and Binomial series through convolution. The exploration is conducted within the domain of the open unit disk. We delve into the analysis of initial Taylor-Maclaurin coefficients $|a_2|$ and $|a_3|$, deriving insights and findings for functions belonging to these new subclasses. Additionally, Fekete-Szegö inequalities are established for these functions. Furthermore, the study unveils a range of new subclasses of Σ, some of which are special cases, yet have not been previously explored in conjunction with telephone numbers. These subclasses emerge as a result of hybrid-type convolution operators. Concluding from our results, we present several corollaries, which stand as fresh contributions in the domain of involution numbers involving hybrid-type convolution operators.

Keywords: univalent functions; analytic functions; bi-univalent functions; binomial series; convolution operator; involution numbers; coefficient bounds

MSC: 30C45; 30C50; 30C55

Citation: Bayram, H.; Vijaya, K.; Murugusundaramoorthy, G.; Yalçın, S. Bi-Univalent Functions Based on Binomial Series-Type Convolution Operator Related with Telephone Numbers. *Axioms* **2023**, *12*, 951. https://doi.org/10.3390/axioms12100951

Academic Editor: Hans J. Haubold

Received: 31 August 2023
Revised: 27 September 2023
Accepted: 3 October 2023
Published: 7 October 2023

1. Introduction

In this article, we will study Bi-Univalent Functions Based on Binomial Series-Type Convolution Operator Related with Telephone Numbers. For this purpose, we will first give the basic definitions and theorems we need. Let $\mathcal{A}$ represent the class of functions that can be written as:

$$f(z) = z + \sum_{n=2}^{\infty} a_n z^n, \tag{1}$$

these functions are analytic in the unit disk which defined below and here a_n represents the coefficients,

$$\mathbb{U} := \{z : z \in \mathbb{C} \quad \text{and} \quad |z| < 1\}.$$

Let $\mathcal{S}$ be the class made up of all functions that are univalent on the open unit disk and taken from class $\mathcal{A}$. The most well-known and important subclasses of this class are the starlike and convex classes. Two conversant subclasses of $\mathcal{A}$ are correspondingly the class of starlike functions and convex functions of order α $(0 \le \alpha < 1)$. These classes are familiarised by Robertson [1] and are defined with their analytical description as

$$\mathcal{S}^*(\alpha) := \left\{h \in \mathcal{A} : \Re\left(\frac{zh'(z)}{h(z)}\right) > \alpha,\ z \in \mathbb{U}\right\}$$

and

$$\mathcal{C}(\alpha) := \left\{h \in \mathcal{A} : \Re\left(1 + \frac{zh''(z)}{h'(z)}\right) > \alpha,\ z \in \mathbb{U}\right\}.$$

It is well known that $\mathcal{S}^*(\alpha) \subset \mathcal{S}$ and $\mathcal{C}(\alpha) \subset \mathcal{S}$. In the interpretation of Alexander's relation, $h \in \mathcal{C}(\alpha)$ if and only if $zh'(z)$ for $z \in \mathbb{U}$, belongs to $\mathcal{S}^*(\alpha)$ for each $0 \leq \alpha < 1$.

For $\alpha = 0$ the class $\mathcal{S}^* := \mathcal{S}^*(0)$ condenses to the well-known class of normalized starlike univalent functions and $\mathcal{C} := \mathcal{C}(0)$ reduces to the normalized convex univalent functions.

The classes formed by the starlike and convex functions and the subclasses of these classes have been studied a lot in the past and still maintain their popularity today.

With the f function of type (1) and $h(z) = z + \sum_{n=2}^{\infty} b_n z^n$, the Hadamard Product of these functions is denoted by $f * h$ and defined as

$$(f * h)(z) = z + \sum_{n=2}^{\infty} a_n b_n z^n. \tag{2}$$

Let the functions f and g be analytic, the subordination of the f function to the g function is denoted by $f(z) \prec g(z)$. The important thing here is to prove the existence of an analytic function ϖ that satisfies the conditions $\varpi(0) = 0$ and $|\varpi(z)| < 1$ when $f(z) = g(\varpi(z))$ is defined on the open unit disk. Lately Ma and Minda [2] amalgamated various subclasses of starlike and convex functions for which either of the quantity $\frac{z f'(z)}{f(z)}$ or $\frac{(z f'(z))'}{f'(z)}$ is subordinate to a more general superordinate function $\Upsilon(z) = 1 + M_1 z + M_2 z^2 + M_3 z^3 + \cdots, M_1 > 0$. For $f \in \mathcal{A}$, the class of Ma-Minda starlike functions is given by $\frac{z f'(z)}{f(z)} \prec \Upsilon(z)$ and Ma-Minda convex functions is by $\frac{(z f'(z))'}{f'(z)} \prec \Upsilon(z)$. They concentrated on some results, such as covering theorems, growth theorems, and distortion bounds. Several subfamilies of the collection $\mathcal{S}$ have been looked at as specific options for the class $\mathcal{S}^*(\Upsilon(z))$ throughout the past few years. In the study that has lately been examined, the families mentioned below are particularly noteworthy.

(i). $\mathcal{S}^*_{\mathcal{L}} \equiv \mathcal{S}^*(\sqrt{1+z})$ [3], $\mathcal{S}^*_{\exp} \equiv \mathcal{S}^*(\exp(z))$ [4], $\mathcal{S}^*_{\tanh} \equiv \mathcal{S}^*(1 + \tanh(z))$ [5],

(ii). $\mathcal{S}^*_{\cos} \equiv \mathcal{S}^*(\cos(z))$ [6], $\mathcal{S}^*_{pet} \equiv \mathcal{S}^*\left(1 + \sinh^{-1} z\right)$ [7], $\mathcal{S}^*_{\cosh} \equiv \mathcal{S}^*(\cosh(z))$ [8],

(iii). $\mathcal{S}^*_{\sin} \equiv \mathcal{S}^*(1 + \sin(z))$ [9], $\mathcal{S}^*_{car} \equiv \mathcal{S}^*\left(1 + z + \frac{1}{2}z^2\right)$ [10],

(iv). $\mathcal{S}^*_{(n-1)\mathcal{L}} \equiv \mathcal{S}^*(\Psi_{n-1}(z))$ [11] with $\Psi_{n-1}(z) = 1 + \frac{n}{n+1} z + \frac{1}{n+1} z^n$ for $n \geq 2$.

Main idea of this article, we made an attempt to define two new subclasses of the function class of bi-univalent functions defined in the open unit disk, involving Binomial series by convolution and find the initial Taylor coefficient estimate $|a_2|$ and $|a_3|$, relating with generalized telephone numbers. Therefore, before moving on to our general section on Coefficient Bounds, we need to give some general definitions, theorems and examples for detailed examination.

1.1. Integral Operator

Fractional calculus was first studied in the late 17th century. Fractional calculus has a wide range of applications, for example, fluid flow models, electrochemical analysis, groundwater flow problems, structural damping models, acoustic wave equations for complex media, quantum theory, economy, finance, biology, human sciences, etc. Since its application area is very wide, it is a multidisciplinary subject and will increase its popularity and importance even more today and in the near future. References [12–16] can be consulted for some studies. Fractional derivative operator is a field that grows day by day and new studies are made. Many operators have been defined recently, which is clear proof of how important the subject is. Some of these operators are defined via a fractional integral. Thanks to these operators, we can process and analyze data in many different disciplines. Some common fractional derivatives operators are: Riemann–Liouville, Hadamard, Caputo and Erdélyi–Kober fractional operators, which have been proposed and implemented. We recall the operator $\mathcal{L}_{\kappa}^{\sigma} : \mathbb{U} \to \mathbb{U}$, studied by Babalola [17], is defined by

$$\mathcal{L}_{\kappa}^{\sigma} f(z) := \left(\rho_{\sigma} * \rho_{\sigma,\kappa}^{-1} * f\right)(z), \tag{3}$$

where

$$\rho_{\sigma,\kappa}(z) = \frac{z}{(1-z)^{\sigma-\kappa+1}}, \quad \sigma-\kappa+1>0, \quad \text{and} \quad \rho_{\sigma} = \rho_{\sigma,0}.$$

and $\rho_{\sigma,\kappa}^{-1}$ is given by

$$\left(\rho_{\sigma,\kappa} * \rho_{\sigma,\kappa}^{-1}\right)(z) = \frac{z}{1-z} \qquad (\sigma,\kappa \in \mathbb{N} := \{1,2,3,\cdots\}).$$

If the function f is defined in type (1) and belongs to class $\mathcal{A}$, the Equation (3) can be written as follows

$$\mathcal{L}_{\kappa}^{\sigma} f(z) = z + \sum_{n=2}^{\infty} \left(\frac{\Gamma(\sigma+n)}{\Gamma(\sigma+1)} \cdot \frac{(\sigma-\kappa)!}{(\sigma+n-\kappa-1)!} \right) a_n\, z^n \qquad (z \in \mathbb{U}).$$

Using the binomial series, we have:

$$(1-\delta)^j = \sum_{\ell=0}^{j} \binom{j}{\ell} (-\delta)^{\ell} \qquad \text{where} \quad j \in \mathbb{N}_0 := \mathbb{N} \cup \{0\} = \{0,1,2,\cdots\}.$$

For a function f belonging to the class $\mathcal{A}$, Srivastava and Sheza M. El-Deeb [18] introduced the linear derivative operator as follows:

$$\mathcal{D}_{n,\delta,\kappa}^{\sigma,0} f(z) = f(z),$$

$$\begin{aligned}
\mathcal{D}_{n,\delta,\kappa}^{\sigma,1} f(z) &= \mathcal{D}_{n,\delta,\kappa}^{\sigma} f(z) \\
&= (1-\delta)^n \mathcal{L}_{\kappa}^{\sigma} f(z) + [1-(1-\delta)^n] z (\mathcal{L}_{\kappa}^{\sigma} f)'(z) \\
&= z + \sum_{j=2}^{\infty} [1+(j-1)c^n(\delta)] \left(\frac{\Gamma(\sigma+j)}{\Gamma(\sigma+1)} \cdot \frac{(\sigma-\kappa)!}{(\sigma+j-\kappa-1)!} \right) a_j\, z^j,
\end{aligned}$$

and, in general,

$$\begin{aligned}
\mathcal{D}_{j,\delta,\kappa}^{\sigma,m} f(z) &= \mathcal{D}_{j,\delta,\kappa}^{\sigma} \left(\mathcal{D}_{j,\delta,\kappa}^{\sigma,m-1} f(z) \right) \\
&= (1-\delta)^j \mathcal{D}_{j,\delta,\kappa}^{\sigma,m-1} f(z) + \left[1-(1-\delta)^j\right] z \left(\mathcal{D}_{j,\delta,\kappa}^{\sigma,m-1} f(z) \right)' \\
&= z + \sum_{n=2}^{\infty} \left[1+(n-1)c^j(\delta)\right]^m \left(\frac{\Gamma(\sigma+n)}{\Gamma(\sigma+1)} \cdot \frac{(\sigma-\kappa)!}{(\sigma+n-\kappa-1)!} \right) a_n\, z^n \\
&= z + \sum_{n=2}^{\infty} \mathcal{V}_n\, a_n\, z^n \qquad (\delta>0;\ j,\sigma,\kappa \in \mathbb{N};\ m \in \mathbb{N}_0 := \mathbb{N} \cup \{0\}),
\end{aligned} \tag{4}$$

where

$$\mathcal{V}_n = \left[1+(n-1)c^j(\delta)\right]^m \left(\frac{\Gamma(\sigma+n)}{\Gamma(\sigma+1)} \cdot \frac{(\sigma-\kappa)!}{(\sigma+n-\kappa-1)!} \right) \tag{5}$$

and

$$c^j(\delta) = -\sum_{\ell=1}^{j} \binom{j}{\ell} (-\delta)^{\ell} \qquad (j \in \mathbb{N}).$$

It follows from (4) that

$$c^j(\delta)\, z \left(\mathcal{D}^{\sigma,m}_{j,\delta,\kappa} f(z)\right)' = \mathcal{D}^{\sigma,m+1}_{j,\delta,\kappa} f(z) - \left[1 - c^j(\delta)\right] \mathcal{D}^{\sigma,m}_{j,\delta,\kappa} f(z). \tag{6}$$

1.2. Generalized Telephone Numbers (GTN)

The usual involution numbers, also used in definition telephone numbers, are assumed by the recurrence relation

$$\mathcal{Q}(n) = \mathcal{Q}(n-1) + (n-1)\mathcal{Q}(n-2) \quad for \quad n \geq 2$$

here the following initial condition is provided

$$\mathcal{Q}(0) = \mathcal{Q}(1) = 1$$

first published in 1800 by Heinrich August Rothe by which they may easily be calculated [19]. One way to explain this recurrence is to partition the $\mathcal{Q}(n)$ connection patterns of the n subscribers to a telephone system into the patterns in which the first person is not calling anyone else and the patterns in which the first person is making a call. There are $\mathcal{Q}(n-1)$ connection patterns in which the first person is disconnected, explaining the first term of the recurrence. If the first person is connected to someone, there are $n-1$ choices for that person, and $\mathcal{Q}(n-2)$ patterns of connection for the remaining $n-2$ people, explaining the second term of the recurrence [20]. $\mathcal{Q}(n)$ is the number of involutions (self-inverse permutations) in the symmetric group (see, for example, [19,20]). Relation between involution numbers and symmetric groups were first studied in the 1800s. Since involutions correspond to standard Young tableaux, it is clear that the nth involution number is also the number of Young tableaux on the set $1, 2, \ldots, n$ (for more information, see [21]). According to John Riordan, the above recurrence relation, in fact, produces the number of connection patterns in a telephone system with n subscribers (see [22]). In 2017, Wlochand Wolowiec-Musial [23] introduced generalized telephone numbers $\mathcal{Q}(\wp, n)$ defined for integers $n \geq 0$and $\wp \geq 1$ by the following recursion:

$$\mathcal{Q}(\wp, n) = \wp\mathcal{Q}(\wp, n-1) + (n-1)\mathcal{Q}(\wp, n-2)$$

here the following initial conditions are provided

$$\mathcal{Q}(\wp, 0) = 1, \mathcal{Q}(\wp, 1) = \wp,$$

and studied some features. In 2019, Bednarz et al. [24] introduced a new generalization of telephone numbers by

$$\mathcal{Q}_\wp(n) = \mathcal{Q}_\wp(n-1) + \wp(n-1)\mathcal{Q}_\wp(n-2); n \geq 2, \wp \geq 1$$

here the following initial conditions are provided

$$\mathcal{Q}_\wp(0) = \mathcal{Q}_\wp(1) = 1.$$

They examined and researched the main features of this class that they introduced. Moreover, they investigated the connections of these numbers with the congruences and gave some proofs. Lately, they derived the exponential generating function and they gave the definiton of the summation formula for $\mathcal{Q}_\wp(n)$

$$e^{x+\wp\frac{x^2}{2}} = \sum_{n=0}^{\infty} \mathcal{Q}_\wp(n)\frac{x^n}{n!} \quad (\wp \geq 1).$$

It is clear that $\mathcal{Q}(n)$ will be obtained when $\wp = 1$. In addition, the following equations are obtained for different values of n:

1. $\mathcal{Q}_\wp(0) = \mathcal{Q}_\wp = 1$
2. $\mathcal{Q}_\wp(2) = 1 + \wp$
3. $\mathcal{Q}_\wp(3) = 1 + 3\wp$
4. $\mathcal{Q}_\wp(4) = 1 + 6\wp + 3\wp^2$
5. $\mathcal{Q}_\wp(5) = 1 + 10\wp + 15\wp^2$
6. $\mathcal{Q}_\wp(6) = 1 + 15\wp + 45\wp^2 + 15\wp^3$.

and due to Deniz [25], now we consider the following analytic function

$$\begin{aligned}\Xi(z) \quad &:= e^{(z+\wp\frac{z^2}{2})} = \\ 1 + z + \tfrac{1+\wp}{2}z^2 \quad &+ \frac{1+3\wp}{6}z^3 + \frac{3\wp^2+6\wp+1}{24}z^4 + \frac{1+10\wp+15\wp^2}{120}z^5 + \cdots. \end{aligned} \tag{7}$$

for $z \in \mathbb{U}$. Here, the Ξ function defined in $\mathbb{U}$ is chosen as an analytic function with a positive real part and Ξ satisfies the conditions $\Xi(0) = 1$, $\Xi'(0) > 0$, and Ξ maps open unit disk onto a region starlike with respect to 1 and symmetric with respect to the real axis. In recent years, researchers who have focused their studies on Generalized Telephone Numbers have defined a new class and presented appropriate solutions by addressing problems such as coefficient relations, Fekete-Szegö inequalities of this class. Based on these studies, similar results were obtained for f^{-1}. In addition, with the help of convolution products for analytic functions normalized in $\mathbb{U}$, different applications and special cases of Fekete-Szegö inequality are examined and some important problems and applications are examined in [26]. In the light of this information, similar discussions can be made for bi-univalent functions.

Now we recall and define a new subclass of bi-univalent functions in the following section.

1.3. Bi-Univalent Functions Σ

Let f belongs of class $\mathcal{S}$. In this case, we know that the function f has an inverse f^{-1}, and this inverse function is defined as follows:

$$f^{-1}(f(z)) = z \qquad (z \in \mathbb{U})$$

and

$$f(f^{-1}(w)) = w \quad \left(|w| < r_0(f); r_0(f) \geq \frac{1}{4}\right),$$

where

$$g(w) = f^{-1}(w) = w - a_2w^2 + (2a_2^2 - a_3)w^3 - (5a_2^3 - 5a_2a_3 + a_4)w^4 + \cdots. \tag{8}$$

A function $f \in \mathcal{A}$ is said to be bi-univalent in $\mathbb{U}$ if both $f(z)$ and $f^{-1}(z)$ are univalent in $\mathbb{U}$. Let Σ denote the class of bi-univalent functions in $\mathbb{U}$ given by (1). Note that the functions

$$f_1(z) = \frac{z}{1-z}, \qquad f_2(z) = \frac{1}{2}\log\frac{1+z}{1-z}, \qquad f_3(z) = -\log(1-z)$$

with their corresponding inverses

$$f_1^{-1}(w) = \frac{w}{1+w}, \qquad f_2^{-1}(w) = \frac{e^{2w}-1}{e^{2w}+1}, \qquad f_3^{-1}(w) = \frac{e^w-1}{e^w}$$

are elements of Σ. In the past years, Srivastava et al.'s reference article [27] has been a pioneer for many researchers and the importance of the subject has been better understood after this article. Afterwards, different studies on this subject were carried out by many researchers. Recently there has been triggering interest to study bi-univalent function class

Σ and obtained non-sharp coefficient estimates on the first two coefficients $|a_2|$ and $|a_3|$ of (1). But the coefficient problem for each of the following Taylor-Maclaurin coefficients:

$$|a_n| \qquad (n \in \mathbb{N} \setminus \{1,2\}; \ \mathbb{N} := \{1,2,3,\cdots\}$$

is still an open problem (for more detail see [28–33]). By using the hybrid-type convolution operator $\mathcal{D}^{\sigma,m}_{n,\delta,\lambda}$ and motivated by certain recent study on bi-univalent functions which still remain popular today [34–39]. We define a subclass in association with generalized telephone numbers (GTN) [25,26].

Definition 1. *The f function belonging to the class Σ in type (1) is said to belong to the class $\mathcal{B}^{\sigma,m;\wp}_{j,\delta,\Sigma}(\lambda, z)$ if f satisfies the following inequalities :*

$$\left(\frac{z^{1-\lambda}(\mathcal{D}^{\sigma,m-1}_{j,\delta,\kappa} f(z))'}{[\mathcal{D}^{\sigma,m-1}_{j,\delta,\kappa} f(z)]^{1-\lambda}} \right) \prec \Xi(z) \tag{9}$$

and

$$\left(\frac{w^{1-\lambda}(\mathcal{D}^{\sigma,m-1}_{j,\delta,\kappa} g(w))'}{[\mathcal{D}^{\sigma,m-1}_{j,\delta,\kappa} g(w)]^{1-\lambda}} \right) \prec \Xi(w), \tag{10}$$

here $0 \leq \lambda \leq 1$; $z, w \in \mathbb{U}$ and it is assumed that the g function is as in (8).

The new subclasses of the Σ class created by the special selection of the parameters in this definition can be defined as in the following two examples.

Example 1. *For $\lambda = 0$, the f function belonging to the class Σ in type (1) is said to belong to the class $\mathcal{S}^{\sigma,m;\wp}_{j,\delta,\Sigma}$ if f satisfies the following inequalities:*

$$\left(\frac{z(\mathcal{D}^{\sigma,m-1}_{j,\delta,\kappa} f(z))'}{\mathcal{D}^{\sigma,m-1}_{j,\delta,\kappa} f(z)} \right) \prec \Xi(z) \tag{11}$$

and

$$\left(\frac{w(\mathcal{D}^{\sigma,m-1}_{j,\delta,\kappa} g(w))'}{\mathcal{D}^{\sigma,m-1}_{j,\delta,\kappa} g(w)} \right) \prec \Xi(w) \tag{12}$$

in here $z, w \in \mathbb{U}$ and it is assumed that the g function is as in (8).

Example 2. *For $\lambda = 1$, the f function belonging to the class Σ in type (1) is said to belong to the class $\mathcal{R}^{\sigma,m;\wp}_{j,\delta,\Sigma}$ if f satisfies the following inequalities:*

$$\left(\mathcal{D}^{\sigma,m-1}_{j,\delta,\kappa} f(z))' \right) \prec \Xi(z) \tag{13}$$

and

$$\left((\mathcal{D}^{\sigma,m-1}_{j,\delta,\kappa} g(w))' \right) \prec \Xi(w) \tag{14}$$

in here $z, w \in \mathbb{U}$ and it is assumed that the g function is as in (8).

In [40], Obradovic et al. gave some criteria for univalence expressing by $\Re(f'(z)) > 0$, for the linear combinations

$$\tau\left(1 + \frac{zf''(z)}{f'(z)}\right) + (1-\tau)\frac{1}{f'(z)} > 0, \qquad (\tau \geq 1, z \in \mathbb{U}).$$

According to the above definitions, Lashin [41] defined the new subclasses of bi-univalent function.

Definition 2. *A function f belonging to the class Σ in type* (1) *is considered to be in the class $\mathcal{M}_{j,\delta,\Sigma}^{\sigma,m;\wp}(\tau,\Xi)$ if f satisfies the following inequalities:*

$$\tau\left(1+\frac{z(\mathcal{D}_{j,\delta,\kappa}^{\sigma,m-1}f(z))''}{(\mathcal{D}_{j,\delta,\kappa}^{\sigma,m-1}f(z))'}\right)+(1-\tau)\frac{1}{(\mathcal{D}_{j,\delta,\kappa}^{\sigma,m-1}f(z))'}\prec\Xi(z) \tag{15}$$

and

$$\tau\left(1+\frac{w(\mathcal{D}_{j,\delta,\kappa}^{\sigma,m-1}g(w))''}{(\mathcal{D}_{j,\delta,\kappa}^{\sigma,m-1}g(w))'}\right)+(1-\tau)\frac{1}{(\mathcal{D}_{j,\delta,\kappa}^{\sigma,m-1}g(w))'}\prec\Xi(w) \tag{16}$$

where $z,w\in\mathbb{U}$, $\tau\geq 1$, and it is assumed that the function g is as defined in (8).

Example 3. *A function f belonging to the class Σ in type* (1) *is considered to be in the class $\mathcal{M}_{j,\delta,\Sigma}^{\sigma,m;\wp}(1,\Xi)\equiv\mathcal{K}_{j,\delta,\Sigma}^{\sigma,m;\wp}(\Xi)$ if f satisfies the following inequalities:*

$$\left(1+\frac{z(\mathcal{D}_{j,\delta,\kappa}^{\sigma,m-1}f(z))''}{(\mathcal{D}_{j,\delta,\kappa}^{\sigma,m-1}f(z))'}\right)\prec\Xi(z)\ \text{and}\ \left(1+\frac{w(\mathcal{D}_{j,\delta,\kappa}^{\sigma,m-1}g(w))''}{(\mathcal{D}_{j,\delta,\kappa}^{\sigma,m-1}g(w))'}\right)\prec\Xi(w)$$

where $z,w\in\mathbb{U}$, and it is assumed that the function g is as defined in (8).

2. Coefficient Bounds

To establish our main results, we require the following lemma.

Lemma 1 (see [42]). *If $h\in\mathcal{P}$, then $|c_k|\leq 2$ for each k, where $\mathcal{P}$ is the family of all functions h, analytic in $\mathbb{U}$, for which*

$$\Re\{h(z)\}>0 \qquad (z\in\mathbb{U}),$$

where

$$h(z)=1+c_1z+c_2z^2+\cdots \qquad (z\in\mathbb{U}).$$

We begin by estimating the coefficients $|a_2|$ and $|a_3|$ for functions in the class $\mathcal{B}_{j,\delta,\Sigma}^{\sigma,m;\wp}(\lambda,\Xi)$. Let $P(z)$ be defined by

$$P(z):=\frac{1+\varpi(z)}{1-\varpi(z)}=1+c_1z+c_2z^2+\cdots.$$

It is evident that

$$\begin{aligned}\varpi(z)&=\frac{P(z)-1}{P(z)+1}\\&=\frac{1}{2}\left[c_1z+\left(c_2-\frac{c_1^2}{2}\right)z^2+\left(c_3-c_1c_2+\frac{c_1^3}{4}\right)z^3+\cdots\right].\end{aligned} \tag{17}$$

Since $\varpi(z)$ is a Schwarz function, it follows that $\Re(p_1(z))>0$ and $p_1(0)=1$. Therefore,

$$\begin{aligned}\Psi(\varpi(z))&=e^{\left(\frac{P(z)-1}{P(z)+1}+\kappa\frac{\left[\frac{P(z)-1}{P(z)+1}\right]^2}{2}\right)}\\&=1+\frac{c_1}{2}z+\left(\frac{c_2}{2}+\frac{(\wp-1)c_1^2}{8}\right)z^2+\left(\frac{c_3}{2}+(\wp-1)\frac{c_1c_2}{4}+\frac{(1-3\wp)}{48}c_1^3\right)z^3+\ldots\end{aligned} \tag{18}$$

Define the functions $p(z)$ and $q(z)$ as follows:

$$p(z) := \frac{1+u(z)}{1-u(z)} = 1 + p_1 z + p_2 z^2 + \cdots$$

and

$$q(z) := \frac{1+v(z)}{1-v(z)} = 1 + q_1 z + q_2 z^2 + \cdots$$

or, equivalently,

$$u(z) := \frac{p(z)-1}{p(z)+1} = \frac{1}{2}\left[p_1 z + \left(p_2 - \frac{p_1^2}{2}\right)z^2 + \cdots\right]$$

and

$$v(z) := \frac{q(z)-1}{q(z)+1} = \frac{1}{2}\left[q_1 z + \left(q_2 - \frac{q_1^2}{2}\right)z^2 + \cdots\right].$$

Subsequently, $p(z)$ and $q(z)$ are analytic in $\mathbb{U}$ with $p(0) = 1 = q(0)$. Furthermore, since both u and v map from $\mathbb{U}$ to $\mathbb{U}$, the functions $p(z)$ and $q(z)$ exhibit a positive real part in $\mathbb{U}$, and they satisfy the inequalities:

$$|p_i| \leq 2 \quad \text{and} \quad |q_i| \leq 2. \tag{19}$$

For the scope of our study, we introduce the notation:

$$\mathcal{V}_2 = \mathcal{V}_{\vartheta,m}^{a,c}(2) = \left[1 + c^j(\delta)\right]^m \left(\frac{\Gamma(\sigma+2)}{\Gamma(\sigma+1)} \cdot \frac{(\sigma-\lambda)!}{(\sigma+1-\lambda)!}\right), \tag{20}$$

$$\mathcal{V}_3 = \left[1 + 2c^j(\delta)\right]^m \left(\frac{\Gamma(\sigma+3)}{\Gamma(\sigma+1)} \cdot \frac{(\sigma-\lambda)!}{(\sigma+2-\lambda)!}\right). \tag{21}$$

In the subsequent theorem, we embark on the initial exploration of the Taylor-Maclaurin coefficients $|a_2|$ and $|a_3|$ for functions belonging to this novel subclass $\mathcal{B}_{j,\delta,\Sigma}^{\sigma,m;\wp}(\lambda,\Xi)$.

Theorem 1. *Let assume that the f function is as in* (1) *and in the class $\mathcal{B}_{j,\delta,\Sigma}^{\sigma,m;\wp}(\lambda,\Xi)$. Then*

$$|a_2| \leq \min\left\{ \begin{array}{l} \frac{1}{(\lambda+1)\mathcal{V}_2}, \\ \sqrt{\frac{2}{|\{(\lambda-1)(\lambda+2)-(\wp-1)(\lambda+1)^2\}\mathcal{V}_2^2+2(\lambda+2)\mathcal{V}_3|}} \end{array} \right. \tag{22}$$

and

$$|a_3| \leq \min\left\{ \begin{array}{l} \frac{1}{(\lambda+1)^2\mathcal{V}_2^2} + \frac{1}{(2+\lambda)\mathcal{V}_3}, \\ \frac{2}{\{(\lambda-1)(\lambda+2)-(\wp-1)(\lambda+1)^2\}\mathcal{V}_2^2+2(\lambda+2)\mathcal{V}_3} + \frac{1}{(2+\lambda)\mathcal{V}_3}. \end{array} \right. \tag{23}$$

Proof. It follows from (9) and (10) that

$$\left(\frac{z^{1-\lambda}(\mathcal{D}_{j,\delta,\kappa}^{\sigma,m-1}f(z))'}{[\mathcal{D}_{j,\delta,\kappa}^{\sigma,m-1}f(z)]^{1-\lambda}}\right) = \Xi(u(z)) \tag{24}$$

and

$$\left(\frac{w^{1-\lambda}(\mathcal{D}_{j,\delta,\kappa}^{\sigma,m-1}g(w))'}{[\mathcal{D}_{j,\delta,\kappa}^{\sigma,m-1}g(w)]^{1-\lambda}}\right) = \Xi(v(w)), \tag{25}$$

where $p(z)$ and $q(w)$ in $\mathcal{P}$ and have the following forms:

$$\Xi(u(z)) = 1 + \frac{1}{2}p_1 z + \Big(\frac{p_2}{2} + \frac{(\wp-1)p_1^2}{8}\Big)z^2 + \cdots \tag{26}$$

and

$$\Xi(v(w)) = 1 + \frac{1}{2}q_1 w + \Big(\frac{q_2}{2} + \frac{(\wp-1)q_1^2}{8}\Big)w^2 + \cdots, \tag{27}$$

respectively. Now, by equating the coefficients in (24) and (25), we have

$$(1+\lambda)\mathcal{V}_2 a_2 = \frac{1}{2}p_1, \tag{28}$$

$$\left[\frac{(\lambda-1)(\lambda+2)}{2}\mathcal{V}_2^2 a_2^2 + (\lambda+2)\mathcal{V}_3 a_3\right] = \frac{p_2}{2} + \frac{(\wp-1)p_1^2}{8}, \tag{29}$$

$$-(\lambda+1)\mathcal{V}_2 a_2 = \frac{1}{2}q_1 \tag{30}$$

and

$$\left[\left(2(\lambda+2)\mathcal{V}_3 + \frac{(\lambda-1)(\lambda+2)}{2}\mathcal{V}_2^2\right)a_2^2 - (\lambda+2)\mathcal{V}_3 a_3\right] = \frac{q_2}{2} + \frac{(\wp-1)q_1^2}{8}. \tag{31}$$

From (28) and (30), we can determine that

$$a_2 = \frac{p_1}{2(1+\lambda)\mathcal{V}_2} = \frac{-q_1}{2(1+\lambda)\mathcal{V}_2}, \tag{32}$$

which implies

$$p_1 = -q_1 \tag{33}$$

and

$$8(\lambda+1)^2\mathcal{V}_2^2 a_2^2 = p_1^2 + q_1^2. \tag{34}$$

Thus we have

$$a_2^2 = \frac{p_1^2 + q_1^2}{8(\lambda+1)^2\mathcal{V}_2^2} \tag{35}$$

and

$$(\lambda+1)^2\mathcal{V}_2^2 a_2^2 = \frac{p_1^2 + q_1^2}{8}. \tag{36}$$

By adding (29) and (31), and utilizing (32) as well as (33), we get

$$\left[(\lambda-1)(\lambda+2)\mathcal{V}_2^2 + 2(\lambda+2)\mathcal{V}_3\right]a_2^2 = \frac{p_2+q_2}{2} + \frac{(\wp-1)}{8}(p_1^2 + q_1^2). \tag{37}$$

Thus, by using (36)

$$a_2^2 = \frac{p_2 + q_2}{2[\{(\lambda-1)(\lambda+2) - (\wp-1)(\lambda+1)^2\}\mathcal{V}_2^2 + 2(\lambda+2)\mathcal{V}_3]} \tag{38}$$

Applying Lemma 1 to the coefficients p_2 and q_2, yields the immediate result

$$|a_2|^2 \leq \frac{2}{|\{(\lambda-1)(\lambda+2) - (\wp-1)(\lambda+1)^2\}\mathcal{V}_2^2 + 2(\lambda+2)\mathcal{V}_3|}. \tag{39}$$

Hence,

$$|a_2| \leq \sqrt{\frac{2}{|\{(\lambda-1)(\lambda+2)-(\wp-1)(\lambda+1)^2\}\mathcal{V}_2^2+2(\lambda+2)\mathcal{V}_3|}}.$$

This yields the bound on $|a_2|$ as stated in (22). To establish the bound on $|a_3|$, we subtract (31) from (29), resulting in

$$\left[2(\lambda+2)\mathcal{V}_3 a_3 - 2(\lambda+2)\mathcal{V}_3 a_2^2\right] = \frac{1}{2}(p_2-q_2)+\frac{\wp-1}{8}(p_1^2-q_1^2) \tag{40}$$

Using (32), (33) and (40) we can deduce that

$$\begin{aligned} a_3 &= a_2^2+\frac{p_2-q_2}{4(2+\lambda)\mathcal{V}_3} \\ &= \frac{p_1^2+q_1^2}{8(\lambda+1)^2\mathcal{V}_2^2}+\frac{p_2-q_2}{4(2+\lambda)\mathcal{V}_3}. \end{aligned} \tag{41}$$

Applying Lemma 1 once more to for the coefficients p_2, q_2, we immediately obtain

$$|a_3| \leq \frac{1}{(\lambda+1)^2\mathcal{V}_2^2}+\frac{1}{(2+\lambda)\mathcal{V}_3}$$

also,

$$|a_3| \leq \frac{2}{|\{(\lambda-1)(\lambda+2)-(\wp-1)(\lambda+1)^2\}\mathcal{V}_2^2+2(\lambda+2)\mathcal{V}_3|}+\frac{1}{(2+\lambda)\mathcal{V}_3}.$$

This completes the proof of Theorem 1. □

As a consequence of our results, by appropriately setting the parameter, we present the following corollaries, which are novel and have not been studied for the case of involution numbers involving hybrid-type convolution operators.

When we fix $\lambda = 0$ in Theorem 1, the following corollary emerges.

Corollary 1. *Let assume that the f function is as in* (1) *and in the class* $\mathcal{S}_{j,\delta,\Sigma}^{\sigma,m;\wp}(\Xi)$. *Then*

$$|a_2| \leq \min\left\{ \begin{array}{l} \frac{1}{\mathcal{V}_2}, \\ \sqrt{\frac{2}{|4\mathcal{V}_3-(\wp+1)\mathcal{V}_2^2|}} \end{array} \right. \tag{42}$$

and

$$|a_3| \leq \min\left\{ \begin{array}{l} \frac{1}{\mathcal{V}_2^2}+\frac{1}{2\mathcal{V}_3}, \\ \frac{2}{|-(1+\wp)\mathcal{V}_2^2+4\mathcal{V}_3|}+\frac{1}{2\mathcal{V}_3}. \end{array} \right. \tag{43}$$

Fixing $\lambda = 1$ in Theorem 1, we have the following corollary.

Corollary 2. *Let assume that the f function is as in* (1) *and in the class* $\mathcal{R}_{j,\delta,\Sigma}^{\sigma,m;\wp}(\Xi)$. *Then*

$$|a_2| \leq \min\left\{ \begin{array}{l} \frac{1}{2\mathcal{V}_2}, \\ \sqrt{\frac{1}{3\mathcal{V}_3-2(\wp-1)\mathcal{V}_2^2}} \end{array} \right. \tag{44}$$

and

$$|a_3| \leq \min\left\{ \begin{array}{l} \frac{1}{4\mathcal{V}_2^2}+\frac{1}{3\mathcal{V}_3} \\ \frac{2}{|-4(\wp-1)\mathcal{V}_2^2+6\mathcal{V}_3|}+\frac{1}{3\mathcal{V}_3}. \end{array} \right. \tag{45}$$

In the subsequent theorem, we are embarking on the initial exploration of the Taylor-Maclaurin coefficients $|a_2|$ and $|a_3|$ for functions within this novel subclass $\mathcal{M}_{j,\delta,\Sigma}^{\sigma,m;\wp}(\tau,\Xi)$.

Theorem 2. *Let assume that the f function is as in* (1) *and* $f \in \mathcal{M}_{j,\delta,\Sigma}^{\sigma,m;\wp}(\tau,\Xi)$, $\tau \geq 1$. *Then*

$$|a_2| \leq \min\left\{ \begin{array}{l} \frac{1}{2(2\tau-1)\mathcal{V}_2}, \\ \frac{1}{\sqrt{|(1+\tau)-2(2\tau-1)^2(\wp-1)|\mathcal{V}_2^2}} \end{array} \right. \tag{46}$$

and

$$|a_3| \leq \min\left\{ \begin{array}{l} \frac{2}{3(3\tau-1)\mathcal{V}_3} + \frac{1}{4(2\tau-1)^2\mathcal{V}_2^2}, \\ \frac{2}{3(3\tau-1)\mathcal{V}_3} + \frac{1}{|(1+\tau)-2(2\tau-1)^2(\wp-1)|\mathcal{V}_2^2}. \end{array} \right. \tag{47}$$

Proof. It follows from (15) and (16) that

$$\tau\left(1+\frac{(z\mathcal{D}_{j,\delta,\kappa}^{\sigma,m-1}f(z))''}{(\mathcal{D}_{j,\delta,\kappa}^{\sigma,m-1}f(z))'}\right)+(1-\tau)\frac{1}{(\mathcal{D}_{j,\delta,\kappa}^{\sigma,m-1}f(z))'}=\Xi(u(z)) \tag{48}$$

and

$$\tau\left(1+\frac{w(\mathcal{D}_{j,\delta,\kappa}^{\sigma,m-1}g(w))''}{(\mathcal{D}_{j,\delta,\kappa}^{\sigma,m-1}g(w))'}\right)+(1-\tau)\frac{1}{(\mathcal{D}_{j,\delta,\kappa}^{\sigma,m-1}g(w))'}=\Xi(v(w)). \tag{49}$$

From (48) and (49), we have

$$\begin{aligned} 1+2(2\tau-1)\mathcal{V}_2a_2z+\Big[3(3\tau-1)\mathcal{V}_3a_3+4(1-2\tau)\mathcal{V}_2^2a_2^2\Big]z^2+\cdots \\ =1+\frac{1}{2}p_1z+\left(\frac{p_2}{2}+\frac{(\wp-1)p_1^2}{8}\right)z^2+\cdots, \end{aligned}$$

and

$$\begin{aligned} 1-2(2\tau-1)\mathcal{V}_2a_2w+\Big(2(5\tau-1)\mathcal{V}_2^2a_2^2-3(3\tau-1)\mathcal{V}_3a_3\Big)w^2-\cdots \\ =1+\frac{1}{2}q_1w+\left(\frac{q_2}{2}+\frac{(\wp-1)q_1^2}{8}\right)w^2+\cdots. \end{aligned}$$

By equating the coefficients, we obtain

$$2(2\tau-1)\mathcal{V}_2a_2=\frac{1}{2}p_1, \tag{50}$$

$$3(3\tau-1)\mathcal{V}_3a_3+4(1-2\tau)\mathcal{V}_2^2a_2^2=\frac{p_2}{2}+\frac{(\wp-1)p_1^2}{8}, \tag{51}$$

$$-2(2\tau-1)\mathcal{V}_2a_2=\frac{1}{2}q_1, \tag{52}$$

and

$$2(5\tau-1)\mathcal{V}_2^2a_2^2-3(3\tau-1)\mathcal{V}_3a_3=\frac{q_2}{2}+\frac{(\wp-1)q_1^2}{8}. \tag{53}$$

Using (50) and (52), we obtain

$$p_1=-q_1 \tag{54}$$

From (50) by using (19),

$$|a_2| \leq \frac{1}{2(2\tau-1)\mathcal{V}_2}. \tag{55}$$

Also

$$32(2\tau-1)^2\mathcal{V}_2^2 a_2^2 = p_1^2+q_1^2$$
$$a_2^2 = \frac{p_1^2+q_1^2}{32(2\tau-1)^2\mathcal{V}_2^2}. \tag{56}$$

Thus by (19), we get

$$|a_2| \leq \frac{1}{4(2\tau-1)\mathcal{V}_2} = \frac{1}{4(2\tau-1)\mathcal{V}_2}. \tag{57}$$

Now from (51), (53) and using (56), we obtain

$$\Big(2(1+\tau) - 4(2\tau-1)^2(\wp-1)\Big)\mathcal{V}_2^2 a_2^2 = \frac{p_2+q_2}{2}. \tag{58}$$

Thus, by (58) we obtain

$$a_2^2 = \frac{p_2+q_2}{4[(1+\tau)-2(2\tau-1)^2(\wp-1)]\mathcal{V}_2^2}$$
$$|a_2| \leq \frac{1}{\sqrt{|(1+\tau)-2(2\tau-1)^2(\wp-1)|\mathcal{V}_2^2}}.$$

By using (51) and (53), and then substituting (54), we get

$$a_3 = \frac{p_2-q_2}{6(3\tau-1)\mathcal{V}_3} + a_2^2. \tag{59}$$

Taking the modulus of both sides, we obtain

$$|a_3| \leq \frac{2}{3(3\tau-1)\mathcal{V}_3} + |a_2^2|. \tag{60}$$

Using (55) and (57), we get

$$|a_3| \leq \frac{2}{3(3\tau-1)\mathcal{V}_3} + \frac{1}{4(2\tau-1)^2\mathcal{V}_2^2}.$$

Now by using (58) in (60),

$$|a_3| \leq \frac{2}{3(3\tau-1)\mathcal{V}_3} + |a_2^2|$$
$$= \frac{2}{3(3\tau-1)\mathcal{V}_3} + \frac{1}{|(1+\tau)-2(2\tau-1)^2(\wp-1)|\mathcal{V}_2^2}.$$

□

Corollary 3. *Let assume that the f function is as in* (1) *and* $f \in \mathcal{K}_{j,\delta,\Sigma}^{\sigma,m;\wp}(\Xi)$. *Then*

$$|a_2| \leq \min\left\{\begin{array}{l} \frac{1}{2\mathcal{V}_2}, \\ \frac{1}{\sqrt{|2-2(\wp-1)|\mathcal{V}_2^2}} \end{array}\right. \tag{61}$$

and

$$|a_3| \leq \min\left\{\begin{array}{l} \frac{2}{6\mathcal{V}_3} + \frac{1}{4\mathcal{V}_2^2}, \\ \frac{2}{6\mathcal{V}_3} + \frac{1}{|2-2(\wp-1)|\mathcal{V}_2^2}. \end{array}\right. \tag{62}$$

3. Fekete-Szegö Inequalities

For $f \in \mathcal{A}$, Fekete and Szegö [43] introduced the generalized functional $|a_3 - \aleph a_2^2|$, where $\aleph$ is some real number. In [44] Zaprawa provided the Fekete and Szegö results for $f \in \Sigma$. We prove Fekete-Szegö inequalities for functions f in the new subclasses $\mathcal{B}^{\sigma,m;\wp}_{j,\delta,\Sigma}(\lambda,\Xi)$ and $\mathcal{M}^{\sigma,m;\wp}_{j,\delta,\Sigma}(\tau,\Xi)$ using the following lemmas proven by Zaprawa [44].

Lemma 2 ([44]). *Let $k \in \mathbb{R}$ and $z_1, z_2 \in \mathbb{C}$. If $|z_1| < R$ and $|z_2| < R$ then*

$$|(k+1)z_1 + (k-1)z_2| \leq \begin{cases} 2|k|R, & |k| \geq 1 \\ \\ 2R & |k| \leq 1. \end{cases} \tag{63}$$

Lemma 3 ([44]). *Let $k, l \in \mathbb{R}$ and $z_1, z_2 \in \mathbb{C}$. If $|z_1| < R$ and $|z_2| < R$ then*

$$|(k+l)z_1 + (k-l)z_2| \leq \begin{cases} 2|k|R, & |k| \geq |l| \\ \\ 2|l|R & |k| \leq |l|. \end{cases} \tag{64}$$

Now, we obtain Fekete-Szegö inequalities for $f \in \mathcal{B}^{\sigma,m;\wp}_{j,\delta,\Sigma}(\lambda,\Xi)$:

Theorem 3. *For $\aleph \in \mathbb{R}$, let assume that the f function is as in* (1) *and $f \in \mathcal{B}^{\sigma,m;\wp}_{j,\delta,\Sigma}(\lambda,\Xi)$, then*

$$\left|a_3 - \aleph a_2^2\right| \leq \begin{cases} \frac{1}{(2+\lambda)\mathcal{V}_3} & ; \quad 0 \leq |h(\aleph)| \leq \frac{1}{4(2+\lambda)\mathcal{V}_3} \\ 4|h(\aleph)| & ; \quad |h(\aleph)| \geq \frac{1}{4(2+\lambda)\mathcal{V}_3} \end{cases}$$

where

$$h(\aleph) = \frac{1-\aleph}{2\left[\{(\lambda-1)(\lambda+2) - (\wp-1)(\lambda+1)^2\}\mathcal{V}_2^2 + 2(\lambda+2)\mathcal{V}_3\right]}. \tag{65}$$

Proof. From (41), we have

$$a_3 - \aleph a_2^2 = \frac{p_2 - q_2}{4(2+\lambda)\mathcal{V}_3} + (1-\nu)a_2^2. \tag{66}$$

By substituting (38) in (66), we have

$$\begin{aligned} a_3 - \aleph a_2^2 &= \frac{p_2 - q_2}{4(2+\lambda)\mathcal{V}_3} \\ &+ \frac{(1-\aleph)(p_2+q_2)}{2\left[\{(\lambda-1)(\lambda+2) - (\wp-1)(\lambda+1)^2\}\mathcal{V}_2^2 + 2(\lambda+2)\mathcal{V}_3\right]} \\ &= \left(h(\aleph) + \frac{1}{4(2+\lambda)\mathcal{V}_3}\right)p_2 + \left(h(\nu) - \frac{1}{4(2+\lambda)\mathcal{V}_3}\right)q_2, \end{aligned} \tag{67}$$

where

$$h(\aleph) = \frac{1-\aleph}{2\left[\{(\lambda-1)(\lambda+2) - (\wp-1)(\lambda+1)^2\}\mathcal{V}_2^2 + 2(\lambda+2)\mathcal{V}_3\right]}.$$

Thus by taking modulus of (67), we conclude that

$$\left|a_3 - \aleph a_2^2\right| \leq \begin{cases} \frac{1}{(2+\lambda)\mathcal{V}_3} & ; \quad 0 \leq |h(\aleph)| \leq \frac{1}{4(2+\lambda)\mathcal{V}_3} \\ 4|h(\aleph)| & ; \quad |h(\aleph)| \geq \frac{1}{4(2+\lambda)\mathcal{V}_3} \end{cases} \tag{68}$$

where $h(\aleph)$ is given by (65). □

By taking $\aleph = 1$ in above Theorem one can easily state the following:

Remark 1. *Let the function f be assumed by* (1) *and $f \in \mathcal{B}_{j,\delta,\Sigma}^{\sigma,m;\wp}(\lambda,\Xi)$. Then*

$$\left|a_3 - a_2^2\right| \leq \frac{1}{(2+\lambda)\mathcal{V}_3}.$$

By taking $\lambda = 0$ and $\lambda = 1$, we can state the following:

Corollary 4. *For $\aleph \in \mathbb{R}$, let assume that the f function is as in* (1) *and $f \in \mathcal{S}_{j,\delta,\Sigma}^{\sigma,m;\wp}(\Xi)$, then*

$$\left|a_3 - \aleph a_2^2\right| \leq \begin{cases} \frac{1}{2\mathcal{V}_3} & ; \quad 0 \leq |h(\aleph)| \leq \frac{1}{8\mathcal{V}_3} \\ 4|h(\aleph)| & ; \quad |h(\aleph)| \geq \frac{1}{8\mathcal{V}_3} \end{cases}$$

where $h(\aleph) = \frac{1-\aleph}{2\left[4\mathcal{V}_3 - (\wp+1)\mathcal{V}_2^2\right]}$.

Corollary 5. *For $\aleph \in \mathbb{R}$, let assume that the f function is as in* (1) *and $f \in \mathcal{R}_{j,\delta,\Sigma}^{\sigma,m;\wp}(\Xi)$, then*

$$\left|a_3 - \aleph a_2^2\right| \leq \begin{cases} \frac{1}{3\mathcal{V}_3} & ; \quad 0 \leq |h(\aleph)| \leq \frac{1}{12\mathcal{V}_3} \\ 4|h(\aleph)| & ; \quad |h(\aleph)| \geq \frac{1}{12\mathcal{V}_3} \end{cases}$$

where $h(\aleph) = \frac{1-\aleph}{2\left[6\mathcal{V}_3 - 4(\wp-1)\mathcal{V}_2^2\right]}$.

Now, we prove Fekete-Szegö inequalities for $f \in \mathcal{M}_{j,\delta,\Sigma}^{\sigma,m;\wp}(\tau,\Xi)$.

Theorem 4. *For $\nu \in \mathbb{R}$, let assume that the f function is as in* (1) *and $f \in \mathcal{M}_{j,\delta,\Sigma}^{\sigma,m;\wp}(\tau,\Xi)$, then*

$$\left|a_3 - \nu a_2^2\right| \leq \begin{cases} \dfrac{2}{3(3\tau-1)\mathcal{V}_3} & ; 0 \leq |h(\nu)| \leq \dfrac{1}{6(3\tau-1)\mathcal{V}_3} \\ 4|h(\nu)| & ; |h(\nu)| \geq \dfrac{1}{6(3\tau-1)\mathcal{V}_3} \end{cases}$$

where

$$h(\nu) = \frac{1-\nu}{4[(1+\tau) - 2(2\tau-1)^2(\wp-1)]\mathcal{V}_2^2}.$$

Proof. From (59), we have

$$a_3 - \nu a_2^2 = \frac{p_2 - q_2}{6(3\tau-1)\mathcal{V}_3} + +(1-\nu)a_2^2. \tag{69}$$

By substituting (58) in (69), we have

$$\begin{aligned} a_3 - \nu a_2^2 &= \frac{p_2 - q_2}{6(3\tau-1)\mathcal{V}_3} + a_2^2 + \frac{(p_2+q_2)(1-\nu)}{4[(1+\tau) - 2(2\tau-1)^2(\wp-1)]\mathcal{V}_2^2} \\ &= \left(h(\nu) + \frac{1}{6(3\tau-1)\mathcal{V}_3}\right)p_2 + \left(h(\nu) - \frac{1}{6(3\tau-1)\mathcal{V}_3}\right)q_2, \end{aligned} \tag{70}$$

where

$$h(\nu) = \frac{1-\nu}{4[(1+\tau) - 2(2\tau-1)^2(\wp-1)]\mathcal{V}_2^2}. \tag{71}$$

Thus by taking modulus of (70), we get

$$\left|a_3 - \nu a_2^2\right| \leq \begin{cases} \dfrac{2}{3(3\tau-1)\mathcal{V}_3} & ; 0 \leq |h(\nu)| \leq \dfrac{1}{6(3\tau-1)\mathcal{V}_3} \\ 4|h(\nu)| & ; |h(\nu)| \geq \dfrac{1}{6(3\tau-1)\mathcal{V}_3} \end{cases} \tag{72}$$

where $h(\nu)$ is given by (71). □

By taking $\nu = 1$ in above theorem, we can easily state the following:

Remark 2. *Let assume that the f function is as in* (1) *and $f \in \mathcal{M}_{\Sigma}^{a,b,c}(\tau, \Xi)$. Then*

$$\left|a_3 - a_2^2\right| \leq \frac{2}{3(3\tau-1)\mathcal{V}_3}.$$

Corollary 6. *For $\nu \in \mathbb{R}$, let assume that the f function is as in* (1) *and $f \in \mathcal{K}_{j,\delta,\Sigma}^{\sigma,m;\wp}(\Xi)$, then*

$$\left|a_3 - \nu a_2^2\right| \leq \begin{cases} \dfrac{2}{6\mathcal{V}_3} & ; 0 \leq |h(\nu)| \leq \dfrac{1}{12\mathcal{V}_3} \\ 4|h(\nu)| & ; |h(\nu)| \geq \dfrac{1}{12\mathcal{V}_3} \end{cases}$$

where $h(\nu) = \frac{1-\nu}{4[2-2(\wp-1)]\mathcal{V}_2^2}$.

4. Discussion

The research presented in this paper follows the same path as the previous studies that introduced new classes of bi-univalent functions, building upon the pioneering article by Srivastava et al. [27], which involves generalized telephone numbers. We then extended this approach to define a new function class and derived results concerning the initial Taylor coefficients for this class.

Furthermore, by specific parameter choices, our newly defined subclasses $\mathcal{B}_{j,\delta,\Sigma}^{\sigma,m;\wp}(\lambda, \Xi)$ and $\mathcal{M}_{j,\delta,\Sigma}^{\sigma,m;\wp}(\tau, \Xi)$ give rise to various other subclasses of analytic functions, such as $\mathcal{S}_{j,\delta,\Sigma}^{\sigma,m;\wp}(\Xi)$, $\mathcal{R}_{j,\delta,\Sigma}^{\sigma,m;\wp}(\Xi)$, and $\mathcal{K}_{j,\delta,\Sigma}^{\sigma,m;\wp}(\Xi)$. These subclasses have not been previously explored in connection with telephone numbers. Furthermore, by tailoring the parameters, we've attempted to discretize the new results, presenting novel discussions in this direction.

The main contributions of our work lie in providing new and improved results for the initial Taylor-Maclaurin coefficients $|a_2|$ and $|a_3|$, which further enhances the understanding of the discussed classes.

5. Conclusions

Our motivation in this study is to unlock a plethora of interesting and valuable applications of a diverse array of telephone numbers within the realm of Geometric Function Theory. We firmly believe that this research will serve as a catalyst, inspiring numerous researchers to expand upon this concept by delving into meromorphic bi-univalent functions. Additionally, new classes could be formulated based on specific hybrid-type convolution operators, incorporating Poisson, Borel, and Pascal distribution series. Another avenue to explore is subordination with Gegenbauer and Legendre polynomials, as seen in recent studies [35–39,45] within the context of the Σ class.

By defining subclasses akin to starlike functions concerning the symmetric points of Σ in relation to telephone numbers, we could potentially unify and extend various classes of analytic bi-univalent functions. This approach could pave the way for comprehensive discussions on new extensions and detailed examinations of enhanced improvements to initial Taylor-Maclaurin coefficients $|a_2|$ and $|a_3|$.

Moreover, our future plans include delving into second Hankel determinant and Toeplitz determinant inequality results, as previously explored in [45,46].

Author Contributions: Conceptualization, H.B., K.V., G.M. and S.Y.; methodology, H.B., K.V., G.M. and S.Y.; software, H.B., K.V., G.M. and S.Y.; validation, H.B., K.V., G.M. and S.Y.; formal analysis, H.B., K.V., G.M. and S.Y.; investigation, H.B., K.V., G.M. and S.Y.; resources, H.B., K.V., G.M. and S.Y.; data curation, H.B., K.V., G.M. and S.Y.; writing—original draft preparation, H.B., K.V., G.M. and S.Y.; writing—review and editing, H.B., K.V., G.M. and S.Y.; visualization, H.B., K.V., G.M. and S.Y.; supervision, H.B., G.M. and S.Y.; project administration, H.B. and G.M.; funding acquisition, H.B., G.M. and S.Y. All authors have read and agreed to the published version of the manuscript.

Funding: This research received no external funding.

Institutional Review Board Statement: Not applicable.

Informed Consent Statement: Not applicable.

Conflicts of Interest: The authors declare no conflict of interest.

References

1. Robertson, M.S. On the theory of univalent functions. *Ann. Math.* **1936**, *37*, 374–408. [CrossRef]
2. Ma, W.C.; Minda, D. A unified treatment of some special classes of functions. In *Proceedings of the Conference on Complex Analysis, 1992*; Conference Proceedings and Lecture Notes in Analysis I; International Press Inc.: Cambridge, MA, USA, 1994; pp. 157–169.
3. Sokół, J.; Stankiewicz, J. Radius of convexity of some subclasses of strongly starlike functions. *Zeszyty Nauk. Politech. Rzeszowskiej Mat.* **1996**, *19*, 101–105.
4. Mendiratta, R.; Nagpal, S.; Ravichandran, V. On a subclass of strongly starlike functions associated with exponential function. *Bull. Malays. Math. Sci. Soc.* **2015**, *38*, 365–386. [CrossRef]
5. Ullah, K.; Srivastava, H.M.; Rafiq, A.; Darus, M.; Shutaywi, M. Radius problems for starlike functions associated with the tan hyperbolic function. *J. Funct. Spaces* **2021**, *2022*, 9967640. [CrossRef]
6. Bano, K.; Raza, M. Starlike functions associated with cosine function. *Bull. Iran. Math. Soc.* **2012**, *47*, 1513–1532. [CrossRef]
7. Arora, K.; Kumar, S.S. Starlike functions associated with a petal shaped domain. *Bull. Korean Math. Soc.* **2022**, *59*, 993–1010.
8. Alotaibi, A.; Arif, M.; Alghamdi, M.A.; Hussain, S. Starlikness associated with cosine hyperbolic function. *Mathematics* **2020**, *8*, 1118. [CrossRef]
9. Cho, N.E.; Kumar, V.; Kumar, S.S.; Ravichandran, V. Radius problems for starlike functions associated with the sine function. *Bull. Iran. Math. Soc.* **2019**, *45*, 213–232. [CrossRef]
10. Gupta, P.; Nagpal, S.; Ravichandran, V. Inclusion relations and radius problems for a subclass of starlike functions. *J. Korean Math. Soc.* **2021**, *58*, 1147–1180.
11. Gandhi, S.; Gupta, P.; Nagpal, S.; Ravichandran, V. Starlike functions associated with an Epicycloid. *Hacet. J. Math. Stat.* **2022**, *51*, 1637–1660. [CrossRef]
12. Samko, G.; Kilbas, A.; Marichev, O. *Fractional Integrals and Derivatives: Theory and Applications*; Gordon and Breach: Amsterdam, The Netherlands, 1993.
13. Gorenflo, R.; Mainardi, F. Fractional calculus: Integral and differential equations of fractional order. In *Fractals and Fractional Calculus in Continuum Mechanics*; Carpinteri, A., Mainardi, F., Eds.; Springer: New York, NY, USA, 1997; pp. 277–290.
14. Podlubny, I. *Fractional Differential Equations*; Academic Press: San Diego, CA, USA, 1999.
15. Hilfer, R. *Applications of Fractional Calculus in Physics*; World Scientific Publishing Company: Singapore, 2000.
16. Kilbas, A.A.; Srivastava, H.M.; Trujillo, J.J. *Theory and Applications of Fractional Differential Equations*; Elsevier: Amsterdam, The Netherlands, 2006.
17. Babalola, K.O. New subclasses of analytic and univalent functions involving certain convolution operator. *Math. Cluj* **2008**, *50*, 3–12.
18. Srivastava, H.M.; El-Deeb, S.M. Hölder's inequalities for a class of analytic functions connected with a certain hybrid-type convolution operator, preprint.
19. Knuth, D.E. *The Art of Computer Programming*; Addison-Wesley: Boston, MA, USA, 1973; Volume 3.
20. Chowla, S.; Herstein, I.N.; Moore, W.K. On recursions connected with symmetric groups I. *Can. J. Math.* **1951**, *3*, 328–334. [CrossRef]
21. Beissinger, J.S. Similar constructions for Young tableaux and involutions, and their applications to shiftable tableaux. *Discret. Math.* **1987**, *67*, 149–163. [CrossRef]
22. Riordan, J. *Introduction to Combinatorial Analysis*; Dover: Mineola, TX, USA, 2002.
23. Włoch, A.; Wołowiec-Musiał, M. On generalized telephone number, their interpretations and matrix generators. *Util. Math.* **2017**, *10*, 531–539.
24. Bednarz, U.; Wolowiec-Musial, M. On a new generalization of telephone numbers. *Turk. J. Math.* **2019**, *43*, 1595–1603. [CrossRef]

25. Deniz, E. Sharp coefficient bounds for starlike functions associated with generalized telephone numbers. *Bull. Malays. Math. Sci. Soc.* **2021**, *44*, 1525–1542. [CrossRef]
26. Murugusundaramoorthy, G.; Vijaya, K. Certain Subclasses of Analytic Functions Associated with Generalized Telephone Numbers. *Symmetry* **2022**, *14*, 1053. [CrossRef]
27. Srivastava, H.M.; Mishra, A.K.; Gochhayat, P. Certain subclasses of analytic and bi-univalent functions. *Appl. Math. Lett.* **2010**, *23*, 1188–1192. [CrossRef]
28. Brannan, D.A.; Clunie, J.; Kirwan, W.E. Coefficient estimates for a class of star-like functions. *Can. J. Math.* **1970**, *22*, 476–485. [CrossRef]
29. Brannan, D.A.; Clunie, J.G. (Eds.) *Aspects of Contemporary Complex Analysis*; Academic Press: London, UK, 1980.
30. Brannan, D.A.; Taha, T.S. On some classes of bi-univalent functions. *Studia Univ. Babeş-Bolyai Math.* **1986**, *31*, 70–77.
31. Lewin, M. On a coefficient problem for bi-univalent functions. *Proc. Am. Math. Soc.* **1967**, *18*, 63–68. [CrossRef]
32. Netanyahu, E. The minimal distance of the image boundary from the origin and the second coefficient of a univalent function in $|z| < 1$. *Arch. Rational Mech. Anal.* **1969**, *32*, 100–112.
33. Taha, T.S. Topics in Univalent Function Theory. Ph.D. Thesis, University of London, London, UK, 1981.
34. Xu, Q.-H.; Gui, Y.-C.; Srivastava, H.M. Coefficient estimates for a certain subclass of analytic and bi-univalent functions. *Appl. Math. Lett.* **2012**, *25*, 990–994. [CrossRef]
35. Srivastava, H.M.; Wanas, A.K.; Murugusundaramoorthy, G. A certain family of bi-univalent functions associated with the Pascal distribution series based upon the Horadam polynomials. *Surv. Math. Appl.* **2021**, *16*, 193–205.
36. Murugusundaramoorthy, G.; Guney, H.O.; Vijaya, K. Coefficient bounds for certain suclasses of Bi-prestarlike functions associated with the Gegenbauer polynomial. *Adv. Stud. Contemp. Math.* **2022**, *32*, 5–15.
37. Srivastava, H.M.; Wanas A.K.; Güney, H.Ö. New Families of Bi-univalent Functions Associated with the Bazilevič Functions and the λ-Pseudo-Starlike Functions. *Iran J. Sci. Technol. Trans. Sci.* **2021**, *45*, 1799–1804. [CrossRef]
38. El-Deeb, S.M.; Murugusundaramoorty, G.; Alburaikan, A. Abi-Bazileviĉ functions based on the Mittag-Leffler-Type Borel distribution associated with Legendre polynomials. *J. Math. Comput. Sci.* **2021**, *24*, 235–245. [CrossRef]
39. Srivastava, H.M.; Murugusundaramoorty, G.; El-Deeb, S.M. Faber polynomial coefficient estimates of bi-close-to-convex functions connected with Borel distribution of the Mittag-Leffler-type. *J. Nonlinear Var. Anal.* **2021**, *5*, 103–118.
40. Obradovic, M.; Yaguchi, T.; Saitoh, H. On some conditions for univalence and starlikeness in the unit disc. *Rend. Math. Ser. VII* **1992**, *12*, 869–877.
41. Lashin, A.Y. Coefficient Estimates for Two Subclasses of Analytic and Bi-Univalent Functions. *Ukr. Math. J.* **2019**, *70*, 1484–1492. [CrossRef]
42. Pommerenke, C. *Univalent Functions*; Vandenhoeck & Ruprecht: Göttingen, Germany, 1975.
43. Fekete, M.; Szegö, G. Eine Bemerkung über ungerade schlichte Functionen. *J. Lond. Math. Soc.* **1933**, *8*, 85–89. [CrossRef]
44. Zaprawa, P. On the Fekete-Szegö problem for classes of bi-univalent functions. *Bull. Belg. Math. Soc. Simon Stevin* **2014**, *21*, 169–178. [CrossRef]
45. Srivastava, H.M.; Murugusundaramoorty, G.; Bulboacă, T. The second Hankel determinant for subclasses of Bi-univalent functions associated with a nephroid domain. *Rev. Real Acad. Cienc. Exactas Fis. Nat. Ser. A-Mat.* **2022**, *116*, 145. [CrossRef]
46. Yalçın, S.; Altınkaya, S.; Murugusundaramoorty, G.; Vijaya, K. Hankel inequalities for a subclass of bi-univalent functions based on Salagean type q-difference operator. *J. Math. Fund. Sci.* **2020**, *52*, 189–201. [CrossRef]

axioms

MDPI

Article

A New Pseudo-Type κ-Fold Symmetric Bi-Univalent Function Class

Sondekola Rudra Swamy [1] and Luminita-Ioana Cotîrlă [2,*]

1 Department of Information Science and Engineering, Acharya Institute of Technology, Bengaluru 560 107, Karnataka, India; swamy2704@acharya.ac.in
2 Department of Mathematics, Tehnical University of Cluj-Napoca, 400114 Cluj-Napoca, Romania
* Correspondence: luminita.cotirla@math.utcluj.ro

Abstract: We introduce and study a new pseudo-type κ-fold symmetric bi-univalent function class that meets certain subordination conditions in this article. For functions in the newly formed class, the initial coefficient bounds are obtained. For members in this class, the Fekete–Szegö issue is also estimated. In addition, we uncover pertinent links to previous results and give a few observations.

Keywords: regular; subordination; Fekete–Szegö inequality; bi-univalent

MSC: 30C45; 30C50

1. Preliminaries

Let $\{\varsigma \in \mathbb{C} : |\varsigma| < 1\} = \mathfrak{D}$, where $\mathbb{C}$ is the set of all complex numbers. Let $\mathcal{A}$ denote the class of all regular functions of the type

$$s(\varsigma) = \varsigma + \sum_{j=2}^{\infty} d_j \varsigma^j \quad (1)$$

with $s(0) = s'(0) - 1 = 0$, $\varsigma \in \mathfrak{D}$ and $\mathcal{S}$ denote the subfamily of functions $\in \mathcal{A}$ which are univalent in $\mathfrak{D}$. For $\tau \geq 1$, the class of τ-pseudo-convex functions is defined as

$$\mathcal{K}^\tau = \left\{ s \in \mathcal{A} : \Re\left(\frac{\{(\varsigma s'(\varsigma))'\}^\tau}{s(\varsigma)} \right) > 0, \quad \varsigma \in \mathfrak{D} \right\},$$

the class of τ-pseudo-starlike functions is given by

$$\mathcal{S}^\tau = \left\{ s \in \mathcal{A} : \Re\left(\frac{\varsigma\{s'(\varsigma)\}^\tau}{s(\varsigma)} \right) > 0, \quad \varsigma \in \mathfrak{D} \right\}$$

and the class of τ-pseudo-bounded turning is introduced as

$$\mathcal{R}^\tau = \left\{ s \in \mathcal{A} : \Re(s'(\varsigma))^\tau > 0, \quad \right\}, \ (\varsigma \in \mathfrak{D}),$$

The class $\mathcal{K}^\tau$ was explored by Guney and Murugusundaramoorthy [1] and the class $\mathcal{S}^\tau$ was examined in [2]. We note that $\mathcal{S}^1 = \mathcal{S}$. Al Amiri and Reade [3] presented the class $\mathfrak{M}(\nu)$ $(\nu < 1)$ of functions $s \in \mathcal{A}$ with $s'(\varsigma) \neq 0$ *in* $\mathfrak{D}$ which satisfy

$$\Re\left(\nu \frac{(\varsigma s'(\varsigma))'}{s'(\varsigma)} + (1-\nu) s'(\varsigma) \right) > 0, \quad (\varsigma \in \mathfrak{D}).$$

Citation: Swamy, S.R.; Cotîrlă, L.-I. A New Pseudo-Type κ-Fold Symmetric Bi-Univalent Function Class. *Axioms* **2023**, *12*, 953. https://doi.org/10.3390/axioms12100953

Academic Editor: Georgia Irina Oros

Received: 25 August 2023
Revised: 7 October 2023
Accepted: 7 October 2023
Published: 10 October 2023

In [4], Sukhjit Singh and Sushma Gupta gave certain criteria for univalence by proving $\Re(s'(\varsigma)) > 0$, whenever

$$\Re\left(\nu\frac{(\varsigma s'(\varsigma))'}{s'(\varsigma)} + (1-\nu)s'(\varsigma)\right) > \xi, \quad (0 \leq \nu < 1, 0 \leq \xi < 1, \varsigma \in \mathfrak{D}).$$

The Koebe theorem (see [5]) ensures that $s(\mathfrak{D})$, $s \in \mathcal{S}$, contains a disc of radius $1/4$. Thus, any function s admits an inverse $g = s^{-1}$ defined by $g(s(\varsigma)) = \varsigma$, and $s(g(\varkappa)) = \varkappa$, $|\varkappa| < r_0(s)$, $r_0(s) \geq 1/4, \varsigma \in \mathfrak{D}, \varkappa \in \mathfrak{D}$, where

$$g(\varkappa) = \varkappa - d_2\varkappa^2 + (2d_2^2 - d_3)\varkappa^3 - (5d_2^3 - 5d_2d_3 + d_4)\varkappa^4 + \cdots \tag{2}$$

If $s \in \mathcal{S}$ and $s^{-1} \in \mathcal{S}$, then a member s of $\mathcal{A}$ given by (1) is called bi-univalent in $\mathfrak{D}$ and the collection of such functions in $\mathfrak{D}$ is symbolized by σ. For a brief study, and to know some interesting properties of the family σ, see [6]. Some subfamilies of the family σ that are comparable to the well-known subfamilies of the family S have been introduced by Tan [7], Brannan and Taha [8], and Srivastava et al. [9]. In fact, as sequels to the above subfamilies of σ, a number of different subfamilies of σ have since then been explored by many authors (see, for example, [10–14]). Most of these works are devoted to the study of the Fekete–Szegö issue of functions in various subfamilies of σ.

Let $\mathbb{N} = \{1, 2, 3, \cdots\}$ and $\mathbb{R} = (-\infty, +\infty)$.

If, for $\kappa \in \mathbb{N}$, $s(e^{\frac{2\pi i}{\kappa}}\varsigma) = e^{\frac{2\pi i}{\kappa}}s(\varsigma)$, $\varsigma \in \mathfrak{D}$, then a regular function s is called a κ-fold symmetric (κ-FS). The function s, defined by $s(\varsigma) = (f(\varsigma^\kappa))^{1/\kappa}$, $\kappa \in \mathbb{N}$, $f \in \mathcal{S}$, is univalent and maps $\mathfrak{D}$ into a κ-fold symmetry region. We indicate by $\mathcal{S}_\kappa$ the class of κ-fold symmetric univalent (κ-FSU) functions in $\mathfrak{D}$. A function $s \in \mathcal{S}_\kappa$ has the following form:

$$s(\varsigma) = \varsigma + \sum_{j=1}^{\infty} d_{\kappa j+1} \cdot \varsigma^{\kappa j+1} \qquad (\kappa \in \mathbb{N}; \varsigma \in \mathfrak{D}). \tag{3}$$

Clearly $\mathcal{S}_1 = \mathcal{S}$.

Similar to the idea of $\mathcal{S}_\kappa$, Srivastava et al. [15] investigated the class σ_κ of κ-fold symmetric bi-univalent (κ-FSBU) functions. A few intriguing findings were made, including the series

$$\begin{aligned} s^{-1}(\varkappa) = \varkappa - d_{\kappa+1}\varkappa^{\kappa+1} + [(1+\kappa)d_{\kappa+1}^2 - d_{2\kappa+1}]\varkappa^{2\kappa+1} \\ - \left[\tfrac{1}{2}(1+\kappa)(2+3\kappa)d_{\kappa+1}^3 - (2+3\kappa)d_{\kappa+1}d_{2\kappa+1} + d_{3\kappa+1}\right]\varkappa^{3\kappa+1} + \cdots. \end{aligned} \tag{4}$$

when $s \in \sigma_\kappa$.

Note that the functions

$$s_1(\varsigma) = \left(\frac{1}{2}log\left(\frac{1+\varsigma^\kappa}{1-\varsigma^\kappa}\right)\right)^{1/\kappa}, s_2(\varsigma) = \left(\frac{\varsigma^\kappa}{1-\varsigma^\kappa}\right)^{1/\kappa}, \quad s_3(\varsigma) = (-log(1-\varsigma^\kappa))^{1/\kappa}, \cdots.$$

with the corresponding inverses

$$g_1(\varkappa) = \left(\frac{e^{2\varkappa^\kappa} - 1}{e^{2\varkappa^\kappa} - 1}\right)^{1/\kappa}, \; g_2(\varkappa) = \left(\frac{\varkappa^\kappa}{1+\varkappa^\kappa}\right)^{1/\kappa}, \; g_3(\varkappa) = \left(\frac{e^{\varkappa^\kappa} - 1}{e^{\varkappa^\kappa}}\right)^{1/m}, \cdots.$$

are elements of σ_κ. We obtain (2) from (4) on taking $\kappa = 1$.

The focus on the initial coefficients of functions in some subfamilies of σ_κ is an interesting topic and this opened an area for many developments. New subfamilies of σ_κ were introduced and examined in depth by many researchers (see, for example, [16–19]). We mention here some recent works on this topic. Initial coefficient bounds for new subfamilies of σ_κ were determined in [20]. The Fekete–Szegö (FS) issue $|d_{2m+1} - \delta d_{m+1}^2|$, $\delta \in \mathbb{R}$ (see [21]) for certain special families of σ_κ was examined by Swamy et al. [22,23]; and another special family of σ_κ satisfying certain subordination conditions was examined by Aldawish et al. [24]; initial coefficients estimates for elements belonging to certain new families of σ_κ were obtained by Breaz and Cotîrlă in [25] (see [26–28]), indicating the developments in this domain.

For functions s_1 and s_2 regular in $\mathfrak{D}$, s_1 is said to subordinate s_2, if there is a Schwarz function ψ in $\mathfrak{D}$, such that $\psi(0) = 0$, $|\psi(z)| < 1$ and $s_1(z) = s_2(\psi(z))$, $z \in \mathfrak{D}$. This subordination is indicated as $s_1 \prec s_2$. If $s_2 \in \mathcal{S}$, then $s_1(z) \prec s_2(z)$ is equivalent to $s_1(0) = s_2(0)$ and $s_1(\mathfrak{D}) \subset s_2(\mathfrak{D})$.

Inspired by the efforts of Al-Amiri [3] and the authors of [19], we introduce a new class $\mathfrak{P}^{\tau}_{\sigma_\kappa}(\eta, \nu, \varphi)$, $\eta \in \mathbb{C}^* = \mathbb{C} - \{0\}, 0 \leq \nu \leq 1$, and $\varphi(\varsigma)$ is a regular function, such that $\Re(\varphi(\varsigma)) > 0$, $\varphi'(0) > 0$, $\varphi(0) = 1$, $\varphi(\mathfrak{D})$ is symmetric with respect to the real axis. In Section 2, we estimate the upper bounds of $|d_{\kappa+1}|$, $|d_{2\kappa+1}|$ and $|d_{2\kappa+1} - \delta d^2_{\kappa+1}|$ ($\delta \in \mathbb{R}$), for functions that belong to the class $\mathfrak{P}^{\tau}_{\sigma_\kappa}(\eta, \nu, \varphi)$. We consider two special cases $\mathfrak{Q}^{\varrho}_{\sigma_\kappa}(\eta, \nu, \tau) = \mathfrak{P}^{\tau}_{\sigma_\kappa}(\eta, \nu, \left(\frac{1+\varsigma}{1-\varsigma}\right)^{\varrho}), 0 < \varrho \leq 1$ and $\mathfrak{X}^{\xi}_{\sigma_\kappa}(\eta, \nu, \tau) = \mathfrak{P}^{\tau}_{\sigma_\kappa}(\eta, \nu, \frac{1+(1-2\xi)\varsigma}{1-\varsigma})$, $0 \leq \xi < 1$, in Section 3 and Section 4, respectively. We also identify connections to existing results and present a few new observations.

2. The Class $\mathfrak{P}^{\tau}_{\sigma_\kappa}(\eta, \nu, \varphi)$

Throughout this paper, $s^{-1}(\varkappa) = g(\varkappa)$ is as in (4), $\eta \in \mathbb{C}^* = \mathbb{C}\backslash\{0\}, \varsigma \in \mathfrak{D}, \varkappa \in \mathfrak{D}$ and $\varphi(\varsigma)$ will be a regular function such that $\Re(\varphi(\varsigma)) > 0$, $\varphi'(0) > 0$, $\varphi(0) = 1$, and $\varphi(\mathfrak{D})$ is symmetric with respect to the real axis. An expansion of $\varphi(\varsigma)$ has the form:

$$\varphi(\varsigma) = 1 + B_1\varsigma + B_2\varsigma^2 + B_3\varsigma^3 + \cdots (B_1 > 0). \tag{5}$$

Let **P** be the class of regular functions of the type $p(\varsigma) = 1 + p_1\varsigma + p_2\varsigma^2 + p_3\varsigma^3 + \cdots$, $\Re(p(\varsigma)) > 0$. A κ-FS function $p_\kappa \in \mathbf{P}$ is of the form $p_\kappa(\varsigma) = 1 + p_\kappa\varsigma^\kappa + p_{2\kappa}\varsigma^{2\kappa} + p_{3\kappa}\varsigma^{3\kappa} + \cdots$ (see [29]).

Let $\mathfrak{h}(\varsigma)$ and $\mathfrak{p}(\varkappa)$ be regular in $\mathfrak{D}$ with $\max\{|\mathfrak{h}(\varsigma)|, |\mathfrak{p}(\varkappa)|\} < 1$ and $\mathfrak{h}(0) = 0 = \mathfrak{p}(0)$. We suppose that $\mathfrak{h}(\varsigma) = h_\kappa\varsigma^\kappa + h_{2\kappa}\varsigma^{2\kappa} + h_{3\kappa}\varsigma^{3\kappa} + \cdots$ and $\mathfrak{p}(\varkappa) = p_\kappa\varkappa^\kappa + p_{2\kappa}\varkappa^{2\kappa} + p_{3\kappa}\varkappa^{3\kappa} + \cdots$. Also, we assume that

$$|h_\kappa| < 1; |h_{2\kappa}| \leq 1 - |h_\kappa|^2; |p_\kappa| < 1; |p_{2\kappa}| \leq 1 - |p_\kappa|^2. \tag{6}$$

After simple computations, using (5), we have

$$\varphi(\mathfrak{h}(\varsigma)) = 1 + B_1h_\kappa\varsigma^\kappa + (B_1h_{2\kappa} + B_2h^2_\kappa)\varsigma^{2\kappa} + \ldots \tag{7}$$

and

$$\varphi(\mathfrak{p}(\varkappa)) = 1 + B_1p_\kappa\varkappa^\kappa + (B_1p_{2\kappa} + B_2p^2_\kappa)\varkappa^{2\kappa} + \ldots. \tag{8}$$

Definition 1. *A function $s \in \sigma_\kappa$ of the form (3) is said to be in the class $\mathfrak{P}^{\tau}_{\sigma_\kappa}(\eta, \nu, \varphi)$ if*

$$\frac{1}{\eta}\left(\nu\frac{\{(\varsigma s'(\varsigma))'\}^{\tau}}{s'(\varsigma)} + (1-\nu)(s'(\varsigma))^{\tau} - 1\right) + 1 \prec \varphi(\varsigma)$$

and

$$\frac{1}{\eta}\left(\nu\frac{\{(\varkappa g'(\varkappa))'\}^{\tau}}{g'(\varkappa)} + (1-\nu)(g'(\varkappa))^{\tau} - 1\right) + 1 \prec \varphi(\varkappa),$$

where $g = s^{-1}$, $\tau \geq 1$, $\eta \in \mathbb{C}^*$, and $0 \leq \nu \leq 1$.

Remark 1. *(i) The subclass $\mathfrak{P}^{\tau}_{\sigma_\kappa}(\eta, 0, \varphi) \equiv \mathscr{H}^{\tau}_{\sigma_\kappa}(\eta, \varphi)$, and was explored in [24].*

(ii) $\mathfrak{P}^{1}_{\sigma_\kappa}(\eta, \nu, \varphi) \equiv \mathscr{I}_{\sigma_\kappa}(\eta, \nu, \varphi)$ is the subclass of functions $s \in \sigma_\kappa$ satisfying

$$\frac{1}{\eta}\left(\nu\frac{(\varsigma s'(\varsigma))'}{s'(\varsigma)} + (1-\nu)s'(\varsigma) - 1\right) + 1 \prec \varphi(\varsigma)$$

and its inverse $g = s^{-1}$ *satisfies*

$$\frac{1}{\eta}\left(\nu\frac{(\varkappa g'(\varkappa))'}{g'(\varkappa)} + (1-\nu)g'(\varkappa) - 1\right) + 1 \prec \varphi(\varkappa),$$

where $\eta \in \mathbb{C}^*$ *and* $0 \leq \nu < 1$.

Theorem 1. *If the function* s *given by (3) belongs to the family* $\mathfrak{P}^{\tau}_{\sigma_\kappa}(\eta,\nu,\varphi)$ *and* $\delta \in \mathbb{R}$, *then*

$$|d_{\kappa+1}| \leq \frac{|\eta|B_1\sqrt{2B_1}}{\sqrt{|\{M(1+\kappa)+[N\tau(\tau-1)+(1-(1+\kappa)\tau)2\nu](1+\kappa)^2\}\eta B_1^2-2L^2B_2|+2L^2B_1}}, \tag{9}$$

$$|d_{2\kappa+1}| \leq \begin{cases} \frac{B_1|\eta|}{M} & ;\, 0 < B_1 < \frac{2L^2}{|\eta|M(1+\kappa)} \\ \frac{B_1|\eta|}{M} + \left(\frac{1+\kappa}{2} - \frac{L^2}{|\eta|B_1M}\right)\frac{2\eta^2B_1^3}{|\{M(1+\kappa)+[N\tau(\tau-1)+(1-(1+\kappa)\tau)2\nu](1+\kappa)^2\}\eta B_1^2-2L^2B_2|+2L^2B_1} & \\ & ;\, B_1 \geq \frac{2L^2}{|\eta|M(1+\kappa)}, \end{cases} \tag{10}$$

and

$$|d_{2\kappa+1} - \delta d_{\kappa+1}^2| \leq \begin{cases} \frac{B_1|\eta|}{M} & ;\, |1+\kappa-2\delta| < J \\ \frac{|\eta|^2B_1^3|\kappa-2\delta+1|}{|\{M(1+\kappa)+[N\tau(\tau-1)+(1-(1+\kappa)\tau)2\nu](1+\kappa)^2\}\eta B_1^2-2L^2B_2|} & ;\, |1+\kappa-2\delta| \geq J, \end{cases} \tag{11}$$

where

$$J = \left|\frac{\{M(1+\kappa)+[N\tau(\tau-1)+2\nu(1-(1+\kappa)\tau)](1+\kappa)^2\}\eta B_1^2 - 2L^2B_2}{\eta M B_1^2}\right|. \tag{12}$$

$$L = (1+\kappa)(\tau(1+\nu\kappa)-\nu), \tag{13}$$

$$M = (\tau(1+2\nu\kappa)-\nu)(1+2\kappa) \tag{14}$$

and

$$N = 1+\nu\kappa(2+\kappa). \tag{15}$$

Proof. Let the function s of the form (3) belong to the family $\mathfrak{P}^{\tau}_{\sigma_\kappa}(\eta,\nu,\varphi)$. Then, we have regular functions $\mathfrak{h}, \mathfrak{p} : \mathfrak{D} \longrightarrow \mathfrak{D}$, $\mathfrak{h}(0) = \mathfrak{p}(0) = 0$ satisfying

$$\frac{1}{\eta}\left(\nu\frac{\{(\varsigma s'(\varsigma))'\}^{\tau}}{s'(\varsigma)} + (1-\nu)(s'(\varsigma))^{\tau} - 1\right) + 1 = \varphi(\mathfrak{h}(\varsigma)), \tag{16}$$

and

$$\frac{1}{\eta}\left(\nu\frac{\{(\varkappa g'(\varkappa))'\}^{\tau}}{g'(\varkappa)} + (1-\nu)(g'(\varkappa))^{\tau} - 1\right) + 1 = \varphi(\mathfrak{p}(\varkappa)). \tag{17}$$

Using (3) in (16) and (17) we obtain:

$$\frac{1}{\eta}\left(\nu\frac{[\{(\varsigma s'(\varsigma))'\}^{\tau}}{s'(\varsigma)} + (1-\nu)(s'(\varsigma))^{\tau} - 1\right) + 1 =$$

$$\frac{1}{\eta}\{Ld_{\kappa+1}\varsigma^{\kappa}+[Md_{2\kappa+1}+$$
$$(1+\kappa)^2\left(\frac{N\tau(\tau-1)}{2}+\nu(1-(1+\kappa)\tau)\right)d_{\kappa+1}^2\Big]\varsigma^{2\kappa}+\cdots\Big\}+1 \quad (18)$$

and

$$\frac{1}{\eta}\left(\nu\frac{\{(\varkappa g'(\varkappa))'\}^{\tau}}{g'(\varkappa)}+(1-\nu)(g'(\varkappa))^{\tau}-1\right)+1=$$

$$\frac{1}{\eta}\Big\{-Ld_{\kappa+1}\varkappa^{\kappa}+\Big[M((1+\kappa)d_{\kappa+1}^2-d_{2\kappa+1})+$$
$$(1+\kappa)^2\left(\frac{N\tau(\tau-1)}{2}+\nu(1-(1+\kappa)\tau)\right)d_{\kappa+1}^2\Big]\varkappa^{2\kappa}+\cdots\Big\}+1, \quad (19)$$

where L, M, and N are as in (13), (14), and (15), respectively.

Comparing (7) and (18), we obtain

$$Ld_{\kappa+1}=\eta B_1 h_{\kappa} \quad (20)$$

and

$$Md_{2\kappa+1}+\left(\frac{N\tau(\tau-1)}{2}+\nu(1-(1+\kappa)\tau)\right)(1+\kappa)^2 d_{\kappa+1}^2=\eta[B_1 h_{2\kappa}+B_2 h_{\kappa}^2]. \quad (21)$$

Comparing (8) and (19), we obtain

$$-Ld_{\kappa+1}=\eta B_1 p_{\kappa} \quad (22)$$

and

$$M((\kappa+1)d_{\kappa+1}^2-d_{2\kappa+1})+\left(\tfrac{N\tau(\tau-1)}{2}+\nu(1-(1+\kappa)\tau)\right)(1+\kappa)^2 d_{\kappa+1}^2$$
$$=\eta[B_1 p_{2\kappa}+B_2 p_{\kappa}^2], \quad (23)$$

From (20) and (22), we obtain

$$h_{\kappa}=-p_{\kappa} \quad (24)$$

and

$$2L^2 d_{\kappa+1}^2=\eta^2 B_1^2(h_{\kappa}^2+p_{\kappa}^2). \quad (25)$$

We add (21) and (23) and then use (25) to obtain

$$[\{M(1+\kappa)+[N\tau(\tau-1)+(1-(1+\kappa)\tau)2\nu](1+\kappa)^2\}\eta B_1^2-2L^2B_2]d_{\kappa+1}^2$$
$$=\eta^2 B_1^3(h_{2\kappa}+p_{2\kappa}) \quad (26)$$

By using (6) and (20) in (26) for the coefficients $h_{2\kappa}$ and $p_{2\kappa}$, we obtain

$$[|\{M(1+\kappa)+[N\tau(\tau-1)+(1-(1+\kappa)\tau)2\nu](1+\kappa)^2\}\eta B_1^2-2L^2B_2|+2L^2B_1]|d_{\kappa+1}|^2$$
$$\leq 2\eta^2 B_1^3, \quad (27)$$

which implies (9).

We subtract (23) from (21) to find the bound on $|d_{2\kappa+1}|$:

$$d_{2\kappa+1}=\frac{\eta B_1(h_{2\kappa}-p_{2\kappa})}{2M}+\left(\frac{1+\kappa}{2}\right)d_{\kappa+1}^2. \quad (28)$$

In view of (20), (24), (28) and applying (6), we obtain

$$|d_{2\kappa+1}| \leq \frac{|\eta|B_1}{M} + \left(\frac{1+\kappa}{2} - \frac{L^2}{|\eta|B_1 M}\right) \times \tag{29}$$

$$\times \frac{2\eta^2 B_1^3}{|\{M(1+\kappa) + [N\tau(\tau-1) + (1-(1+\kappa)\tau)2\nu](1+\kappa)^2\}\eta B_1^2 - 2L^2 B_2| + 2L^2 B_1},$$

which obtains (10), the desired assessment.

From (26) and (28), for $\delta \in \mathbb{R}$, we obtain

$$d_{2\kappa+1} - \delta d_{\kappa+1}^2 = \frac{\eta B_1}{2}\left[\left(\mathfrak{Y}(\delta) + \frac{1}{M}\right)h_{2\kappa} + \left(\mathfrak{Y}(\delta) - \frac{1}{M}\right)p_{2\kappa}\right],$$

where

$$\mathfrak{Y}(\delta) = \frac{\eta B_1^2(\kappa - 2\delta + 1)}{\{M(1+\kappa) + [N\tau(\tau-1) + (1-(1+\kappa)\tau)2\nu](\kappa+1)^2\}\eta B_1^2 - 2L^2 B_2}.$$

In view of (6), we conclude that

$$|d_{2\kappa+1} - \delta d_{\kappa+1}^2| \leq \begin{cases} \frac{|\eta|B_1}{M} & ; 0 \leq |\mathfrak{Y}(\delta)| < \frac{1}{M} \\ |\eta|B_1|\mathfrak{Y}(\delta)| & ; |\mathfrak{Y}(\delta)| \geq \frac{1}{M}, \end{cases}$$

form which we obtain (11) with J as in (12). So the proof is completed. □

Remark 2. *We obtain Corollary 1 of [24] if $\nu = 0$ in Theorem 1.*

Choosing $\tau = 1$ in $\mathfrak{P}_{\sigma_\kappa}^{\tau}(\eta, \nu, \varphi)$, we have the corollary given below:

Corollary 1. *Let $\delta \in \mathbb{R}$ and let the function s given by (3) be in the family $\mathscr{I}_{\sigma_\kappa}(\eta, \nu, \varphi)$. Then,*

$$|d_{\kappa+1}| \leq \frac{|\eta|B_1\sqrt{2B_1}}{\sqrt{|\{(1+\kappa)M_1 - 2\nu\kappa(1+\kappa)^2\}\eta B_1^2 - 2L_1^2 B_2| + 2L_1^2 B_1}},$$

$$|d_{2\kappa+1}| \leq$$

$$\begin{cases} \frac{|\eta|B_1}{M_1} & ; 0 < B_1 < \frac{2L_1^2}{(1+\kappa)M_1|\eta|} \\ \frac{|\eta|B_1}{M_1} + \left(\frac{1+\kappa}{2} - \frac{L_1^2}{B_1 M_1|\eta|}\right)\frac{2\eta^2 B_1^3}{|\{(1+\kappa)M_1 - 2\nu\kappa(1+\kappa)^2\}\eta B_1^2 - 2L_1^2 B_2| + 2L_1^2 B_1} & ; B_1 \geq \frac{2L_1^2}{(1+\kappa)M_1|\eta|} \end{cases}$$

and

$$|d_{2\kappa+1} - \delta d_{\kappa+1}^2| \leq \begin{cases} \frac{|\eta|B_1}{M_1} & ; |\kappa - 2\delta + 1| < J_1 \\ \frac{B_1^3|\kappa - 2\delta + 1||\eta|^2}{|\{(\kappa+1)M_1 - 2\nu\kappa(\kappa+1)^2\}\eta B_1^2 - 2L_1^2 B_2|} & ; |\kappa - 2\delta + 1| \geq J_1, \end{cases}$$

where

$$J_1 = \left|\frac{\{(1+\kappa)M_1 - 2\nu\kappa(1+\kappa)^2\}\eta B_1^2 - 2L_1^2 B_2}{M_1 B_1^2 \eta}\right|,$$

$$L_1 = (1+\kappa)((\kappa-1)\nu + 1) \tag{30}$$

and

$$M_1 = (1+2\kappa)((2\kappa-1)\nu + 1), \tag{31}$$

Remark 3. *If $\nu = 0$ and $\eta = 1$ in Corollary 1 are allowed, then the first and second theorems of Tang et al. [19] are obtained.*

Choosing $\kappa = 1$ in Theorem 1, we have

Corollary 2. *If $s \in \mathfrak{P}^{\tau}_{\sigma_1}(\eta, \nu, \varphi)$ is given by (1) and $\delta \in \mathbb{R}$, then*

$$|d_2| \leq \frac{|\eta| B_1 \sqrt{B_1}}{\sqrt{|\{M_2+2(N_2\tau(\tau-1)+2\nu(1-2\tau))\}\eta B_1^2 - L_2^2 B_2| + L_2^2 B_1}},$$

$$|d_3| \leq \begin{cases} \frac{|\eta| B_1}{M_2} & ; 0 < B_1 < \frac{L_2^2}{|\eta| M_2} \\ \frac{|\eta| B_1}{M_2} + \left(1 - \frac{L_2^2}{|\eta| B_1 M_2}\right) \frac{\eta^2 B_1^3}{|\{M_2+2(N_2\tau(\tau-1)+2\nu(1-2\tau))\}\eta B_1^2 - L_2^2 B_2| + L_2^2 B_1} ; & B_1 \geq \frac{L_2^2}{|\eta| M_2}, \end{cases}$$

and

$$|d_3 - \delta d_2^2| \leq \begin{cases} \frac{|\eta| B_1}{M_2} & ; |1-\delta| < J_2 \\ \frac{|\eta|^2 B_1^3 |1-\delta|}{|\{M_2+2(N_2\tau(\tau-1)+2\nu(1-2\tau))\}\eta B_1^2 - L_2^2 B_2|} ; & |1-\delta| \geq J_2, \end{cases}$$

where

$$J_2 = \left| \frac{\{M_2 + 2(N_2\tau(\tau-1) + 2\nu(1-2\tau))\}\eta B_1^2 - L_2^2 B_2}{\eta M_2 B_1^2} \right|,$$

$$L_2 = 2((1+\nu)\tau - \nu), \tag{32}$$

$$M_2 = 3((1+2\nu)\tau - \nu) \tag{33}$$

and

$$N_2 = 3\nu + 1. \tag{34}$$

Setting $\eta = \tau = 1$ in Corollary 2, we obtain the following.

Corollary 3. *If $s \in \mathfrak{P}^{1}_{\sigma_1}(1, \nu, \varphi)$ is given by (1) and $\delta \in \mathbb{R}$, then*

$$|d_2| \leq \frac{B_1 \sqrt{B_1}}{\sqrt{|(3-\nu)B_1^2 - 4B_2| + 4B_1}},$$

$$|d_3| \leq \begin{cases} \frac{B_1}{3(\nu+1)} & ; 0 < B_1 < \frac{4}{3(\nu+1)} \\ \frac{B_1}{3(\nu+1)} + \left(1 - \frac{4}{3(\nu+1)B_1}\right) \frac{B_1^3}{|(3-\nu)B_1^2 - 4B_2| + 4B_1} ; & B_1 \geq \frac{4}{3(\nu+1)}, \end{cases}$$

and

$$|d_3 - \delta d_2^2| \leq \begin{cases} \frac{B_1}{3(\nu+1)} & ; |1-\delta| < \left| \frac{(3-\nu)B_1^2 - 4B_2}{3(\nu+1)B_1^2} \right| \\ \frac{B_1^3 |1-\delta|}{|(3-\nu)B_1^2 - 4B_2|} ; & |1-\delta| \geq \left| \frac{(3-\nu)B_1^2 - 4B_2}{3(\nu+1)B_1^2} \right|. \end{cases}$$

Remark 4. *When $\nu = 0$ is selected in Corollary 3, we obtain Corollaries 1 and 4 of Tang et al. [19] (also see [30]).*

3. The Class $\mathfrak{Q}^{\tau}_{\sigma_\kappa}(\eta, \nu, \varrho)$

Let $\varphi(\varsigma) = 1 + 2\varrho\varsigma + 2\varrho^2\varsigma^2 + \cdots = \left(\frac{1+\varsigma}{1-\varsigma}\right)^{\varrho}$ in Definition 1. Then, we have the subclass of all $s \in \sigma_\kappa$ satisfying

$$\left| arg\left[\frac{1}{\eta} \left(\nu \frac{\{(\varsigma s'(\varsigma))'\}^{\tau}}{s'(\varsigma)} + (1-\nu)(s'(\varsigma))^{\tau} - 1 \right) + 1 \right] \right| < \frac{\varrho \pi}{2}$$

and

$$\left| arg\left[\frac{1}{\eta} \left(\nu \frac{\{(\varkappa g'(\varkappa))'\}^{\tau}}{g'(\varkappa)} + (1-\nu)(g'(\varkappa))^{\tau} - 1 \right) + 1 \right] \right| < \frac{\varrho \pi}{2},$$

where $g = s^{-1}$, $0 < \varrho \leq 1$, $\eta \in \mathbb{C}^*$, $\tau \geq 1$, and $0 \leq \nu < 1$. We denote this class by $\mathfrak{Q}^{\tau}_{\sigma_\kappa}(\eta, \nu, \varrho) = \mathfrak{P}^{\tau}_{\sigma_\kappa}(\eta, \nu, \left(\frac{1+\varsigma}{1-\varsigma}\right)^{\varrho})$.

Remark 5. *(i) The family* $\mathfrak{Q}^{\tau}_{\sigma_\kappa}(\eta,0,\varrho) \equiv \mathscr{B}^{\tau}_{\sigma_\kappa}(\eta,\varrho)$, *and was explored in [24], where* $\eta \in \mathbb{C}^*$, $\tau \geq 1$ *and* $0 < \varrho \leq 1$.

ii) $\mathfrak{Q}^{1}_{\sigma_\kappa}(\eta,\nu,\varrho) \equiv \mathscr{D}_{\sigma_\kappa}(\eta,\nu,\varrho)$ *is the subfamily of all* $s \in \sigma_\kappa$ *satisfying*

$$\left|arg\left[\frac{1}{\eta}\left(\nu\frac{(\varsigma s'(\varsigma))'}{s'(\varsigma)} + (1-\nu)s'(\varsigma) - 1\right) + 1\right]\right| < \frac{\varrho\pi}{2}$$

and its inverse $g = s^{-1}$ *satisfies*

$$\left|arg\left[\frac{1}{\eta}\left(\nu\frac{(\varkappa g'(\varkappa))'}{g'(\varkappa)} + (1-\nu)g'(\varkappa) - 1\right) + 1\right]\right| < \frac{\varrho\pi}{2},$$

where $0 < \varrho \leq 1$, $\eta \in \mathbb{C}^*$ *and* $0 \leq \nu < 1$.

Taking $\varphi(\varsigma) = \left(\frac{1+\varsigma}{1-\varsigma}\right)^{\varrho}$ in Theorem 1, we obtain

Corollary 4. *If the function s given by (3) belongs to the family* $\in \mathfrak{Q}^{\tau}_{\sigma_\kappa}(\eta,\nu,\varrho)$ *and* $\delta \in \mathbb{R}$, *then*

$$|d_{\kappa+1}| \leq \frac{2\varrho|\eta|}{\sqrt{\varrho|\{M(1+\kappa)+[N\tau(\tau-1)+(1-(1+\kappa)\tau)2\nu](1+\kappa)^2\}\eta - L^2| + L^2}},$$

$$|d_{2\kappa+1}| \leq \begin{cases} \frac{2\varrho|\eta|}{M} & ; 0 < \varrho < \frac{L^2}{M(1+\kappa)|\eta|} \\ \frac{2\varrho|\eta|}{M} + \left(1+\kappa - \frac{L^2}{\varrho M|\eta|}\right)\frac{2\varrho^2\eta^2}{\varrho|\{(1+\kappa)M+[N\tau(\tau-1)+(1-(1+\kappa)\tau)2\nu](1+\kappa)^2\}\eta - L^2| + L^2}; & \varrho \geq \frac{L^2}{M(1+\kappa)|\eta|}, \end{cases}$$

and

$$|d_{2\kappa+1} - \delta d^2_{\kappa+1}| \leq \begin{cases} \frac{2\varrho|\eta|}{M} & ; |\kappa - 2\delta + 1| < J_3 \\ \frac{2\varrho|\kappa-2\delta+1||\eta|^2}{|\{(1+\kappa)M+[\tau(\tau-1)N+(1-(\kappa+1)\tau)2\nu](\kappa+1)^2\}\eta - L^2|}; & |\kappa - 2\delta + 1| \geq J_3, \end{cases}$$

where

$$J_3 = \left|\frac{\{M(1+\kappa) + [N\tau(\tau-1) + (1-(1+\kappa)\tau)2\nu](1+\kappa)^2\}\eta - L^2}{\eta M}\right|,$$

L, M, and N are as in (13), (14), and (15), respectively.

Remark 6. *For* $\nu = 0$ *in Corollary 4, we obtain Corollary 4 in [24].*

Choosing $\tau = 1$ in $\mathfrak{Q}^{\tau}_{\sigma_\kappa}(\eta,\nu,\varphi)$, we obtain the corollary given below:

Corollary 5. *If the function s given by (3) belongs to the family* $\mathscr{D}_{\sigma_\kappa}(\eta,\nu,\varrho)$ *and* $\delta \in \mathbb{R}$, *then*

$$|d_{\kappa+1}| \leq \frac{2\varrho|\eta|}{\sqrt{\varrho|\{M_1(1+\kappa)-2\nu\kappa(1+\kappa)^2\}\eta - L_1^2| + L_1^2}},$$

$$|d_{2\kappa+1}| \leq \begin{cases} \frac{2\varrho|\eta|}{M_1} & ; 0 < \varrho < \frac{L_1^2}{M_1(1+\kappa)|\eta|} \\ \frac{2\varrho|\eta|}{M_1} + \left(1+\kappa - \frac{L_1^2}{\varrho M_1|\eta|}\right)\frac{2\varrho^2\eta^2}{\varrho|\{M_1(1+\kappa)-2\nu\kappa(1+\kappa)^2\}\eta - L_1^2| + L^2}; & \varrho \geq \frac{L_1^2}{(1+\kappa)M_1|\eta|} \end{cases}$$

and

$$|d_{2\kappa+1} - \delta d^2_{\kappa+1}| \leq \begin{cases} \frac{2\varrho|\eta|}{M_1} & ; |\kappa - 2\delta + 1| < J_4 \\ \frac{2\varrho|\kappa-2\delta+1||\eta|^2}{|\{M_1(\kappa+1)-2\nu\kappa(\kappa+1)^2\}\eta - L_1^2|}; & |\kappa - 2\delta + 1| \geq J_4, \end{cases}$$

where

$$J_4 = \left|\frac{\{M_1(1+\kappa) - 2\nu\kappa(1+\kappa)^2\}\eta - L_1^2}{\eta M_1}\right|,$$

L_1 and M_1 are as in (30) and (31), respectively.

Corollary 4 yields the following if $\kappa = 1$:

Corollary 6. *If $s \in \mathfrak{Q}^{\tau}_{\sigma_1}(\eta, \nu, \varrho)$ is given by (1) and $\delta \in \mathbb{R}$, then*

$$|d_2| \le \frac{2|\eta|\varrho}{\sqrt{\varrho|\{2M_2+4(N_2\tau(\tau-1)+2\nu(1-2\tau))\}\eta - L_2^2| + L_2^2}},$$

$$|d_3| \le \begin{cases} \frac{2|\eta|\varrho}{M_2} & ; 0 < \varrho < \frac{L_2^2}{2|\eta|M_2} \\ \frac{2|\eta|\varrho}{M_2} + \left(2 - \frac{L_2^2}{|\eta|\varrho M_2}\right)\frac{2\eta^2\varrho^2}{\varrho|\{2M_2+4(N_2\tau(\tau-1)+2\nu(1-2\tau))\}\eta - L_2^2| + L_2^2}; & \varrho \ge \frac{L_2^2}{2|\eta|M_2}, \end{cases}$$

and

$$|d_3 - \delta d_2^2| \le \begin{cases} \frac{2|\eta|\varrho}{M_2} & ; |1-\delta| < J_5 \\ \frac{2|\eta|^2\varrho|1-\delta|}{|\{2M_2+4(N_2\tau(\tau-1)+2\nu(1-2\tau))\}\eta - L_2^2|} & ; |1-\delta| \ge J_5, \end{cases}$$

where

$$J_5 = \left|\frac{\{2M_2 + 4(N_2\tau(\tau-1) + 2\nu(1-2\tau))\}\eta - L_2^2}{2\eta M_2}\right|,$$

L_2, M_2, and N_2 are as in (32), (33), and (34), respectively.

Corollary 6 would yield the following if $\eta = \tau = 1$.

Corollary 7. *If the function s of the form (1) $\in \mathfrak{Q}^{1}_{\sigma_1}(1, \nu, \varphi)$ and $\delta \in \mathbb{R}$, then*

$$|d_2| \le \frac{\varrho\sqrt{2}}{\sqrt{\varrho(1-\nu)+2}},$$

$$|d_3| \le \begin{cases} \frac{2\varrho}{3(\nu+1)} & ; 0 < \varrho < \frac{2}{3(\nu+1)} \\ \frac{2\varrho}{3(\nu+1)} + \left(1 - \frac{2}{3\varrho(\nu+1)}\right)\frac{2\varrho^2}{\varrho(1-\nu)+2} & ; \varrho \ge \frac{2}{3(\nu+1)}, \end{cases}$$

and

$$|d_3 - \delta d_2^2| \le \begin{cases} \frac{2\varrho}{3(\nu+1)} & ; |1-\delta| < \frac{1-\nu}{3(\nu+1)} \\ \frac{\varrho|1-\delta|}{1-\nu} & ; |1-\delta| \ge \frac{1-\nu}{3(\nu+1)}. \end{cases}$$

Remark 7. *Letting $\nu = 0$ in Corollary 7, we obtain Corollary 2 of Tang et al. [19]. The estimate obtained here for $|d_3|$ is more accurate when compared to that in Theorem 2 of Srivastava et al. [9].*

4. The Class $\mathfrak{X}^{\tau}_{\sigma_\kappa}(\eta, \nu, \xi)$

If $\varphi(\varsigma) = 1 + 2(1-\xi)\varsigma + 2(1-\xi)\varsigma^2 + \cdots = \frac{1+(1-2\xi)\varsigma}{1-\varsigma}$ in Definition 1, then we have the subset of all $s \in \sigma_\kappa$ satisfying

$$\Re\left[\left(\nu\frac{\{(\varsigma s'(\varsigma))'\}^{\tau}}{s'(\varsigma)} + (1-\nu)(s'(\varsigma))^{\tau} - 1\right)\frac{1}{\eta} + 1\right] > \xi$$

and

$$\Re\left[\left(\nu\frac{\{(\varkappa g'(\varkappa))'\}^{\tau}}{g'(\varkappa)} + (1-\nu)(g'(\varkappa))^{\iota} - 1\right)\frac{1}{\eta} + 1\right] > \xi,$$

where $g = s^{-1}$, $\eta \in \mathbb{C}^*$, $0 \le \xi < 1$, $\tau \ge 1$, and $0 \le \nu < 1$. We denote this set by $\mathfrak{X}^{\tau}_{\sigma_\kappa}(\eta, \nu, \xi) = \mathfrak{P}^{\tau}_{\sigma_\kappa}\left(\eta, \nu, \left(\frac{1+(1-2\xi)\varsigma}{1-\varsigma}\right)\right)$.

Remark 8. *(i). The family* $\mathfrak{X}^{\tau}_{\sigma_\kappa}(\eta,0,\xi) \equiv \mathscr{E}^{\tau}_{\sigma_\kappa}(\eta,\xi)$, $\tau \geq 1$, $0 \leq \xi < 1$, *and was studied in [24].*
(ii). $\mathfrak{X}^{1}_{\sigma_\kappa}(\eta,\nu,\xi) \equiv \mathscr{F}_{\sigma_\kappa}(\eta,\nu,\xi)$ *is a set of all* $s \in \sigma_\kappa$ *satisfying*

$$\Re\left[\left(\nu\frac{(\varsigma s'(\varsigma))'}{s'(\varsigma)} + (1-\nu)s'(\varsigma) - 1\right)\frac{1}{\eta} + 1\right] > \xi$$

and its inverse $g = s^{-1}$ *satisfies*

$$\Re\left[\left(\nu\frac{(\varkappa g'(\varkappa))'}{g'(\varkappa)} + (1-\nu)g'(\varkappa) - 1\right)\frac{1}{\eta} + 1\right] > \xi,$$

where $\eta \in \mathbb{C}^*, 0 \leq \xi < 1$, *and* $0 \leq \nu < 1$.

Allowing $\varphi(\varsigma) = \frac{1+(1-2\xi)\varsigma}{1-\varsigma}, 0 \leq \xi < 1$, in Theorem 1, we obtain

Corollary 8. *Let the function s of the form (3) belong to the class* $\mathfrak{X}^{\tau}_{\sigma_\kappa}(\eta,\nu,\xi)$ *and* $\delta \in \mathbb{R}$. *Then,*

$$|d_{\kappa+1}| \leq \frac{(1-\xi)2|\eta|}{\sqrt{|\{(1+\kappa)M + (1+\kappa)^2[N\tau(\tau-1) + (1-(1+\kappa)\tau)2\nu]\}(1-\xi)\eta - L^2| + L^2}},$$

$$|d_{2\kappa+1}| \leq$$

$$\begin{cases} \frac{(1-\xi)2|\eta|}{M} & ; 1 - \frac{L^2}{(1+\kappa)M|\eta|} < \xi < 1 \\ \frac{(1-\xi)2|\eta|}{M} + \left(1+\kappa - \frac{L^2}{(1-\xi)M|\eta|}\right)\frac{2(1-\xi)^2|\eta|^2}{|\{(1+\kappa)M + [N\tau(\tau-1)+(1-(1+\kappa)\tau)2\nu](1+\kappa)^2\}(1-\xi)\eta - L^2| + L^2} & \\ & ; 0 \leq \xi \leq 1 - \frac{L^2}{(1+\kappa)M|\eta|} \end{cases}$$

and

$$|d_{2\kappa+1} - \delta d^2_{\kappa+1}| \leq \begin{cases} \frac{(1-\xi)2|\eta|}{M} & ; |\kappa - 2\delta + 1| < J_6 \\ \frac{2(1-\xi)^2|\eta|^2|\kappa-2\delta+1|}{|\{(1+\kappa)M + [N\tau(\tau-1)+(1-(1+\kappa)\tau)2\nu](1+\kappa)^2\}(1-\xi)\eta - L^2|}; & |\kappa - 2\delta + 1| \geq J_6, \end{cases}$$

where

$$J_6 = \left|\frac{\{(1+\kappa)M + (1+\kappa)^2[N\tau(\tau-1) + (1-(1+\kappa)\tau)2\nu]\}(1-\xi)\eta - L^2}{M(1-\xi)\eta}\right|.$$

L, M, and N are as in (13), (14), and (15), respectively.

Remark 9. *We obtain Corollary 7 of Aldawish et al. [24] if* $\nu = 0$ *in Corollary 8. In addition, we obtain Corollary 11 of Swamy et al. [22] when* $\eta = \tau = 1$.

Corollary 9. *Let the function s of the form (3) belong to the class* $\mathscr{F}^{\tau}_{\sigma_\kappa}(\eta,\nu,\xi)$ *and* $\delta \in \mathbb{R}$. *Then,*

$$|d_{\kappa+1}| \leq \frac{(1-\xi)2|\eta|}{\sqrt{|\{(1+\kappa)M_1 - 2\nu\kappa(1+\kappa)^2\}(1-\xi)\eta - L_1^2| + L_1^2}},$$

$$|d_{2\kappa+1}| \leq$$

$$\begin{cases} \frac{(1-\xi)2|\eta|}{M_1} & ; 1 - \frac{L_1^2}{(\kappa+1)M_1|\eta|} < \xi < 1 \\ \frac{(1-\xi)2|\eta|}{M_1} + \left(1+\kappa - \frac{L_1^2}{(1-\xi)M_1|\eta|}\right)\frac{2(1-\xi)^2|\eta|^2}{|\{(1+\kappa)M_1 - 2\nu\kappa(1+\kappa)^2\}\eta(1-\xi) - L_1^2| + L_1^2} & \\ & ; 0 \leq \xi \leq 1 - \frac{L_1^2}{(1+\kappa)M_1|\eta|} \end{cases}$$

and

$$|d_{2\kappa+1} - \delta d^2_{\kappa+1}| \leq \begin{cases} \frac{2|\eta|(1-\xi)}{M_1} & ; |\kappa - 2\delta + 1| < J_7 \\ \frac{2|\eta|^2(1-\xi)^2|\kappa-2\delta+1|}{|\{(1+\kappa)M_1 - 2\nu\kappa(1+\kappa)^2\}(1-\xi)\eta - L_1^2|} & ; |\kappa - 2\delta + 1| \geq J_7, \end{cases}$$

where

$$J_7 = \left| \frac{\{(1+\kappa)M_1 - 2\nu\kappa(1+\kappa)^2\}(1-\xi)\eta - L_1^2}{M_1(1-\xi)\eta} \right|,$$

L_1 and M_1 are as in (30) and (31), respectively.

If we let $\kappa = 1$ in Corollary 8, then we have

Corollary 10. *Let the function s of the form (1) belong to the class $\mathfrak{X}_{\sigma_1}^{\tau}(\eta,\nu,\xi)$ and $\delta \in \mathbb{R}$. Then,*

$$|d_2| \leq \frac{2(1-\xi)|\eta|}{\sqrt{|\{2M_2+4(N_2\tau(\tau-1)+2\nu(1-2\tau))\}(1-\xi)\eta - L_2^2| + L_2^2}},$$

$$|d_3| \leq \begin{cases} \frac{2(1-\xi)|\eta|}{M_2} & ; 1 - \frac{L_2^2}{2M_2|\eta|} < \xi < 1 \\ \frac{2(1-\xi)|\eta|}{M_2} + \left(2 - \frac{L_2^2}{(1-\xi)M_2|\eta|}\right) \frac{2(1-\xi)^2|\eta|^2}{|\{2M_2+4(N\tau(\tau-1)+2\nu(1-2\tau))\}(1-\xi)\eta - L_2^2| + L_2^2} & \\ & ; 0 \leq \xi \leq 1 - \frac{L_2^2}{2M_2|\eta|} \end{cases}$$

and

$$|d_3 - \delta d_2^2| \leq \begin{cases} \frac{2(1-\xi)|\eta|}{3(\nu+1)} & ; |1-\delta| < J_8 \\ \frac{2(1-\xi)^2|\eta|^2|1-\delta|}{|\{2M_2+4(N_2\tau(\tau-1)+2\nu(1-2\tau))\}(1-\xi)\eta - L_2^2|} & ; |1-\delta| > J_8, \end{cases}$$

where

$$J_8 = \left| \frac{\{2M_2 + 4(N\tau(\tau-1) + 2\nu(1-2\tau))\}(1-\xi)\eta - L_2^2}{2M_2(1-\xi)\eta} \right|,$$

L_2, M_2, and N_2 are as in (32), (33), and (34), respectively.

If $\eta = \tau = 1$ in Corollary 10, then we obtain

Corollary 11. *If $s \in \mathfrak{X}_{\sigma_1}^{1}(1,\nu,\varphi)$ is of the form (1) and $\delta \in \mathbb{R}$, then*

$$|d_2| \leq \frac{\sqrt{2}(1-\xi)}{\sqrt{|(3-\nu)(1-\xi)-2|+2}},$$

$$|d_3| \leq \begin{cases} \frac{2(1-\xi)}{3(1+\nu)} & ; \frac{3\nu+1}{3(1+\nu)} < \xi < 1 \\ \frac{2(1-\xi)}{3(1+\nu)} + \left(1 - \frac{2}{3(1-\xi)(1+\nu)}\right) \frac{2(1-\xi)^2}{|(1-\xi)(3-\nu)-2|+2} & ; 0 \leq \xi \leq \frac{3\nu+1}{3(1+\nu)}, \end{cases}$$

and

$$|d_3 - \delta d_2^2| \leq \begin{cases} \frac{2(1-\xi)}{3(1+\nu)} & ; |1-\delta| < \left| \frac{(1-\xi)(3-\nu)-2}{3(1-\xi)(1+\nu)} \right| \\ \frac{2|1-\delta|(1-\xi)^2}{|(1-\xi)(3-\nu)-2|} & ; |1-\delta| \geq \left| \frac{(3-\nu)(1-\xi)-2}{3(1-\xi)(1+\nu)} \right|, \end{cases}$$

Remark 10. *Putting $\nu = 0$ in Corollary 11, we obtain Corollary 3 of Tang et al. [19]. The estimates obtained here for $|d_2|$ and $|d_3|$ are more accurate when compared to those estimates of Theorem 2 in [9].*

5. Conclusions

In this paper, a new class $\mathfrak{P}_{\sigma_\kappa}^{\tau}(\eta,\nu,\varphi)$ is explored and the upper bounds of $|d_{\kappa+1}|$, $|d_{2\kappa+1}|$, and $|d_{2\kappa+1} - \delta d_{\kappa+1}^2|$ $\delta \in \Re$, are estimated for elements in $\mathfrak{P}_{\sigma_\kappa}^{\tau}(\eta,\nu,\varphi)$. Two special cases $\mathfrak{Q}_{\upsilon_\kappa}^{\varrho}(\eta,\nu,\tau) = \mathfrak{P}_{\upsilon_\kappa}^{\tau}(\eta,\nu,\left(\frac{1+\varsigma}{1-\varsigma}\right)^{\varrho}), 0 < \varrho \leq 1$ and $\mathfrak{X}_{\upsilon_\kappa}^{\xi}(\eta,\nu,\tau) = \mathfrak{P}_{\upsilon_\kappa}^{\tau}(\eta,\nu,\frac{1+(1-2\xi)\varsigma}{1-\varsigma})$, $0 \leq \xi < 1$, have been considered. In addition, we have uncovered pertinent links to previous results and given a few observations. This paper could inspire researchers towards further investigations using the (i) integro-differential operator [31], (ii) q-differential operator [32], (iii) q-integral operator [33], and (iv) Hohlov operator [34].

Author Contributions: S.R.S. and L.-I.C.: implementation and original draft; S.R.S.: analysis, methodology, software, and conceptualization; L.-I.C.: validation, resources, and editing. All authors have read and agreed to the published version of the manuscript.

Funding: This research received no external funding.

Data Availability Statement: Not applicable.

Acknowledgments: The authors are appreciative of the reviewers who provided insightful criticism, suggestions, and counsel that helped them to modify and enhance the paper's final version.

Conflicts of Interest: The authors declare no conflict of interest.

References

1. Guney, H.O.; Murugusundaramoorthy, G. New classes of pseudo-type bi-univalent fumctions. *Rev. Real Acad. Cienc. Exactas, Fis. Nat. Ser. A Mat.* **2020**, *114*, 65. [CrossRef]
2. Babalola, K.O. On λ-pseudo-starlke functions. *J. Class. Anal.* **2012**, 3, 137–147.
3. Al-Amiri, H.S.; Reade, M.O. On a linear combination of some expressions in the theory of univalent functions. *Monatsh. Math.* **1975**, *80*, 257–264. [CrossRef]
4. Sukhjit, S.; Sushma, G. On a problem of H. S. Almiri and M. O. Reade. *Demonstr. Math.* **2005**, *38*, 303–311.
5. Duren, P.L. *Univalent Functions*; Springer: New York, NY, USA, 1983.
6. Lewin, M. On a coefficient problem for bi-univalent functions. *Proc. Am. Math. Soc.* **1967**, *18*, 63–68. [CrossRef]
7. Tan, D.L. Coefficient estimates for bi-univalent functions. *Chin. Ann. Math. Ser. A* **1984**, *5*, 559–568.
8. Brannan, D.A.; Taha, T.S. On some classes of bi-univalent functions. *Math. Anal. Appl.* **1985**, *3*, 18–21.
9. Srivastava, H.M.; Mishra, A.K.; Gochhayat, P. Certain subclasses analytic and bi-univalent functions. *Appl. Math. Lett.* **2010**, *23*, 1188–1192. [CrossRef]
10. Srivastava, H.M.; Gaboury, S.; Ghanim, F. Coefficients estimate for some general subclasses of analytic and bi-univalent functions. *Afr. Mat.* **2017**, *28*, 693–706. [CrossRef]
11. Frasin, B.A.; Aouf, M.K. New subclass of bi-univalent functons. *Appl. Math. Lett.* **2011**, *24*, 1569–1573. [CrossRef]
12. Deniz, E. Certain subclasses of bi-univalent functions satisfying subordinate conditions. *J. Class. Anal.* **2013**, *2*, 49–60. [CrossRef]
13. Tang, H.; Deng, G.; Li, S. Coefficient estimates for new subclasses of Ma-Minda bi-univalent functions. *J. Ineq. Appl.* **2013**, *317*, 10. [CrossRef]
14. Frasin, B.A. Coefficient bounds for certain classes of bi-univalent functions. *Hacet. J. Math. Stat.* **2014**, *43*, 383–389. [CrossRef]
15. Srivastava, H.M.; Sivasubramanian, S.; Sivakumar, R. Initial coefficients estimate for some subclasses of m-fold symmetric bi-univalent functions. *Tbilisi Math J.* **2014**, *7*, 1–10. [CrossRef]
16. Srivastava, H.M.; Gaboury, S.; Ghanim, F. Initial coefficients estimate for some subclasses of m-fold symmetric bi-univalent functions. *Acta Math. Sci. Ser. B.* **2016**, *36*, 863–971. [CrossRef]
17. Srivastava, H.M.; Zireh, A.; Hajiparvaneh, S. Coefficients estimate for some subclasses of m-fold symmetric bi-univalent functions. *Filomat* **2018**, *32*, 3143–3153. [CrossRef]
18. Srivastava, H.M.; Wanas, A.K. Initial Maclaurin coefficients bounds for new subclasses of m-fold symmetric bi-univalent functions defined by a linear combination. *Kyungpook Math. J.* **2019**, *59*, 493–503.
19. Tang, H.; Srivastava, H.M.; Sivasubramanian, S.; Gurusamy, P. Fekete-Szegö functional problems of m-fold symmetric bi-univalent functions. *J. Math. Ineq.* **2016**, *10*, 1063–1092. [CrossRef]
20. Wanas, A.K.; Páll-Szabó, A.O. Coefficient bounds for new subclasses of analytic and m-fold symmetric bi-univalent functions. *Stud. Univ. Babes-Bolai Math.* **2021**, *66*, 659–666. [CrossRef]
21. Fekete, M.; Szegö, G. Eine Bemerkung Über Ungerade Schlichte Funktionen. *J. Lond. Math. Soc.* **1933**, *89*, 85–89. [CrossRef]
22. Swamy, S.R.; Frasin, B.A.; Aldawish, I. Fekete-Szegö functional problem for a special family of m-fold symmetric bi-univalent functions. *Mathematics* **2022**, *10*, 1165. [CrossRef]
23. Swamy S.R.; Cotîrlă, L.-I. On τ-pseudo-ν-convex κ-fold symmetric bi-univalent function family. *Symmetry* **2022**, *14*, 1972. [CrossRef]
24. Aldawish, I.; Swamy, S.R.; Frasin, B.A. A special family of m-fold symmetric bi-univalent functions satisfying subordination condition. *Fractal Fract.* **2022**, *6*, 271. [CrossRef]
25. Breaz, D.; Cotîrlă, L.-I. The study of the new classes of m-fold symmetric bi-univalent Functions. *Mathematics* **2022**, *10*, 75. [CrossRef]
26. Oros, G.I.; Cotîrlă, L.-I. Coefficient Estimates and the Fekete–Szegö problem for new classes of m-fold symmetric bi-univalent functions. *Mathematics* **2022**, *10*, 129. [CrossRef]
27. Shehab, N.H.; Juma, A.R.S. Coefficient bounds of m-fold symmetric bi-univalent functions for certain subclasses. *Int. J. Nonlinear Anal. Appl.* **2021**, *12*, 71–82. [CrossRef]
28. Sabir, P.O.; Srivastava, H.M.; Atshan, W.G.; Mohammed, P.O.; Chorfi, N.; Miguel, V.-C.A family of holomorphic and m-fold symmetric bi-univalent functions endowed with coefficient estimate problems. *Mathematics* **2023**, *11*, 3970. [CrossRef]
29. Pommerenke, C. *Univalent Functions;* Vandenhoeck and Ruprecht: Gottingen, Germany, 1975.

30. Peng, Z.-G.; Han, Q.-Q. On the coefficients of several classes of bi-univalent functions. *Acta. Math. Sci. Ser. B Engl. Ed.* **2014**, 34, 228–240. [CrossRef]
31. Páll-Szabó, Á.O.; Oros, G.I. Coefficient related studies for new classes of bi-univalent functions. *Mathematics* **2020**, *8*, 1110. [CrossRef]
32. Srivastava, H.M.; Mostafa, A.O.; Aouf, M.K.; Zayed, H.M. Basic and fractional q-calculus and associated Fekete-Szegö problem for p-valently q-starlike functions and p-valently q-convex functions of complex order. *Miskolc Math. Notes* **2019**, *20*, 489–509. [CrossRef]
33. Khan, B.; Srivastava, H.M.; Tahir, M.; Darus, M.; Ahmad, Q.Z.; Khan, N. Applications of a certain q-integral operator to he subclasses of analytic and bi-uivalent functions. *AIMS Math.* **2020**, *6*, 1024–1039. [CrossRef]
34. Murugusundaramoorthy, G.; Cotîrlă, L.-I. Bi-univalent functions of complex order defined by Hohlov operator associated with legendrae polynomial. *AIMS Math.* **2022**, *7*, 8733–8750. [CrossRef]

axioms

MDPI

Article

Coefficient Bounds for Some Families of Bi-Univalent Functions with Missing Coefficients †

Ebrahim Analouei Adegani [1,‡], Mostafa Jafari [2,‡], Teodor Bulboacă [3,*,‡] and Paweł Zaprawa [4,‡]

1 Faculty of Mathematical Sciences, Shahrood University of Technology, Shahrood P.O. Box 316-36155, Iran; analoey.ebrahim@shahroodut.ac.ir
2 Department of Mathematics, Faculty of Computer Engineering, Islamic Azad University, Najafabad Branch, Najafabad 66414, Iran; drmostafajafari@pco.iaun.ac.ir
3 Faculty of Mathematics and Computer Science, Babeş-Bolyai University, 400084 Cluj-Napoca, Romania
4 Department of Mathematics, Faculty of Mechanical Engineering, Lublin University of Technology, 20-618 Lublin, Poland; p.zaprawa@pollub.pl
* Correspondence: bulboaca@math.ubbcluj.ro; Tel.: +40-729087153
† Dedicated to the memory of Professor Bogdan Tadeusz Bojarski (1931–2018).
‡ These authors contributed equally to this work.

Abstract: A branch of complex analysis with a rich history is geometric function theory, which first appeared in the early 20th century. The function theory deals with a variety of analytical tools to study the geometric features of complex-valued functions. The main purpose of this paper is to estimate more accurate bounds for the coefficient $|a_n|$ of the functions that belong to a class of bi-univalent functions with missing coefficients that are defined by using the subordination. The significance of our present results consists of improvements to some previous results concerning different recent subclasses of bi-univalent functions, and the aim of this paper is to improve the results of previous outcomes. In addition, important examples of some classes of such functions are provided, which can help to understand the issues related to these functions.

Keywords: analytic and univalent function; bi-univalent function; coefficient estimates; subordination

MSC: 30C45; 30C50; 30C80

Citation: Analouei Adegani, E.; Jafari, M.; Bulboacă, T.; Zaprawa, P. Coefficient Bounds for Some Families of Bi-Univalent Functions with Missing Coefficients. *Axioms* **2023**, *12*, 1071. https://doi.org/10.3390/axioms12121071

Academic Editor: Georgia Irina Oros

Received: 18 October 2023
Revised: 14 November 2023
Accepted: 21 November 2023
Published: 23 November 2023

1. Introduction

The study of univalent functions is traditional, and it is categorized under geometric function theory (GFT) since numerous noteworthy characteristics of univalent functions can be found in the basic geometrical properties. In 1851 [1], the Reimann mapping theorem led to the development of GFT. Nevertheless, it helps to discover new results in a wide range of topics, including contemporary mathematical physics and more established branches of physics, like fluid dynamics, nonlinear integrable systems theory, and the theory of partial differential equations. One of the most fascinating areas of geometric function theory is the theory of univalent functions, which is a well-known classical topic of complex analytic functions. Around the 20th century, many geometric aspects of analytical functions were introduced and studied, like starlikeness, convexity, close-to-convexity, typically real functions, etc.

Let $\mathbb{D} := \{z \in \mathbb{C} : |z| < 1\}$ denote the open unit disk in the complex plane $\mathbb{C}$, and let $\mathcal{A}$ be the class of functions f analytic in $\mathbb{D}$ that has the following representation:

$$f(z) = z + \sum_{k=2}^{\infty} a_k z^k, \ z \in \mathbb{D}. \quad (1)$$

Denote $\mathcal{S}$ as the subclass of all functions of $\mathcal{A}$ that are univalent in $\mathbb{D}$. The study of the characteristics of normalized univalent functions that fall under the class and are defined in the open unit disk $\mathbb{D}$ is the main focus of the geometry theory of functions.

Furthermore, let $\mathcal{B}$ represent the category of all analytic functions ϖ in $\mathbb{D}$ that fulfil the criteria $\varpi(0) = 0$ and $|\varpi(z)| < 1$ for all $z \in \mathbb{D}$. If the image of the open unit disk by a univalent function has some geometrical characteristics, it may be of interest to find an analytic characterization of such functions. The best example of a domain with desirable features is a convex domain and a starlike one with regard to a point. Many subclasses of those analytic univalent functions that map onto these above-mentioned domains were introduced and thoroughly studied, such as the well-known classes $\mathcal{K}$ and $\mathcal{S}^*$ of convex and starlike functions, respectively.

In geometric function theory, determining the bounds for the coefficients $|a_n|$ is a crucial task since it reveals details about the geometric characteristics of these functions. For instance, the growth and distortion bounds, as well as the covering theorems, are given by the bound for the second coefficient $|a_2|$ of functions $f \in \mathcal{S}$.

Every function $f \in \mathcal{S}$ has an inverse f^{-1}, which is defined by

$$f^{-1}(f(z)) = z \ (z \in \mathbb{D}) \quad \text{and} \quad f\left(f^{-1}(w)\right) = w \quad \left(|w| < r_0(f),\ r_0(f) \geq \frac{1}{4}\right),$$

with the expansion of the power series

$$f^{-1}(w) = w + \sum_{k=2}^{\infty} b_k w^k = w - a_2 w^2 + \left(2a_2^2 - a_3\right)w^3 - \left(5a_2^3 - 5a_2a_3 + a_4\right)w^4 + \ldots.$$

A function $f \in \mathcal{A}$ is said to be *bi-univalent* in $\mathbb{D}$ if f is univalent in $\mathbb{D}$ and f^{-1} has a univalent analytic extension in $\mathbb{D}$. For brevity, we will denote this analytic extension by $g := f^{-1}$. The studies of the class of bi-univalent functions in $\mathbb{D}$ was initiated by Levin [2], who proved that

$$|a_2| < 1.51.$$

Following these studies, Branan and Clunie [3] improved Levin's result by the subsequent variant

$$|a_2| \leq \sqrt{2}.$$

Furthermore, Netanyahu [4] showed that for the bi-univalent functions,

$$\max |a_2| = \frac{3}{4}.$$

The fact that the following functions are bi-univalent must be mentioned:

$$f_1(z) = \frac{z}{1-z}, \quad f_2(z) = \log\left(\frac{1}{1-z}\right).$$

And, these correspond to the inverse functions of

$$f_1^{-1}(w) = \frac{w}{1+w}, \quad f_2^{-1}(w) = \frac{e^w - 1}{e^w}.$$

Let Σ denote the family of bi-univalent functions in $\mathbb{D}$. The study of Srivastava et al. [5] provides a brief historical review of the roles in the family Σ along with a few examples. Regarding [5], the class Σ of bi-univalent functions has numerous subfamilies, each of which has a different set of analytic features, and many authors have attempted to explore these families, for example, [6–13]. In a few of these articles, the authors studied some subclasses of bi-univalent functions connected with the Faber and Laguerre polynomials, determined estimates for coefficients and Hankel determinants for different subclasses of bi-univalent functions associated with Hohlov operator and Horadam polynomials, and gave some estimates for the Fekete–Szegő functional. Other related issues can be found in [14–16], while, in general, it is still difficult to determine the extremal functions for bi-univalent functions.

The Faber polynomials expansion method was first described by Faber [17], and he used this method to study the coefficient boundaries of $|a_m|$ for $m \geq 3$. In the mathematical sciences, notably in the field of geometric function theory, these Faber polynomials are crucial. In this regard, in order to obtain the optimal bounds of $|a_n|$ for the coefficients of bi-univalent functions, some researchers used the Faber polynomial expansions [18–23].

Let f and F be two analytic functions in $\mathbb{D}$; the function f is considered *subordinate* to F, denoted by $f(\zeta) \prec F(\zeta)$, if there exists a function $\omega : \mathbb{D} \to \mathbb{D}$ analytic in $\mathbb{D}$ with $\omega(0) = 0$, such that $f = F \circ \omega$. The above function ω is considered a *subordination function* (see [24], p. 125). If $f(\zeta) \prec F(\zeta)$, then $f(0) = F(0)$ and $f(\mathbb{D}) \subset F(\mathbb{D})$, and with the additional assumption that F is univalent in $\mathbb{D}$, the subordination $f(\zeta) \prec F(\zeta)$ is equivalent to $f(0) = F(0)$ and $f(\mathbb{D}) \subset F(\mathbb{D})$ (see [25], p. 15).

The conceptual underpinnings of the current research problem and important research-related issues are shown in this section. A review of comparable studies sheds some light on the advantages and shortcomings of the earlier investigations.

Let h be an analytic function with positive real part in $\mathbb{D}$ and the power series expansion

$$h(z) = 1 + B_1 z + B_2 z^2 + B_3 z^3 + \ldots,\ z \in \mathbb{D}, \quad \text{with} \quad B_1 \neq 0.$$

With the help of the aforementioned type of function, we define a subclass of $\mathcal{A}$ that is a generalization of Definition 1 from [20], assuming the weaker assumption $\lambda \geq 0$ as follows:

Definition 1. *A function $f \in \Sigma$ is said to be in the class $\mathcal{N}_\Sigma(\lambda, \delta, h)$ for $\lambda \geq 0$ and $\delta \geq 0$ if*

$$\mathrm{I}_{\lambda,\delta}[f](z) := (1-\lambda)\frac{f(z)}{z} + \lambda f'(z) + \delta z f''(z) \prec h(z), \quad \textit{and}$$
$$\mathrm{I}_{\lambda,\delta}[g](w) := (1-\lambda)\frac{g(w)}{w} + \lambda g'(w) + \delta w g''(w) \prec h(w), \quad g = f^{-1}.$$

Here, we present an example that helps prove that this class is nonempty and contains functions other than the identity one.

Remark 1. *(i) We emphasize that the class $\mathcal{N}_\Sigma(\lambda, \delta, h)$ is not empty for appropriate choices of the parameters. Thus, letting*

$$h_*(z) = 1 + 0.35z + 0.1z^2,$$

like we may see in Figure 1a made using the MAPLE™ computer software, we have

$$\operatorname{Re} h_*(z) > 0, z \in \mathbb{D},\ B_1 = 0.35 = h'_*(0) \neq 0, B_2 = 0.1,$$

and

$$B_n = 0 \quad \text{for} \quad n \geq 3.$$

It is easy to show that

$$\operatorname{Re}\frac{z h'_*(z)}{h_*(z) - 1} = \operatorname{Re}\frac{2z + 3.5}{z + 3.5} > 0.6 > 0,\ z \in \mathbb{D}.$$

Hence, h_* is a starlike (univalent) function in $\mathbb{D}$ with respect to the point $z_0 = 1$.

The function

$$f_*(z) = \frac{z}{1 + 0.2z} \in \mathcal{S}$$

and its inverse

$$g_*(w) = f_*^{-1}(w) = \frac{w}{1 - 0.2w}$$

are analytic in $\mathbb{D}$*; Hence,* $f_* \in \Sigma$.

Also, for $\lambda = 0.2$ *and* $\delta = 0.1$*, a simple computation shows that*

$$\mathrm{I}_{0.2,0.1}[f_*](z) = \frac{1}{0.2z+1} - \frac{0.04z}{(0.2z+1)^2} + 0.1z\left(-\frac{0.4}{(0.2z+1)^2} + \frac{0.08z}{(0.2z+1)^3}\right) \quad and$$
$$\mathrm{I}_{0.2,0.1}[g_*](w) = \frac{1}{-0.2w+1} + \frac{0.04w}{(-0.2w+1)^2} + 0.1w\left(\frac{0.4}{(-0.2w+1)^2} + \frac{0.08w}{(-0.2w+1)^3}\right).$$

Since h_* *is univalent in* $\mathbb{D}$*, using the inclusions*

$$\mathrm{I}_{0.2,0.1}[f_*](\mathbb{D}) \subset h(\mathbb{D}) \quad and \quad \mathrm{I}_{0.2,0.1}[g_*](\mathbb{D}) \subset h(\mathbb{D})$$

that follow from Figure 1b and Figure 1c, respectively, also made using MAPLE™, we conclude that

$$\mathrm{I}_{0.2,0.1}[f_*](z) \prec h_*(z) \quad and \quad \mathrm{I}_{0.2,0.1}[g_*](w) \prec h_*(w).$$

Therefore, $f_* \in \mathcal{N}_\Sigma(0.2, 0.1, h_*)$*. Therefore, there exists values of the parameters* λ*,* δ*, and functions* h*, such that*

$$\mathcal{N}_\Sigma(\lambda, \delta, h) \setminus \{\mathrm{Id}\} \neq \emptyset,$$

where Id *denotes the identity function. To not lengthen the paper unnecessarily, we omit the MAPLE™ codes for the figures we used throughout the article.*

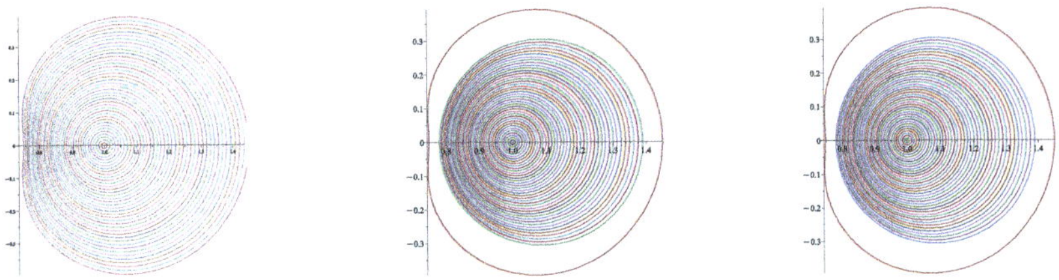

(**a**) The image $h(\mathbb{D})$ (**b**) The inclusion $\mathrm{I}_{0.2,0.1}[f_*](\mathbb{D}) \subset h_*(\mathbb{D})$ (**c**) The inclusion $\mathrm{I}_{0.2,0.1}[g_*](\mathbb{D}) \subset h_*(\mathbb{D})$

Figure 1. Figures for Remark 1.

(ii) If, in the above example, the values of $|\lambda|$ *and* $|\delta|$ *decrease to 0, then the behavior of the functions* $\mathrm{I}_{\lambda,\delta}[f_*]$ *and* $\mathrm{I}_{\lambda,\delta}[g_*]$ *becomes very similar to that of the functions* $\frac{f_*(z)}{z}$ *and* $\frac{g_*(z)}{z}$*. In some examples we made using MAPLE™ software, we saw that the above set inclusions hold. Hence, these new functions belong to the classes of Definition 1. These indicate a consequence of the general fact that*

$$\lim_{(\lambda,\delta)\to(0,0)} \mathrm{I}_{\lambda,\delta}[f_*](z) = \frac{f_*(z)}{z} \quad and \quad \lim_{(\lambda,\delta)\to(0,0)} \mathrm{I}_{\lambda,\delta}[g_*](z) = \frac{f_*(z)}{z},\ z \in \mathbb{D};$$

that is,

$$\mathcal{N}_\Sigma(0,0,h) = \mathcal{N}_\Sigma\left(0,0,\frac{f(z)}{z}\right) \text{ for all } f \in \Sigma.$$

(iii) If, in similar examples, the values of $|\lambda|$ *and* $|\delta|$ *increase, then there are some cases when the subordinations of Definition 1 do or do not hold, as follows (to not lengthen the paper, we omit the corresponding graphical representations):*

(a) $\widetilde{f}(z) = \dfrac{z}{1+0.1z} \in \mathcal{N}_\Sigma(1.1, 0.3, h_*)$;
(b) $f_*(z) = \dfrac{z}{1+0.2z} \notin \mathcal{N}_\Sigma(1.1, 0.3, h_*)$, if $h_*(z) = 1 + 0.35z + 0.1z^2$.

In a similar way, the authors of [26] defined the following family of analytic functions:

$$\mathscr{S}(v,\rho;h) = \left\{ f \in \mathcal{A} : 1 + \frac{1}{\rho}\left(\frac{zf'(z) + vz^2 f''(z)}{(1-v)f(z) + vzf'(z)} - 1\right) \prec h(z),\, 0 \le v \le 1,\, \rho \in \mathbb{C} \setminus \{0\} \right\}$$

and obtained a bound for the general coefficients of the bi-univalent functions of this class by using the Faber polynomials subject to a series of assumptions.

In our paper, we replace the assumptions for the function h from [26] with some weaker ones as stated above (i.e., omitting the conditions that $h(\mathbb{D})$ is symmetric with respect of the real axis and $B_1 > 0$).

Here, we present an example that helps to better understand the above explanation for the function h and proves that this family is nonempty, containing other functions than the identity one.

Remark 2. *In the below example, we consider a case when $h(\mathbb{D})$ is not symmetric with respect of the real axis and $B_1 \neq 0$, as we assumed in Definition 1. We show that for some values of the parameters, the class $\mathscr{S}(v,\rho;h)$ is not empty. Taking*

$$\widehat{h}(z) = 1 + 0.35(1+i)z + 0.1z^2,$$

since $\widehat{h}(\overline{z}) \neq \overline{\widehat{h}(z)}$ for all $z \in \mathbb{D}$, it follows that the domain $\widehat{h}(\mathbb{D})$ is not symmetric with respect of the real axis and

$$B_1 = 0.35(1+i) = \widehat{h}'(0) \neq 0.$$

Like we may see in Figure 2a, we have $\operatorname{Re}\widehat{h}(z) > 0$, $z \in \mathbb{D}$, and Figure 2b, also made with MAPLE™ software, shows that

$$\operatorname{Re} \mathrm{J}(z) := \operatorname{Re} \frac{z\widehat{h}'(z)}{\widehat{h}(z) - 1} = \operatorname{Re} \frac{3.5(1+i) + 2z}{3.5(1+i) + z} > 0.7 > 0,\ z \in \mathbb{D}.$$

Hence, $\widehat{h}$ is a starlike (univalent) function with respect to the point $z_0 = 1$. Denoting

$$\mathrm{L}_{v,\rho}[f](z) := 1 + \frac{1}{\rho}\left(\frac{zf'(z) + vz^2 f''(z)}{(1-v)f(z) + vzf'(z)} - 1\right),$$

with the same notation as in Remark 1, we have (see Figure 2c)

$$\mathrm{L}_{0.5,4}[f_*](\mathbb{D}) \subset \widehat{h}(\mathbb{D}).$$

Using the fact that $\widetilde{h}$ is univalent in $\mathbb{D}$, the above inclusion shows that

$$\mathrm{L}_{4,0.5}[f_*](z) \prec \widehat{h}(z),\ i.e.\ f_* \in \mathscr{S}\left(0.5, 4; \widetilde{h}\right).$$

In conclusion, for the above choices of functions and the corresponding parameters, we have

$$\mathscr{S}(v,\rho;h) \setminus \{\mathrm{Id}\} \neq \varnothing.$$

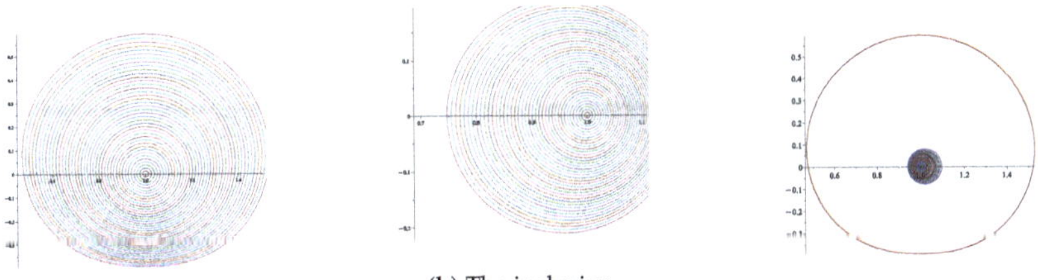

(**a**) The image $\widehat{h}(\mathbb{D})$

(**b**) The inclusion $\mathrm{J}(\mathbb{D}) \subset \{w \in \mathbb{C} : \operatorname{Re} w > 0\}$

(**c**) The inclusion $\mathrm{L}_{0.5,4}[f_*](\mathbb{D}) \subset \widehat{h}(\mathbb{D})$

Figure 2. Figures for Remark 2.

In [18], the researchers proved the following result for analytic functions of the family $\mathscr{S}(\nu, \rho; h)$:

Theorem ([18] Theorem 4). *Let* $f(z) = z + \sum_{k=n}^{\infty} a_k z^k$ $(n \geq 2)$ *and its inverse map* $g = f^{-1}$ *be in* $\mathscr{S}(\nu, \rho; h)$ *with* $|B_2| \leq B_1$. *Then,*

(i)

$$|a_n| \leq \min\left\{ \frac{|\rho| B_1}{(n-1)[1+\nu(n-1)]}; \sqrt{\frac{2|\rho| B_1}{n(2n-2)[1+\nu(2n-2)]}} \right\},$$

(ii)

$$\left| n a_n^2 - a_{2n-1} \right| \leq \frac{|\rho| B_1}{(2n-2)[1+\nu(2n-2)]}.$$

The goal of the current study is to estimate upper bounds for the coefficients $|a_n|$ for those functions that belong to the set of bi-univalent functions with missing coefficients and defined by the $\mathcal{N}_\Sigma(\lambda, \delta, h)$. This paper aims to improve some of the results from [18,27]. Additionally, connections to some previously obtained results are made.

The below lemmas are required to prove our results.

Lemma 1 ([28,29]). *Let* $f \in \mathcal{S}$ *be given by* (1). *Then, the coefficients of its inverse map* $g = f^{-1}$ *are given in terms of the Faber polynomials of* f *with*

$$g(w) = f^{-1}(w) = w + \sum_{n=2}^{\infty} \frac{1}{n} K_{n-1}^{-n}(a_2, a_3, \ldots, a_n) w^n,$$

where

$$\begin{aligned} K_{n-1}^{-n} = & \frac{(-n)!}{(-2n+1)!(n-1)!} a_2^{n-1} + \frac{(-n)!}{(2(-n+1))!(n-3)!} a_2^{n-3} a_3 \\ & + \frac{(-n)!}{(-2n+3)!(n-4)!} a_2^{n-4} a_4 + \frac{(-n)!}{(2(-n+2))!(n-5)!} a_2^{n-5} \left[a_5 + (-n+2) a_3^2 \right] \\ & + \frac{(-n)!}{(-2n+5)!(n-6)!} a_2^{n-6} [a_6 + (-2n+5) a_3 a_4] + \sum_{j \geq 7} a_2^{n-j} V_j, \end{aligned}$$

such that V_j $(7 \leq j \leq n)$ *is a homogeneous polynomial in the variables* $a_2, a_3, \ldots, a_n$ *and the expressions such as (for example)* $(-m)!$ *are to be interpreted symbolically by*

$$(-m)! \equiv \Gamma(1-m) := (-m)(-m-1)(-m-2)\ldots, \quad m \in \mathbb{N}_0 := \mathbb{N} \cup \{0\}, \ \mathbb{N} := \{1, 2, \ldots\}.$$

We see that the initial three terms of K_{n-1}^{-n} are given by

$$K_1^{-2} = -2a_2, \quad K_2^{-3} = 3\left(2a_2^2 - a_3\right), \quad \text{and} \quad K_3^{-4} = -4\left(5a_2^3 - 5a_2a_3 + a_4\right).$$

Typically, for every real number p, the expansion of K_n^p is given below (see [28] for details; see also [29], p. 349):

$$K_n^p = pa_{n+1} + \frac{p(p-1)}{2}D_n^2 + \frac{p!}{(p-3)!3!}D_n^3 + \ldots + \frac{p!}{(p-n)!n!}D_n^n.$$

Lemma 2 ([30]). *Let $f(z) = z + \sum\limits_{k=n}^{\infty} a_k z^k$, $n \geq 2$ be a univalent function in $\mathbb{D}$ and*

$$f^{-1}(w) = w + \sum_{k=n}^{\infty} b_k w^k \quad \left(|w| < r_0(f),\ r_0(f) \geq \frac{1}{4}\right).$$

Then,

$$b_{2n-1} = na_n^2 - a_{2n-1}, \quad \text{and} \quad b_k = -a_k \quad \text{for} \quad n \leq k \leq 2n-2.$$

Lemma 3 ([31] Exercise 9, p. 172). *Assume that $\omega(z) = \sum\limits_{j=1}^{\infty} p_j z^j \in \mathcal{B}$. Then,*

$$|p_n| \leq 1,\ n \geq 2.$$

This lemma represents a special case of the result in [31] [Exercise 9, p. 172] obtained from this exercise for $p_0 = 0$.

2. Main Results

First, we prove the next lemma.

Lemma 4. *Let $u(z) = u_1 z + u_2 z^2 + u_3 z^3 + \cdots \in \mathcal{B}$ and s be a complex number. Then, for all $n \in \mathbb{N}$, the following inequality holds:*

$$\left|u_{2n} - su_n^2\right| \leq 1 + (|s| - 1)\left|u_n^2\right| \leq \max\{1; |s|\}.$$

Moreover, the functions $u(z) = z$ and $u(z) = z^2$ prove that the above inequality is sharp for $|s| \geq 1$ and for $|s| < 1$, respectively.

Proof. For $u(z) = u_1 z + u_2 z^2 + u_3 z^3 + \cdots \in \mathcal{B}$ and a fixed $n \in \mathbb{N}$, let

$$\varepsilon_k := e^{2k\pi i/n}, \quad k \in \{1, 2, \ldots, n\}$$

be the nth order complex roots of the unit. If we define the function $v : \mathbb{D} \to \mathbb{C}$ by

$$v(z) := \frac{1}{n}\sum_{k=1}^{n} u(\varepsilon_k z),\ z \in \mathbb{D}, \tag{2}$$

using the well-known relation

$$\sum_{k=1}^{n} \varepsilon_k^m = \begin{cases} 0, & \text{if} \quad m \in \mathbb{N} \quad \text{is not a multiple of } n, \\ n, & \text{if} \quad m \in \mathbb{N} \quad \text{is a multiple of } n, \end{cases}$$

it follows that

$$v(z) = u_n z^n + u_{2n} z^{2n} + \ldots,\ z \in \mathbb{D}. \tag{3}$$

Since u is an analytic function in $\mathbb{D}$, from Definition (2), it follows that v ia also analytic in $\mathbb{D}$ and $v(0) = 0$. Moreover, since $u \in \mathcal{B}$, we have

$$|v(z)| \leq \frac{1}{n}\sum_{k=1}^{n}\left|u\left(e^{-2ik\pi/n}z\right)\right| < \frac{n}{n} = 1,\ z \in \mathbb{D}.$$

Therefore, $v \in \mathcal{B}$.

Because the function $\chi(z) := z^n$ is a surjective endomorphism of the unit disk $\mathbb{D}$, setting $\zeta := z^n$ in (3) and using the fact that $v \in \mathcal{B}$, we deduce that the function $\psi : \mathbb{D} \to \mathbb{C}$ by

$$\psi(\zeta) := u_n\zeta + u_{2n}\zeta^2 + u_{3n}\zeta^3 + \ldots,\ \zeta \in \mathbb{D}$$

belongs to the class $\mathcal{B}$. Now, using [32] (page 10, inequality (7)) for the function $\psi \in \mathcal{B}$, we obtain the desired outcome with the aforementioned power series expansion. □

We now prove the following main theorem using the aforementioned lemmas and a new method.

Theorem 1. *Let the function* $f(z) = z + \sum\limits_{k=n_0}^{\infty} a_k z^k \in \mathcal{N}_\Sigma(\lambda, \delta, h)$, $n_0 \geq 2$. *Then,*

$$|a_{n_0}| \leq \min\left\{\frac{|B_1|}{1+(n_0-1)(\lambda+n_0\delta)};\ \sqrt{\frac{2|B_1|\max\left\{1;\left|\frac{B_2}{B_1}\right|\right\}}{n_0(1+(2n_0-2)[\lambda+(2n_0-1)\delta])}}\right\}, \tag{4}$$

and

$$\left|n_0 a_{n_0}^2 - a_{2n_0-1}\right| \leq \frac{|B_1|\max\left\{1;\left|\frac{B_2}{B_1}\right|\right\}}{1+(2n_0-2)[\lambda+(2n_0-1)\delta]}. \tag{5}$$

Proof. If $f(z) = z + \sum\limits_{k=n_0}^{\infty} a_k z^k \in \mathcal{N}_\Sigma(\lambda, \delta, h)$, then there are two functions as defined by the quasi-subordination $u, v \in \mathcal{B}$ of the form

$$u(z) = \sum_{k=1}^{\infty} u_k z^n \quad \text{and} \quad v(z) = \sum_{k=1}^{\infty} v_k z^k,$$

satisfying

$$(1-\lambda)\frac{f(z)}{z} + \lambda f'(z) + \delta z f''(z) = 1 + \sum_{k=n_0}^{\infty}[1+(k-1)(\lambda+k\delta)]a_k z^{k-1} = h(u(z)) \tag{6}$$

and

$$(1-\lambda)\frac{g(w)}{w} + \lambda g'(w) + \delta w g''(w) = 1 + \sum_{k=2}^{\infty}[1+(k-1)(\lambda+k\delta)]b_k w^{k-1} = h(v(w)), \tag{7}$$

respectively, where, according to Lemma 1,

$$b_k = \frac{1}{k}K_{n-1}^{-k}(a_2, a_3, \ldots, a_k),\ k \geq 2. \tag{8}$$

We have

$$h(u(z)) = 1 + B_1\left(u_1 z + u_2 z^2 + \ldots\right) + B_2\left(u_1 z + u_2 z^2 + \ldots\right)^2 + \ldots, \tag{9}$$

and, according to (6) and (9), the corresponding coefficients of the power expansions are equal. Hence, we equate these coefficients step by step.

First, from (6), we have $a_k = 0$ for $2 \leq k \leq n_0 - 1$. Thus, the term containing "z" in (9) is equal to zero, that is, $B_1 u_1 = 0$. Using the fact that $B_1 \neq 0$, it follows $u_1 = 0$. Therefore, (9) becomes

$$h(u(z)) = 1 + B_1\left(u_2 z^2 + \dots\right) + B_2\left(u_2 z^2 + \dots\right)^2 + \dots. \tag{10}$$

Secondly, since, in (6), the term containing "z^2" is zero, it follows that, for the corresponding term of (10), we have $B_1 u_2 = 0$. Since $B_1 \neq 0$, it follows that $u_2 = 0$. Hence, (10) becomes

$$h(u(z)) = 1 + B_1\left(u_3 z^3 + \dots\right) + B_2\left(u_3 z^3 + \dots\right)^2 + \dots.$$

We repeat the same method $n_0 - 2$ times and take into account that from the "$n_0 - 3$" step we obtain

$$h(u(z)) = 1 + B_1\left(u_{n_0-2} z^{n_0-2} + \dots\right) + B_2\left(u_{n_0-2} z^{n_0-2} + \dots\right)^2 + \dots. \tag{11}$$

Since the coefficient of term containing "z^{n_0-2}" in (6) is zero, we obtain that the relevant coefficient in (11) is $B_1 u_{n_0-2} = 0$. Thus, the assumption $B_1 \neq 0$ implies $u_{n_0-2} = 0$. Hence, (11) becomes

$$h(u(z)) = 1 + B_1\left(u_{n_0-1} z^{n_0-1} + \dots\right) + B_2\left(u_{n_0-1} z^{n_0-1} + \dots\right)^2 + \dots. \tag{12}$$

Now, by comparing the terms in "z^{n_0-1}" in (6) and (12), we obtain that

$$B_1 u_{n_0-1} = [1 + (n_0 - 1)(\lambda + n_0\delta)]a_{n_0},$$

that is,

$$a_{n_0} = \frac{B_1 u_{n_0-1}}{1 + (n_0 - 1)(\lambda + n_0\delta)}. \tag{13}$$

On the other hand, since $a_k = 0$ for $2 \leq k \leq n_0 - 1$, from (8), we obtain $b_k = 0$ for $2 \leq k \leq n_0 - 1$, and from (8), we have

$$b_{n_0} = \frac{1}{n_0} K_{n_0-1}^{-n_0}(0, 0, \dots, 0, a_{n_0}) = -a_{n_0}.$$

Furthermore, similar to the method described above, from the relation (7), we obtain that the term containing "w^{n_0-1}" is given by

$$B_1 v_{n_0-1} = -[1 + (n_0 - 1)(\lambda + n_0\delta)]a_{n_0},$$

that is,

$$a_{n_0} = -\frac{B_1 v_{n_0-1}}{1 + (n_0 - 1)(\lambda + n_0\delta)}. \tag{14}$$

From (13) and (14), using Lemma 3 and considering the previous reasons, we obtain

$$|a_{n_0}| = |b_{n_0}| \leq \frac{|B_1|}{1 + (n_0 - 1)(\lambda + n_0\delta)}. \tag{15}$$

Also, equating the terms that contain "z^{2n_0-2}" from (6) for $k = 2n_0 - 1$ and those of (12), we obtain

$$\Big(1 + (2n_0 - 2)[\lambda + (2n_0 - 1)\delta]\Big)a_{2n_0-1} = B_1 u_{2n_0-2} + B_2 u_{n_0-1}^2 = B_1\left(u_{2n_0-2} + \frac{B_2}{B_1} u_{n_0-1}^2\right).$$

Thus, based on the previous equality and according to the Lemma 4, it follows that

$$\Big(1+(2n_0-2)[\lambda+(2n_0-1)\delta]\Big)|a_{2n_0-1}|\le|B_1|\max\left\{1;\left|\frac{B_2}{B_1}\right|\right\}.$$

Hence,

$$|a_{2n_0-1}|\le\frac{|B_1|\max\left\{1;\left|\frac{B_2}{B_1}\right|\right\}}{1+(2n_0-2)[\lambda+(2n_0-1)\delta]}. \tag{16}$$

From Definition 1, because $f\in\mathcal{N}_\Sigma(\lambda,\delta,h)$ implies $g\in\mathcal{N}_\Sigma(\lambda,\delta,h)$ and using the above method of proof, we have

$$(1-\lambda)\frac{g(w)}{w}+\lambda g'(w)+\delta w g''(w)=1+\sum_{k=n_0}^{\infty}[1+(k-1)(\lambda+k\delta)]b_k w^{k-1}=h(v(w)).$$

Hence, we obtain

$$|b_{2n_0-1}|\le\frac{|B_1|\max\left\{1;\left|\frac{B_2}{B_1}\right|\right\}}{1+(2n_0-2)[\lambda+(2n_0-1)\delta]}. \tag{17}$$

Furthermore, in view of Lemma 2, using the relations (16) and (17), we deduce that

$$|a_{n_0}|\le\sqrt{\frac{|a_{2n_0-1}|+|b_{2n_0-1}|}{n_0}}\le\sqrt{\frac{2|B_1|\max\left\{1;\left|\frac{B_2}{B_1}\right|\right\}}{n_0\big(1+(2n_0-2)[\lambda+(2n_0-1)\delta]\big)}}, \tag{18}$$

and from (15) and (18), we obtain the inequality (4).

In addition, using (17) and Lemma 2, it follows that

$$|n_0a_{n_0}^2-a_{2n_0-1}|=|b_{2n_0-1}|\le\frac{|B_1|\max\left\{1;\left|\frac{B_2}{B_1}\right|\right\}}{1+(2n_0-2)[\lambda+(2n_0-1)\delta]},$$

which completes our proof. □

Next, this study shows why this theorem improves and generalizes some previous ones by a suitable choice of parameters.

Remark 3. *By choosing λ, δ, and h properly, we obtain from Theorem 1 the bounds that are better, in some ranges of the parameters, than the estimates obtained before.*

1. If

$$h(z)=\frac{1+(1-2\alpha)z}{1-z},\ 0\le\alpha<1,$$

then the bounds are better than those in [20, Theorem 2];

2. If

$$h(z)=\frac{1+(1-2\alpha)z}{1-z},\ 0\le\alpha<1,$$

and $\delta=0$ or $\lambda=1$, then the bounds are better than those in [20] [Corollary 3] and [20] [Corollary 4], respectively;

3. If $\delta=0$, then the bounds are better than those in [33] [Theorems 3.1] in the case of subordination.

In the following part, we emphasize the significance of our present results that improve some previous results concerning different recent subclasses of bi-univalent functions.

Remark 4. *In the proof of Theorem 4 of [18], assume for convenience that* $\rho = 1$, $\vartheta = 0$ *with* $f(z) = z + \sum_{k=n}^{\infty} a_k z^k \in \mathscr{S}(0,1;h)$. *By the definition of the subordination, there exist two functions* $u, v \in \mathcal{B}$ *with*

$$u(z) = \sum_{k=1}^{\infty} u_k z^n \quad \text{and} \quad v(z) = \sum_{k=1}^{\infty} v_k z^k,$$

satisfying

$$\frac{zf'(z)}{f(z)} = h(u(z)) \quad and \quad \frac{wg'(w)}{g(w)} = h(v(w)),$$

respectively.

Since

$$\left.\frac{zf'(z)}{f(z)}\right|_{z=0} = 1,$$

it follows that

$$\frac{zf'(z)}{f(z)} = 1 + \beta_1 z + \ldots + \beta_n z^n + \ldots, \; z \in \mathbb{D}, \tag{19}$$

that is,

$$z + na_n z^n + \ldots = (z + a_n z^n + \ldots)\left(1 + \beta_1 z + \beta_2 z^2 + \ldots\right), \; z \in \mathbb{D}.$$

Equating the corresponding coefficients of the above relation, we obtain

$$\beta_1 = \beta_2 = \cdots = \beta_{n-2} = 0,$$
$$\beta_{n-1} = (n-1)a_n,$$

and from (19), *it follows that*

$$\frac{zf'(z)}{f(z)} = 1 + (n-1)a_n z^{n-1} + \ldots, \; z \in \mathbb{D}.$$

Let us consider again, for convenience, that $n = 3$. *Thus,*

$$f(z) = z + a_3 z^3 + a_4 z^4 + \ldots,$$

then

$$\frac{zf'(z)}{f(z)} = 1 + \beta_2 z^2 + \beta_3 z^3 + \ldots,$$

where

$$\beta_2 = 2a_3, \; \beta_3 = 3a_4, \; \beta_4 = 4a_5 - 2a_3^2.$$

Consequently, if f *has the above form, then it is impossible that* $\beta_2 = 2a_3$ *and* $\beta_4 = 4a_5$ *at the same time. We have* $\beta_4 = 4a_5$ *while* $n_0 = 5$, *but in this case,* $\beta_2 = 0$. *Therefore, the relation (2.11) of [18] and the Theorem 4 of [18] are not correct. Similarly, for the same reason, Theorem 2.6 of [27] is not correct.*

Example 1. *As an example of Theorem 1, if we consider the analytic function in* $\mathbb{D}$ *defined by*

$$f(z) := \frac{1}{\ell}\log\left(\frac{1}{1-\ell z}\right) = z + \frac{\ell z^2}{2} + \frac{\ell^2 z^3}{3} + \ldots, \; z \in \mathbb{D}, \quad with \quad 0 < |\ell| \le 1,$$

then $f \in \mathcal{A}$ *and its inverse is* $f^{-1}(w) = \dfrac{e^{\ell w} - 1}{\ell e^{\ell w}}$, *which have an analytic extension in* $\mathbb{D}$ *denoted as* $g(z) = \dfrac{e^{\ell z} - 1}{\ell e^{\ell z}}$.

Letting

$$h(z) := 1 + 0.35z + 0.1z^2 + 0.1z^3, \; z \in \mathbb{D}, \tag{20}$$

like we may see in Figure 3a made with MAPLE™ computer software, we have

$$\operatorname{Re} h(z) > 0,\ z \in \mathbb{D},\ B_1 = 0.35 = h'(0) \neq 0, B_2 = 0.1, B_3 = 0.1,$$

and

$$B_n = 0 \quad \text{for} \quad n \geq 4.$$

Also, we see that

$$\operatorname{Re} \frac{zh'(z)}{h(z) - 1} = \operatorname{Re} \frac{3z^2 + 2z + 3.5}{z^2 + z + 3.5} > 0.1 > 0,\ z \in \mathbb{D}.$$

Hence, h is a starlike (univalent) function in $\mathbb{D}$ with respect to the point $z_0 = 1$. For some "very small" values of the parameter $|\ell|$ (i.e., close to zero), we have $f \in \mathcal{N}_\Sigma(1.1, 0.15, h)$ with h given by (20) *since the ranges $f(\mathbb{D})$ and $g(\mathbb{D})$ with small neighborhoods of the point $w_0 = 1$ are included in $h(\mathbb{D})$. According to Theorem 1, the inequalities* (4) *and* (5) *reduce to*

$$|\ell| \leq 0.5843487098\ldots \quad \textit{and} \quad |\ell| \leq 0.7156780854\ldots,$$

respectively. Hence,

$$0 < |\ell| \leq 0.5843487098\ldots. \tag{21}$$

(i) Unfortunately, the upper bound of (21) *represents a necessary but not sufficient condition for $f \in \mathcal{N}_\Sigma(1.1, 0.15, h)$ with h given by* (20)*. Let us consider $\lambda = 1.1$ and $\delta = 0.15$. Thus, for $\ell = 0.5843487098$ from Figure 3b,c, we see that*

$$\mathrm{I}_{1.1,0.15}[f](\mathbb{D}) \not\subset h(\mathbb{D}) \quad \textit{and} \quad \mathrm{I}_{1.1,0.15}[g](\mathbb{D}) \not\subset h(\mathbb{D}),$$

but the reverse inclusions are true. Hence, for $\ell = 0.5843487098$, we have $f \notin \mathcal{N}_\Sigma(1.1, 0.15, h)$.

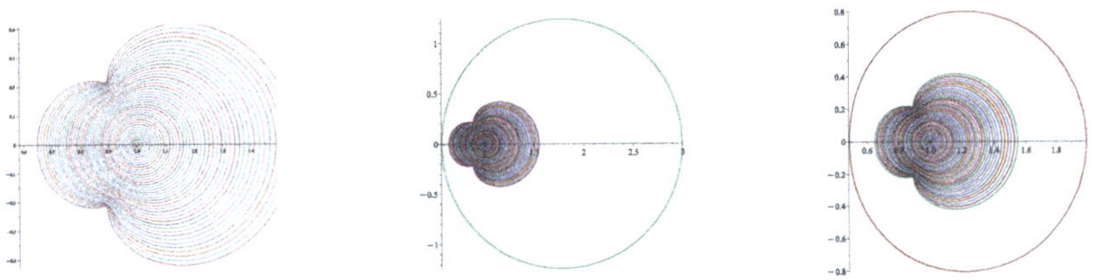

(**a**) The image $h(\mathbb{D})$

(**b**) The inclusion $h(\mathbb{D}) \subset \mathrm{I}_{1.1,0.15}[f](\mathbb{D})$

(**c**) The inclusion $h(\mathbb{D}) \subset \mathrm{I}_{1.1,0.15}[g](\mathbb{D})$

Figure 3. Figures for Example 1(i).

(ii) As we see in Figure 4a,b, for $\lambda = 1.1$, $\delta = 0.15$, and, for example, $\ell = 0.201$, we have the inclusions

$$\mathrm{I}_{1.1,0.15}[f](\mathbb{D}) \subset h(\mathbb{D}) \quad \textit{and} \quad \mathrm{I}_{1.1,0.15}[g](\mathbb{D}) \subset h(\mathbb{D}),$$

and from the fact that h is univalent in $\mathbb{D}$, it follows that both of the subordinations of Definition 1 hold, i.e., $f \in \mathcal{N}_\Sigma(1.1, 0.15, h)$.

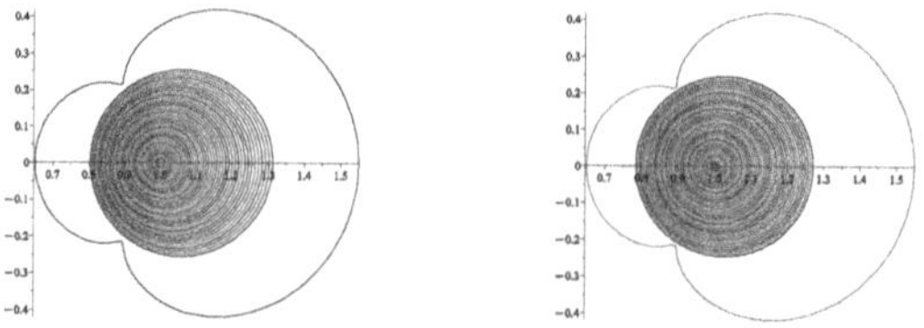

(**a**) The inclusion $I_{1.1,0.15}[f](\mathbb{D}) \subset h(\mathbb{D})$ (**b**) The inclusion $I_{1.1,0.15}[g](\mathbb{D}) \subset h(\mathbb{D})$

Figure 4. Figures for Example 1(ii).

3. Conclusions

The present studies have been extensively made in order to make conclusions that support the justification for the current research, taking into account the aims, methodology, conclusions, and results of the investigations. The coefficient boundaries of analytic functions can be found with the use of the Faber polynomial expansion approach, which has been proven to be effective.

We have defined a new subclass of bi-univalent functions in this article, along with several useful examples. In the concluding part, we underline that by utilizing subordination, we were able to determine the bounds for the coefficient $|a_n|$ for the class of bi-univalent functions with missing coefficients, emphasizing the novelty of the methods used for the proofs and comments.

Moreover, by applying Lemma 4, the inequalities of Theorem 1 for these function classes represent an improvement of a few results for some ranges of the parameters.

We expect that this method can be applied to the classes of harmonic and meromorphic functions in some future works.

Author Contributions: Conceptualization, E.A.A., M.J., T.B. and P.Z.; methodology, E.A.A., M.J., T.B. and P.Z.; software, E.A.A., M.J., T.B. and P.Z.; validation, E.A.A., M.J., T.B. and P.Z.; formal analysis, E.A.A., M.J., T.B. and P.Z.; investigation, E.A.A., M.J., T.B. and P.Z.; resources, E.A.A., M.J., T.B. and P.Z.; writing—original draft preparation, E.A.A., M.J., T.B. and P.Z.; writing—review and editing, E.A.A., M.J., T.B. and P.Z.; visualization, E.A.A., M.J., T.B. and P.Z.; supervision, E.A.A., M.J., T.B. and P.Z.; project administration, E.A.A., M.J., T.B. and P.Z. All authors have read and agreed to the published version of the manuscript.

Funding: This research received no external funding.

Data Availability Statement: Data are contained within the article.

Acknowledgments: The authors are grateful to the reviewers of this article, who gave valuable remarks, comments, and advice in order to improve the quality of the paper. Also, the first author would like to convey his sincere gratitude and particular thanks to Sylwia Położyńska-Figiel and Zbigniew Figiel, as well as their gracious family, for their extraordinary generosity, assistance, and ongoing direction during his family's stay in the Pasikurowice, Wroclaw, Poland, area. He wants to express his gratitude for having friends who are always there for him and who are so kind and understanding.

Conflicts of Interest: The authors declare no conflict of interest.

References

1. Riemann, B. *Grundlagen fürr eine Allgemeine Theorie der Funktionen einer Verändlichen Complexen Grösse, Inaugraldissertation, Göttingen 1851*; Zweiter Unveränderter Abdruck: Göttinger, Germany, 1867.
2. Lewin, M. On a coefficient problem for bi-univalent functions. *Proc. Am. Math. Soc.* **1967**, *18*, 63–68. [CrossRef]
3. Brannan, D.A.; Clunie, J. Aspects of contemporary complex analysis. In Proceedings of the NATO Advanced Study Institute, University of Durham, Durham, UK, 29 August–10 September 1979; Academic Press: New York, NY, USA, 1979.
4. Netanyahu, E. The minimal distance of the image boundary from the origin and the second coefficient of a univalent function in $|z| < 1$. *Arch. Ration. Mech. Anal.* **1967**, *32*, 100–112.

5. Srivastava, H.M.; Mishra, A.K.; Gochhayat, P. Certain subclasses of analytic and biunivalent functions. *Appl. Math. Lett.* **2010**, *23*, 1188–1192. [CrossRef]
6. Güney, H.Ö.; Murugusundaramoorthy, G. New classes of pseudo-type bi-univalent functions. *Rev. Real Acad. Cienc. Exactas Fis. Nat. Ser. Mat.* **2020**, *114*, 65. [CrossRef]
7. Hameed Mohammed, N. Coefficient bounds for a new class of bi-univalent functions associated with subordination. *Math. Anal. Convex Optim.* **2021**, *2*, 73–82.
8. Kareem Wanas, A.; Alb Lupaş, A. Applications of Laguerre polynomials on a new family of bi-prestarlike functions. *Symmetry* **2022**, *14*, 645. [CrossRef]
9. Murugusundaramoorthy, G.; Bulboacă, T. Estimate for initial MacLaurin coefficients of certain subclasses of bi-univalent functions of complex order associated with the Hohlov operator. *Ann. Univ. Paedagog. Crac. Stud. Math.* **2018**, *17*, 27–36. [CrossRef]
10. Srivastava, H.M.; Altınkaya, Ş.; Yalçin, S. Certain subclasses of bi-univalent functions associated with the Horadam polynomials. *Iran. J. Sci. Technol. Trans. A Sci.* **2019**, *43*, 1873–1879. [CrossRef]
11. Srivastava, H.M.; Gaboury, S.; Ghanim, F. Coefficient estimates for a general subclass of analytic and bi-univalent functions of the Ma-Minda type. *Rev. R. Acad. Cienc. Exactas Fís. Nat. Ser. A Mat.* **2018**, *112*, 1157–1168. [CrossRef]
12. Srivastava, H.M.; Khan, S.; Ahmad, Q.Z.; Khan, N.; Hussain, S. The Faber polynomial expansion method and its application to the general coe cient problem for some subclasses of bi-univalent functions associated with a certain q-integral operator. *Stud. Univ. Babes-Bolyai Math.* **2018**, *63*, 419–436. [CrossRef]
13. Zaprawa, P. On the Fekete-Szegő problem for classes of bi-univalent functions. *Bull. Belg. Math. Soc. Simon Stevin* **2014**, *21*, 169–178. [CrossRef]
14. Analouei Adegani, E.; Alimohammadi, D.; Bulboacă, T.; Cho, N.E.; Bidkham, M. On the logarithmic coefficients for some classes defined by subordination. *AIMS Math.* **2023**, *8*, 21732–21745. [CrossRef]
15. Hameed Mohammed, N.; Adegani, E.A.; Bulboacă, T.; Cho, N.E. A family of holomorphic functions defined by differential inequality. *Math. Inequal. Appl.* **2022**, *25*, 27–39. [CrossRef]
16. Jafari, M.; Bulboacă, T.; Zireh, A.; Adegani, E.A. Simple criteria for univalence and coefficient bounds for a certain subclass of analytic functions. *Commun. Fac. Sci. Univ. Ank. Ser. A1 Math. Stat.* **2020**, *69*, 394–412. [CrossRef]
17. Faber, G. Uber polynomische Entwickelungen. *Math. Ann.* **1903**, *57*, 1569–1573. [CrossRef]
18. Analouei Adegani, E.; Cho, N.E.; Alimohammadi, D.; Motamednezhad, A. Coefficient bounds for certain two subclasses of bi-univalent functions. *AIMS Math.* **2021**, *6*, 9126–9137. [CrossRef]
19. Analouei Adegani, E.; Motamednezhad, A.; Bulut, S. Coefficient estimates for a subclass of meromorphic bi-univalent functions defined by subordination. *Stud. Univ. Babeş-Bolyai Math.* **2020**, *65*, 57–66. [CrossRef]
20. Bulut, S. Faber polynomial coefficient estimates for a subclass of analytic bi-univalent functions. *Filomat* **2016**, *30*, 1567–1575. [CrossRef]
21. Hamidi, S.G.; Jahangiri, J.M. Faber polynomial coefficients of bi-subordinate functions. *C. R. Math. Acad. Sci. Paris* **2016**, *354*, 365–370. [CrossRef]
22. Srivastava, H.M.; Sümer Eker, S.; Ali, R.M. Coeffcient bounds for a certain class of analytic and bi-univalent functions. *Filomat* **2015**, *29*, 1839–1845. [CrossRef]
23. Srivastava, H.M.; Sümer Eker, S.; Hamidi, S.G.; Jahangiri, J.M. Faber polynomial coefficient estimates for bi-univalent functions defined by the Tremblay fractional derivative operator. *Bull. Iran. Math. Soc.* **2018**, *44*, 149–157. [CrossRef]
24. Antonino, J.A.; Miller, S.S. An extension of Briot-Bouquet differential subordinations with an application to Alexander integral transforms. *Complex Var. Elliptic Equ.* **2016**, *61*, 124–136. [CrossRef]
25. Miller S.S.; Mocanu, P.T. *Differential Subordination. Theory and Applications*; Series on Monographs and Textbooks in Pure and Applied Mathematics; Marcel Dekker Inc.: New York, NY, USA; Basel, Switzerland, 2000; Volume 225.
26. Deniz, E.; Jahangiri, J.M.; Hamidi, S.G.; Kina, S. Faber polynomial coefficients for generalized bi-subordinate functions of complex order. *J. Math. Inequal.* **2018**, *12*, 645–653. [CrossRef]
27. Alimohammadi, D.; Cho, N.E.; Analouei Adegani, E. Coefficient bounds for subclasses of analytic and bi-univalent functions. *Filomat* **2020**, *34*, 4709–4721. [CrossRef]
28. Airault, H.; Bouali, A. Differential calculus on the Faber polynomials. *Bull. Sci. Math.* **2006**, *130*, 179–222. [CrossRef]
29. Airault, H.; Ren, J. An algebra of differential operators and generating functions on the set of univalent functions. *Bull. Sci. Math.* **2002**, *126*, 343–367. [CrossRef]
30. Alrefal, O.; Ali, M. General coefficient estimates for bi-univalent functions: A new approach. *Turk. J. Math.* **2020**, *44*, 240–251. [CrossRef]
31. Nehari, Z. *Conformal Mapping*; McGraw-Hill: New York, NY, USA, 1952.
32. Keogh, F.R.; Merkes, E.P. A Coefficient inequality for certain classes of analytic functions. *Proc. Am. Math. Soc.* **1969**, *20*, 8–12. [CrossRef]
33. Zireh, A.; Analouei Adegani, E.; Bidkham, M. Faber polynomial coefficient estimates for subclass of bi-univalent functions defined by quasi-subordinate. *Math. Slovaca* **2018**, *68*, 369–378. [CrossRef]

axioms

Article

Results of Third-Order Strong Differential Subordinations

Madan Mohan Soren [1], Abbas Kareem Wanas [2] and Luminiţa-Ioana Cotîrlă [3,*]

[1] Department of Mathematics, Berhampur University (Bhanja Bihar), Brahmapur 760007, India; mms.math@buodisha.edu.in
[2] Department of Mathematics, College of Science, University of Al-Qadisiyah, Al Diwaniyah 58001, Iraq; abbas.kareem.w@qu.edu.iq
[3] Department of Mathematics, Technical University of Cluj-Napoca, 400114 Cluj-Napoca, Romania
* Correspondence: luminita.cotirla@math.utcluj.ro

Abstract: In this paper, we present and investigate the notion of third-order strong differential subordinations, unveiling several intriguing properties within the context of specific classes of admissible functions. Furthermore, we extend certain definitions, presenting novel and fascinating results. We also derive several interesting properties of the results of third-order strong differential subordinations for analytic functions associated with the Srivastava–Attiya operator.

Keywords: admissible function; analytic function; strong differential subordination; dominants; multivalent function

MSC: 30C45

Citation: Soren, M.M.; Wanas, A.K.; Cotîrlă, L.-I. Results of Third-Order Strong Differential Subordinations. *Axioms* **2024**, *13*, 42. https://doi.org/10.3390/axioms13010042

Academic Editors: Hans J. Haubold and Clemente Cesarano

Received: 18 October 2023
Revised: 29 December 2023
Accepted: 2 January 2024
Published: 10 January 2024

1. Introduction and Definitions

Differential subordination is a fundamental technique in geometric function theory of complex analysis used by many authors in investigations to obtain interesting new results. The notion of strong differential subordination was first used by Antonino and Romaguera [1] (see [2]) to study Briot–Bouquet's strong differential subordination. They introduced this concept as an extension of the classical notion of differential subordination, due to Miller and Mocanu [3] (see [4]). The concept was beautifully developed for the theory of strong differential subordination in 2009 [5], where the authors extended the concepts familiar to the established theory of differential subordination [4]. There have been many interesting and fruitful usages of a wide variety of first-order and second-order strong differential subordinations for analytic functions. Recently, many researchers have worked in this direction and proved several significant results that can be seen in [6–8]. Various strong differential subordinations were established by linking different types of operators to the study. The Sălăgean differential operator was employed for introducing a new class of analytic functions in [9], and the Ruscheweyh differential operator in [10] for defining a new class of univalent functions and for studying strong differential subordinations. The Sălăgean and Ruscheweyh operators were used together in the study presented in [11], and a multiplier transformation provided new strong differential subordinations in [12–14]. The Komatu integral operator was applied for obtaining new strong differential subordinations results [15,16], and other differential operators proved effective for studying strong differential subordinations [17]. The fractional derivative operator was used in [18], and the fractional integral of the extended Dziok–Srivastava operator was used in [19]. Multivalent meromorphic functions and the Liu–Srivastava operator were involved in obtaining strong differential subordinations in [20]. The topic remains of interest at present, as proven by recently published works (see, for details, [21–23]). Thus, in this current paper, we introduced and investigated the concept of third-order strong differential subordinations, unveiling several intriguing properties within the context of specific classes of admissible functions.

Let $\mathbb{N}$ denote the set of positive integers. Suppose $\mathcal{H} = \mathcal{H}(\mathcal{U})$ denotes the class of analytic functions in the *open* unit disc

$$\mathcal{U} = \{z : z \in \mathbb{C} \text{ and } |z| < 1\},$$

where $\mathbb{C}$ is the set of complex numbers. For $n \in \mathbb{N}, b \in \mathbb{C}$, define the class of functions

$$\mathcal{H}[b,n] := \left\{f : f \in \mathcal{H}; f(z) = b + b_n z^n + b_{n+1}z^{n+1} + \dots\right\}.$$

Given $f, F \in \mathcal{H}$. The function f is *subordinate* to F, denoted by $f(z) \prec F(z)$, if there exists an analytic function ω in $\mathcal{U}$ satisfying the conditions $\omega(0) = 0$ and $|\omega(z)| < 1$ so that $f(z) = F(\omega(z)) \quad (z \in \mathcal{U})$. Further, if the function F is univalent in $\mathcal{U}$, then (see [3,4]) $f \prec F \Longleftrightarrow f(0) = F(0)$ and $f(\mathcal{U}) \subset F(\mathcal{U})$. Suppose that $\mathcal{F}(z,\zeta)$ is analytic in $\mathcal{U} \times \overline{\mathcal{U}}$ and $f(z)$ is analytic and univalent in $\mathcal{U}$. We say that $\mathcal{F}(z,\zeta)$ is strongly subordinate to $f(z)$. Simply write

$$\mathcal{F}(z,\zeta) \prec\prec f(z),$$

if $\mathcal{F}(z,\zeta) \quad (\zeta \in \overline{\mathcal{U}})$ as a function of z is subordinate to $f(z)$. Here, also observe that (cf. [2,5,24])

$$\mathcal{F}(z,\zeta) \prec\prec f(z) \Longleftrightarrow \mathcal{F}(0,\zeta) = f(0) \text{ and } \mathcal{F}(\mathcal{U} \times \overline{\mathcal{U}}) \subset f(\mathcal{U})$$

For $p \in \mathbb{N}$, we denote $\mathcal{A}(p)$ as the class of analytic functions defined by

$$f(z) = z^p + \sum_{k=1}^{\infty} a_{k+p} z^{k+p}. \tag{1}$$

Mishra and Gochhayat [25] introduced and studied the *fractional differintegral operator*. For $f \in \mathcal{A}(p)$, the transform

$$\mathcal{I}^{\lambda}_{p,\delta} : \mathcal{A}(p) \longrightarrow \mathcal{A}(p)$$

is expressed by

$$\mathcal{I}^{\lambda}_{p,\delta} f(z) := z^p + \sum_{k=1}^{\infty} \left(\frac{p+\delta}{p+k+\delta}\right)^{\lambda} a_{p+k} z^{p+k} \tag{2}$$

$$(p+\delta \in \mathbb{C} \setminus \mathbb{Z}_0^-;\ \mathbb{Z}_0^- := \{0,-1,-2,\dots\};\ \lambda \in \mathbb{C}).$$

The operator $\mathcal{I}^{\lambda}_{p,\delta}$ can be seen as a generalization of the Srivastava–Attiya operator [26] (see [27–29]); it is also popularly known as the Srivastava–Attiya operator for multivalent functions (see, for example, [30–32]). Furthermore, $\mathcal{I}^{\lambda}_{p,\delta}$ generalizes several previously studied familiar differential operators as well as integral operators by Bernardi [33], Cho and Kim [34], Jung et al. [35], Libera [36], Sălăgean [37] and Uralegaddi and Somanatha [38]. For a detailed discussion [25], also see [39–41].

They [25] derived from (2) the relation

$$z\left(\mathcal{I}^{\lambda}_{p,\delta} f(z)\right)' = (p+\delta)\mathcal{I}^{\lambda-1}_{p,\delta} f(z) - \delta \mathcal{I}^{\lambda}_{p,\delta} f(z). \tag{3}$$

In terms of the third order, there have been only three articles [1,42–44] for the corresponding third-order implication connected to a special case. Let Π and Δ be sets in $\mathbb{C}$. Suppose p is an analytic function in $\mathcal{U}$ and

$$\Xi(r_1, s_1, t_1, u_1; z, \zeta) : \mathbb{C}^4 \times \mathcal{U} \times \overline{\mathcal{U}} \longrightarrow \mathbb{C}.$$

We have determined properties of the function p that imply the following inequality holds:

$$\left\{\Xi(\mathrm{p}(z), z\mathrm{p}'(z), z^2\mathrm{p}''(z), z^3\mathrm{p}'''(z); z, \zeta)\right\} \subset \Pi \quad \Longrightarrow \mathrm{p}(\mathcal{U}) \subset \Delta. \tag{4}$$

A natural question arises as to what conditions on Ξ, Π and Δ are needed so that the implication (4) holds.
In this present article, we consider conditions on Π, Δ and Ξ so that the inequality (4) holds. We see that there are three different cases to consider in analyzing this inequality's truth:
Problem 1. Given Π and Δ, we find Ξ so that (4) holds, and Ξ is an admissible function.
Problem 2. Given Ξ and Π, we find the 'smallest' Δ that satisfies (4).
Problem 3. Given Ξ and Δ, we find the Π that satisfies (4). Furthermore, we find the 'largest' such Π.

The relation (4) can be rephrased in strong subordination terms, when either Π or Δ is a simply connected domain. If Δ is a simply connected domain with $\Delta \neq \mathbb{C}$, and $p(z)$ is analytic in $\mathcal{U}$, then a conformal mapping $q(z)$ of $\mathcal{U}$ onto Δ can be performed so that $q(0) = p(0)$. In such case, (4) can be written as follows:

$$\left\{\Xi(p(z), zp'(z), z^2p''(z), z^3p'''(z); z, \zeta)\right\} \subset \Pi \quad \Longrightarrow p \prec q. \tag{5}$$

Similarly, if Π is a simply connected domain, then there is a conformal mapping h of $\mathcal{U}$ onto Π so that $h(0) = \Xi(p(0), 0, 0, 0; 0, 0)$. If

$$\Xi(p(z), zp'(z), z^2p''(z), z^3p'''(z); z, \zeta)$$

is analytic in $\mathcal{U}$, then (5) can be reduced to

$$\left\{\Xi(p(z), zp'(z), z^2p''(z), z^3p'''(z); z, \zeta)\right\} \prec\prec h(z) \quad \Longrightarrow p \prec q. \tag{6}$$

There are three key ingredients in a differential implication of the form of (5): the Ξ, the set Π and the dominating function q. If two of these entities were given, one would hope to find conditions on the third so that (6) would be satisfied. In this present article, we start with a given set Π and a given q, and determine a set of admissible operators Ξ so that inequality (4) holds. This leads to some of the definitions that will be used in our main results.

Definition 1. *Suppose $\Xi : \mathbb{C}^4 \times \mathcal{U} \times \overline{\mathcal{U}} \longrightarrow \mathbb{C}$ and h is univalent in $\mathcal{U}$. If $p \in \mathcal{H}$ and satisfies the third-order strong differential subordination*

$$\Xi(p(z), zp'(z), z^2p''(z), z^3p'''(z); z, \zeta) \prec\prec h(z), \tag{7}$$

then p is said to be a solution of the strong differential subordination. Moreover, if $p \prec q$ for all p satisfying (7), then the univalent function q is a dominant of the solutions for the strong differential subordination. A dominant $\tilde{q}$ that satisfies $\tilde{q} \prec q$ for all dominants q of (7) is the best dominant of (7).

For $\Pi \subset \mathbb{C}$, with Ξ and p given in Definition 1, relation (7) can be written as follows:

$$\left\{\Xi(p(z), zp'(z), z^2p''(z), z^3p'''(z); z, \zeta)\right\} \subset \Pi. \tag{8}$$

Condition (8) will also be referred to as strong differential subordination, and can be further extended to the definitions of the solution, dominant and best dominant.

Definition 2 ([1]). *Let $\mathcal{Q}$ denote the collection of all injective and analytic functions q on $\overline{\mathcal{U}} \backslash E(q)$, where*

$$E(q) = \left\{\xi : \xi \in \partial\mathcal{U} \text{ and } \lim_{z \to \xi} q(z) = \infty\right\},$$

and $\min |q'(\xi)| = \rho > 0 \quad (\xi \in \partial\mathcal{U} \backslash E(q))$. *Also, $\mathcal{Q}(b)$ is the class of functions q with $q(0) = b$.*

We will use the following lemmas from the third-order differential subordinations to find dominants of strong differential subordinations.

Lemma 1 ([1]). *Let $\mathcal{U}_{r_0} = \{z : |z| < r_0\}$, with $0 < r_0 < 1$. Let $p(z) = b + b_n z^n + b_{n+1} z^{n+1} + \ldots$ be analytic in $\mathcal{U}$ with $n \geq 2$ and $p(z) \not\equiv b$, and let $q \in \mathcal{Q}(b)$. If there exist points $z_0 = r_0 e^{i\theta_0} \in \mathcal{U}$ and $\xi_0 \in \partial\mathcal{U} \backslash E(q)$ such that $p(z_0) = q(\xi_0)$, $p(\overline{\mathcal{U}}_{r_0}) \subset q(\mathcal{U})$,*

$$\Re \frac{\xi_0 q''(\xi_0)}{q'(\xi_0)} \geq 0, and \tag{9}$$

$$\left| \frac{z p'(z)}{q'(\xi)} \right| \leq n \tag{10}$$

where $z \in \overline{\mathcal{U}}_{r_0}$ and $\xi \in \partial\mathcal{U} \backslash E(q)$, then there exists a real constant $k \geq n \geq 2$ such that

$$z_0 p'(z_0) = n \xi_0 q'(\xi_0), \tag{11}$$

$$\Re\left(\frac{z_0 p''(z_0)}{p'(z_0)} + 1 \right) \geq n \left[\Re \frac{\xi_0 q''(\xi_0)}{q'(\xi_0)} + 1 \right], \tag{12}$$

$$\Re\left(\frac{z_0^2 p'''(z_0)}{p'(z_0)} + 1 \right) \geq n^2 \left[\Re \frac{\xi_0^2 q'''(\xi_0)}{q'(\xi_0)} \right] + 1,$$

or

$$\Re\left(\frac{z_0^2 p'''(z_0)}{p'(z_0)} \right) \geq n^2 \left[\Re \frac{\xi_0^2 q'''(\xi_0)}{q'(\xi_0)} \right]. \tag{13}$$

Consider a special case when q is univalent in Lemma 1. If

$$q(w) = M \frac{Mw + b}{M + \bar{b}w}, \tag{14}$$

with $|b| < M$, then $q(\overline{\mathcal{U}}) = \mathcal{U}_M$, $q(0) = b$ and $E(q) = \phi$.

Lemma 2 ([1]). *Let $\mathcal{U}_{r_0} = \{z : |z| < r_0\}$, with $0 < r_0 < 1$. Suppose q given in (14) and $p(z) = b + b_n z^n + b_{n+1} z^{n+1} + \ldots$ is analytic in $\mathcal{U}$ with $n \geq 2$ and $p(z) \not\equiv b$. If there exist points $z_0 = r_0 e^{i\theta_0} \in \mathcal{U}_M$ and $w_0 \in \partial\mathcal{U}$ such that $p(z_0) = q(w_0)$, $p(\mathcal{U}_{r_0}) \subset \mathcal{U}_M$ and*

$$|zp'(z)||[M + \bar{b}e^{i\theta}]|^2 \leq nM[M^2 - |b|^2] \tag{15}$$

when $z \in \overline{\mathcal{U}}_{r_0}$ and $\theta \in [0, 2\pi]$, then

$$z_0 p'(z_0) = n q(w_0) \frac{|q(w_0) - b|^2}{|q(w_0)|^2 - |b|^2},$$

$$\Re\left(\frac{z_0 p''(z_0)}{p'(z_0)} + 1 \right) \geq n \left(\frac{|q(w_0) - b|^2}{|q(w_0)|^2 - |b|^2} \right), \quad and$$

$$\Re\left(\frac{z_0^2 p'''(z_0)}{p'(z_0)} \right) \geq 6n^2 \frac{[|q(w_0) - b|^2]^2}{[|q(w_0)|^2 - |b|^2]^2}.$$

Our main objective in this article is to systematically investigate several potentially useful results that are based upon third-order strong differential subordinations and their applications in geometric function theory of complex analysis. Our results give interesting new properties and, together with other papers that appeared in recent years, could emphasize the perspective of the importance of third-order strong differential subordination theory and the generalized Srivastava–Attiya operator.

The organization of this article is as follows. In Section 2 below, we derive the notion of third-order strong differential subordination, some definitions and the interesting main results. We consider some suitable classes of admissible functions and investigate several third-order strong differential subordination properties of multivalent functions involving the Srivastava–Attiya operator defined by (2) in Section 3. Some corollaries and consequences of our main results are also presented in Sections 2 and 3. Finally, in the last Section 4, some potential directions for related further research are presented.

2. Main Results

Unless indicated otherwise, we assume throughout the sequel that $p \geq 2$, $z \in \mathcal{U}$ and $\zeta \in \overline{\mathcal{U}}$. We establish the third-order strong differential subordinations theorem. In this connection, we state the following definition.

Definition 3. *Suppose $\Pi \in \mathbb{C}$ and $q \in \mathcal{Q}$. The class of admissible functions $\Xi_n[\Pi, q]$ consists of those functions*

$$\Xi : \mathbb{C}^4 \times \mathcal{U} \times \overline{\mathcal{U}} \longrightarrow \mathbb{C}$$

that fulfill the following admissibility condition:

$$\Xi(r_1, s_1, t_1, u_1; z, \zeta) \notin \Pi \tag{16}$$

whenever $r_1 = q(\xi)$, $s_1 = n\xi q'(\xi)$,

$$\Re\left(\frac{t_1}{s_1} + 1\right) \geq n\left[\Re\frac{\xi q''(\xi)}{q'(\xi)} + 1\right]$$

and

$$\Re\left(\frac{u_1}{s_1}\right) \geq n^2\left[\Re\frac{\xi^2 q'''(\xi)}{q'(\xi)}\right],$$

for $\xi \in \partial\mathbb{U}\backslash E(q)$.

Here, $\Xi_1[\Pi, q]$ is denoted as $\Xi[\Pi, q]$. We refer to two special subcases of this definition. If $\Xi : \mathbb{C}^3 \times \mathcal{U} \times \overline{\mathcal{U}} \longrightarrow \mathbb{C}$, then (16) becomes $\Xi(r_1, s_1, t_1; z, \zeta) \notin \Pi$ when $r_1 = q(\xi), s_1 = n\xi q'(\xi)$ and

$$\Re\left(\frac{t_1}{s_1} + 1\right) \geq n\left[\Re\frac{\xi q''(\xi)}{q'(\xi)} + 1\right], \quad \text{for } \xi \in \partial\mathbb{U}\backslash E(q).$$

If $\Xi : \mathbb{C}^2 \times \mathcal{U} \times \overline{\mathcal{U}} \longrightarrow \mathbb{C}$, then (16) becomes $\Xi(q(\xi), n\xi q'(\xi); z, \zeta) \notin \Pi$ when $\xi \in \partial\mathcal{U}\backslash E(q)$. We also deduce from Definition 3 the inclusion relations $\Xi_n[\Pi', q] \subset \Xi_n[\Pi, q]$ if $\Pi' \subset \Pi$.

The following theorem is a key result in the notion of third-order strong differential subordination.

Theorem 1. *Consider $p \in \mathcal{H}[b, n]$ and $q \in \mathcal{Q}(b)$ fulfills*

$$\Re\frac{\xi q''(\xi)}{q'(\xi)} \geq 0 \quad \text{and} \quad \left|\frac{zp'(z)}{q'(\xi)}\right| \leq n, \tag{17}$$

where $\xi \in \partial\mathcal{U}\backslash E(q)$. If Π is a set in $\mathbb{C}$, $\Xi \in \Xi_n[\Pi, q]$ and

$$\Xi(p(z), zp'(z), z^2p''(z), z^3p'''(z); z, \zeta) \subset \Pi, \tag{18}$$

then

$$p(z) \prec q(z).$$

Proof. If we assume that $p \nprec q$, then there exist points $z_0 = r_0 e^{i\theta_0} \in \mathcal{U}$ and $\xi_0 \in \partial\mathcal{U}\backslash E(q)$ such that $p(z_0) = q(\xi_0)$ and $p(\overline{\mathcal{U}}_{r_0}) \subset q(\mathcal{U})$. From (17), we see that (9) and (10) of Lemma 1 are satisfied when $z \in \mathcal{U}$ and $\xi \in \partial\mathcal{U}\backslash E(q)$. The conditions of that lemma are satisfied; we conclude that (11)–(13) also follow. Using these conditions with $r_1 = p(z_0), s_1 = z_0 p'(z_0), t_1 = z_0^2 p''(z_0), u_1 = z_0^3 p'''(z_0)$ and $z = z_0$ in Definition 3 leads to

$$\Xi(p(z_0), z_0 p'(z_0), z_0^2 p''(z_0), z_0^3 p'''(z_0); z, \zeta) \notin \Pi,$$

which contradicts (18); thus, we have

$$p(z) \prec q(z).$$

□

In Theorem 1, inequalities (17) and (18) are the most necessary for solving third-order differential subordination. If third-order terms in (18) are missing, then they are not required to satisfy (17).

The next result is a special case where the behavior of q on $\partial\mathcal{U}$ is not known in Theorem 1.

Corollary 1. *Suppose q is univalent in $\mathcal{U}$, $q(0) = b$ and set $q_\rho(z) \equiv q(\rho z)$ for $\rho \in (0,1)$. Consider that $p \in \mathcal{H}[b, n]$ and q_ρ fulfill*

$$\Re\frac{\xi q_\rho''(\xi)}{q_\rho'(\xi)} \geq 0 \quad \text{and} \quad \left|\frac{zp'(z)}{q_\rho'(\xi)}\right| \leq n,$$

when $\xi \in \partial\mathcal{U}\backslash E(q)$. If Π is a set in $\mathbb{C}$ and $\Xi \in \Xi_n[\Pi, q_\rho]$, then

$$\Xi(p(z), zp'(z), z^2 p''(z), z^3 p'''(z); z, \zeta) \subset \Pi$$

implies

$$p(z) \prec q(z).$$

Proof. Given q_ρ is univalent in $\partial\mathcal{U}$, and hence $E(q_\rho) = \phi$ and $q_\rho \in \mathcal{Q}(b)$. Since the class $\Xi_n[\Pi, q_\rho]$ is an admissible functions and from Theorem 1 we obtain $p \prec q_\rho$. Since $q_\rho \prec q$, here we conclude that $p \prec q$. □

In Definition 3, there are no specific conditions on Π. When $\Pi \neq \mathbb{C}$ is a simply connected domain and there is a conformal mapping h of $\mathcal{U}$ onto Π, we denote the class $\Xi_n[h(\mathcal{U}), q]$ by $\Xi_n[h, q]$. The next two results are directly from Theorem 1 and Corollary 1.

Theorem 2. *Consider $p \in \mathcal{H}[b, n]$ and $q \in \mathcal{Q}(b)$ and that they fulfill*

$$\Re\frac{\xi q''(\xi)}{q'(\xi)} \geq 0 \quad \text{and} \quad \left|\frac{zp'(z)}{q'(\xi)}\right| \leq n,$$

where $\xi \in \partial\mathcal{U}\backslash E(q)$. If $\Xi \in \Xi_n[h, q]$ and $\Xi(p(z), zp'(z), z^2 p''(z), z^3 p'''(z); z, \zeta)$ is analytic in $\mathcal{U}$, then

$$\Xi(p(z), zp'(z), z^2 p''(z), z^3 p'''(z); z, \zeta) \prec\prec h(z)$$

implies

$$p(z) \prec q(z).$$

Corollary 2. *Suppose q is univalent in $\mathcal{U}$, with $q(0) = b$, and set $q_\rho(z) \equiv q(\rho z)$ for $\rho \in (0,1)$. Consider that $p \in \mathcal{H}[b, n]$ and q_ρ fulfill*

$$\Re\frac{\xi q_\rho''(\xi)}{q_\rho'(\xi)} \geq 0 \quad \text{and} \quad \left|\frac{zp'(z)}{q_\rho'(\xi)}\right| \leq n$$

where $\xi \in \partial\mathcal{U}\backslash E(q)$. *If* $\Xi \in \Xi_n[h, q_\rho]$ *and* $\Xi(p(z), zp'(z), z^2p''(z), z^3p'''(z); z, \zeta)$ *is analytic in* $\mathcal{U}$, *then*

$$\Xi(p(z), zp'(z), z^2p''(z), z^3p'''(z); z, \zeta) \prec\prec h(z)$$

implies

$$p(z) \prec q(z).$$

We next specify the connection between the best dominant of a strong differential subordination and the solution of a corresponding differential equation.

Theorem 3. *Consider* $p \in \mathcal{H}[b, n]$, $\Xi : \mathbb{C}^4 \times \mathcal{U} \times \overline{\mathcal{U}} \longrightarrow \mathbb{C}$ *and that*

$$\Xi(p(z), zp'(z), z^2p''(z), z^3p'''(z); z, \zeta)$$

is analytic in $\mathcal{U}$. *Suppose h is univalent in* $\mathcal{U}$ *and the differential equation*

$$\Xi(p(z), zp'(z), z^2p''(z), z^3p'''(z); z, \zeta) = h(z) \tag{19}$$

has a solution $q \in \mathcal{Q}(b)$ *and*

$$\Re\frac{\xi q''(\xi)}{q'(\xi)} \geq 0 \quad \text{and} \quad \left|\frac{zp'(z)}{q'(\xi)}\right| \leq n,$$

where $\xi \in \partial\mathcal{U}\backslash E(q)$. *If* $\Xi \in \Xi_n[h, q]$, *then*

$$\Xi(p(z), zp'(z), z^2p''(z), z^3p'''(z); z, \zeta) \prec\prec h(z) \tag{20}$$

implies that

$$p(z) \prec q(z)$$

and q is the best dominant.

Proof. From Theorem 1, we have that q is a dominant of (20). Again, q fulfills (19) and it is a solution of (20). Thus, q will be dominated by all dominants of (20). Therefore, q is the best dominant. □

We further pursue the family of admissible functions and theorems, when $q(\mathcal{U})$ is a disc. Since q is given by (14), the class denoted by $\Xi_n[\Pi, M, b]$. When $\Pi = \Delta$, the class denoted by $\Xi_n[M, b]$. Since $q(w) = Me^{i\theta}$ with $0 \leq \theta \leq 2\pi$ when $|w| = 1$, from Lemma 2 we derived the following.

Definition 4. *Consider q to be given by (14),* $n \geq 2$, *and* Π *is a set in* $\mathbb{C}$. *For* $\theta \in [0, 2\pi]$, *the class* $\Xi_n[\Pi, M, b]$ *which consists of those functions*

$$\Xi : \mathbb{C}^4 \times \mathcal{U} \times \overline{\mathcal{U}} \longrightarrow \mathbb{C}$$

that fulfill the following admissibility condition

$$\Xi(r_1, s_1, t_1, u_1; z, \zeta) \notin \Pi$$

whenever $r_1 = Me^{i\theta}, s_1 = nM\frac{|M - \bar{b}e^{i\theta}|^2}{M^2 - |b|^2}e^{i\theta}$

$$\Re\frac{t_1}{s_1}+1\geq n\frac{|M-\bar{b}e^{i\theta}|^2}{M^2-|b|^2} \quad and$$
$$\Re\frac{u_1}{s_1}\geq 6n^2\Re\frac{\left[\bar{b}M-|b|^2\right]^2}{\left[M^2-|b|^2\right]^2},$$
$$for\ z\in\mathcal{U},\zeta\in\overline{\mathcal{U}}. \tag{21}$$

When $b=0,\ 0\leq\theta\leq 2\pi$, we see from (21) that $\Xi_n[\Pi,M,0]$ consists of those functions

$$\Xi:\mathbb{C}^4\times\mathcal{U}\times\overline{\mathcal{U}}\longrightarrow\mathbb{C}$$

that fulfill

$$\Xi(Me^{i\theta},nMe^{i\theta},L,N;z,\zeta)\notin\Pi$$

when

$$\Re(Le^{-i\theta})\geq(n^2-n)M \text{ and } \quad \Re(Ne^{-i\theta})\geq 0. \tag{22}$$

The following result is the immediate consequence.

Theorem 4. *Consider that the q given in (14) and $p\in\mathcal{H}[b,n]$ satisfy*

$$|zp'(z)||M+\bar{b}e^{i\theta}|^2\leq Mn\left[M^2-|b|^2\right],$$

where $z\in\mathcal{U}$ and $0\leq\theta\leq 2\pi$. If $\Xi\in\Xi_n[\Pi,M,b]$, then

$$\Xi(p(z),zp'(z),z^2p''(z),z^3p'''(z);z,\zeta)\subset\Pi$$

implies

$$p(z)\prec q(z).$$

Next, we obtain the following corollary when $b=0$ in Theorem 4.

Corollary 3. *Consider that $q(w)=Mw$ and $p\in\mathcal{H}[0,n]$ fulfill*

$$|zp'(z)|\leq Mn$$

when $z\in\mathcal{U}$. If Π is a set in $\mathbb{C}$ and $\Xi\in\Xi_n[\Pi,M,0]$ as characterized by (22), then

$$\Xi(p(z),zp'(z),z^2p''(z),z^3p'''(z);z,\zeta)\subset\Pi$$

implies

$$p(z)\prec Mz.$$

In this particular case, Theorem 4 becomes

Theorem 5. *Consider that the q given in (14) and $p\in\mathcal{H}[b,n]$ satisfy (17). If Π is a set in $\mathbb{C}$ and (i) $\Xi\in\Xi_n[\Pi,M,b]$, then*

$$\Xi(p(z),zp'(z),z^2p''(z),z^3p'''(z);z,\zeta)\subset\Pi\Longrightarrow|p(z)|<M.$$

(ii) If $\Xi\in\Xi_n[M,b]$, then

$$|\Xi(p(z),zp'(z),z^2p''(z),z^3p'''(z);z,\zeta)|<M\Longrightarrow|p(z)|<M.$$

3. Applications with the Operator

By using the operator $\mathcal{I}_{p,\delta}^{\lambda}$, we establish the family of admissible functions to discuss the strong subordination properties.

Definition 5. *Suppose Π is a set in $\mathbb{C}$ and $q \in \mathcal{Q}$. The family of admissible functions $\Theta_I[\Pi, q]$ consists of functions*

$$\Theta : \mathbb{C}^4 \times \mathcal{U} \times \overline{\mathcal{U}} \longrightarrow \mathbb{C}$$

fulfilling the admissibility

$$\Theta(\alpha, \beta, \gamma, \eta; z, \zeta) \notin \Pi$$

when $\alpha = q(\xi), \beta = \frac{k\xi q'(\xi)+\delta q(\xi)}{p+\delta}$,

$$\Re\left(\frac{(p+\delta)^2\gamma - \delta^2\alpha}{(p+\delta)\beta - \delta\alpha} - 2\delta\right) \geq k\left[\Re\frac{\xi q''(\xi)}{q'(\xi)} + 1\right]$$

and

$$\Re\left(\frac{(p+\delta)^2(\eta(p+\delta) - 3\gamma(1+\delta)) + (3+2\delta)\delta^2\alpha}{(p+\delta)\beta - \delta\alpha} + 2 + 3(2+\delta)\delta\right) \geq k^2\left[\Re\frac{\xi^2 q'''(\xi)}{q'(\xi)}\right],$$

for $\xi \in \partial\mathcal{U}\backslash E(q)$ *and* $k \geq p$.

Theorem 6. *Consider* $\mathcal{I}_{p,\delta}^{\lambda} f(z) \in \mathcal{H}[0, p]$ *with* $p \geq 2$, $q \in \mathcal{Q}(0)$ *and that they satisfy*

$$\Re\frac{\xi q''(\xi)}{q'(\xi)} \geq 0 \quad \text{and} \quad \left|\frac{z(\mathcal{I}_{p,\delta}^{\lambda} f(z))'}{q'(\xi)}\right| \leq k, \tag{23}$$

when $\xi \in \partial\mathcal{U}\backslash E(q)$ *and* $k \geq p$. *If* Π *is a set in* $\mathbb{C}$, $\Theta \in \Theta_I[\Pi, q]$ *and* $f(z) \in \mathcal{A}(p)$ *satisfies*

$$\Theta(\mathcal{I}_{p,\delta}^{\lambda} f(z), \mathcal{I}_{p,\delta}^{\lambda-1} f(z), \mathcal{I}_{p,\delta}^{\lambda-2} f(z), \mathcal{I}_{p,\delta}^{\lambda-3} f(z); z, \zeta) \subset \Pi, \tag{24}$$

then

$$\mathcal{I}_{p,\delta}^{\lambda} f(z) \prec q(z).$$

Proof. Let

$$g(z) := \mathcal{I}_{p,\delta}^{\lambda} f(z). \tag{25}$$

Differentiating (25) with respect to z, and using the identity (3), we obtain

$$\mathcal{I}_{p,\delta}^{\lambda-1} f(z) = \frac{zg'(z) + \delta g(z)}{p+\delta}. \tag{26}$$

Again, by differentiating (26), we have

$$\mathcal{I}_{p,\delta}^{\lambda-2} f(z) = \frac{z^2 g''(z) + (1+2\delta)zg'(z) + \delta^2 g(z)}{(p+\delta)^2}. \tag{27}$$

Further computations show that

$$\mathcal{I}_{p,\delta}^{\lambda-3} f(z) = \frac{z^3 g'''(z) + 3(1+\delta)z^2 g''(z) + (1+3\delta+3\delta^2)zg'(z) + \delta^3 g(z)}{(p+\delta)^3}. \tag{28}$$

Set the transformations from $\mathbb{C}^4$ to $\mathbb{C}$ by

$$\alpha = r_1, \quad \beta = \frac{s_1 + \delta r_1}{p+\delta}, \quad \gamma = \frac{t_1 + (1+2\delta)s_1 + \delta^2 r_1}{(p+\delta)^2},$$
$$\eta = \frac{u_1 + 3(1+\delta)t_1 + (1+3\delta+3\delta^2)s_1 + \delta^3 r_1}{(p+\delta)^3}. \tag{29}$$

Let

$$\Xi(r_1, s_1, t_1, u_1; z, \zeta) = \Theta(\alpha, \beta, \gamma, \eta; z, \zeta)$$
$$= \Theta\left(r_1, \frac{s_1 + \delta r_1}{p+\delta}, \frac{t_1 + (1+2\delta)s_1 + \delta^2 r_1}{(p+\delta)^2}, \frac{u_1 + 3(1+\delta)t_1 + (1+3\delta+3\delta^2)s_1 + \delta^3 r_1}{(p+\delta)^3}; z, \zeta\right). \tag{30}$$

Using Equations (25)–(28), and from (30), we obtain

$$\Xi(g(z), zg'(z), z^2g''(z), z^3g'''(z); z, \zeta) = \Theta(\mathcal{I}_{p,\delta}^{\lambda} f(z), \mathcal{I}_{p,\delta}^{\lambda-1} f(z), \mathcal{I}_{p,\delta}^{\lambda-2} f(z), \mathcal{I}_{p,\delta}^{\lambda-3} f(z); z, \zeta).$$

Therefore, the inclusion (24) leads to

$$\Xi(g(z), zg'(z), z^2g''(z), z^3g'''(z); z, \zeta) \in \Pi.$$

Now,

$$\frac{t_1}{s_1} + 1 = \frac{(p+\delta)^2\gamma - \delta^2\alpha}{(p+\delta)\beta - \delta\alpha} - 2\delta$$

and

$$\frac{u_1}{s_1} = \frac{(p+\delta)^2(\eta(p+\delta) - 3\gamma(1+\delta)) + (3+2\delta)\delta^2\alpha}{(p+\delta)\beta - \delta\alpha} + 2 + 3(2+\delta)\delta.$$

Hence, the admissibility condition in Definition 5 for $\Theta \in \Theta_I[\Pi, \mathrm{q}]$ is equivalent to Definition 3. Thus, by use of (23) and applying Theorem 1, we obtain

$$g(z) \prec \mathrm{q}(z)$$

or

$$\mathcal{I}_{p,\delta}^{\lambda} f(z) \prec \mathrm{q}(z).$$

□

The hypothesis of Theorem 6 requires that the behavior of q on the boundary is not known.

Corollary 4. *Consider* q *to be univalent in* $\mathcal{U}$, *with* $\mathrm{q}(0) = 0$, *and set* $\mathrm{q}_\rho(z) \equiv \mathrm{q}(\rho z)$ *for* $\rho \in (0,1)$. *Let* $\mathcal{I}_{p,\delta}^{\lambda} f(z) \in \mathcal{H}[0,p]$ *for* $p \geq 2$ *and let* $\mathcal{I}_{p,\delta}^{\lambda} f(z)$ *and* q_ρ *satisfy* (23). *If* Π *is a set in* $\mathbb{C}$ *and* $\Theta \subset \Theta_I[\Pi, \mathrm{q}_\rho]$ *and* $f(z) \subset \mathcal{A}(p)$ *fulfill*

$$\Theta(\mathcal{I}_{p,\delta}^{\lambda} f(z), \mathcal{I}_{p,\delta}^{\lambda-1} f(z), \mathcal{I}_{p,\delta}^{\lambda-2} f(z), \mathcal{I}_{p,\delta}^{\lambda-3} f(z); z, \zeta) \subset \Pi,$$

then

$$\mathcal{I}_{p,\delta}^{\lambda} f(z) \prec \mathrm{q}(z).$$

Proof. Proof of the corollary is an immediate consequence of using Theorem 6, and we obtain

$$\mathcal{I}_{p,\delta}^{\lambda} f(z) \prec \mathrm{q}_\rho(z).$$

Since $\mathrm{q}_\rho \prec \mathrm{q}$, we conclude that

$$\mathcal{I}_{p,\delta}^{\lambda} f(z) \prec \mathrm{q}(z).$$

□

In Definition 5, there are no special conditions on Π . When $\Pi \neq \mathbb{C}$, then there is some conformal mapping h of $\mathcal{U}$ onto Π. Let it be denoted by $\Theta_I[h, q]$. We then obtain the results that are an immediate consequence of Theorem 6 and Corollary 4.

Theorem 7. *Consider that $\mathcal{I}_{p,\delta}^{\lambda} f(z) \in \mathcal{H}[0, p]$ with $p \geq 2$ and $q \in \mathcal{Q}(0)$ and that they satisfy* (23). *If Π is a set in $\mathbb{C}$, $\Theta \in \Theta_I[\Pi, q]$, $f(z) \in \mathcal{A}(p)$ and*

$$\Theta(\mathcal{I}_{p,\delta}^{\lambda} f(z), \mathcal{I}_{p,\delta}^{\lambda-1} f(z), \mathcal{I}_{p,\delta}^{\lambda-2} f(z), \mathcal{I}_{p,\delta}^{\lambda-3} f(z); z, \zeta)$$

is analytic in $\mathcal{U}$, then

$$\Theta(\mathcal{I}_{p,\delta}^{\lambda} f(z), \mathcal{I}_{p,\delta}^{\lambda-1} f(z), \mathcal{I}_{p,\delta}^{\lambda-2} f(z), \mathcal{I}_{p,\delta}^{\lambda-3} f(z); z, \zeta) \prec\prec h(z)$$

implies

$$\mathcal{I}_{p,\delta}^{\lambda} f(z) \prec q(z).$$

Corollary 5. *Consider q to be univalent in $\mathcal{U}$, with $q(0) = 0$, and set $q_\rho(z) \equiv q(\rho z)$ for $\rho \in (0, 1)$. Let $\mathcal{I}_{p,\delta}^{\lambda} f(z) \in \mathcal{H}[0, p]$ for $p \geq 2$ and let $\mathcal{I}_{p,\delta}^{\lambda} f(z)$ and q_ρ satisfy* (23). *If Π is a set in $\mathbb{C}$, $\Theta \in \Theta_I[\Pi, q_\rho]$,$f(z) \in \mathcal{A}(p)$ and*

$$\Theta(\mathcal{I}_{p,\delta}^{\lambda} f(z), \mathcal{I}_{p,\delta}^{\lambda-1} f(z), \mathcal{I}_{p,\delta}^{\lambda-2} f(z), \mathcal{I}_{p,\delta}^{\lambda-3} f(z); z, \zeta)$$

is analytic in $\mathcal{U}$, then

$$\Theta(\mathcal{I}_{p,\delta}^{\lambda} f(z), \mathcal{I}_{p,\delta}^{\lambda-1} f(z), \mathcal{I}_{p,\delta}^{\lambda-2} f(z), \mathcal{I}_{p,\delta}^{\lambda-3} f(z); z, \zeta) \prec\prec h(z)$$

implies

$$\mathcal{I}_{p,\delta}^{\lambda} f(z) \prec q(z).$$

We next indicate the connection between the best dominant and the solution of a strong differential subordination.

Theorem 8. *Consider that $\mathcal{I}_{p,\delta}^{\lambda} f(z) \in \mathcal{H}[0, p]$ with $p \geq 2$, $\Theta : \mathbb{C}^4 \times \mathcal{U} \times \overline{\mathcal{U}} \longrightarrow \mathbb{C}$ and that*

$$\Theta(\mathcal{I}_{p,\delta}^{\lambda} f(z), \mathcal{I}_{p,\delta}^{\lambda-1} f(z), \mathcal{I}_{p,\delta}^{\lambda-2} f(z), \mathcal{I}_{p,\delta}^{\lambda-3} f(z); z, \zeta)$$

is analytic in $\mathcal{U}$. Suppose h is univalent in $\mathcal{U}$ and $q \in \mathcal{Q}(0)$ is a solution of the following differential equation

$$\Theta(\mathcal{I}_{p,\delta}^{\lambda} f(z), \mathcal{I}_{p,\delta}^{\lambda-1} f(z), \mathcal{I}_{p,\delta}^{\lambda-2} f(z), \mathcal{I}_{p,\delta}^{\lambda-3} f(z); z, \zeta) = h(z) \tag{31}$$

and satisfies (23). *If Π is a set in $\mathbb{C}$, $\Theta \in \Theta_I[h, q]$ and $f(z) \in \mathcal{A}(p)$ fulfills*

$$\Theta(\mathcal{I}_{p,\delta}^{\lambda} f(z), \mathcal{I}_{p,\delta}^{\lambda-1} f(z), \mathcal{I}_{p,\delta}^{\lambda-2} f(z), \mathcal{I}_{p,\delta}^{\lambda-3} f(z); z, \zeta) \prec\prec h(z), \tag{32}$$

then

$$\mathcal{I}_{p,\delta}^{\lambda} f(z) \prec q(z)$$

and q is the best dominant.

Proof. From Theorem 6, we conclude that q is a dominant of (32). Since q satisfies (31), q is a solution of (32). Thus, q is dominated by all dominants of (32). Therefore, q is the best dominant. □

Our next outcomes are for the specialized case of q being a disc, where q is given by (14) and the class $\Theta_I[\Pi, M, b]$. Also, we denote the class $\Theta_I[M, b]$, when $\Pi = \Delta$. And

$q(w) = Me^{i\theta}$ with $0 \leq \theta \leq 2\pi$ when $|w| = 1$. Notably, the case $q(z) = Mz,\ M > 0$ denotes the admissible functions class $\Theta_I[\Pi, M]$.

Definition 6. *If Π is a set in $\mathbb{C}$, $M > 0$ and $p \geq 2$. The admissible functions class $\Theta_I[\Pi, M]$ consists of those functions*

$$\Theta : \mathbb{C}^4 \times \mathcal{U} \times \overline{\mathcal{U}} \longrightarrow \mathbb{C}$$

such that

$$\Theta\left(Me^{i\theta}, \frac{k+\delta}{p+\delta}Me^{i\theta}, \frac{L + ((1+2\delta)k + \delta^2)Me^{i\theta}}{(p+\delta)^2}, \frac{N + 3(1+\delta)L + ((1+3\delta+3\delta^2)k + \delta^3)Me^{i\theta}}{(p+\delta)^2}; z, \zeta\right) \notin \Pi$$

whenever

$$\Re Le^{-i\theta} \geq (k^2 - k)M, \quad \Re Ne^{-i\theta} \geq 0$$
$$\textit{for} 0 \leq \theta \leq 2\pi \textit{ and } k \geq p.$$

Corollary 6. *Consider $q(z) = Mz$ and $\mathcal{I}^{\lambda}_{p,\delta}f(z) \in \mathcal{H}[0, p]$ with $p \geq 2$ to satisfy*

$$|z(\mathcal{I}^{\lambda}_{p,\delta}f(z))'| \leq Mk,$$

when $z \in \mathcal{U}$ and $k \geq p$. If $\Theta \in \Theta_I[\Pi, M]$, $f(z) \in \mathcal{A}(p)$ satisfies

$$\Theta(\mathcal{I}^{\lambda}_{p,\delta}f(z), \mathcal{I}^{\lambda-1}_{p,\delta}f(z), \mathcal{I}^{\lambda-2}_{p,\delta}f(z), \mathcal{I}^{\lambda-3}_{p,\delta}f(z); z, \zeta) \subset \Pi,$$

then

$$\mathcal{I}^{\lambda}_{p,\delta}f(z) \prec q(z).$$

Corollary 7. *Consider $q(z) = Mz$ and $\mathcal{I}^{\lambda}_{p,\delta}f(z) \in \mathcal{H}[0, p]$ with $p \geq 2$. If Π is a set in $\mathbb{C}$ and (i) $\Theta \in \Theta_I[\Pi, M]$, $f(z) \in \mathcal{A}(p)$ satisfies*

$$\Theta(\mathcal{I}^{\lambda}_{p,\delta}f(z), \mathcal{I}^{\lambda-1}_{p,\delta}f(z), \mathcal{I}^{\lambda-2}_{p,\delta}f(z), \mathcal{I}^{\lambda-3}_{p,\delta}f(z); z, \zeta) \subset \Pi \Longrightarrow |p(z)| < M.$$

(ii) If $f(z) \in \mathcal{A}(p)$ and $\Theta \in \Theta_I[M]$, it satisfies

$$|\Theta(\mathcal{I}^{\lambda}_{p,\delta}f(z), \mathcal{I}^{\lambda-1}_{p,\delta}f(z), \mathcal{I}^{\lambda-2}_{p,\delta}f(z), \mathcal{I}^{\lambda-3}_{p,\delta}f(z); z, \zeta)| < M \Longrightarrow |p(z)| < M.$$

4. Conclusions

This paper is intended to propose a new line of investigation for third-order strong differential subordination theories using some specific classes of admissible functions. In each theorem, the dominant and the best dominant, respectively, are established, replacing the functions considered as the dominant and the best dominant from the theorems with remarkable functions and using the properties which produce interesting corollaries. Using the operator, strong subordination results are obtained. The third-order strong differential subordination outcomes such as those here may serve as inspiration for future research on this subject, and in the theory of differential subordinations and superordinations of the third and higher orders as well. Here, we only used and explored the third-order strong differential subordinations.

Author Contributions: All authors contributed equally to the present investigation. All authors have read and approved the final manuscript.

Funding: This research received no external funding.

Data Availability Statement: Data are contained within the article.

Acknowledgments: The authors are thankful to the reviewer(s) for their very careful reading of the article and fruitful comments and suggestions.

Conflicts of Interest: The authors declare no conflict of interest.

References

1. Antonino, J.A.; Miller, S.S. Third-order differential inequalities and subordinations in the complex plane. *Complex Var. Ellip. Equ.* **2011**, *56*, 439–454. [CrossRef]
2. Antonino, J.A. Strong differentail subordination and applications to univalency conditions. *J. Korean Math. Soc.* **2006**, *43*, 311–322. [CrossRef]
3. Miller, S.S.; Mocanu, P.T. Differential subordinations and univalent functions. *Mich. Math. J.* **1981**, *28*, 157–172. [CrossRef]
4. Miller, S.S.; Mocanu, P.T. *Differential Subordination: Theory and Applications, Monographs and Textbooks in Pure and Applied Mathematics*; Marcel Dekker: New York, NY, USA; Basel, Switzerland, 2000; Volume 225.
5. Oros, G.I.; Oros, G. Strong differentail subordination. *Turk. J. Math.* **2009**, *33*, 249–257.
6. Abd, E.H.; Atshan, W.G. Strong subordination for p-valent functions involving a linear operator. *J. Phys. Conf. Ser.* **2021**, *1818*, 012113. [CrossRef]
7. Aghalary, R.; Arjomandinia, P. On a first order strong differential subordination and application to univalent functions. *Commun. Korean Math. Soc.* **2022**, *37*, 445–454.
8. Srivastava, H.M.; Wanas, A.K. Strong differential sandwich results of λ-pseudo-starlike functions with respect to symmetrical points. *Math. Mor.* **2019**, *23*, 45–58. [CrossRef]
9. Sakar, F.M. Estimate for Initial Tschebyscheff Polynomials Coefficients on a Certain Subclass of Bi-univalent Functions Defined by Salagean Differential Operator. *Acta Univ. Apulensis* **2018**, *54*, 45–54.
10. Juma, A.R.S.; Saloomi, M.H. Coefficient Bounds for Certain Subclass of Analytic Functions Defined By Quasi-Subordination. *Iraqi J. Sci.* **2018**, *59*, 1115–1121.
11. Alb Lupaş, A. Certain strong differential subordinations using Sălăgean and Ruscheweyh operators. *Adv. Appl. Math. Anal.* **2011**, *6*, 27–34.
12. Shehab, N.H.; Juma, A.R.S. Third Order Differential Subordination for Analytic Functions Involving Convolution Operator. *Baghdad Sci. J.* **2022**, *19*, 581–592. [CrossRef]
13. Al-Shbeil, I.; Khan, S.; Tchier, F.; Tawfiq, F.M.O.; Shatarah, A.; Cătaş, A. Sharp Estimates Involving a Generalized Symmetric Sălăgean q-Differential Operator for Harmonic Functions via Quantum Calculus. *Symmetry* **2023**, *15*, 2156. [CrossRef]
14. Swamy, S.R. Some strong differential subordinations using a new generalized multiplier transformation. *Acta Univ. Apulensis Math. Inform.* **2013**, *34*, 285–291.
15. Cho, N.E. Strong differential subordination properties for analytic functions involving the Komatu integral operator. *Bound. Value Probl.* **2013**, *2013*, 44. [CrossRef]
16. Jeyaraman, M.P.; Suresh, T.K.; Reddy, E.K. Strong differential subordination and superordination of analytic functions associated with Komatu operator. *Int. J. Nonlinear Anal. Appl.* **2013**, *4*, 26–44.
17. Khan, N.; Khan, K.; Tawfiq, F.M.; Ro, J.S.; Al-shbeil, I. Applications of Fractional Differential Operator to Subclasses of Uniformly q-Starlike Functions. *Fractal Fract.* **2023**, *7*, 715. [CrossRef]
18. Amsheri, S.M.; Zharkova, V. Some strong differential subordinations obtained by fractional derivative operator. *Int. J. Math. Anal.* **2012**, *6*, 2159–2172.
19. Deniz, E.; ; Çağlar, M.; Orhan, H. The Fekete-Szegö problem for a class of analytic functions defined by Dziok-Srivastava operator. *Kodai Math. J.* **2012**, *35*, 439–462. [CrossRef]
20. Cho, N.E.; Kwon, O.S.; Srivastava, H.M. Strong differential subordination and superordination for multivalently meromorphic functions involving the Liu-Srivastava operator. *Integral Transform. Spec. Funct.* **2010**, *21*, 589–601. [CrossRef]
21. Jeyaraman, M.P.; Suresh, T.K. Strong differential subordination and superordination of analytic functions. *J. Math. Anal. Appl.* **2012**, *385*, 854–864. [CrossRef]
22. Soren, M.M. Sandwich results for analytic functions involving with iterations of the Owa-Srivastava operator and its combination. *Asian-Eur. J. Math.* **2014**, *7*, 1450063. [CrossRef]
23. Wanas, A.K.; Majeed, A.H. New strong differential subordination and superordination of meromorphic multivalent quasi-convex functions. *Kragujev. J. Math.* **2020**, *44*, 27–39. [CrossRef]
24. Antonino, J.A.; Romaguera, S. Strong differentail subordination to Briot-Bouquet differentail equations. *J. Differ. Equ.* **1994**, *114*, 101–105. [CrossRef]
25. Mishra, A.K.; Gochhayat, P. Invariance of some subclass of multivalent functions under a differintegral operator. *Complex Var. Ellip. Equ.* **2010**, *55*, 677–689. [CrossRef]
26. Srivastava, H.M.; Attiya, A.A. An integral operator associated with the Hurwitz-Lerch Zeta function and differential subordination. *Integral Transform. Spec. Funct.* **2007**, *18*, 207–216. [CrossRef]
27. Liu, J.-L. Subordinations for certain multivalent analytic functions associated with the generalized Srivastava-Attiya operator. *Integral Transform. Spec. Funct.* **2008**, *19*, 893–901. [CrossRef]

28. Mishra, A.K.; Soren, M.M. A generalization of the Srivastava—Attiya transform and associated classes. *Integral Transform. Spec. Funct.* **2011**, *23*, 831–846. [CrossRef]
29. Wang, Z.-G.; Li, Q.-G.; Jiang, Y.-P. Certain subclasses of multivalent analytic functions involving the generalized Srivastava-Attiya operator. *Integral Transform. Spec. Funct.* **2010**, *21*, 221–234. [CrossRef]
30. Liu, J.-L. Sufficient conditions for strongly starlike functions involving the generalized Srivastava-Attiya operator. *Integral Transform. Spec. Funct.* **2011**, *22*, 79–90. [CrossRef]
31. Murugusundaramoorthy, G. Subordination results for spiral-like functions associated with the Srivastava-Attiya operator. *Integral Transform. Spec. Funct.* **2011**, *23*, 97–103. [CrossRef]
32. Noor, K.I.; Bukhari, S.Z.H. Some subclasses of analytic and spiral-like functions of complex order involving the Srivastava-Attiya integral operator. *Integral Transform. Spec. Funct.* **2010**, *21*, 907–916. [CrossRef]
33. Bernardi, S.D. Convex and starlike univalent functions. *Trans. Am. Math. Soc.* **1969**, *135*, 429–446. [CrossRef]
34. Cho, N.E.; Kim, J.A. Inclusion properties of certain subclasses of analytic functions defined by a multiplier transformation. *Comput. Math. Appl.* **2006**, *52*, 323–330. [CrossRef]
35. Jung, I.B.; Kim, Y.C.; Srivastava, H.M. The Hardy space of analytic functions associated with certain one-parameter families of integral operators. *J. Math. Anal. Appl.* **1993**, *176*, 138–147. [CrossRef]
36. Libera, R.J. Some classes of regular univalent functions. *Proc. Am. Math. Soc.* **1965**, *16*, 755–758. [CrossRef]
37. Sălăgean, G.S. Subclasses of univalent functions. *Lect. Notes Math.* **1983**, *1013*, 362–372.
38. Uralegaddi, B.A.; Somanatha, C. Certain integral operators for starlike functions. *J. Math. Res. Expos.* **1995**, *15*, 14–16.
39. Wang, Z.-G.; Liu, Z.-H.; Sun, Y. Some properties of the generalized Srivastava-Attiya operator. *Integral Transform. Spec. Funct.* **2010**, *23*, 223–236. [CrossRef]
40. Yuan, S.-M.; Liu, Z.-M. Some properties of two subclasses of *k*-fold symmetric functions associated with Srivastava-Attiya operator. *Appl. Math. Comput.* **2011**, *218*, 1136–1141. [CrossRef]
41. Cho, N.E.; Kim, I.H.; Srivastava, H.M. Sandwich-type theorems for multivalent functions associated with the Srivastava-Attiya operator. *Appl. Math. Comput.* **2010**, *217*, 918–928. [CrossRef]
42. Goldstein, M.; Hall, R.; Sheil-Small, T.; Smith, H. Convexity preservation of inverse Euler operators and a problem of S. Miller. *Bull. Lond. Math. Soc.* **1982**, *14*, 537–541. [CrossRef]
43. Ponnusamy, S.; Juneja, O.P. *Third Order Differential Inequalities in the Complex Plane, Current Topic in Analytic Function Theory*; World Scientific: Singapore; London, UK, 1992.
44. Yıldırım, Z.; Deniz, E.; Kazımoğlu, S. Some Families of Meromorphic Functions Involving a Differential Operator. In Proceedings of the 5th International Conference on Mathematics "An Istanbul Meeting for World Mathematicians", Istanbul, Turkey, 1–3 December 2021.

MDPI
St. Alban-Anlage 66
4052 Basel
Switzerland
www.mdpi.com

Axioms Editorial Office
E-mail: axioms@mdpi.com
www.mdpi.com/journal/axioms

www.ingramcontent.com/pod-product-compliance
Lightning Source LLC
Chambersburg PA
CBHW061451210926
51850CB00008B/1682
* 9 7 8 3 7 2 5 8 0 8 1 6 8 *